# Wonders of Learning
# BIG WORKBOOK
# Year Two

**What every Year Two child needs to know!**

© 2022 North Parade Publishing
Editorial team: Jennifer G. Bove, Kris Anah Allard, Joel Riemer
UK editor: J. Emmerson-Hicks
Published by North Parade Publishing, 3-6 Henrietta Mews, Bath BA2 6LR, United Kingdom
Printed in China, Guangdong Province 2022
First Printing
24 23 22 21 20  1 2 3 4 5
All rights are reserved. No part of this publication may be reproduced, stored in a retrieval system or transmitted in any form or by any means, electronic, mechanical, photocopying, recording or otherwise, without the prior permission of the Publisher.

# Contents

Spoken Language .................... 5
Spelling ........................... 13
Punctuation and Grammar ..... 47
Handwriting ....................... 71
Reading – Comprehension ..... 83
Writing – Composition ......... 109
Numbers and Place Value ...... 135
Addition and Subtraction ......157
Multiplication and Division .....195
Fractions .......................... 227
Measurement ................... 247
Geometry ..........................281
Statistics ......................... 305
Science ........................... 313
Geography ...................... 349
History ............................ 361
Hands-on ........................ 375
Answers .......................... 397

# Dear Family,

What does it mean when we say that *Wonders of Learning* workbooks have been crafted with your child in mind?

Of course, we have not met your child. But we understand the uniqueness of each child's learning path, as well as the developmental stages that children have in common. Each page is designed to facilitate effective and enjoyable learning, either as a supplement to school-based learning or as part of a home-based course of study. Classic "pencil-and-paper" activities are complemented by pages that provide hands-on and enquiry-based learning opportunities.

Because children learn at different rates, pages are designed so that some children may complete them on their own while others may need more help from you. In the earliest years, your child will need you to read instructions aloud.

You are your child's first teacher and, whether your child attends school or studies at home, you will always be an important teacher. The earliest learning happens naturally and through repetition. Children learn about words and concepts each time you call something by its name – the difference between a cat and a dog, for example. They learn to count each time you use numbers to describe objects or events in everyday life. And many children learn to read by unconsciously memorising picture books that are read to them frequently.

Have fun working through this book with your child. Encourage curiosity as you explore new concepts and practice familiar ones. And throughout daily life, read to your child as often as possible, name and count what you see, and keep answering children's questions!

We have put our hearts into providing a resource that will be meaningful and memorable for your child, and we hope that you enjoy the results.

Yours sincerely,

*The publishers*

# Spoken Language

# telling tales

The following pictures show the story of Little Red Riding Hood. Use them as prompts to tell the traditional fairy tale aloud to a friend or an adult.

Now colour in the picture below.

SPOKEN LANGUAGE

# questions and answers

Tell someone about your day. What time did you get up in the morning? What did you eat? What did you do? Who did you see? Where did you go?

Then ask your friend about *their* day. Think of five questions to ask them.

Tell someone about a special day in your life. It could be a birthday, a holiday, or a special day out. What did you do? Who did you see? Where did you go? Who were you with? What made it so special?

Then ask your friend about a special day in *their* life. Think of five questions to ask them.

Tell someone about your favourite book. What kind of book is it—funny or scary, exciting or sad? What happens in it? Who are the main characters? What is the best bit? Why is it your favourite book?

Then ask your friend about *their* favourite book. Think of five questions to ask them. Would you like to read it yourself?

Tell someone about your favourite game. Explain to them how to play it. Make sure your instructions are in the right order, and are clear and easy to understand.

Then ask your friend about *their* favourite game. Ask them how to play it. Do you understand the rules? Would you be able to play it now?

Describe a pet that you have, or would like to have. What does it look like? How big is it? What does it like to do? What does it eat? What makes it special to you?

Then ask your friend about a pet that *they* have or would like to have. Think of five questions to ask them.

Make up your own animal. How many legs, or fins, or wings does it have? How many eyes? How big is it? Is it furry or scaly? Can it swim or fly? Make it as strange and colourful as you like. Draw a picture of it, but keep it hidden.

Describe your animal to a friend. Be careful to tell them everything about it. Ask them to draw a picture of it. How does it compare with yours?

### Did you know?

The duck-billed platypus, found only in Australia, is a very strange creature. It has a bill (mouth) like a duck, a beaver-like tail, otter-like fur and webbed feet. Males have a poisonous stinger on the heels of their rear feet!

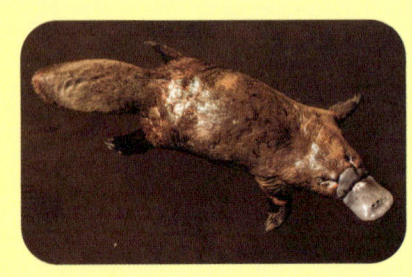

# explain yourself

You're going on a trip! You already have some things packed, and only have room to pack three more items. Choose three of the things from each box, then explain to a friend why you chose those things and not the others.

You're going camping! You already have the tent packed and your clothes and food. Choose three more things to take with you.

You're going to the beach! You already have your towel and swimsuit packed. Choose three more things to take with you.

You're going on a polar expedition! You already have a tent and food packed. Choose three more things to take with you.

# off by heart

Set yourself a challenge. Learn a poem off by heart and then repeat it to a friend or adult. Memorise the poem below, or choose one of your own.

## Bed In Summer

In winter I get up at night
And dress by yellow candle light.
In summer, quite the other way,
I have to go to bed by day.
I have to go to bed and see
The birds still hopping on the tree,
Or hear the grown-up people's feet
Still going past me in the street.
And does it not seem hard to you,
When all the sky is clear and blue,
And I should like so much to play,
To have to go to bed by day?

*by Robert Louis Stevenson*

# Spelling

# quick quiz

Spell the **compound** words below. Then write how many **syllables** each compound word has.

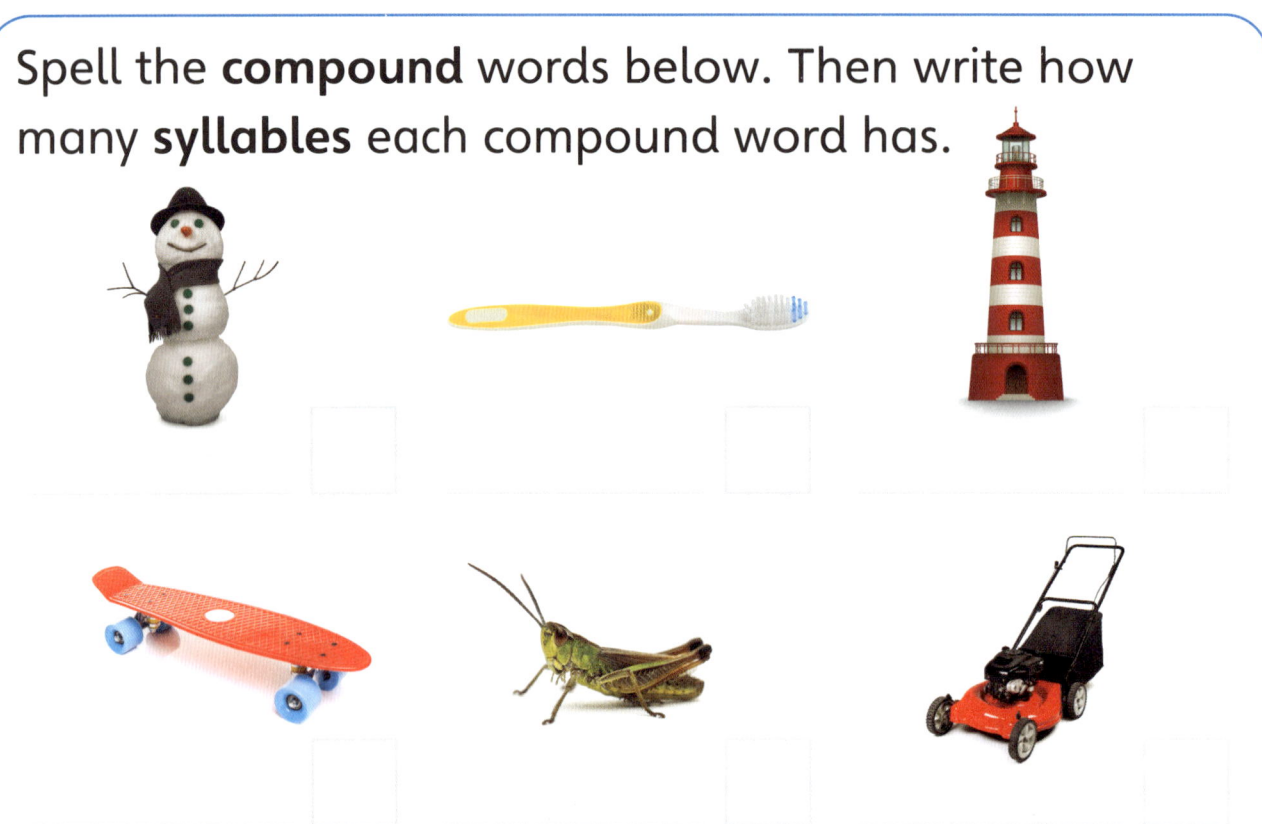

Spell these words with the letter blends **ph** and **wh**.

Circle the picture that **rhymes** with the word.

| | | | |
|---|---|---|---|
| sight | write | shout | bell |
| pleasure | ring | treasure | perfume |
| word | bird | bee | iguana |

Circle the two words with the same **vowel sound**.

| | | | |
|---|---|---|---|
| light |  thief |  pie |  shield |
|  clear |  chair |  bread |  bear |
|  crow |  group |  owl |  count |

15

# words with j, g, ge, dge

Join the words to the correct spelling.

jug • hedgehog • giraffe • allergic • fudge • orange • bridge • j • ge • dge • g • injured • village • fridge • gentle

Unscramble the letters to find the word.

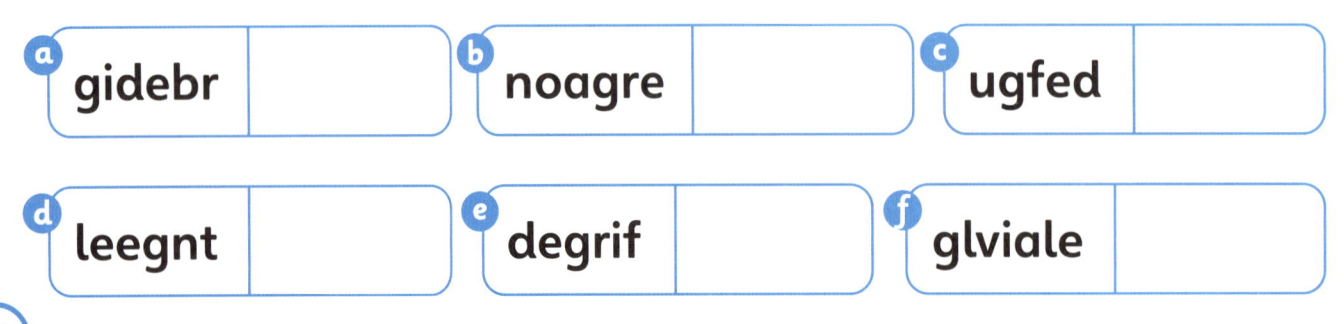

a. gidebr
b. noagre
c. ugfed
d. leegnt
e. degrif
f. glviale

# soft c

Circle the pictures with the **soft c** sound.

ice   lettuce   circle   cone   cycle
cylinder   scooter   rice   crayon

Complete the story by filling in the missing **soft c** words.

| prince | Cinderella | noticed | danced |
| palace | race | cinders | Once | traced |

___ upon a time, poor ___ lived with her cruel stepmother and stepsisters. They made her sleep in the fireplace among the ___ .

One day, the ___ held a great ball in the ___ . With the help of her fairy godmother, Cinderella was able to go.

She ___ all night with the prince, but when the magic stopped, she had to ___ away.

The prince ___ she had left behind one of her glass slippers. He ___ Cinderella using the slipper, and they lived happily ever after.

# silent letters – k, g, w

Say each word out loud. Then circle the word which has a silent letter at the beginning.

|  ram |  rabbit |  rat |  wren |

| 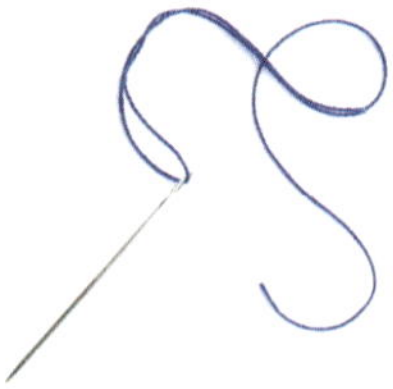 needle |  knot |  necklace |  necktie |

|  napkins |  noodles |  gnaw |  nuts |

Fill in the missing letters with **kn**, **gn** or **wr**.

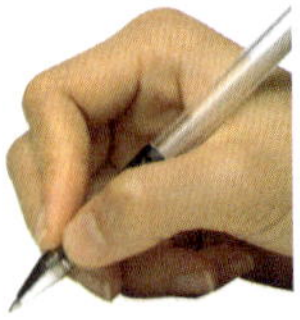

___ite     ___ock     ___ome

___arly    ___iggle   ___ife

Fill in the missing words using one of the words with a silent letter from the word bank below.

| gnat | knight | unwrap | knew | wreath |
|------|--------|--------|------|--------|
| knots | wrong | wrecked | knit | gnome |

Ali couldn't wait to _____ his present.

The clever girl _____ the answer.

The ship was _____ in the storm.

Sailors can tie lots of different _____.

He swatted the annoying _____ away.

Granny likes to sit and _____ by the fire.

I called the _____ number by mistake.

The _____ put on his shiny armour.

Grandad has a _____ in his garden.

In the ancient Olympics, winners were crowned with a laurel _____.

# 'ul' sound at the end of a word – spelt le, el or al

Join the words to the correct ending.

Circle the correct spelling for each picture.

table
tabel
tabal

towle
towel
towal

comicle
comicel
comical

loyle
loyel
loyal

camle
camel
camal

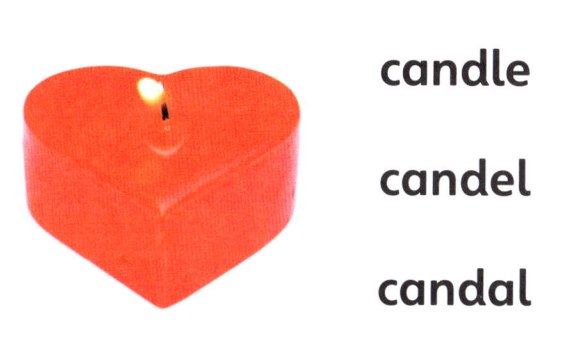
candle
candel
candal

funnle
funnel
funnal

regle
regel
regal

# il at the end of a word

Circle the words with the **il** spelling at the end.

basil    little    colourful
nostril    pencil    pupil    fossil    graceful

See how many **il** words you can find in the word-search below. Circle each word when you find it.

| t | m | f | o | s | s | i | l | s | w | k | h |
|---|---|---|---|---|---|---|---|---|---|---|---|
| o | o | u | q | p | l | v | i | g | i | l | g |
| n | m | b | l | u | n | o | s | t | r | i | l |
| s | w | a | k | p | y | e | w | g | n | l | p |
| i | x | s | z | i | s | r | l | e | h | e | u |
| l | c | i | b | l | x | y | f | r | j | n | r |
| n | v | l | u | f | c | q | i | b | k | t | e |
| b | p | e | n | c | i | l | d | i | e | i | w |
| n | j | l | e | k | y | i | o | l | m | l | t |

# plurals

! If a noun ends in an '**sh**', '**ch**', '**ss**', '**s**', '**x**' or '**z**', add '**es**' to the end of the word.

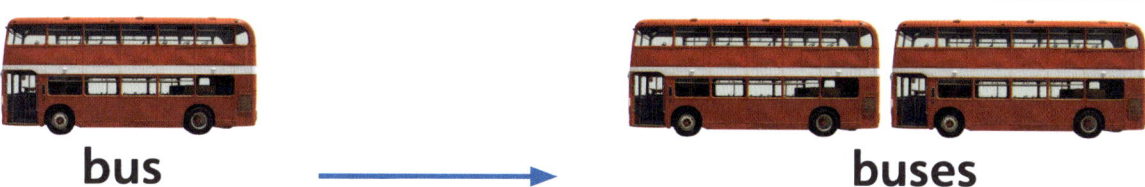

bus → buses

! If a noun ends in **consonant** and then a '**y**', drop the '**y**' and add '**ies**' to the end of the word.*

lorry → lorries

! If a noun ends in **consonant** and then an '**o**', just add '**es**' to the end of the word.

tomato → tomatoes

Write the correct plural.

*When a noun ends in **ey** and is pronounced '**ee**', the plural is formed by the addition of **–s** (donkeys, monkeys, valleys etc).

Fill in the gaps with the correct plural or singular noun.

| | | | |
|---|---|---|---|
| | butterfly | | |
| | | dresses | |
| | toy | | |
| | | benches | |
| | paintbrush | | |
| | domino | | |
| | coach | | |
| | | boxes | |
| | | cherries | |
| | fox | | |
| | bicycle | | |
| | ostrich | | |
| | | heroes | |
| | berry | | |

# y at the end of verbs

> **!** As with nouns, if a verb ends in **consonant** and then a '**y**', drop the '**y**' and add '**ies**' to the end of the word to make the *3rd person singular present tense*.

spy ⟶ he spies a flower

Draw lines to match the two forms of the same word.

| hurry | flies | envies | reply | carries | cry | dries |
|---|---|---|---|---|---|---|
| cries | replies | dry | fly | hurries | envy | carry |

Use the right ending of each verb to complete the sentences below.

| fry | dry | try | worry | cry |
|---|---|---|---|---|

My mother _____ when my brother is late.

Jen _____ her hardest in class.

The baby _____ when she drops her toy.

Mr Sharp _____ an egg every morning for breakfast.

Grandma _____ her clothes on the washing line.

# more spelling patterns

> ! The '**or**' sound is usually spelt **a** before **l** and **ll**.

**ball**  **call**  **talk**  **chalk**

Use each of these words in a short sentence below.

> ! Sometimes the short '**u**' sound is spelt **o**.

Look at the pictures below. Can you spot any patterns with the spelling? What letter(s) follow the **o** each time? Join the words which follow the same pattern.

mother   brother   dove   gloves

nothing   money   honey   monkey   love

> After **w** and **qu** the short '**o**' sound is usually spelt **a**.

Circle the words in which the short '**o**' sound is spelt **a**.

> Sometimes the '**ur**' sound is spelt **or** after **w**.

Use each of these words in a short sentence below.

> **Sometimes the 'or' sound is spelt a after w.**

    **warm**        **warning**        **war**        **towards**

Use each of these words in a short sentence below.

> **The 'zh' sound can be spelt si or su.**

    **treasure**        **measure**        **television**        **decision**

Use each of these words in a short sentence below.

The 'shun' sound is often spelt **tion**.

Circle the words in which the 'shun' sound is *not* spelt **tion**.

**petrol station**

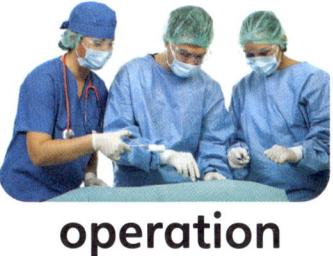
**operation**

**position**

**competition**

**expression**

**magician**

**solution**

Practice writing these words ending in **tion**.

motion

action

decision

fiction

national

Choose *one* of the above words to write in a sentence.

# suffixes with words ending in e

> To add a suffix to a word ending in a consonant and **e**, we usually drop the **e** before adding **ed**, **ing**, **er** or **est**.

Fill in the spaces in the word charts below.

| root word | +ed suffix | +ing suffix |
|---|---|---|
| dance | | |
| smile | | |
| cycle | | |
| bake | | |
| chase | | |
| taste | | |

| root word | +er suffix | +est suffix |
|---|---|---|
| nice | | |
| large | | |
| wide | | |
| cute | | |
| wise | | |
| brave | | |

suffixes with words ending in e

# suffixes with words ending in y

> **!** To add a suffix to a word ending in a consonant and **y**, we change the **y** to **i** before adding **ed**, **er** or **est**.*

Use the right ending for each word to complete the sentences below.

| happy happier happiest | funny funnier funniest |
| pretty prettier prettiest | easy easier easiest |

Sam's joke was funny, but Jodie's was _____.

That was the _____ day of my life.

The red rose was the _____ flower in the garden.

I found the game much _____ the second time.

| copy copied copying | cry cried crying |
| fly flied flying | reply replied replying |

The eagle was _____ high overhead.

Dan _____ when he fell off his bicycle.

Alex was told off for _____ during the test.

Someone _____ to the advert the very next day.

> *The **y** is not changed to an **i** before adding **–ing** as it would result in **ii**! The only words with **ii** are **skiing** and **taxiing**.

# doubling up

! To add **ed, ing, er, est** or **y** to words of one syllable ending in a single consonant after a single vowel we **double** the last letter to keep the short vowel sound.

Complete the words.

Don't double the letters **w**, **x** and **y**.

pat + ed = _____     big + est = _____
hum + ing = _____    fun + y = _____
run + er = _____     clap + ed = _____

**Did you know?**
Hummingbirds are the only birds that can hover for such a long time – and they are the only ones that can fly backwards!

Write a sentence with each suffix. Choose a different word from the word bank for each one.

| big | swim | fat | flop | shop |
| spot | mud | run | travel | knit |

+ ed _____

+ ing _____

+ er _____

+ est _____

+ y _____

## contractions

> **Contractions** are words that are shortened by missing out letters. An **apostrophe** is used to show that letters are missing from a word.

Circle the correct contraction in each sentence.

**It'is / It's**  a beautiful day.

**You're / Your'e**  late for lunch.

We  **hav'nt / haven't**  started to eat.

**Well / We'll**  wait for you.

Write the contraction for each pair of words.

is not _____        I will _____

she is _____        does not _____

I am _____          we are _____

they are _____      can not _____

Write a sentence about this picture using one of the contractions above.

## apostrophes to show possession

! The **apostrophe** when followed by an **s** can be used to show something belongs to someone or something.

Rewrite each sentence below using an apostrophe to show possession. The first is done for you.

This is the rabbit that belongs to Luke.
This is Luke's rabbit.

This is the laptop that belongs to Ada.

This is the bowl that belongs to the cat.

This is the bike that belongs to my brother.

Add the missing **apostrohe** and **s** to these phrases.

Sam    trophy

the dog    ball

the girl    sign

# real or nonsense

Use the skills you have gained to sound out the words below. Say them out loud, then decide whether they are real or nonsense. Use lines to join the real words to the treasure chest, and the nonsense words to the bin!

pration  hedgehog  decision
pluce  shiggle
lettuce  shibber
wrapped
pleasure
tagil
wander
weasure
squim
magical  know
wamper
fiction
pating  radge
pupil  sign  squash

Choose three of the above words to make sentences.

# homophones

> **Homophones** are words that sound the same but have different spellings and meanings.

Circle the correct homophone to complete each of the sentences below.

It was a dark and rainy **night / knight**.

A **night / knight** wears a suit of armour.

The **son / sun** was very hot at midday.

Mr Baker's **son / sun** is a teacher.

Come over **here / hear** so you can see better.

I can **here / hear** the radio from the bedroom.

The **be / bee** buzzed busily around the flower.

Caleb wants to **be / bee** a doctor when he grows up.

Tia wore a **blue / blew** spotty dress.

The wind **blue / blew** Grandma's hat off.

The guests ate everything – the table was **bare / bear**!

The polar **bare / bear** had two cute cubs.

I always get sick when I am at **see / sea**.

I can **see / sea** the birds at the bird table.

Choose the correct homophone from the word bank to complete each of the sentences below.

| where | wear | bored | board | sail | sale |

I bought some cheap shoes in the _____ .

If you're _____ , why not read a book?

My little sister likes to _____ stripy clothes!

I would love to _____ on the sea.

Put the chess pieces on the _____ .

_____ did you go on holiday?

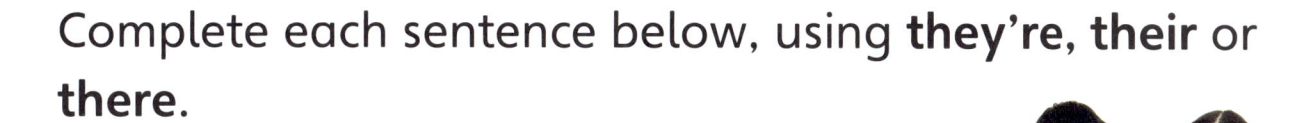

Complete each sentence below, using **they're, their** or **there**.

What's that over _____ ?

The twins are reading _____ books.

_____ going to be late if they don't hurry.

Complete each sentence below, using **too, two** or **to**.

May we order _____ pizzas, please?

I'm going out _____ play now. Are you coming _____ ?

# homophone bingo!

Cut out the word cards on page 377, then put them in a pile, face down. Choose one of the bingo cards below. Take turns with a friend to pick a word card. If it is a homophone for one of the words on your bingo card, cover your picture. If it doesn't match, put it back. The first to cover all their pictures is the winner!

| | | | |
|---|---|---|---|
| hear | weak | blue | tale |
| plane | mail | bear | doe |

| | | | |
|---|---|---|---|
| sore | weigh | see | flu |
| one | buoy | flower | whale |

# homographs

> **Homographs** are words that have the same spelling but have different meanings.

Circle the correct meaning for each underlined word.

Do you use your <u>right</u> hand?
  not left    correct

I need to <u>wind</u> up the clock.
  breeze    turn to tighten

We ran to catch the <u>train</u>.
  teach    rail vehicle

She wore a pretty <u>bow</u> in her hair.
  ribbon tie    bend over

How long will this rain <u>last</u>?
  continue    at the end

What is today's <u>date</u>?
  type of fruit    day and month

Dad used the <u>saw</u> to cut wood.
  tool    past tense of see

The page had a <u>tear</u> in it.
  rip    liquid from eye

I can't wait to open my <u>present</u>!
  right now    gift

> Homographs can be pronounced the same or differently.

39

## common exception words

For each of the common exception words below, read the word, say it out loud, then cover it with some paper or your hand. Next, write the word down. Finally, check to see if you got it right.

> Some words are exceptions in some accents but not in others – for example, fast and path.

| Look and say | Cover and write | Check and write again |
|---|---|---|
| floor | | |
| child | | |
| both | | |
| old | | |
| hour | | |
| every | | |
| even | | |
| great | | |
| pretty | | |
| Christmas | | |

| Look and say | Cover and write | Check and write again |
|---|---|---|
| beautiful | | |
| after | | |
| fast | | |
| father | | |
| path | | |
| sure | | |
| busy | | |
| eye | | |
| because | | |
| could | | |
| who | | |
| people | | |
| water | | |
| again | | |

Here are some more common exception words. Can you find and circle them in the grid below?

poor    mind    cold    everybody    break    last
hold    steak   past    move         should   told
improve any     money   path         many     prove

```
i q m a n y y u t o l d
m w d f h j k m l c v b
p e s c v b n o m i n d
r r t y a n y n y i o p
o t e r t y u e i o m l
v y a c o l d y l h o s
e u k s p d f h k j v a
q i w e a r t y u i e o
a o s d t p r o v e g s
m n u v h b c x z l k h
h o l d t y u b k v l o
v p b n m l p a s t a u
a o r t y u i o p b s l
j o k b r e a k l s t d
b r e v e r y b o d y n
```

Choose from the common exception words in the word bank below to complete the sentences.

> clothes    Mrs    door    bath    half    Mr    gold
> behind    parents    grass    whole    would    sugar

The dog really enjoyed his _____ !

Remember to close the _____ on your way out!

Do you like _____ in your coffee?

The pirates found a chest full of _____ .

Jake's _____ are called _____ and _____ Jones.

Will you eat a _____ pizza or just _____ ?

We need a new lawnmower to cut the _____ .

Susie came from _____ to win the race.

_____ you like another cookie?

The twins always wear different _____ .

# correct the spelling mistake

Each sentence below has a spelling mistake which has been underlined. Write the correct spelling in the box.

Poor Tilly's nose was <u>saw</u>.

Mum said to <u>rap</u> up warm.

Ali <u>cant</u> come out to play.

The <u>childrun</u> ran to the park.

The detective searched for <u>clue's</u>.

The mouse <u>nawed</u> at the rope.

Circle the spelling mistake in each sentence, then write the correct spelling in the box.

The second clown was funnyer.

Their going to be late.

The flowers were very pritty.

There were a lot of peeple.

Yesterday we went too the zoo.

Have you seen the whether report?

Read the short passage below.
Circle all the spelling mistakes in it.

**There are 15 mistakes to look out for!**

> Their is a nome in Grandads garden. It sits on the parth beside the grars. It has a bloo cowt, an orinj hat and a litle watering can. In winter, Grandad puts a scarf around it's neck in case it gets cowld. Peeple pasing by smile becos they think its funny.

Write the passage out below in neat, with the correct spellings and punctuation.

# alphabetical order

> **Dictionaries** list words in **alphabetical** order—starting with A and ending with Z.

Put these animals in **alphabetical** order.

elephant
giraffe
crocodile
monkey
zebra
lion
tiger
antelope
hippopotamus
cheetah

1. _____
2. _____
3. _____
4. _____
5. _____
6. _____
7. _____
8. _____
9. _____
10. _____

Now put these fruit and vegetables in **alphabetical** order.

orange
cherries
banana
cauliflower
strawberry
melon
potatoes
pepper
carrot
apple

1. _____
2. _____
3. _____
4. _____
5. _____
6. _____
7. _____
8. _____
9. _____
10. _____

# Punctuation and Grammar

## capital letters and full stops

Each sentence below is missing punctuation. Underline the words that need a capital letter and add the missing full stops.

our dog doesn't like getting wet

it sometimes snows in january

giraffes have very long necks

kara likes to go ice skating

the zoo was very busy on monday

my cousin plays the guitar really well

Now correct the passage below. Underline the words that need a capital letter and add the missing full stops.

on saturday we went to visit my grandparents it was sunny so we ate our lunch in the garden my little sister olivia had too much cake and felt ill we stayed overnight and came back on sunday i had fun

Remember to use **capital letters** for the **names of people and places, days of the week, months of the year**, and the pronoun **I**.

Each sentence below is missing punctuation. Rewrite it with the correct punctuation.

finlay plays football every saturday

aunty carol bakes the best pies

london is the capital city of england

i dropped my icecream on the floor

Answer each question with a full sentence. Use capital letters and full stops.

What is your name?

How old are you?

What colour are your eyes?

Where do you live?

# the right ending

> A **statement** tells you something, and ends with a **full stop**. A **command** tells you to do something, and also ends with a **full stop**. An **exclamation** shows surprise or strong emotion, and ends with an **exclamation mark**. A **question** asks something, and ends with a **question mark**.

Draw a line to match the sentence to the correct form.

There are seven days in a week.

Would you like an ice cream?

What a pretty dress that is!

Dogs make good pets.

Where are you going?

Sit down on the floor.

What a scary ride!

Shut the door.

What a shame!

How did you do that?

Make your bed neatly.

I can't wait for the party!

My favourite colour is red.

Who wants to go swimming?

Paris is pleasant in the spring.

Put your hands on your head.

**statement**

**command**

**exclamation**

**question**

Add a question mark, full stop or exclamation mark to finish off each sentence.

Gorillas live in the jungle

How I wish I could fly like a bird

How high can a frog jump

What an colourful fish

What do koalas eat

Kittens can be very playful

Use one of these command words to complete each sentence. Make sure to use a capital letter.

| wash | listen | brush | drink | tidy | line |

_____ up at the front of the class.

_____ up all your milk.

_____ your hands properly.

_____ carefully to the instructions.

_____ up your room.

_____ your teeth.

**Did you know?**
Simon Says is a popular game based on commands. It is played all around the world!

PUNCTUATION AND GRAMMAR

51

For each of the pictures below write a short sentence. One should be a statement, one a command, one an exclamation and one a question. Write what kind of sentence it is in the box.

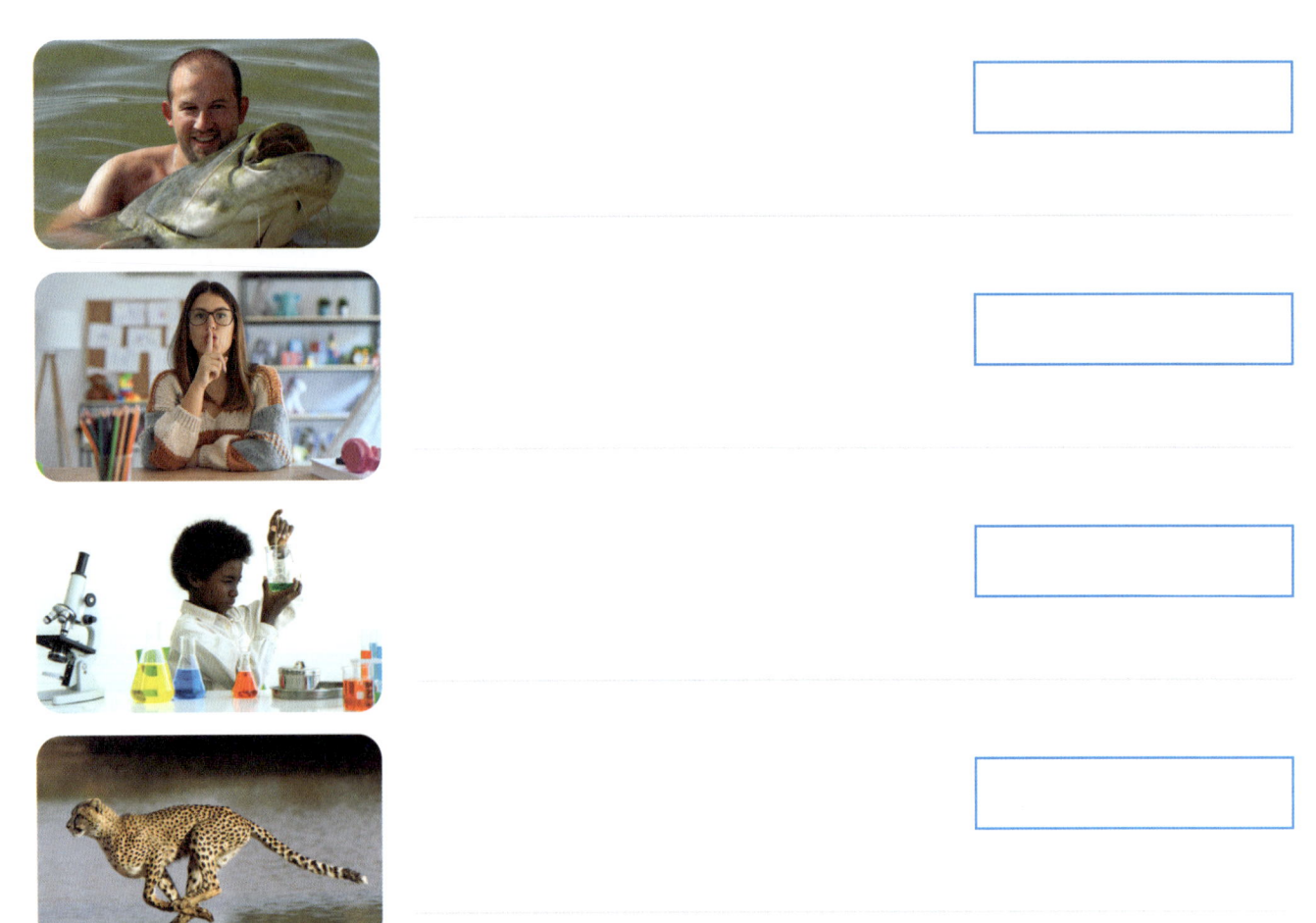

Turn these statements into questions by changing the punctuation, and by rearranging or changing words.

Tokyo is the world's largest city.

Blue whales are the largest animals on earth.

Turn these questions into commands.

Would you like a glass of water?

Are you going to go to sleep now?

Imagine what these children are thinking, and write a speech bubble for each one of them. Make one a command, one an exclamation and one a question.

## commas in a list

Add the missing commas to the sentences below.

> When writing a list, put a comma between each item, except for the last item where you use 'and'. eg I like dogs, cats, ducks and pigs.

Mum bought apples  oranges  grapes and bananas.

To make the cake you need flour  sugar  chocolate and eggs.

My favourite sports are tennis  cricket and football.

Rewrite these sentences using commas and adding an 'and' in the right place.

I need to buy new trousers shoes socks for school.

The colours of the rainbow are red orange yellow green blue indigo violet.

My school bag is full of notebooks books folders pens.

Use three adjectives to describe each thing. Remember to use commas and to add an 'and' before the last adjective. Use your own words, or choose from the word bank. You can use the same word more than once.

| hard | cheeky | wild | cuddly | fierce | warm | furry | small |
| shiny | fluffy | naughty | tasty | wooden | juicy | shiny |
| soft | cute | tall | sweet | cosy | red | sharp | long |
| big | woollen | scary | funny | orange | white | colourful |

The cat is

The strawberry is

The axe is

The bus is

The dog is

The frog is

The hat is

The dinosaur is

The cub is

**PUNCTUATION AND GRAMMAR**

55

# nouns and expanded noun phrases

> **Common nouns** are the names of things (places, objects or ideas). **Proper nouns** are the names of a particular person, place or thing. They always begin with a capital letter.

Circle the **common nouns** in blue and the **proper nouns** in red. Leave the words that aren't nouns.

| | | | | |
|---|---|---|---|---|
| water | London | Samuel | weak | market |
| Shakespeare | when | tree | Jemima | |
| teacher | alligator | go | balloon | Europe |

> An **expanded noun phrase** tells you **more** about the **noun** (for example, *the stormy sea*).

Underline the **expanded noun phrase** in each of these sentences.

The scared mouse hid away.

James spilt his hot coffee.

Her cosy slippers keep Gran warm.

The friendly old lady waved hello.

The big purple balloon burst.

Use an **adjective** to expand each noun phrase. There might be more than one in each sentence!

The _____ fireman went inside the building.

The _____ wind blew all the leaves off the tree.

I bought some _____ flowers for my mum.

The _____ snake slithered closer!

The _____ girls played in the _____ water.

Write a sentence for each picture below. Use adjectives to make your sentences interesting.

# more suffixes

We can add suffixes to a noun to make an **adjective**, or to an adjective to make an **adverb**. We can make new **nouns** by adding suffixes to a root word.

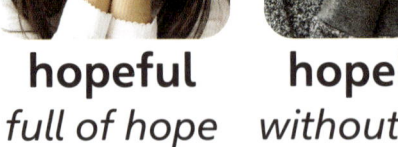

**hopeful**
full of hope

**hopeless**
without hope

Draw a line to join the root word to the suffix.

| ill | slow | spot | punish | forget |
|---|---|---|---|---|
| ment | ful | ly | less | ness |

Add a suffix to each word to make a new word.

help

treat

dark

quick

joy

care

Use one of the words above to write a sentence about this picture.

> When the root word has more than one syllable and ends in a consonant and then **y**, we change the **y** to **i** before adding the suffix.

Complete the words and then write a short sentence for each one.

merry + ment =

lazy + ly =

plenty + ful =

penny + less =

happy + ness =

# prefixes

> **Prefixes** are a group of letters that change the meaning of a word when they are added to the start. For example, **un** means *not*, or *opposite of*, while **re** means *again*, or *back*.

Write the meaning of each word. The first is done for you.

| | |
|---|---|
| unlike | not like |
| undressed | |
| uneven | |
| unsure | |

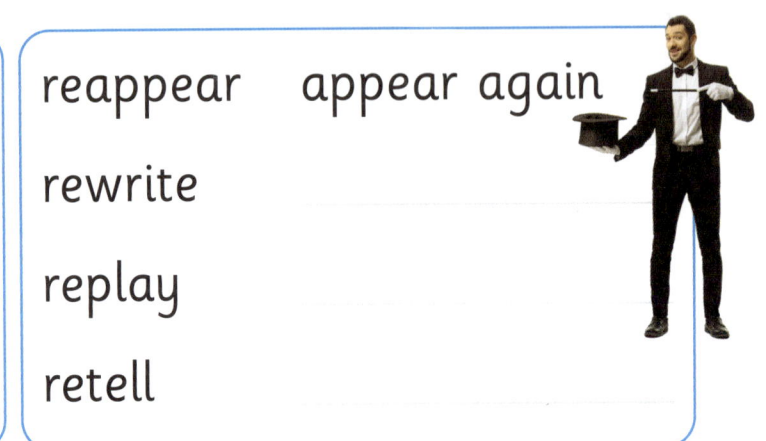

| | |
|---|---|
| reappear | appear again |
| rewrite | |
| replay | |
| retell | |

Write the root word to finish each meaning.

| | | |
|---|---|---|
| untie | = | opposite of |
| unwrap | = | opposite of |
| unwind | = | opposite of |

Add the suffix **un** or **re** to each of these words to make a new word.

| happy | read | safe | lock | use |

Write a sentence using one of your new words.

# conjunctions

> A **conjunction** links two words or phrases together.
> **Co-ordinating conjunctions** (such as *and*, *but* and *or*) link two words or phrases together as an equal pair.
> **Subordinating conjunctions** (such as *when*, *if* and *that*) introduce a subordinate clause.

Choose **and, but, or** or **so** to complete each sentence.

Would you like fruit ____ cake for dessert?

I like apples ____ grapes.

I did well in the test ____ I got a sticker.

My boots are pretty ____ they are too small for me.

Should they go by train ____ by car?

The farmer fed the pigs ____ the chickens.

Sammy was late ____ he had to run.

Jess is young ____ she can hit the ball hard.

Make each set of two sentences into one, using **but** or **so**. Remember to change the punctuation.

I would like to go outside. It's raining.

Lydia was tired. She went to sleep.

Choose **when** or **that** to complete each sentence.

Call me _____ you get home.

We went to a hotel _____ had a big pool.

You can go outside _____ you've finished dinner.

I know a song _____ you will like.

Choose **because** or **if** to complete each sentence.

Zoe felt ill _____ she ate too many cakes.

I don't know _____ I can play today.

You can borrow my umbrella _____ you like.

Gran opened the window _____ it was hot.

Join the word groups to make complete sentences, then circle the **conjunction** in each sentence.

Max was allowed to go — so she put on her coat.

Grace was cold — when he had finished his homework.

You can buy the jacket — because he had run all the way home.

Ade was hot — or you can buy the top.

# verbs

> A **verb** is a word used to describe an action, state or occurrence. It is also known as a '**doing word**'.

Circle the **verb** in each sentence below.

My cat chases birds.

I swim very fast.

The mouse ran away.

The tree grew tall.

Jake plays cricket.

The balloon popped.

Choose one of the verbs below to complete each sentence.

swim    think    wash    clap    play    visit

I like to _____ my grandparents at the weekend.

It is important to _____ your hands regularly.

Do you _____ this dress is pretty?

After school we _____ in the park.

_____ loudly when the show stops.

Will you _____ in the sea?

Choose one of the verbs above to write your own sentence. Circle the verb.

# adverbs

> An **adverb** is a word that describes that describes how an action is carried out.

Circle the **adverb** in each sentence below.

| | |
|---|---|
| The sun shone brightly. | She sang loudly. |
| We walked quickly. | They whispered softly. |
| He sighed sadly. | She danced gracefully. |

Choose one of the adverbs below for each sentence.

**sternly   quietly   quickly   gently   happily   carefully**

Ryan was in a rush so he tied his laces _____ .

The bird sang _____ in the tree.

We talk _____ in the library.

Ella carried the books _____ .

The rain pattered _____ against the window.

The policeman frowned _____ .

Write a sentence about this picture. Use an adverb.

# past and present

> The **present tense** is used for things happening *now* or for things that are continuous. The **past tense** is used for things that happened **in the past**.

What **tense** is each sentence written in? Tick the right box.

|  | present | past |
|---|---|---|
| Theo and Megan walk to school together. | ☐ | ☐ |
| Yesterday Ted visited his aunt. | ☐ | ☐ |
| When I get up I brush my teeth. | ☐ | ☐ |
| You did really well in the test! | ☐ | ☐ |

Change these **present tense** sentences to the **past tense**.

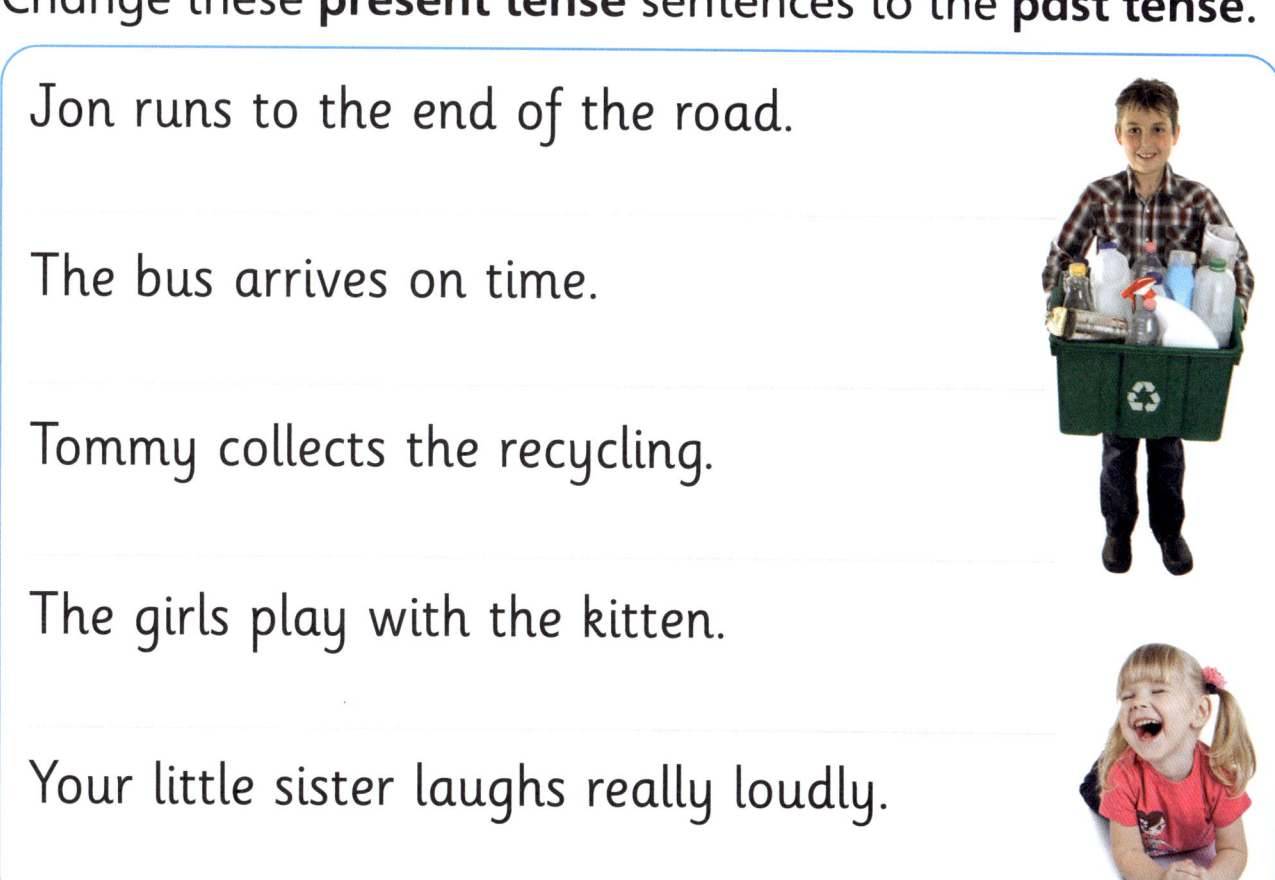

Jon runs to the end of the road.

The bus arrives on time.

Tommy collects the recycling.

The girls play with the kitten.

Your little sister laughs really loudly.

> The **present progressive** and **past progressive** tenses (or **present continuous** and **past continuous**) are used when we are describing **actions that continue for a period of time** in the present or in the past.

What **tense** is each sentence written in? Tick the right box.

|  | present progressive | past progressive |
|---|---|---|
| The baby is crying. | ☐ | ☐ |
| It was snowing heavily. | ☐ | ☐ |
| Granny was sewing a scarf. | ☐ | ☐ |
| The kettle is boiling. | ☐ | ☐ |

Change these sentences from the **present progressive tense** to the **past progressive tense**.

The horses are running fast.

I am making dinner for everybody.

They are playing in the garden.

Ross is taking a selfie.

Write a sentence for each picture, using the right tense.

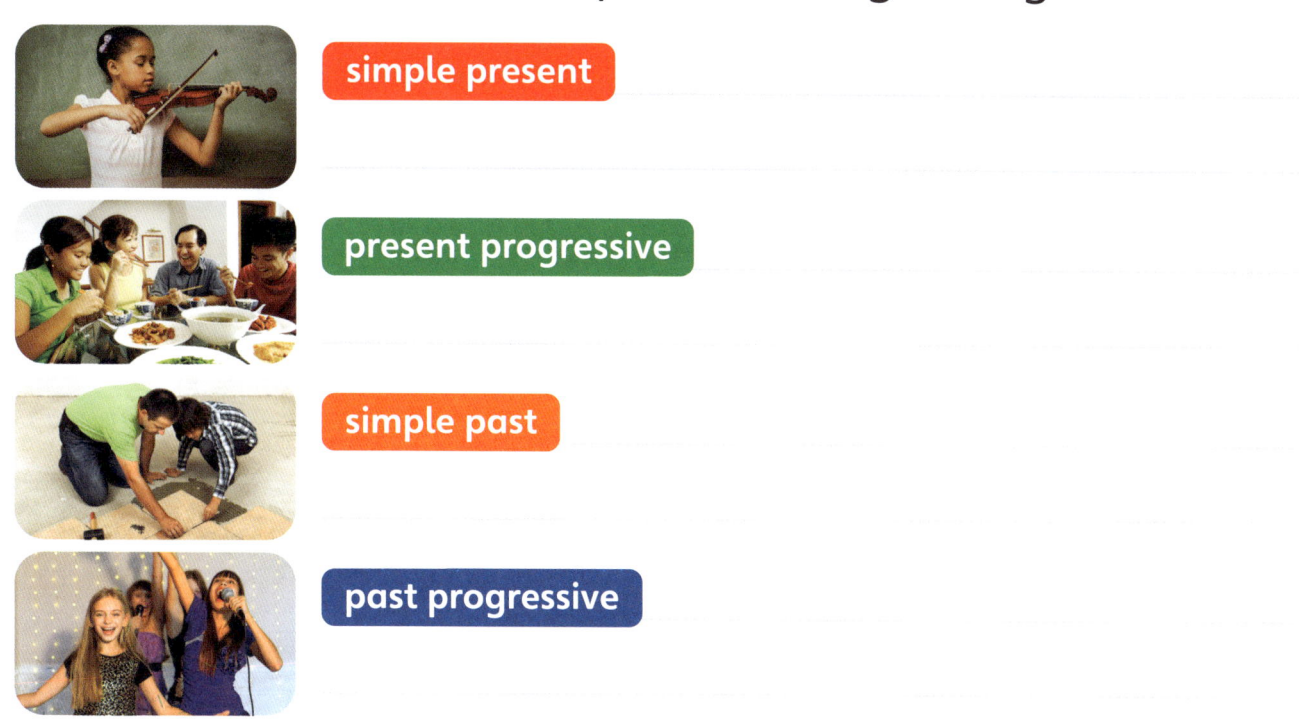

simple present

present progressive

simple past

past progressive

Cut out the sentences on page 379. Stick them into the correct box.

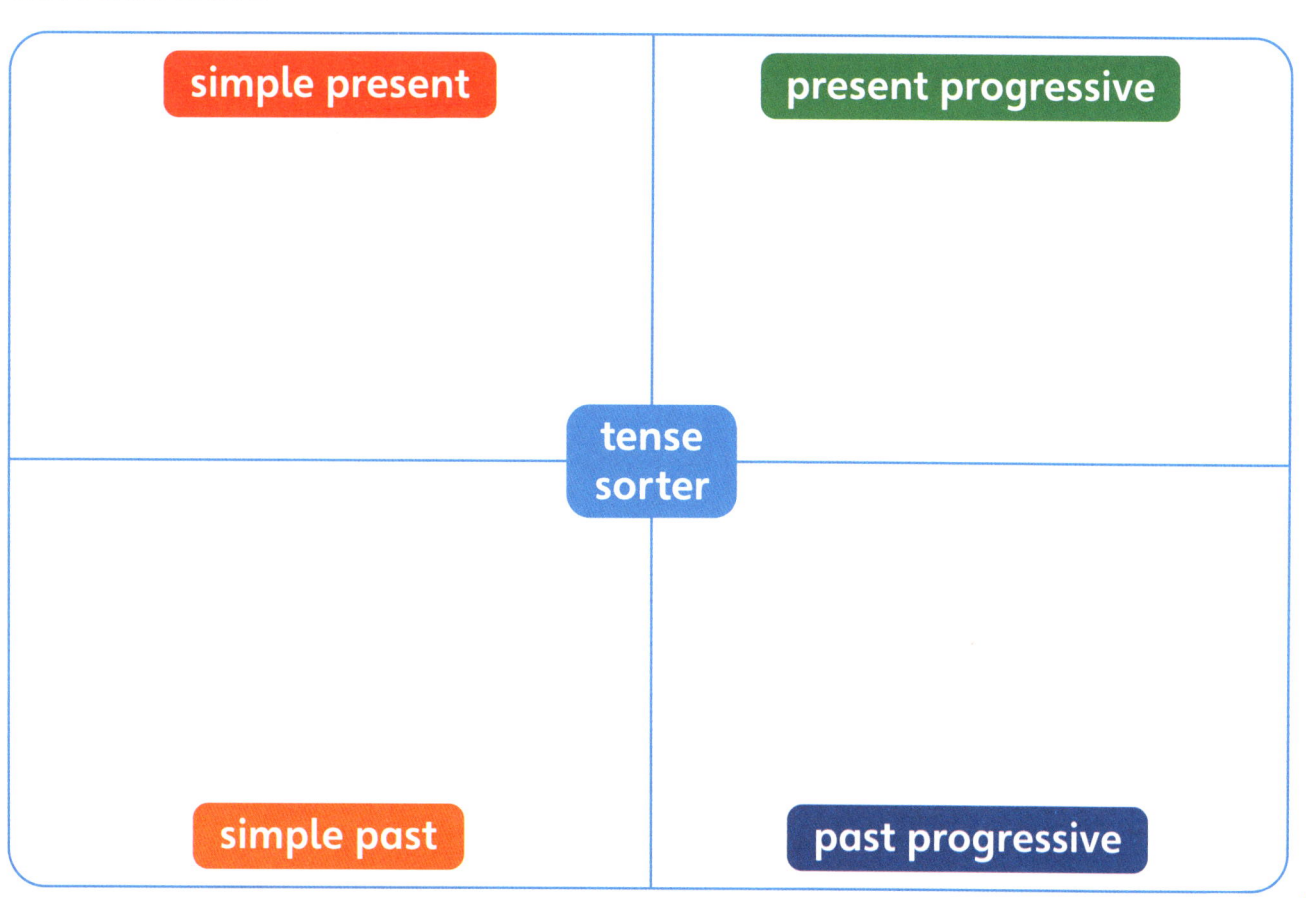

| simple present | present progressive |
|---|---|
| | |
| simple past | past progressive |

tense sorter

# quiz time

**1** Circle each word that is missing a **capital letter**.

My brother and i got a new kitten on saturday. We named her snowy because she has white fur!

**2** Tick the sentence with the correct **punctuation**.

they built a snowman in the garden.

They built a snowman in the garden

They built a snowman in the garden.

**3** The four sentences below are all missing their end **punctuation**. Complete each sentence and then circle the **exclamation** in green, and the **question** in orange.

I need a new hat ☐    Find me a new hat ☐

What a nice hat that is ☐    Where can I find a hat ☐

**4** Tick the sentence with the correct **punctuation**.

They had pie potatoes and peas, for dinner.

They had pie potatoes and peas for dinner.

They had pie, potatoes and peas for dinner.

**5** Join the word to the correct **definition**.

- adjective — A sentence telling someone to do something.
- command — A word that describes a verb.
- adverb — A group of letters that can be added to the end of a word to alter the meaning.
- suffix — A word that describes a noun.

**6** One word is underlined in each sentence below. Write in the box whether that word is a **noun, verb, adjective** or **adverb**.

Samir <u>swims</u> at the weekend. ☐

My kitten is very <u>playful</u>. ☐

The children ran <u>eagerly</u> to the door. ☐

The teacher read a <u>poem</u> to the class. ☐

**7** To which word below can you **not** add the **suffix 'ly'** to make an adjective?

sharp     bright     big     clever

**8** To which word below can you add the **prefix 'un'** to make a new word?

patient     hard     happy     read

**9** Choose the correct **conjunction** from **or, because** or **but** so that the sentence makes sense.

Would you like pie _____ pizza for dinner?

I would like to come _____ I'm not allowed out.

She's tired _____ she didn't sleep well last night.

**10** Circle the correct word so the sentence makes sense.

I don't think **their / they're / there** coming.

It's **their / they're / there** dog.

It costs far **to / two / too** much.

Are you going **to / two / too** the show later?

**11** Circle the word to use to complete each sentence.

He **couldnt / couldn't** stop the goal.

**Milo's / Milos** favourite colour is red.

**12** Complete the sentences filling in the **past** forms of the verb in brackets.

Carlos _____ the trumpet at the concert. (play)

Cinderella _____ all night with the prince. (dance)

The water _____ in the sunshine. (sparkle)

# Handwriting

# joining letters

Trace each letter carefully, then write the letters yourself.

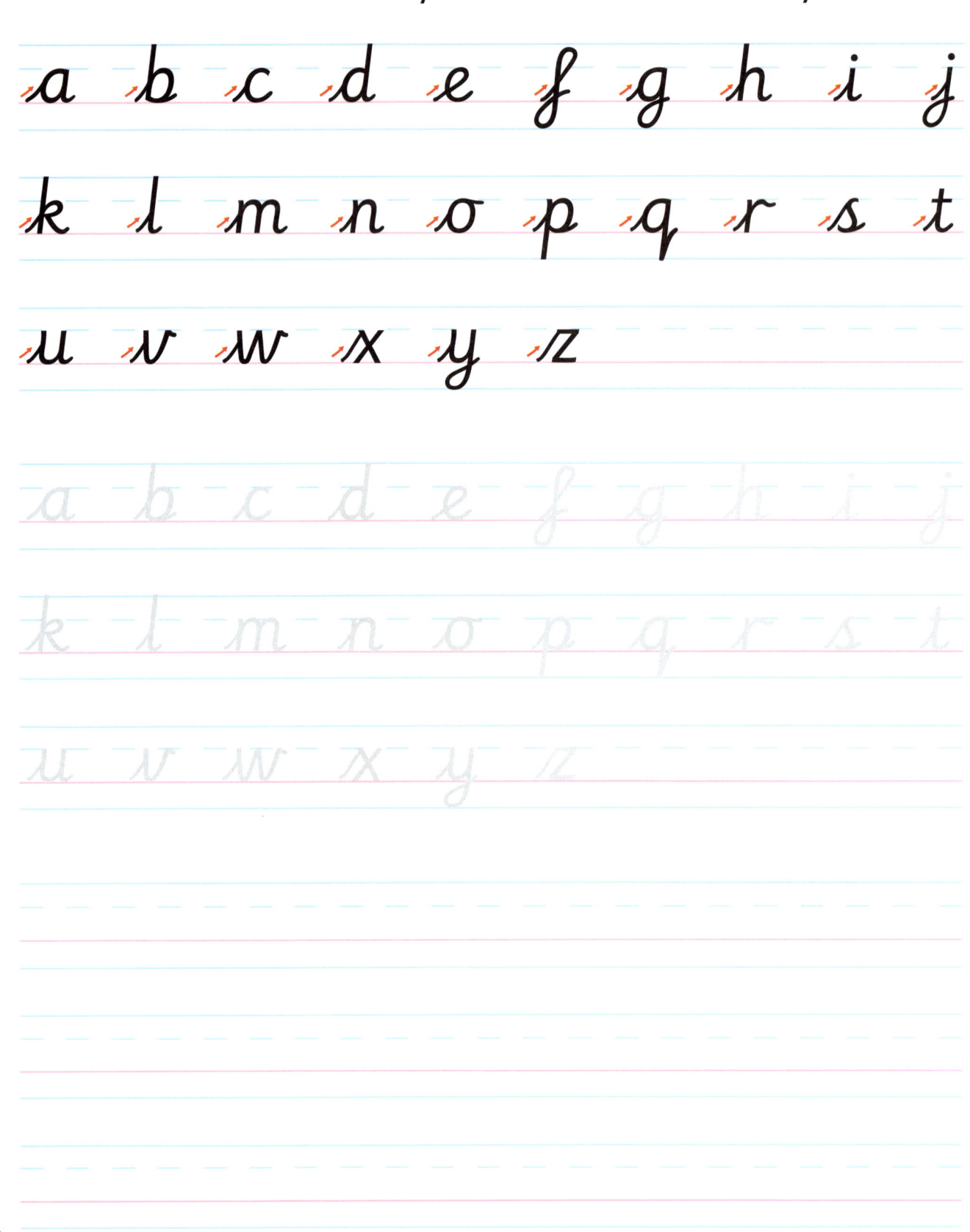

a b c d e f g h i j
k l m n o p q r s t
u v w x y z

Trace each word, then write it yourself. Pay attention to the size of the letters.

again

break

child

door

father

grass

half

improve

jump

koala koala

loyal loyal

many many

nobody nobody

only only

people people

quick quick

robot robot

sugar sugar

told told

under

vowel

would

xylophone

your

zebra

# alphabet sentences

Trace each phrase or sentence, then write it yourself.

Watch out for the spacing between words!

*Adorable animals asleep.*

*Blueberry bread is the best.*

*Crisp carrots are crunchy.*

alphabet sentences

Dad does the dishes

Eva was eager and excited

Feed the fish for me

Gramps' gloves are green

Hares hop on the hill.

Isla's icecream is immense!

Jules jumped for joy.

Kind kangaroos with kites

*Lily likes licking lollipops.*

*Mondays make me mad!*

*Nats naughty nanny goat*

*Owls in the old oak tree*

Pippa's pretty purple purse.

Quentin's quest was quick.

Rory's red robot rattles.

Sophie sings super songs

*Tarts are a tasty treat.*

*Umar's umbrella is ugly.*

*Violet vases are very nice.*

*Wishing for warm weather.*

*Xavier has an extra xylophone.*

*Yasmin's yoyo is yellow.*

*Zany zebras at the zoo.*

# Reading

## types of text

Text comes in many different forms. From the *Encyclopedia Britannica* to an advert for shampoo, there are many different purposes for text, and ways in which it can be presented. Circle the types of text that you have read below, and add any other types you can think of.

> leaflet   diary   magazine   letter   novel   poem
> storybook   advert   biography   form   menu
> travel guide   poster   recipe   instruction manual

Text can mostly be divided into two categories: *fiction (made up)* and *non-fiction (based on facts)*. Write three examples of each type in the boxes.

| fiction | non-fiction |
|---|---|
|  |  |

Text is written differently for different purposes. Match up the type of writing with the text form.

persuasive text          poetry
instructive text         novel
rhyming text             advert
literary text            recipe

> Keep a note of all your favourite words and phrases on the tear-out poster on the next page. Write down vocabulary that you like as you come across it, or paste words or phrases from newspapers, magazines or leaflets.

## my favourite
## words and phrases

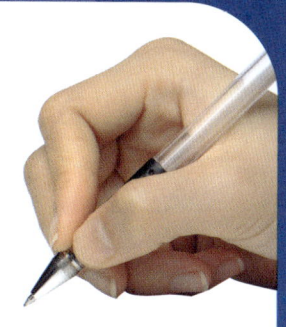

# The Disappearing Sandwich

Ana made a sandwich. She left it on the table while she got a drink. When she came back, it was gone!

"Where ever did it go?" Ana wondered.

Just then she heard a noise. She peeked under the table. She saw her dog's tail wagging. "Oh, Charlie!" she said giggling. "That was *my* sandwich, not *yours*!"

Circle the answers.

What was missing?

- Ana's drink
- Ana's sandwich
- Ana's pet

Who took Ana's food?

- her dog
- her brother
- her cat

What comes next? Write one or two sentences.

# Rosie's Morning

Rosie got into the car and fastened her seatbelt.

"Did you put your lunch in your backpack?" Mum asked. Rosie nodded. Mum started the car and they drove through the streets.

They stopped in front of a big building. Lots of children with backpacks were going inside. Rosie jumped out and joined them excitedly. She waved to her mother.

"Have a fun day!" Mum said.

Where is Rosie going?

How do you think she is feeling?

What else might be in her backpack?

# A Day with Dad

"Let's go!" Ted said, as he and Dad hurried outside. The rising sun painted everything pink. The streets were empty. No one else was awake yet.

Soon they were at the lake. Ted carried the fishing poles. His dad carried the tackle box. They spent the whole day fishing.

At what time of day does the story start?

Underline words in the story that tell you the time of day.

Circle the word that tells where Ted and Dad go.

How long do they stay there?

**Did you know?**
Some fish live in the ocean. They are called saltwater fish. Others are freshwater fish. They live in lakes, ponds and streams. Some fish, like this salmon, spend part of their lives in each kind of water.

# The Unexpected Visitor

"What are you doing for the summer hols?" asked Lucca.

"We're going camping in Wales as usual," replied Milo.

"Lucky you," said Lucca enviously. "My mum won't let us go camping."

"Why not?" asked Milo curiously.

"She only ever went camping once. When she woke up, there was a cow in the tent! She's never dared try again!" laughed Lucca.

Where is Milo going on holiday?

Is it the first time he has been camping?

Has Lucca been camping?

Do you think he would like to go? Why?

# The Big Surprise

JOSH: What do you think the big surprise is?
MAIA: I've no idea! I can't wait to find out.
JOSH: They're coming now, so you won't have to! (MUM and DAD enter the room)
MUM: I guess you'd like to hear the news?
MAIA: Yes please, Mum! Do tell us!

Plays don't use speech marks.

**DAD:** How would you like to go skiing this Christmas?
**JOSH:** Really? I've always wanted to try skiing!
**MAIA:** Yippee!

Why are Maia and Josh excited at the start of the play?

How do they react to the news?

Do you think they have been skiing before?

# The Walk to School

"You'll be late for school," warned Mum.

"I don't care!" said Nina miserably. She trudged slowly down the drive. Things had been fine at her old school. Her friends had been kind. Not like the girls at this school!

She walked with her head low, her slow, reluctant steps bringing her closer and closer to the dreaded place. How she wished she didn't have to go!

How is Nina feeling?

Why do you think Nina doesn't want to go to school?

Circle all the descriptive words in the passage which give you a clue to how she is feeling.

# Mum's Unusual Job

One evening, Max was eating supper alone with Dad. "How long will it be until Mum comes home?" Max asked.

"She'll be back in a month," Dad said.

"Can we check to see where she is?" Max asked. His father nodded, and they went over to the computer. They looked at a map to find out where Mum was.

"She'll be overhead shortly after bedtime," Dad said.

"Can I stay up and wave to her?" Max pleaded hopefully.

"OK," Dad said, smiling. "Let's go and get the telescope."

They set up the telescope outside, and wrapped up warm. Max waited patiently as the night sky got darker. When would Mum come by?

"Look!" Dad said. Max looked up. A bright spot flew across the sky. Max and Dad waved.

"There goes the space station!" Dad said.

"I am so proud of Mum," Max said. "Her job is out of this world!"

Write or circle each answer.

Where are Max and Dad during the story?

Why do they check the map?

Underline the word "**pleaded**" in the story. Circle the word which means almost the same as pleaded.

worried    demanded    begged    replied

What is Max's mother's job?

Where does she work?

on a rocket ship    on a space station
at the computer

Would you like your parent to be an astronaut? Why / why not?

# A Birthday Wish

Sam said, "We don't want a birthday party this year."

Sara added, "We don't even want a cake."

Mum turned to look at them. She was surprised. "You see, what we'd really, really like is a dog!" Sara continued hopefully.

"Oh," said Mum. "We'll see."

The twins sighed. "*We'll see*" usually meant "*no*". In fact, it almost *always* meant "*no*"!

Some weeks later, on the morning of their birthday, Sam and Sara came downstairs to find Dad alone in the kitchen. "I'm making breakfast," he said, smiling. "Then we're meeting Mum."

"Where?" Sam asked eagerly.

"You'll see," Dad answered mysteriously. "Off you go and get ready!"

The meeting spot was a brick building. Sam and Sara were puzzled as they got out of the car. "Where are we?" Sara wondered.

"Wait," Sam said, his eyes widening. "Do you hear barking?" Sara nodded excitedly. Could it be? Was their wish coming true?

Mum came out of the building. "Come on in," she said. "You have a big decision to make!"

They spent the morning at the animal shelter. They liked every single dog! Finally, they chose a floppy-eared puppy with black, brown and white patches and a waggly tail.

"This is the best birthday ever!" Sam said, as the happy twins hugged Mum and Dad – and the dog!

Write or circle the answers.

How do the twins feel when Mum says, "We'll see"?

What tells you how much Sam and Sara want a dog?

> They say they won't argue any more.
> They offer to go without a party or cake.

What clues are there in the story that they are going to get a dog for their birthday?

Underline the word "**puzzled**" in the story. Circle the word which means almost the same as puzzled.

confused    excited    happy    scared

What is the best birthday present you've ever had and why?

# The Boy Who Cried Wolf

Every morning, Aiden took his sheep up to the field. He stayed with them all day while they grazed. At sunset, he took the sheep home. It was boring and lonely.

One day, Aiden had an idea to make things more fun. He ran to the village. "Help! Help!" he cried. "There's a wolf!"

The worried villagers raced up the hill. When they got to the field, they found the sheep grazing peacefully.

"The wolf must have run away," Aiden said cheekily.

Some of the villagers stayed with Aiden to keep an eye out. Aiden enjoyed their company greatly.

A few days later, Aiden felt lonely again. Once more, he raced to the village, crying "Wolf! Wolf!" and the people ran to help him.

Once again, when they got to the field there was no sign of a wolf. The villagers realised that Aiden had been lying to them, and they stormed away angrily. Aiden had to remain by himself with the sheep until it was time to go home.

One afternoon not long after this, Aiden spied a dark shadow lurking near the field. A wolf! Terror filled him. He ran to the village as fast as he could. "Help! Help! There's a wolf in the field!"

No one believed him. Alone, Aiden ran back to the field. The sheep had scattered to get away from the wolf. Aiden had to spend all night searching for them.

**Did you know?**
This story is based on one of Aesop's Fables, called The Shepherd's Boy. Aesop was a writer from Ancient Greece, who is thought to have lived around 600 BC.

Circle the *closest* meanings for these words from the story.

| | | |
|---|---|---|
| **grazed** | slept | ate grass |
| **peacefully** | quietly | excitedly |
| **stormed away** | left angrily | got wet |
| **lurking** | waiting | running |
| **scattered** | got together | ran off |

Write the answers to these questions.

What did Aiden do because he was lonely?

_____

What did Aiden have to do at the end of the story?

_____

What could Aiden have done instead of lying?

_____

All of Aesop's Fables had a message – a lesson to tell – known as the **moral** of the story. Colour the sheep that is telling the key message of this story.

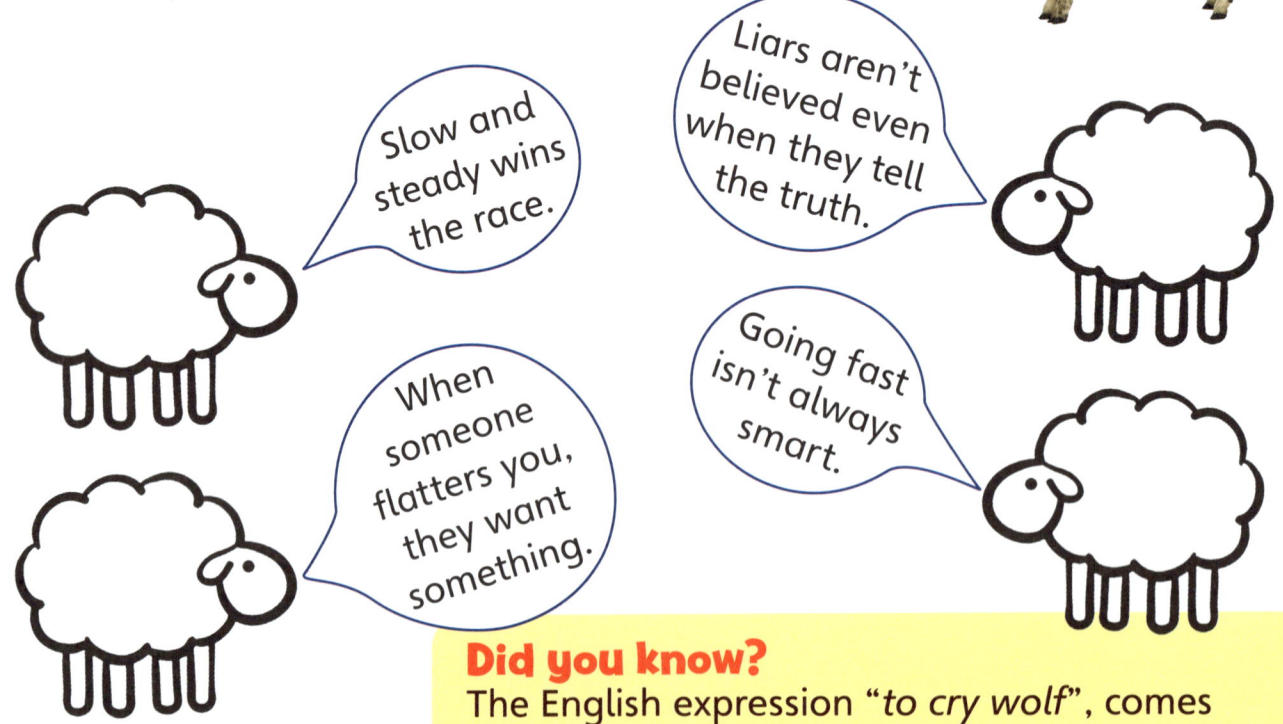

- Slow and steady wins the race.
- Liars aren't believed even when they tell the truth.
- When someone flatters you, they want something.
- Going fast isn't always smart.

**Did you know?**
The English expression "*to cry wolf*", comes from this story. It means "to give a false alarm."

# Who Has Seen the Wind?

*Who has seen the wind?*
*Neither I nor you:*
*But when the leaves hang trembling,*
*The wind is passing through.*

*Who has seen the wind?*
*Neither you nor I:*
*But when the trees bow down their heads,*
*The wind is passing by.*

*by Christina Rossetti*

Write the answers to these questions.

Does the poet think that anyone has seen the wind?

If nobody has seen the wind, how do we know it is there?

Which two words rhyme in the first verse?

Which two words rhyme in the second verse?

# What is Pink?

*Poets' Corner*

*What is pink? A rose is pink
By the fountain's brink.
What is red? A poppy's red
In its barley bed.
What is blue? The sky is blue 
Where the clouds float through.
What is white? A swan is white  
Sailing in the light.
What is yellow? Pears are yellow,
Rich and ripe and mellow.
What is green? The grass is green,  
With small flowers between.
What is violet? Clouds are violet
In the summer twilight.
What is orange? Why, an orange, 
Just an orange!*

by Christina Rossetti

Write the answers to these questions.

How many colours are mentioned in the poem? ☐

Write the rhyming words for these colours.

pink ☐           yellow ☐

blue ☐           green ☐

The poet paints a picture in our mind by comparing things to colours. Choose your own comparisons for these colours.

Red like

White like

Green like

The last line of the poem is different. How? What effect does this have?

**Now compare the two poems by Christina Rossetti.**

What is the first poem about?

What is the second poem about?

Both poems talk about nature. Are there any other ways they are similar?

How are they different?

Which poem do you prefer, and why?

# day by day

Here are two pages from Ted's diary. Read them, then answer the questions below.

**Friday morning . . .**
This morning I got up at half past seven. I brushed my teeth and put on my school uniform. I had breakfast with Mum and Dad. They had coffee. I had orange juice and cereal. I put my dishes in the dishwasher. Then I got my coat and bag and walked to school.

**Saturday morning . . .**
This morning I got up at half past eight. I brushed my teeth and put on my jeans and top. I had breakfast with Mum and Dad. They had coffee. Dad made pancakes. I had two! I put my dishes in the dishwasher. Then I got my jacket and we all drove to Granny's house.

Write what happened only on **Friday** in the left circle. Write what happened only on **Saturday** in the right circle. Write what happened on **both days** in the middle.

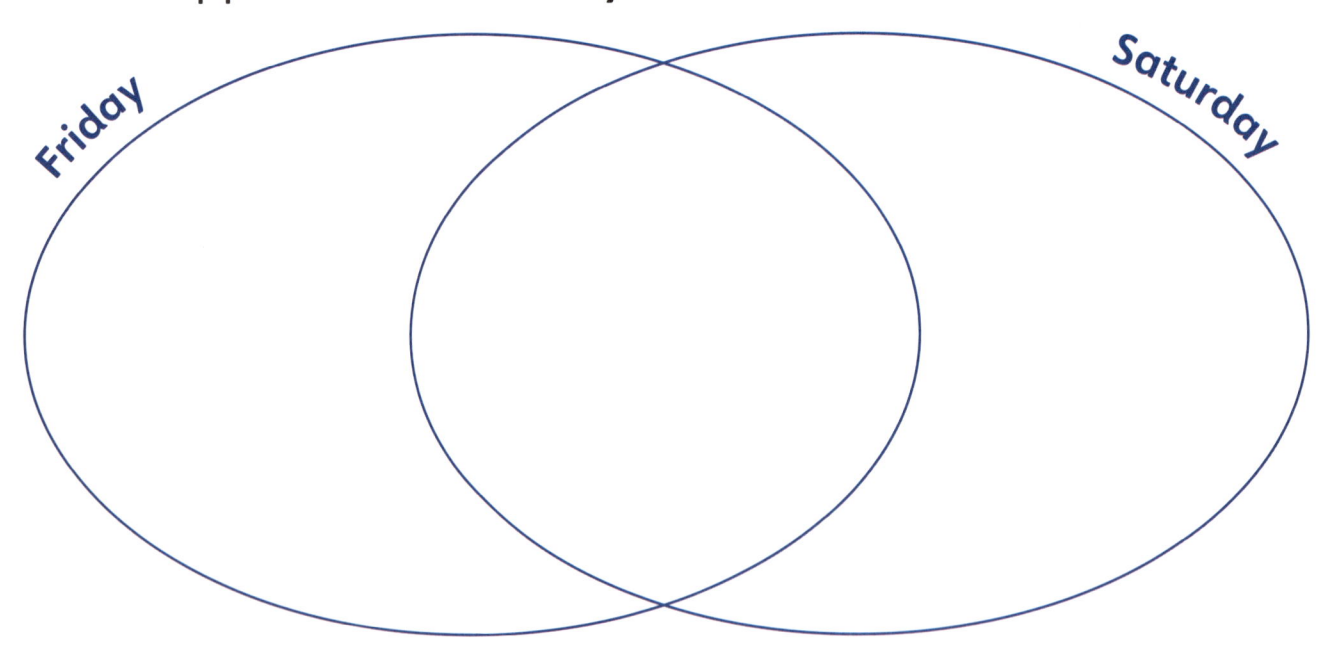

How were the mornings alike?

# The Story of Winnie-the-Pooh

A A Milne was an English writer. His most famous books were Winnie-the-Pooh, and The House at Pooh Corner. They tell the adventures of a young boy named Christopher Robin and his best friend, Winnie-the-Pooh, in the Hundred Acre Woods. The boy was named after Milne's own son, and the lovable bear and his animal friends were inspired by his son's stuffed toys!

The books have been widely loved. They have been sold across the world and translated into 50 different languages. They have also been made into popular films.

Where was A A Milne from?


Who was Christopher Robin named after?


Who was Christopher Robin's best friend?


Where did Christopher Robin and Winnie-the-Pooh play?


**Did you know?**
January 18th is National Winnie the Pooh Day in memory of A A Milne's birthday!

## comparing texts

The following texts all relate to rainy weather, but they are written very differently and for different purposes.

### Storm Causes Chaos

Gale force winds of up to 60mph and heavy rain battered the south of the country last night as Storm Fraser moved in from the Atlantic. The village of Wiltley recorded record rainfall of 45mm in 24 hours— nearly a month's rainfall in a single day. Some homes were left without power, and some roads have been blocked. Motorists have been advised to check their route before setting off.

*newspaper article*

### New Rainbow Umbrella!

Your perfect umbrella awaits you! The brand new Rainbow Umbrella is completely waterproof, with a strong, sturdy frame. It will lift your mood on the darkest day with its bright, cheerful colours!

This stunning umbrella is only £9.99! Don't miss out— buy now while stocks last!

*advert*

### The Storm

I huddled miserably inside the old shed as the wind howled and the endless rain lashed down all around me. It pounded on the roof and beat at the walls like an angry monster, creeping in slowly but surely under the broken door.

I felt trapped! I felt hunted!

*creative writing*

### TODAY'S WEATHER FORECAST

A cold and windy start to the day, with maximum temperatures of 10° centigrade.

Heavy showers expected to move into the area, with a chance of thunderstorms. 15-20mm of rain. Flash flood warnings in place.

*weather forecast*

Read the texts on the opposite page, then answer the questions.

Which text gives the most information?

Write two facts from the newspaper article.

Why do you think it doesn't use many adjectives?

Which text is not factual?

What makes it different from the other texts?

What does the author refer to the storm as?

What makes the umbrella advert persuasive?

List all the adjectives in the umbrella advert.

Would it make you buy the umbrella? Why / why not?

# Helping Birds

Peregrine falcons are special birds. They are great hunters and can fly very fast. In fact, the peregrine falcon can reach over 200 miles per hour (320km/h) when it is diving for food! This makes it not only the fastest bird in the world, but the fastest member of the animal kingdom!

However, at one time, these falcons were in danger. There were not many of them left. Baby falcons were not hatching from eggs. Part of the problem was the chemicals that farmers used as weedkillers.

Tom Cade, an American scientist who studied birds, had an idea. He and other scientists got eggs. They hatched the eggs. They raised the chicks by hand. Then they set them free.

The falcons found new homes in the country and in cities. They had babies of their own. In the towns and cities they made their nests on tall buildings and bridges, instead of cliffs and rock faces. People were excited to see the beautiful birds.

Thanks to Tom Cade and other scientists, peregrine falcons are not in danger anymore!

Circle the answers.

What does "raised the chicks by hand" mean?

They raised the baby falcons themselves.

They used a machine to raise the chicks.

The falcons flew only to the right.

Which word means "baby bird"?

egg        chick        falcon        scientist

Why did the author write this story?

to make people laugh

to tell about how eggs hatch

to tell how a scientist helped birds

Put these events into the correct order. Write 1, 2, 3, or 4 in each box.

| The scientists set the falcons free. | An American scientist had an idea. | The scientists got falcon eggs. | Peregrine falcons were in danger. |

**Did you know?**
Peregrine falcons are among the world's most common birds of prey and live on all continents except Antarctica.

# Hot or Cold?

The planet that we live on, planet Earth, is a huge sphere! The North Pole is at the top and the South Pole is at the bottom. The **Equator** is like a belt around the middle. We call the half above the Equator the **Northern Hemisphere**. Below the Equator is the **Southern Hemisphere**.

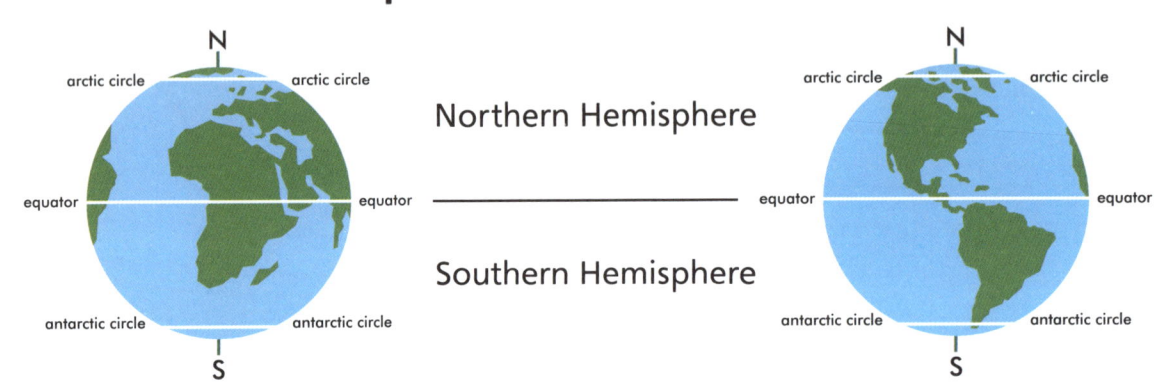

**Seasons** are **opposite** in the two hemispheres. The United Kingdom is in the *Northern Hemisphere*. Here, December, January, and February are winter months, when it is colder. In countries such as Australia, in the *Southern Hemisphere*, December, January, and February are summer months, when it is warmer. In Australia, some people celebrate Christmas Day on the beach!

June, July, and August are the warmest months in the Northern Hemisphere, but they are the coldest months in the Southern Hemisphere. At the Equator, it is hot all year!

### Did you know?
The Equator is not a visible line, but in Uganda people can see where it is, thanks to markers like this. At these locations, you could stand with one foot in the Northern Hemisphere and the other foot in the Southern Hemisphere!

Now answer these questions.

In which hemisphere is the United Kingdom?

In which hemisphere is Australia?

Where is it hot all year round?

Circle the picture that could show **January's** weather in the **Southern Hemisphere**.

Circle the picture that could show **July's** weather in the **Southern Hemisphere**

## step by step

Following directions helps us to do new things. We cook new foods by reading recipes. We put things together by reading instructions.

**Follow these directions for drawing a cat's face.**

1. Draw a circle.
2. In the middle of the circle, draw an upside-down triangle for a nose.
3. Draw small circles above each top corner of the triangle for eyes.
4. Add three lines on each side coming out from the sides of the triangle for whiskers.
5. Add two triangles at the top of the circle on the left and right for ears.

Did your final drawing look like a cat's face? If not, what went wrong? Look back at the instructions. Did you miss something, or were the directions not clear enough? How could you make them better?

# Writing

# super sentences

Make each sentence more interesting by adding more information. Use adjectives, adverbs, prepositions and conjunctions. Use the word bank to help you, and add your own words to it.

> swiftly   loudly   cheeky   because   happy   beautiful
> scary   hungry   green   wild   with   ferocious   huge
> countryside   hopefully   under   holiday   across   sleek

Jonny saw a dinosaur.

The horses ran.

The dog is hiding.

The children cheered.

# for sale!

Imagine that you are selling this bike.

First, think of some adjectives to describe the bike.

Now use those adjectives in one or more sentences on the poster to explain why someone would like this bike.

**FOR SALE!**

# best pet ever

What makes a good pet? Use the word bank to help you complete the tasks below. Add your own words to it.

**cuddly**  **loyal**  **intelligent**  **adorable**  **quiet**  **furry**
**fun**  **beautiful**  **interesting**  **affectionate**  **cunning**
**exotic**  **playful**  **unusual**  **mischievous**  **cute**  **easy**

Describe some of the animals, using expanded noun sentences. Use commas to separate words in a list.

The hamster is

The rabbit is

The parrot is

There are advantages and disadvantages of each pet. Complete each sentence. The first is done for you.

> The horse would be fun to ride **but** it would be hard to look after.
>
> The fish is beautiful **but**
>
>
> The dog would be fun to play with **but**

Which animal do you prefer and why?

> The dog or the budgie?
>
>
> The tortoise or the cat?

Now choose one of the animals (or any other) and say why this animal makes the best pet of all to have.

# a great day out

Think of a great day out that you have had. Write about it below. Use the questions to help guide you with your writing. Use conjunctions to make your sentences interesting.

**Where** did you go?
**Who** did you go with?
**How** did you get there?
**What** did you do first?
**What** did you do next?
**What** did you do after that?
**What** did you eat?
**When** did you leave?
**What** was the weather like?

Remember to use the correct punctuation, leave spaces between the words, and check your spelling!

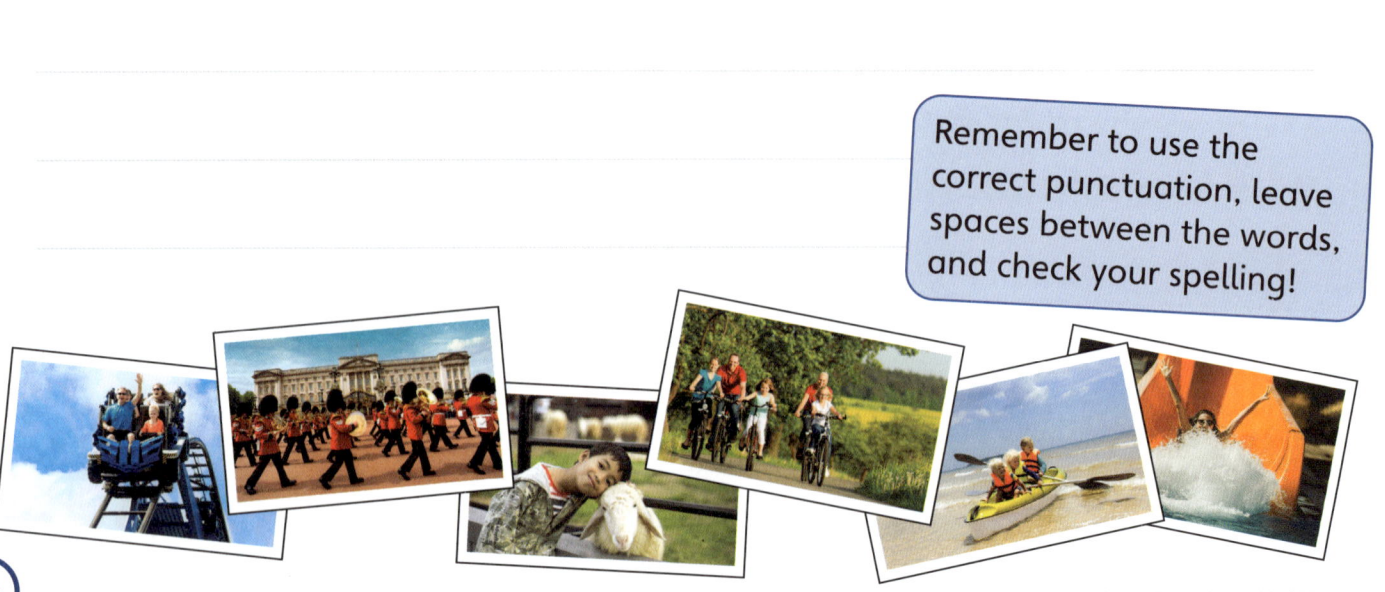

# all in order

Imagine that you are going to teach someone how to tie up their shoelaces. Write the steps.

First,


Next,


Then,


Last,

# best film ever

Do you have a favourite film? What is it called?

Explain briefly what the film is about.

Who are the main characters?

Where is the film set?

Explain why you like the film. The questions below will help give you some ideas. Use conjunctions and expanded noun sentences.

- Is it exciting?
- Does it have a good story?
- Is it funny?
- Do you like the actors?
- Does it have good special effects?

## correcting your own work

Write three sentences explaining which is your favourite season. Write quickly—you will correct it later.

Look over your work carefully. Check your spelling.
Check for capital letters and punctuation.
Mark up any corrections.
Write it out again below, in your best handwriting.

# what's up?

Look at each picture. Write what you think happened just *before*. Use full sentences, and watch out for punctuation and spacing!

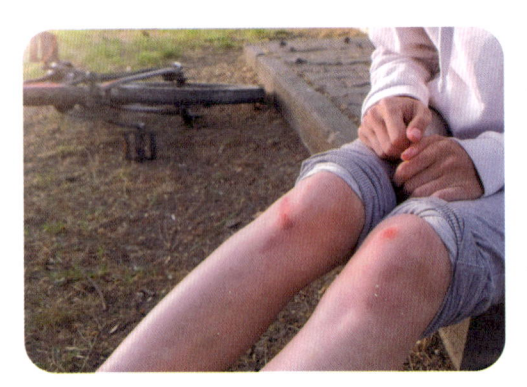

Look at each picture. Write what you think will happen *next*.

## getting organised

The story below has got mixed up. The events are out of order. Number them in order from 1 to 4.

Marcus said, "No! That would be stealing."
"But how do we know who it belongs to? How can we return it to them?" asked Jack.
"I don't know," replied Marcus unhappily.

Just then, their classmate Tom came rushing into the park. He looked really worried, and ran up to Marcus and Jack.

It was a wallet! There was nothing inside it to show who it belonged to, but there was more than £20 inside! Jack told Marcus that he should keep the money.

Jack and Marcus were riding their skateboards in the park. Marcus spotted a dark shape in the leaves. He jumped off his board and went to take a closer look.

Write an end for the story.

# metaphors and similes

> A **metaphor** is a figure of speech that *directly* refers to one thing by mentioning another. A **simile** compares two things using the words *like* or *as*.

Circle the **similes** in red, and the **metaphors** in blue.

- She was as slow as a snail.
- He is my knight in shining armour.
- I slept like a log.
- My sister is a night owl.
- They fight like cat and dog.
- Life is a rollercoaster.

Circle the word that will complete the simile.

| | | | |
|---|---|---|---|
| She is as blind as a | dog | tree | bat |
| The night was black as | dirt | coal | metal |
| He was as brave as a | lion | mouse | frog |

Write your own similes.

The clouds were as white as

The day was as hot as

The tall trees looked like a row of

# mixing it up

Some words are overused. For each sentence, choose one of the words from the word bank to replace **said**.

> whispered   groaned   announced   begged   yelled

"Get out of my garden!" ~~said~~ the angry man.

"That really hurt!" ~~said~~ Billy, clutching his arm.

"Keep quiet! They haven't seen us," ~~said~~ Zoe.

"We will leave at 9.30," ~~said~~ the teacher.

"Please let me go!" ~~said~~ the terrified mouse.

Think of some more alternatives to **said** and also for **went**. Write them in the boxes below.

| said | went |
|---|---|
|  |  |

# more tricks of the trade

> **Onomatopoeia** is when a word names a sound, but also sounds like that sound.

**BOOM!**

Join the sounds to the animals that would make them.

| oink | buzz | moo | hiss | baa | quack |

Complete the sentences below. Choose one of the words from the word bank.

| screeched | slurped | zoomed | sizzled |

The sausages _____ in the hot pan.
The owl _____ eerily in the dark night.
The racing car _____ past us.
The thirsty boy _____ his milk eagerly.

Think of something that makes each of these sounds.

| splash | | miaow | |
| pop | | smash | |
| crunch | | beep | |

# a sensory poem

Some poems use sensory words and onomatopoeia to encourage the reader to imagine the scene.

Underline the words in the poem on the right that use onomatopoeia.

**The Sound of Snow**

Snow is falling all around.
I listen hard and hear new sounds.
I start to walk—creak, creak, creak.
Under my boots the snow goes squeak.

The wind picks up and shakes a bush.
Flying snowflakes now go whoosh.
With chattering teeth and frosty face,
I rush inside to a nice warm place!

Write down as many sensory words as you can about *fireworks*.

Use those words to help you write your own poem.

# an acrostic poem

> In an **acrostic** poem, the first letters spell a word when you read down the lines.

**S**wimming in the sea
**U**nder the hot sun
**M**aking sandcastles
**M**errily playing
**E**ating ice creams
**R**elaxing together

Choose two of the words below to write your own acrostic poems.

**friends**   **spring**   **school**   **winter**   **happy**   **stars**

Illustrate the poems with your own drawings!

# a haiku

! A **haiku** is a form of poetry. The first and third lines have five syllables each. The second line has seven syllables. Haiku are often about nature, but they can be about anything.

 1 2 3 4 5
Chilly wintertime,
1 2 3 4 5 6 7
a graceful skier races
 1 2 3 4 5
down the perfect slope.

Choose a picture. Write a haiku about it. Remember to use adjectives, especially sensory words.

(5 syllables)

(7 syllables)

(5 syllables)

**Did you know?**
The haiku was invented in Japan. Now, people all over the world write haiku.

# recipe for a story

> **Setting, characters** and **plot** are the main ingredients of a story.
>
> **setting:** where and when the story takes place
> **characters:** the people or animals in the story
> **plot:** what happens in the story

Cut out the story ingredients on page 379. Paste them in the correct box below.

| setting | characters | plot |
|---|---|---|
|  |  |  |

Choose one ingredient from each box and write a short story.

# Alone in the Woods

Max and his friends, Jared and Harris, had been playing in the woods. They had discovered an old, abandoned building, half hidden by trees, and had set up camp there, noble knights defending their fortress. But now they traipsed home together because it was time for dinner.

Just as they left the woods, Max realised he had left his jumper behind. "You go on," he urged his friends. "There's no point us all being late!" and he headed back into the trees.

By the time he arrived at the fortress, the light was beginning to fade. He hurried into the deserted building to look for his jumper. How dark it was! The corners were dusty and filled with cobwebs, and as he searched, the building seemed to grow dimmer and dimmer. He shivered. How eerie and unpleasant it seemed now that he was on his own.

All of a sudden, the silence was broken by a strange wail. Max stood still, scarcely daring to breathe, his heart thudding as loud as a drum. He heard the rustle of leaves, and then a bone-chilling screech echoed through the building, filling him with terror.

What was out there? What was hiding in the shadows?

Read the unfinished story on the opposite page. Then answer the questions.

Where is the story set?

Who are the characters in the story?

What problem does Max have?

What do you think is lurking in the old building? What do you think Max will do? Write your own ending to the story. Remember to use full, interesting sentences, and the correct punctuation.

# planning your story

Create a main **character** for a story you will write.

> brave    energetic    injured    cowardly    shy
> strong    young    lonely    fearless

Choose one of the characters above, and use ideas from the word bank to describe your character.

Choose a **setting** for your story. It could be one of the pictures below, or somewhere else. It could be in the present, the past or the future. Describe it below.

Now think about the **plot**. Does your character have to overcome a problem? Is there something that they want, or some mystery to solve? Look at the ideas on the next page, and then write a short outline of your plot.

looking for a friend    injured and scared    lost in a strange place    litter on the beach    trapped in a burning building

the beginning

the middle

the end

It might help to draw some **storyboard** pictures.

Think of a suitable **title** for your story. Try to grab the reader's attention!

Now write out your story on the next page.

Remember to use the correct punctuation, leave spaces between the words, and check your spelling!

# points of view

Here is a picture board for the story of *Goldilocks and the Three Bears*.

Imagine you are Goldilocks. Tell the story from your point of view below.

Imagine you are Baby Bear. How did you feel when you found that a strange girl had eaten your porridge and slept in your bed? Tell *your* story below.

Now imagine you are a reporter for a local newspaper. You heard about the break-in. Write a short article for the newspaper below.

**BREAK-IN AT BEARS' COTTAGE!**

Finally, what do *you* think about what Goldilocks did? Discuss the story with a friend or adult.

# Numbers

# numbers and words

Match the number to the word.

| 62 | thirty-three | ninety-four | 56 |
| 33 | one hundred | forty | 40 |
| 17 | twenty-nine | seventy-seven | 77 |
| 100 | seventeen | eighty-one | 94 |
| 29 | sixty-two | fifty-six | 81 |

Write these numbers in words.

- 39 _____
- 91 _____
- 16 _____
- 48 _____

- 22 _____
- 75 _____
- 80 _____
- 53 _____

Write these numbers in numerals.

| eighty-six | ☐ | ninety | ☐ |
| forty-two | ☐ | seventy-three | ☐ |
| twenty-seven | ☐ | thirty-five | ☐ |
| sixty-nine | ☐ | fifty-eight | ☐ |

## ordering numbers

Reorder each sequence of numbers from smallest to biggest in the boxes on the right.

a) 76  93  21  50  56  →

b) 68  35  41  87  19  →

c) 28  77  16  30  52  →

Cut out the numbers on page 381 and organise them below in order of size, from smallest (1) to biggest (9).

| 1 | 2 | 3 |
|---|---|---|
| 4 | 5 | 6 |
| 7 | 8 | 9 |

# comparing numbers

Circle the correct sign (<, >, or =) to compare these numbers.

| | | |
|---|---|---|
| 81 | < > = | 69 |
| thirty-eight | < > = | eighty-three |
| 43 | < > = | 46 |
| 76 | < > = | seventy-nine |
| 51 | < > = | 44 |
| 6 + 3 + 2 | < > = |  6 + 5 |
| 5 + 5 + 5 | < > = | three + nine |
| 20 + 6 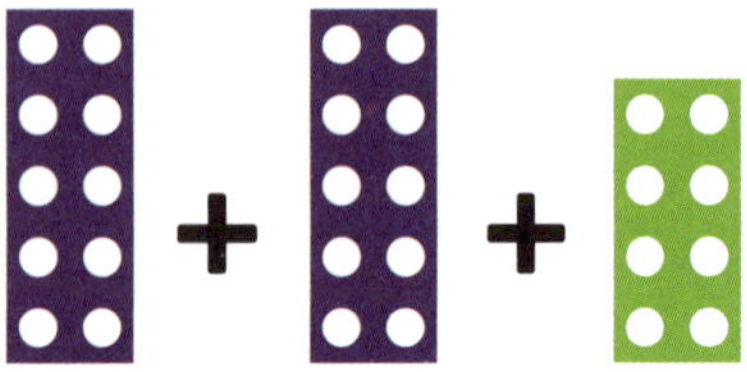 | < > = | 10 + 10 + 10 |

Colour the areas with **true** statements purple. Colour those with **false** statements yellow.

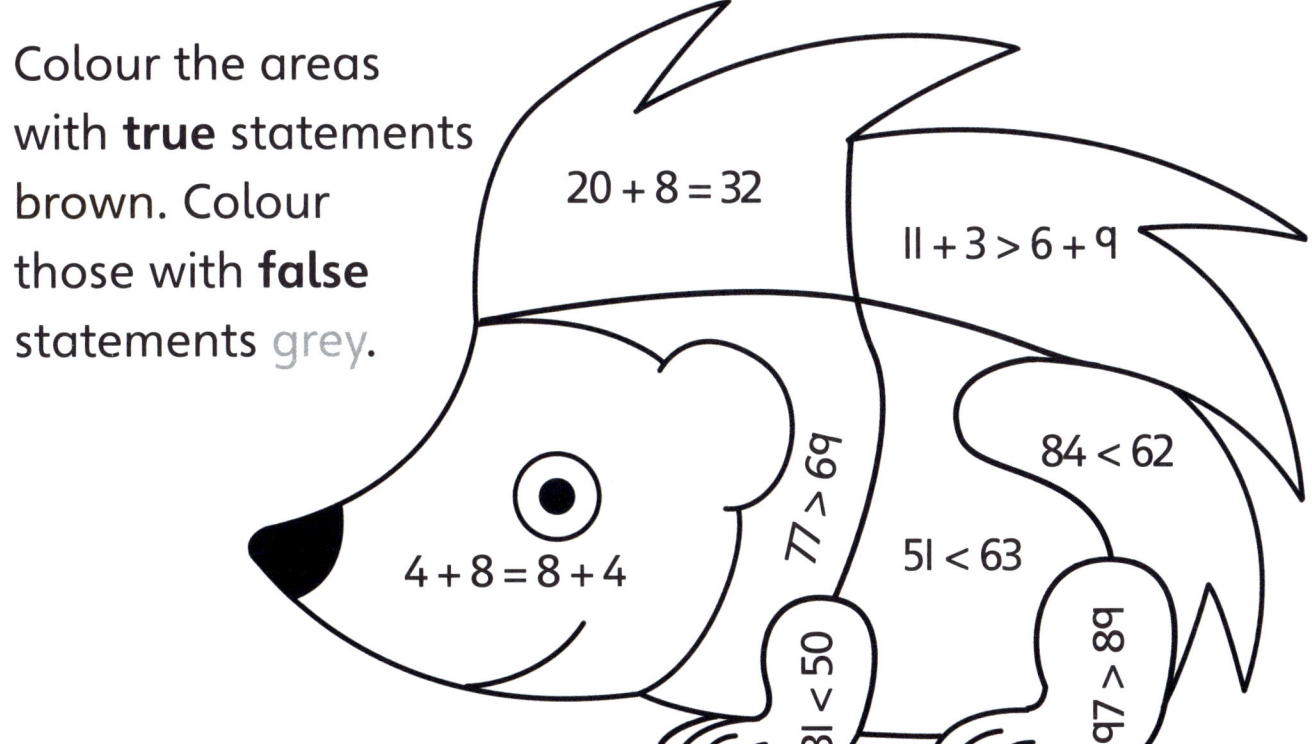

- $8 + 2 = 5 + 6$
- $12 - 3 > 8$
- $38 < 47$
- $91 > 83$
- $73 > 88$
- $6 + 7 = 7 + 6$
- $52 > 61$
- $6 + 14 < 18$

Colour the areas with **true** statements brown. Colour those with **false** statements grey.

- $20 + 8 = 32$
- $11 + 3 > 6 + 9$
- $4 + 8 = 8 + 4$
- $77 > 69$
- $84 < 62$
- $51 < 63$
- $31 < 50$
- $97 > 89$

# odd and even

Colour the squares with **odd** numbers blue and those with **even** numbers green.

| 41 | 22 | 33 | 44 | 49 | 59 | 92 | 25 | 32 | 54 |
|----|----|----|----|----|----|----|----|----|----|
| 34 | 17 | 76 | 29 | 62 | 90 | 11 | 74 | 29 | 49 |
| 58 | 72 | 80 | 13 | 14 | 61 | 82 | 16 | 37 | 66 |

**1** Circle the *largest* **even** number.

59   64   88   99   43   92   71

**2** Circle the *smallest* **odd** number.

22   47   19   33   12   55   40

**3** Circle all the **odd** numbers.

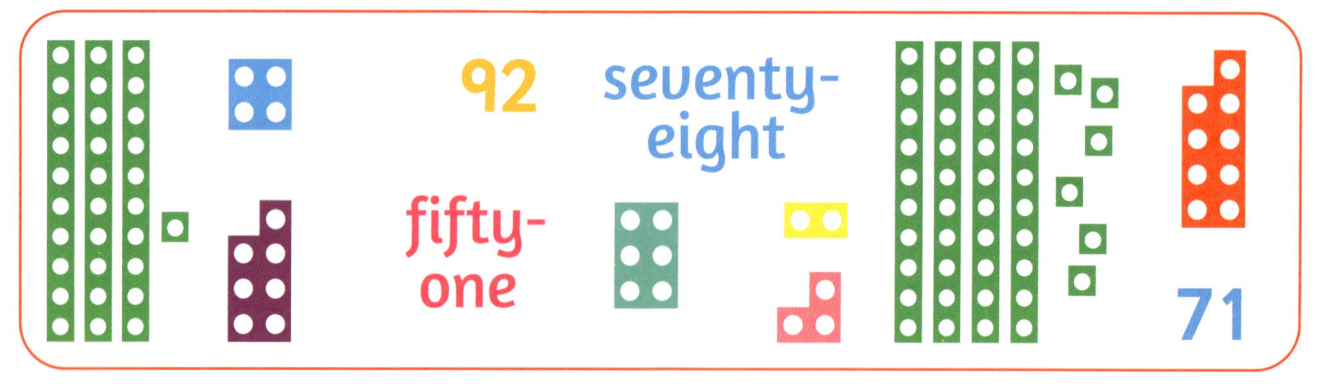

92   seventy-eight   fifty-one   71

**4** Write ✓ for true or ✗ for false.

**Odd** numbers can be shared between 2 equally.

Adding 2 **odd** numbers together will always give an **even** number.

## counting in steps

**1** Count in **2**s and fill in the missing numbers.

8, __, 12, __, __, 18, __, 22

**2** Count in **3**s and fill in the missing numbers.

6, 9, __, 15, __, __, __, 27

**3** Cut out the numbers on page 381 and place them in the correct order to fill in the gaps by counting in **3**s.

| 0 | 3 | | | | |
|---|---|---|---|---|---|
| 18 | | | | | |
| 36 | | | | | |

**4** Count in **5**s and fill in the missing numbers.

15, 20, __, __, __, 40, __, __, 55, __, 65

**5** Count in **10**s and fill in the missing numbers.

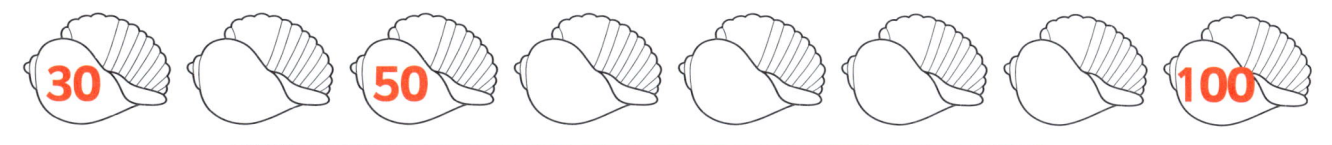

30, __, 50, __, __, __, __, 100

Colour in the objects when you have finished!

# NUMBERS

**1** Complete each sequence below.

| 22 | 24 | 26 |
| 91 | 81 | 71 |
| 55 | 50 | 45 |
| 30 | 28 | 26 |
| 14 | 24 | 34 |

**2** Colour the mistake in each sequence.

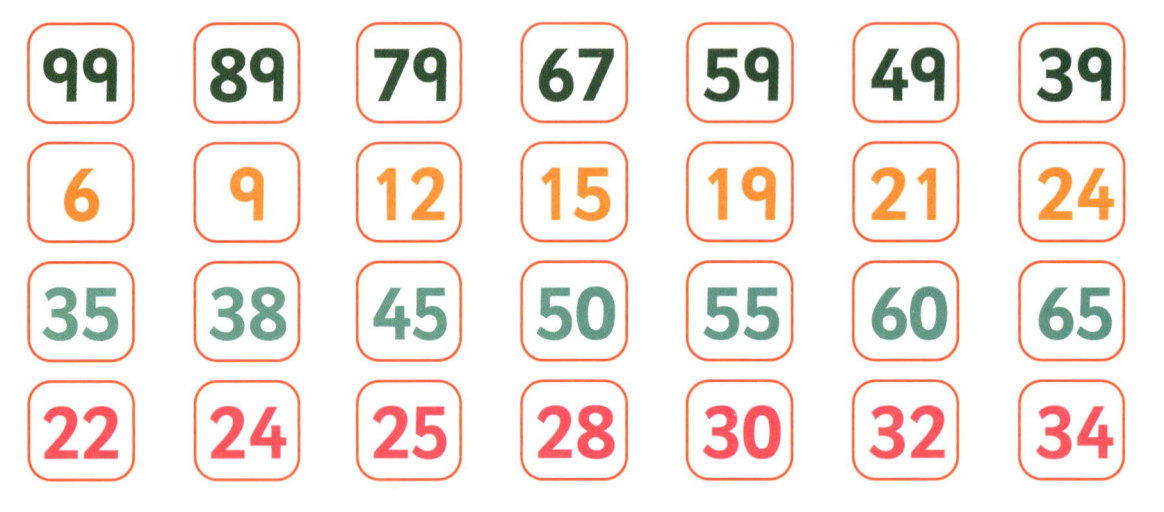

| 99 | 89 | 79 | 67 | 59 | 49 | 39 |
| 6 | 9 | 12 | 15 | 19 | 21 | 24 |
| 35 | 38 | 45 | 50 | 55 | 60 | 65 |
| 22 | 24 | 25 | 28 | 30 | 32 | 34 |

**3** Count in **2**s to find the total number of objects.

There are ☐ muffins.

There are ☐ flipflops.

142

**4** Count in **3**s to find the total number of objects.

There are _____ dinosaurs.

There are _____ stones.

**5** Count in **5**s to find the total number of objects.

There are _____ lollies.

There are _____ paint cans.

**5** Count in **10**s to find the total number of objects.

There are _____ crayons.

**Did you know?**
The average child wears down over 700 crayons by their 10th birthday!

143

# number lines

Fill in the missing numbers on these number lines.

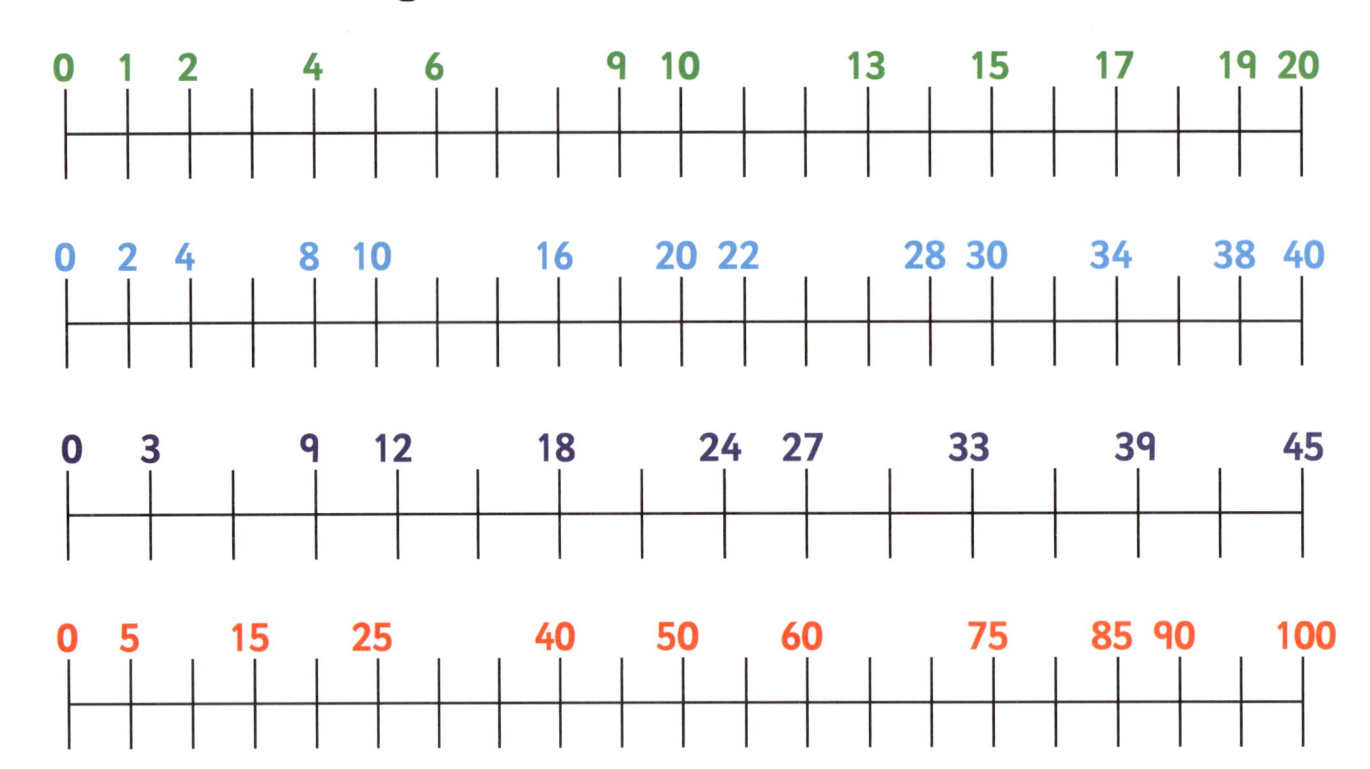

0  1  2  _  4  _  6  _  _  9  10  _  _  13  _  15  _  17  _  19  20

0  2  4  _  8  10  _  _  16  _  _  20  22  _  _  _  28  30  _  _  34  _  _  38  40

0  3  _  _  9  _  12  _  _  18  _  _  24  27  _  _  33  _  _  39  _  _  _  45

0  5  _  15  _  25  _  _  40  _  50  _  60  _  _  75  _  85  90  _  100

Place the number **20** on the number line.

0 _____ 100

Place the number **30** on the number line.

0 _____ 50

Place the number **80** on the number line.

0 _____ 100

Place the number **16** on the number line.

0 |—|—|—|—|—|—|—|—|—|—| 20

Place the number **25** on the number line.

0 |—|—|—|—|—|—| 30

*Estimate* where the number **45** will sit on the number line.

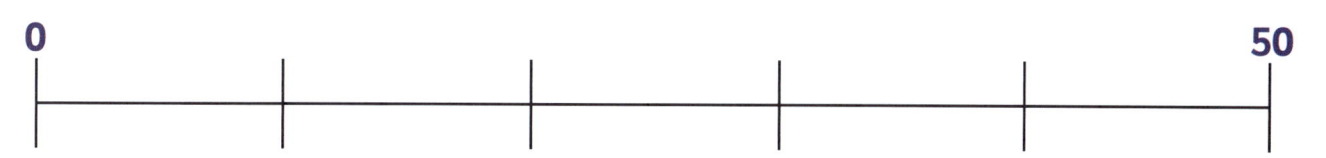

0 |—|—|—|—|—| 50

*Estimate* where the number **8** will sit on the number line.

0 |———————————| 20

Which of these numbers might the arrow be pointing to? Circle the correct answer.

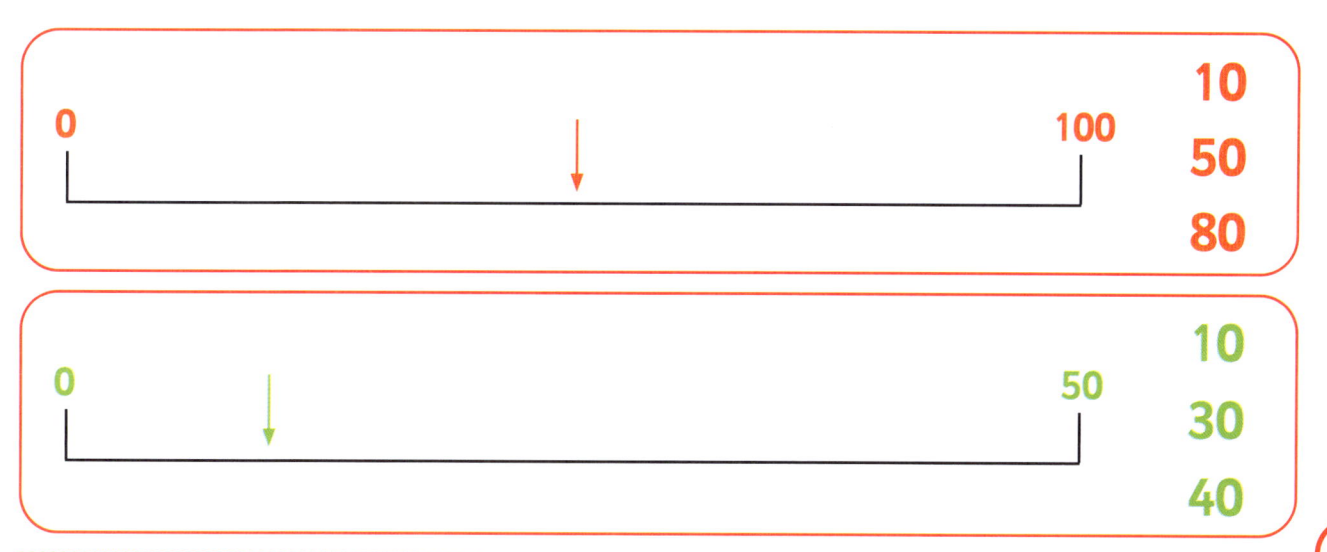

0 ————↓———— 100

10
50
80

0 —↓———————— 50

10
30
40

# place value

**1** Write the number that each abacus shows.

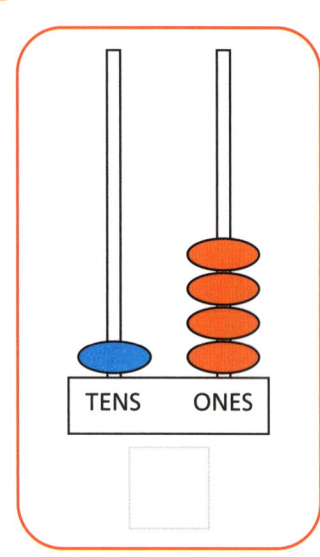

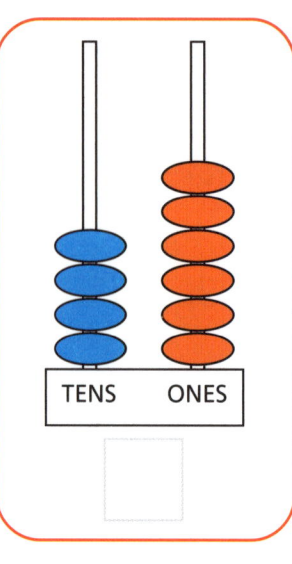

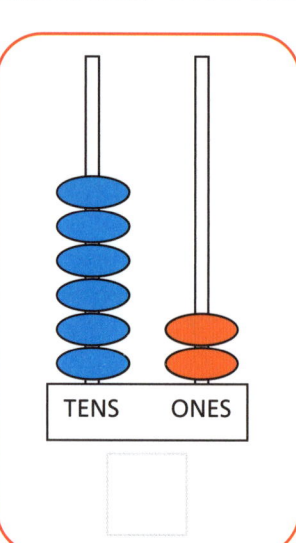

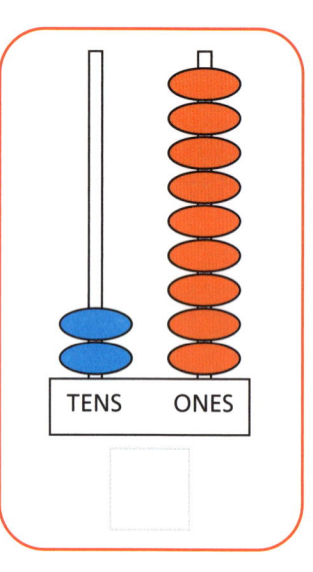

[Abacus 1: 1 ten, 4 ones = 14]
[Abacus 2: 4 tens, 5 ones = 45]
[Abacus 3: 5 tens, 2 ones = 52]
[Abacus 4: 2 tens, 9 ones = 29]

**2** Draw beads on each abacus to show the number.

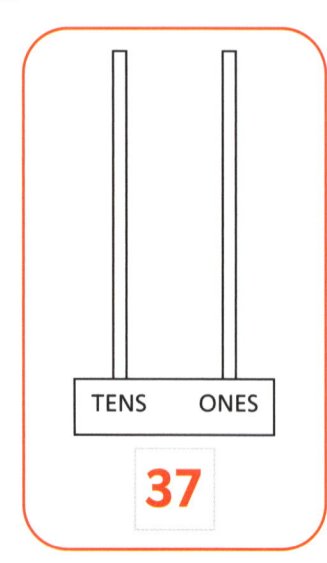

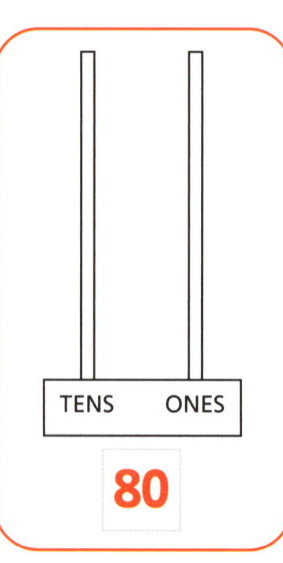

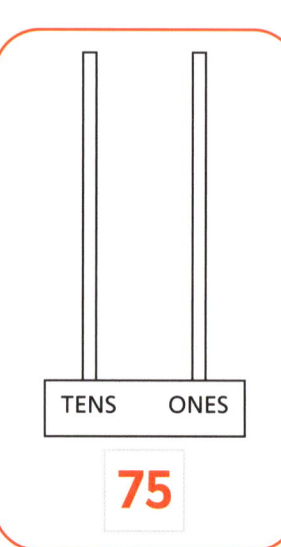

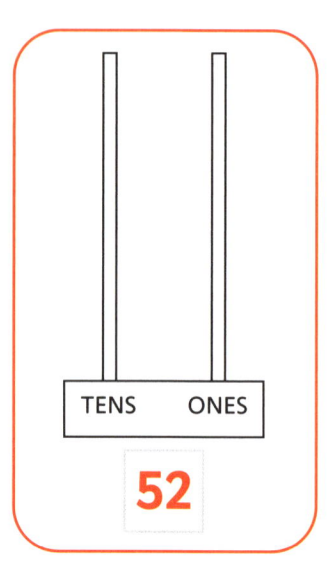

37   80   75   52

**3** Fill in the gaps.

65 = ☐ tens + ☐ ones     3 tens + 3 ones = ☐

92 = ☐ tens + ☐ ones     7 tens + 0 ones = ☐

28 = ☐ tens + ☐ ones     8 tens + 6 ones = ☐

**4** Circle all the numbers that have **3** *ones*.

| 23 | 37 | 53 | 30 | 62 | 74 | 83 | 38 | 93 | 44 |

**5** Circle all the numbers that have **2** *tens*.

| 27 | 12 | 90 | 29 | 51 | 62 | 20 | 32 | 25 | 49 |

**6** Circle groups of 10. Count the total number of birds.

☐ tens + ☐ ones = ☐

**7** Circle groups of 10. Count the total number of bananas.

☐ tens + ☐ ones = ☐

**Did you know?**
Bananas can be yellow, green, red, brown or even purple when they are ripe!

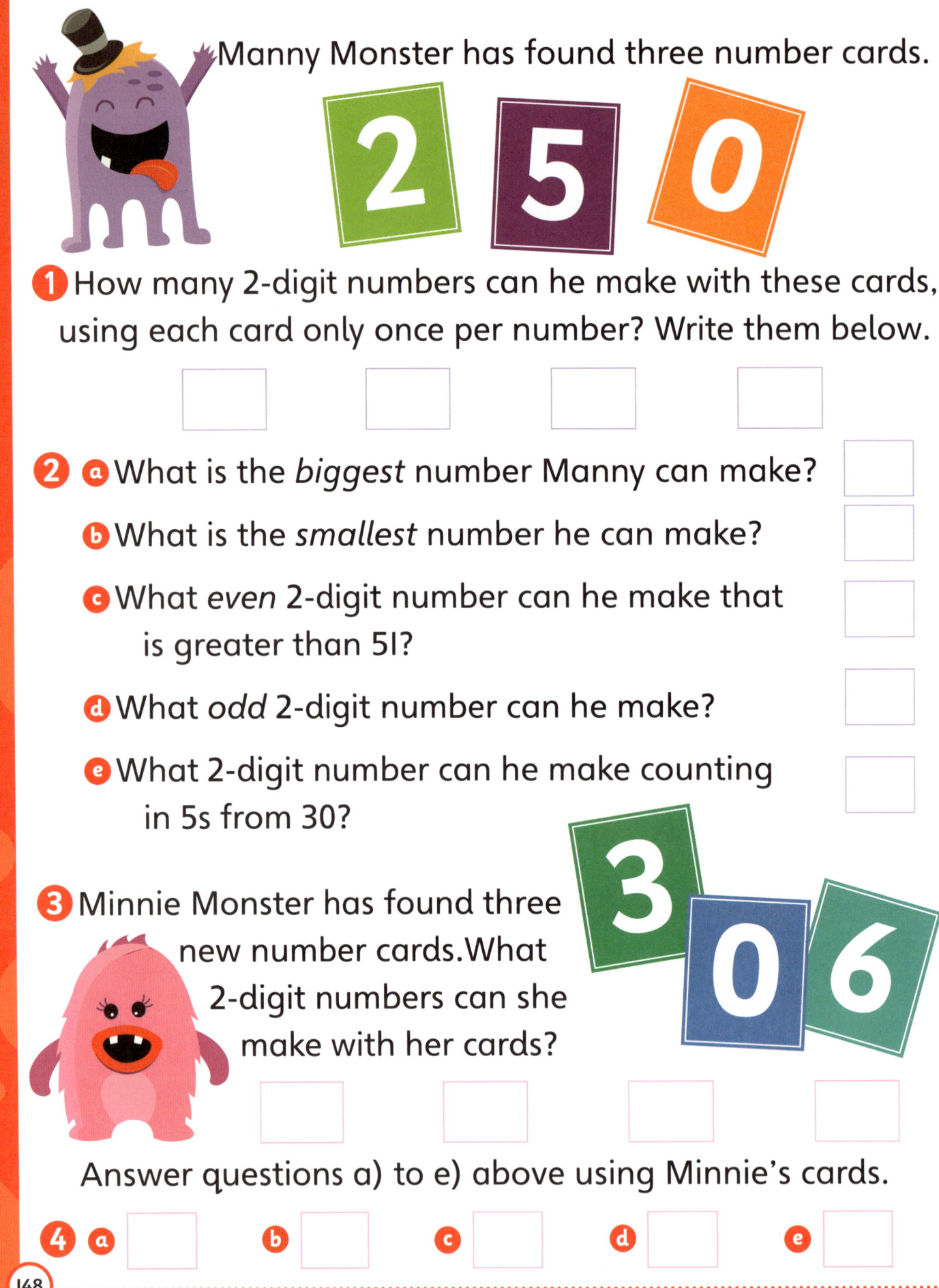

# NUMBERS

Manny Monster has found three number cards.

**2  5  0**

**1** How many 2-digit numbers can he make with these cards, using each card only once per number? Write them below.

☐  ☐  ☐  ☐

**2 a)** What is the *biggest* number Manny can make? ☐

  **b)** What is the *smallest* number he can make? ☐

  **c)** What *even* 2-digit number can he make that is greater than 51? ☐

  **d)** What *odd* 2-digit number can he make? ☐

  **e)** What 2-digit number can he make counting in 5s from 30? ☐

**3** Minnie Monster has found three new number cards. What 2-digit numbers can she make with her cards?

**3  0  6**

☐  ☐  ☐  ☐

Answer questions a) to e) above using Minnie's cards.

**4 a)** ☐   **b)** ☐   **c)** ☐   **d)** ☐   **e)** ☐

148

Complete the table by filling in the gaps.

| | | | |
|---|---|---|---|
| | ☐ tens + ☐ ones | 25 = 20 + 5 | |
| | ☐ tens + ☐ ones | ☐ = ☐ + ☐ | |
| | ☐ tens + ☐ ones | ☐ = 30 + 2 | |
| | ☐ tens + ☐ ones | ☐ = ☐ + ☐ | |
| 27 | ☐ tens + ☐ ones | ☐ = ☐ + ☐ | |

Complete each fact family.

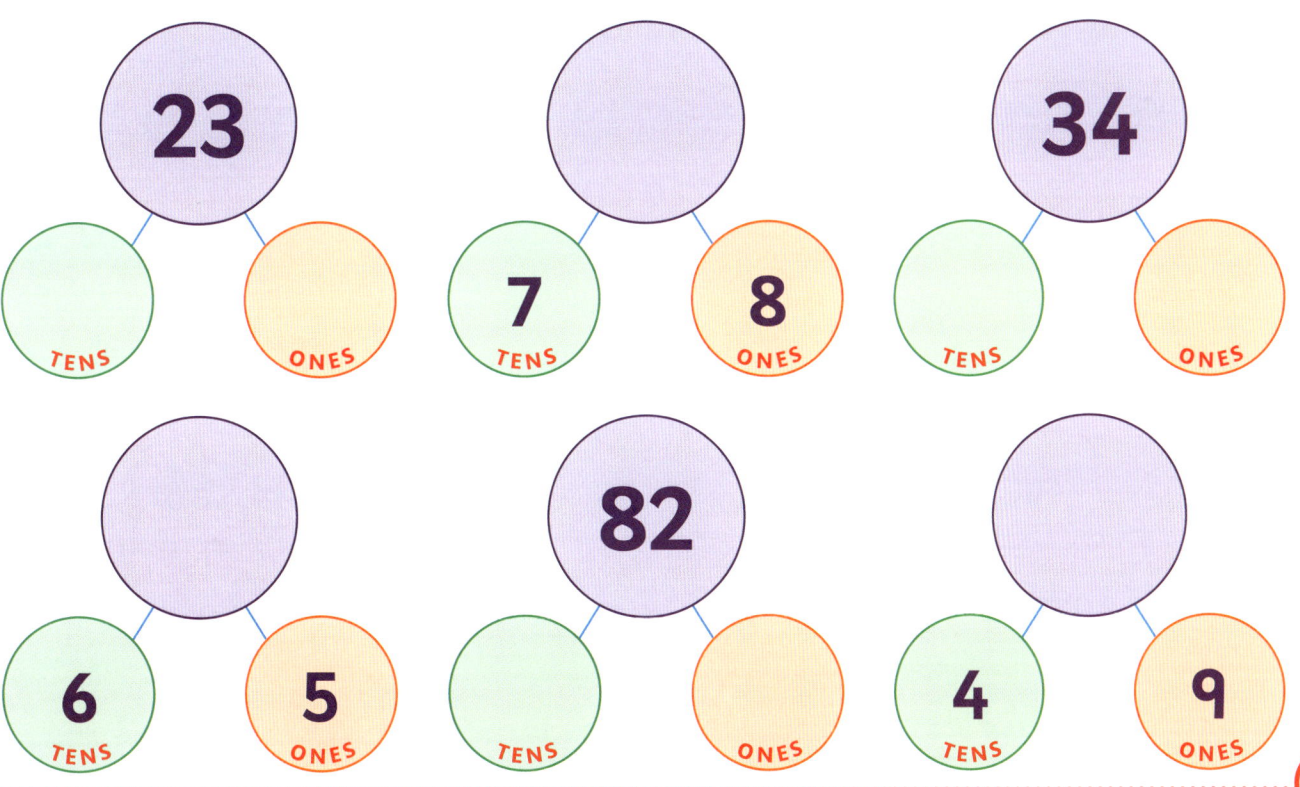

23 — TENS ☐, ONES ☐

☐ — TENS 7, ONES 8

34 — TENS ☐, ONES ☐

☐ — TENS 6, ONES 5

82 — TENS ☐, ONES ☐

☐ — TENS 4, ONES 9

# partitioning numbers

Partition each number in three more ways.

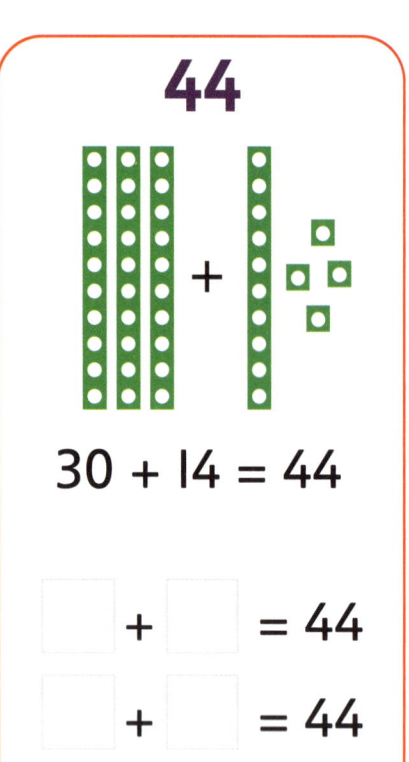

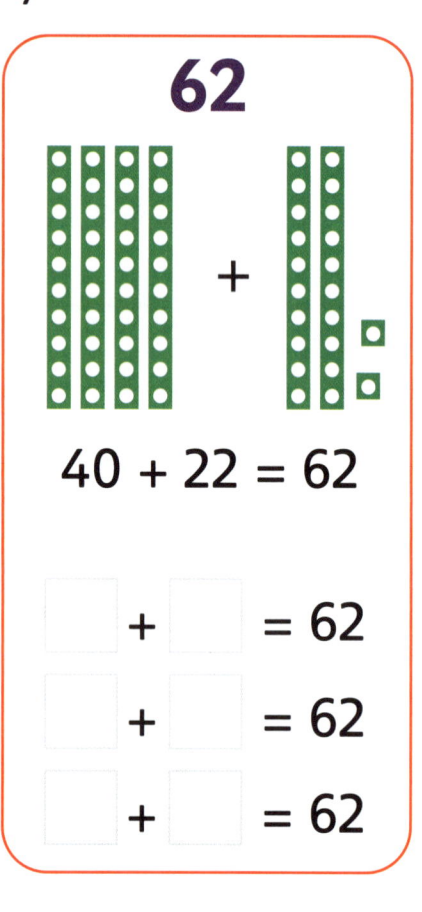

**44**

30 + 14 = 44

☐ + ☐ = 44
☐ + ☐ = 44
☐ + ☐ = 44

**59**

50 + 9 = 59

☐ + ☐ = 59
☐ + ☐ = 59
☐ + ☐ = 59

**62**

40 + 22 = 62

☐ + ☐ = 62
☐ + ☐ = 62
☐ + ☐ = 62

Join the numbers that make up the same total.

50 + 6        20 + 26
30 + 6        40 + 46
60 + 6        50 + 16
40 + 6        60 + 36
90 + 6        10 + 26
80 + 6        30 + 26

# place value bingo!

Cut out the cards on page 383. Put them in a pile, face down. Choose one of the bingo cards below. Take turns with a friend to pick a card and match it to the number shown on your bingo card. If it doesn't match, put it back. The first to cover all their numbers wins!

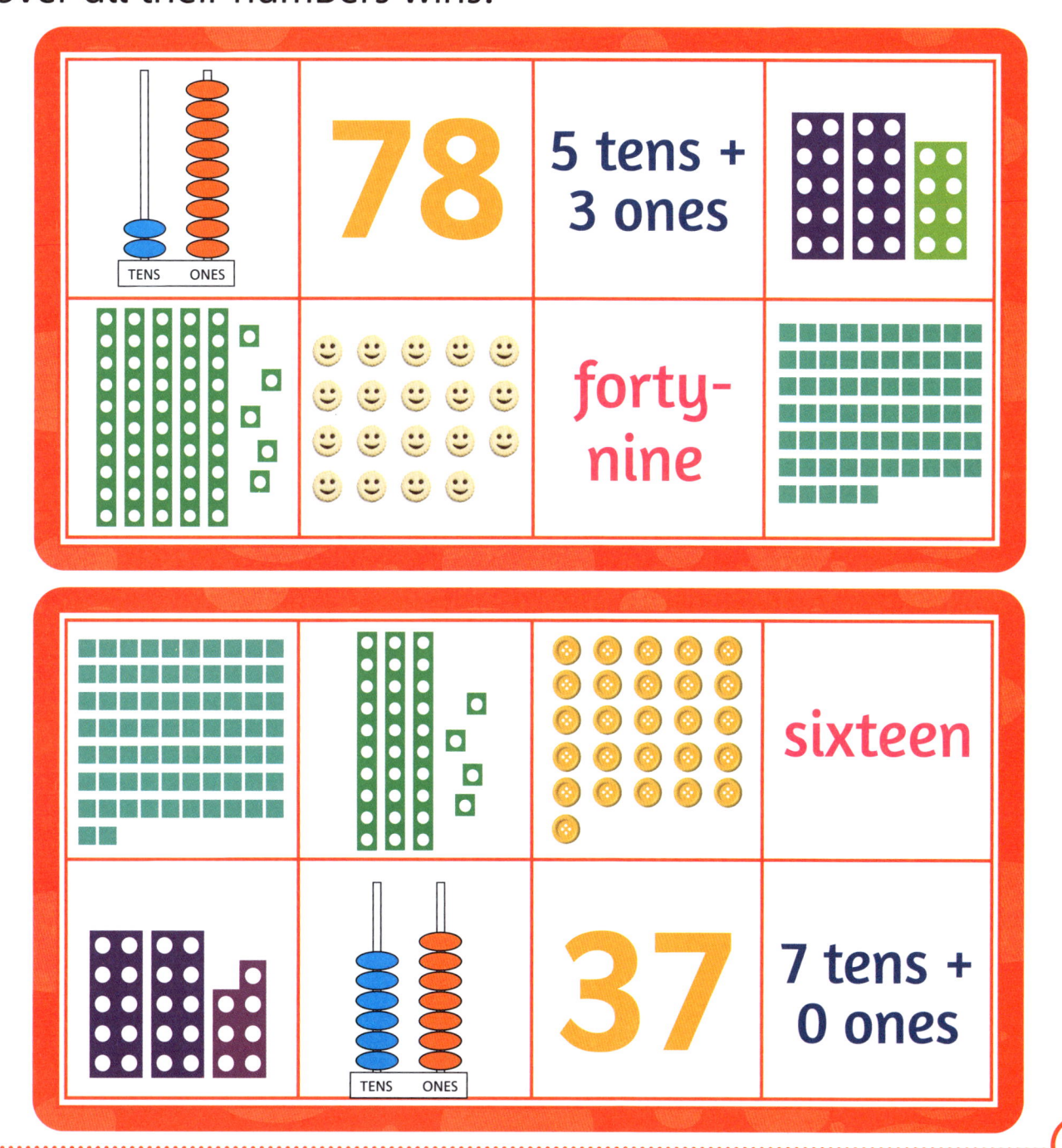

| | | | |
|---|---|---|---|
| (abacus) | 78 | 5 tens + 3 ones | (blocks) |
| (green tens and ones) | (smiley faces) | forty-nine | (green squares) |

| | | | |
|---|---|---|---|
| (green squares) | (green tens and ones) | (yellow buttons) | sixteen |
| (purple blocks) | (abacus) | 37 | 7 tens + 0 ones |

# number puzzles

**1** In a competition to see who could do the most star jumps, Lizzy jumped 35 and Dan jumped 38. Tia jumped 6 more than Lizzy.

Who won the competition? ............

How many star jumps did the winner jump? ☐

**2** Abdul bakes 10 cakes. He gives 2 to a friend.
Isla bakes 12 cakes. She gives 5 of her cakes away.

Who has the most cakes now? ............

How many cakes does he/she have left? ☐

**3** Tariq has made some numbers. He tells Sam that all of his numbers are even. Sam says he is wrong.

Who is right?

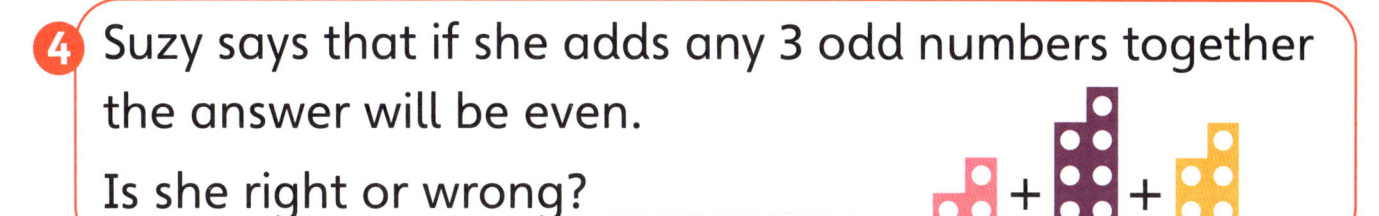

**4** Suzy says that if she adds any 3 odd numbers together the answer will be even.

Is she right or wrong?

**5** Jack has 70 sweets. Jenny has 10 sweets.

Jack gives away some of his sweets to Jenny. Now he has 40 left.

How many sweets did Jack give away?

How many sweets does Jenny have now?

**6** What would be the **8th** number in this sequence?

21  31  41  51  61

**7** What would be the **9th** number in this sequence?

80  75  70  65  60

**8** Read the clues to work out the number.

It is a number between 19 and 40.

It is an odd number.

The digits add up to 9.

The number has a 2 in the tens column.

What is the number?

9. Tom, Tilly and Tania go to the school fete.

Tom spends all his money buying a doughnut for 15p and a toy for 65p.

Tilly also buys a doughnut for 15p, and she buys a book for 50p. She has 15p left.

Tania buys 2 books for 30p each, and a toy for 15p. She has 20p left.

How much money did each child have at the start?

Tom ☐ p     Tilly ☐ p     Tania ☐ p

Who *spent* the most money?

10. Evie puts the **same** number on each number line.

She places it where the arrow points to on the **top** line.

What is the number? ☐

Put the number in the correct place on the **bottom** line.

11. Joseph has 4 tens and 2 ones. Maia has 2 tens more than Joseph.

How many does Maia have? ☐

**12** Read the clues to work out the number.

- It is a number between 16 and 28.
- It is an even number.
- Half this number is 12.
- The number has a 4 in the ones column.

What is the number? ☐

**13** Use the number cards on the right to make as many different 2-digit numbers as you can. Only use each card once per number.

**2  3  4**

**a** Order them from smallest to largest.

☐  ☐  ☐  ☐  ☐  ☐

**b** Choose from your numbers to complete these number sentences.

☐ < ☐        ☐ > ☐

**14** Ginger has 5 balls of wool.
Luna has 1 more ball than Ginger.
Sooty has 4 balls of wool.
Smokey has 3 more than Sooty.

How many balls of wool does Luna have? ☐

Which kitten has the most wool?

# sudoku challenge

Fill in the missing numbers on the 4 x 4 grids below.

The rules are simple. Each square has to contain a single number – 1, 2, 3 or 4. Each column can only contain each number once, and the same applies to each row and each section. The trick is working out how to fit all the numbers in without repeating them in a section, row or column!

Tip: start with the number 4!

**Did you know?**
The name "*Sudoku*" stems from two Japanese words: *su*, which means *number*, and *doku*, which means *single*.

# Addition and Subtraction

# sum or difference

Calculate the difference between each of the numbers shown below. Then write the sum (total) of the two numbers.

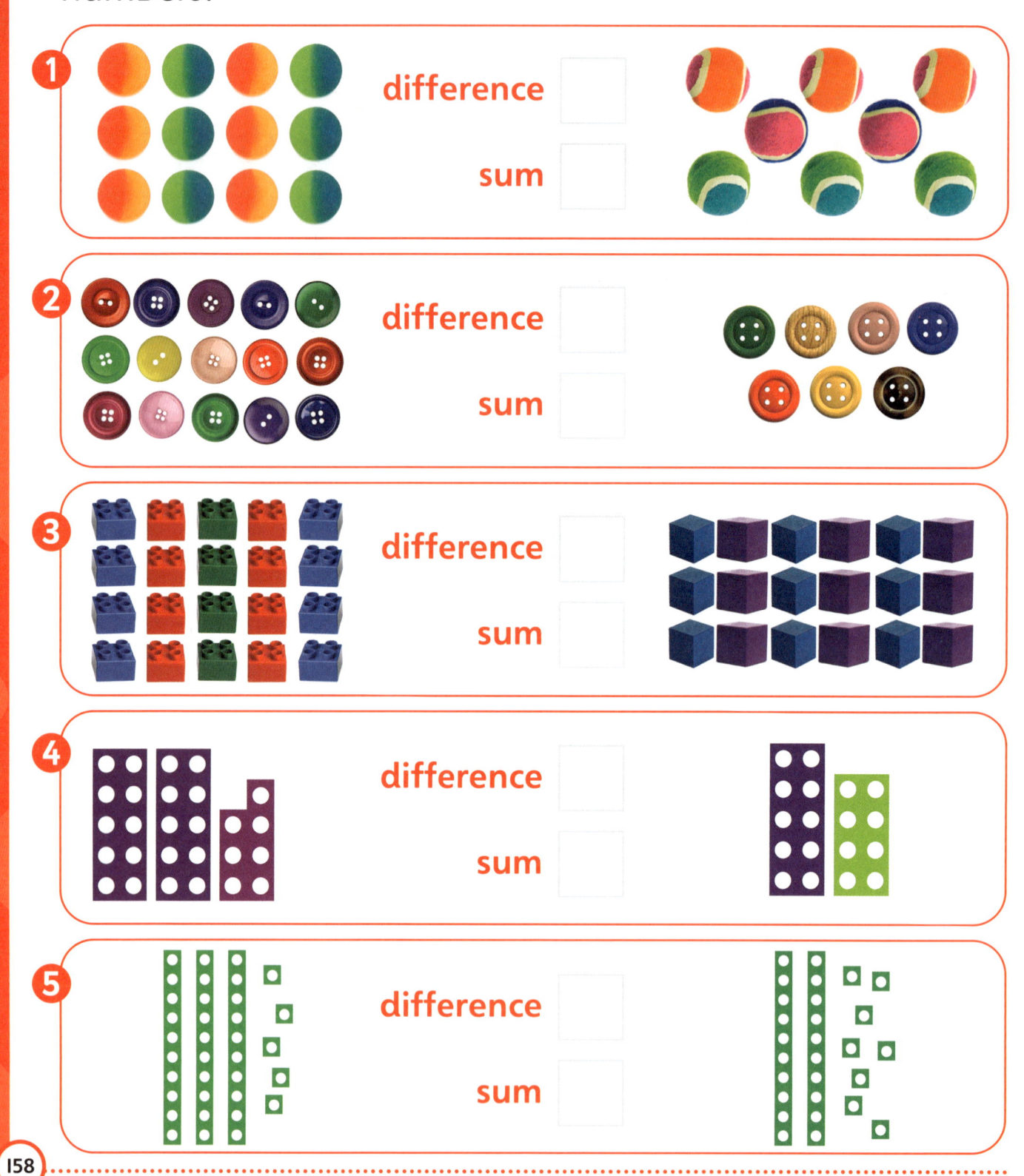

**1** difference ☐ sum ☐

**2** difference ☐ sum ☐

**3** difference ☐ sum ☐

**4** difference ☐ sum ☐

**5** difference ☐ sum ☐

Complete the number sentences for these numbers.

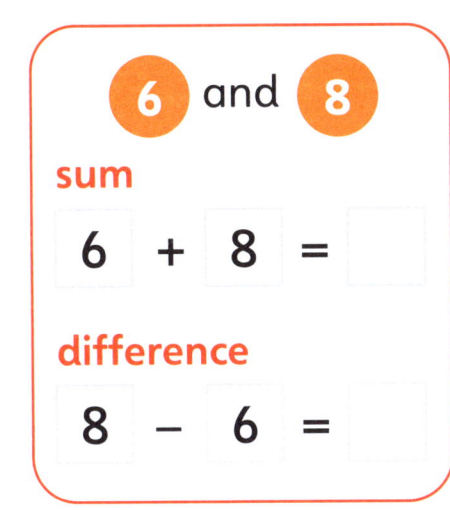

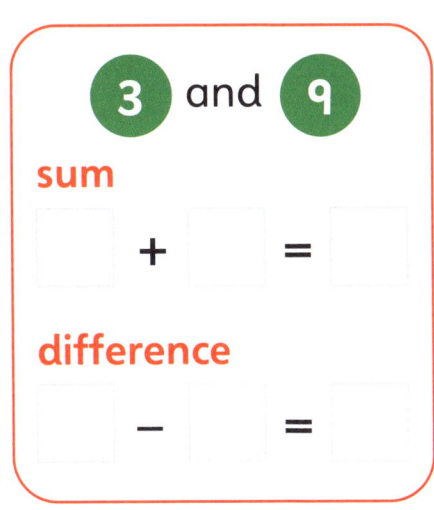

**6 and 8**
sum
6 + 8 = ☐
difference
8 − 6 = ☐

**3 and 9**
sum
☐ + ☐ = ☐
difference
☐ − ☐ = ☐

**7 and 7**
sum
☐ + ☐ = ☐
difference
☐ − ☐ = ☐

Play the game below with a friend. You will need two dice. Take it in turns to throw both dice. Work out the sum of the dice or the difference between them, and then choose a number to colour in on the grid below.

The first one to colour in 4 squares in a row—either horizontally, vertically or diagonally—is the winner.

| 4 | 12 | 1 | 5 | 8 | 3 |
|---|----|---|---|---|---|
| 0 | 2 | 7 | 4 | 6 | 2 |
| 3 | 4 | 9 | 0 | 2 | 7 |
| 1 | 6 | 5 | 4 | 11 | 4 |
| 9 | 3 | 8 | 7 | 1 | 8 |
| 5 | 10 | 0 | 2 | 5 | 6 |

# numberline arithmetic

Solve the sums below. Use the number line to help you.

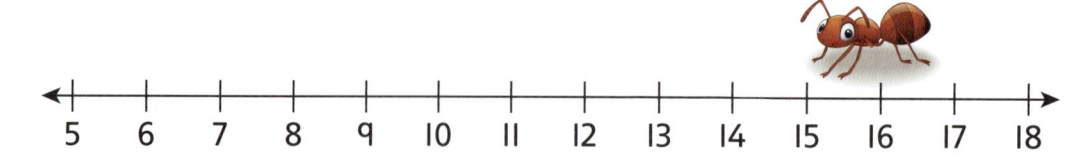

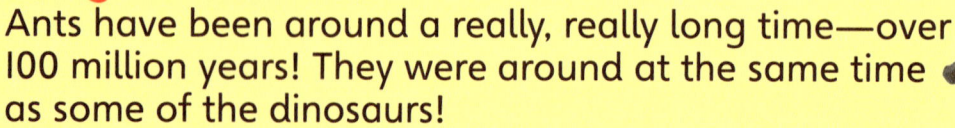

**a** 6 + 8 =   **b** 18 − 8 =

**c** 11 + 7 =   **d** 16 − 9 =

**e** 6 + 10 =   **f** 15 − 7 =

### Did you know?
Ants have been around a really, really long time—over 100 million years! They were around at the same time as some of the dinosaurs!

What colour flamingo is on each sum? Solve the sum, then colour the flamingo to match.

**g** 10 + 9 =   **h** 20 − 8 =

**i)** 8 + 7 =

**j)** 20 − 12 =

Here are some more flamingos. Solve the sums, then colour each flamingo to match.

0 1 2 3 4 5 6 7 8 9 10 11 12 13 14 15 16 17 18 19 20

**k)** 15 + 4 =

**l)** 20 − 15 =

**m)** 7 + 9 =

**n)** 20 − 11 =

**o)** 6 + 7 =

**p)** 20 − 18 =

### Did you know?
The pink colour of flamingos comes from the same substance that makes carrots orange. But flamingos don't eat carrots! They eat shrimp, snails and algae. The more of these they eat, the pinker their colour.

Write the number where the girl is standing. Do the addition. Draw the point where she stops. Then complete the related subtraction to bring her back to where she started!

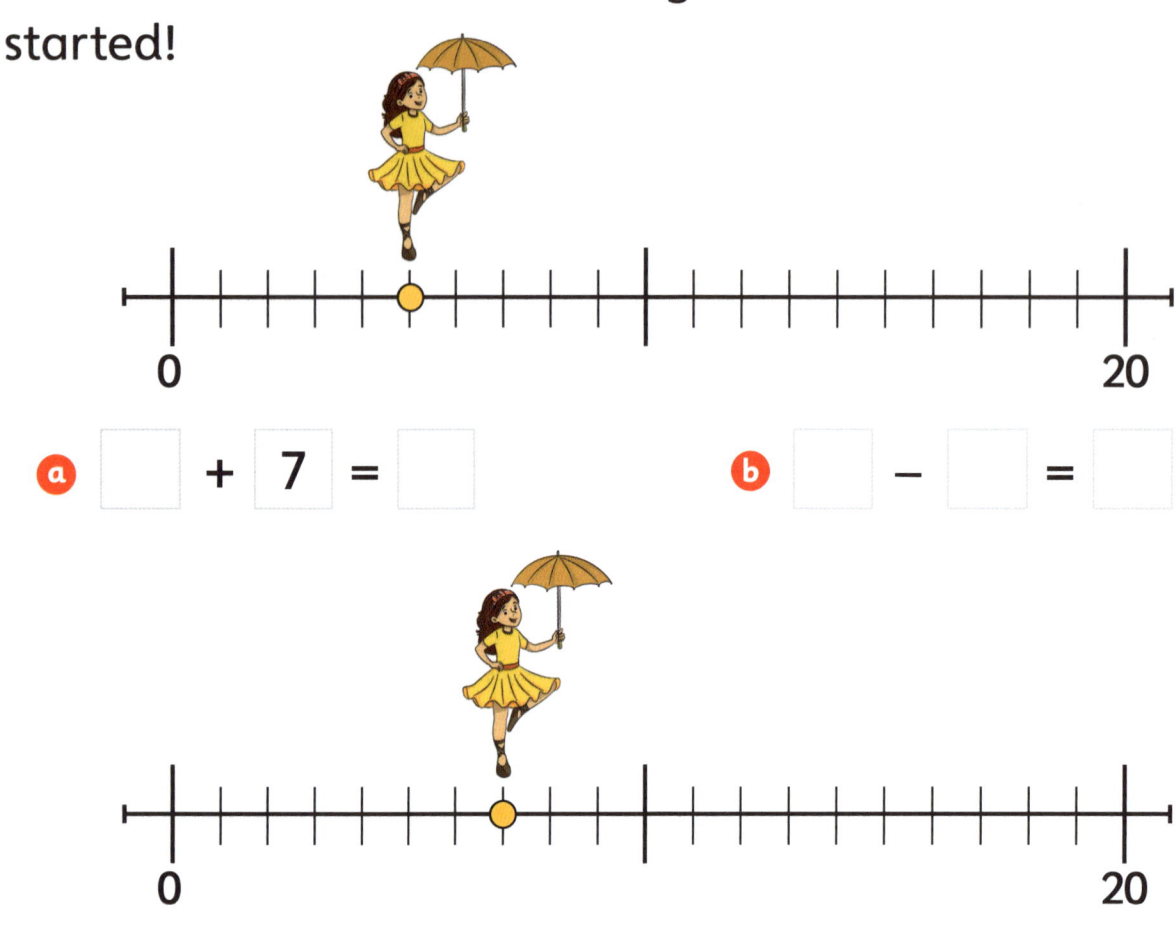

a) ☐ + 7 = ☐   b) ☐ − ☐ = ☐

c) ☐ + 9 = ☐   d) ☐ − ☐ = ☐

Solve the following matching sums.

e) 3 + 8 = ☐   f) 11 − 8 = ☐

g) 7 + 9 = ☐   h) 16 − 9 = ☐

i) 8 + 7 = ☐   j) 15 − 7 = ☐

k) 8 + 6 = ☐   l) 14 − 6 = ☐

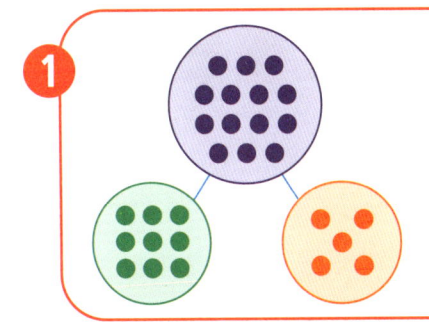

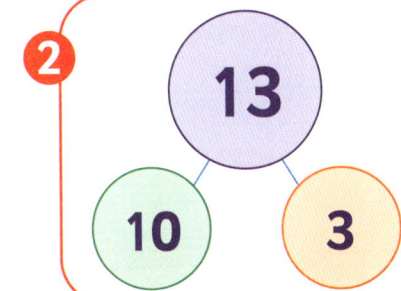

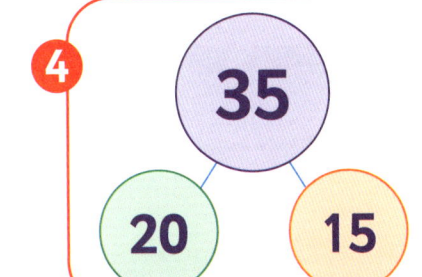

# fact families

Complete the number sentences for each fact family.

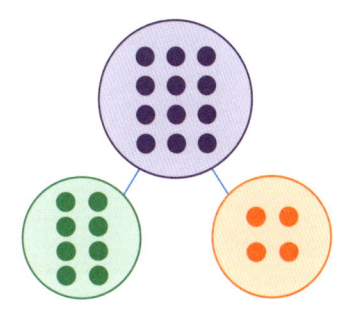

8 + 4 = 12   12 − 4 = 8
4 + 8 = 12   12 − 8 = 4

**1**
☐ + ☐ = ☐   ☐ − ☐ = ☐
☐ + ☐ = ☐   ☐ − ☐ = ☐

**2** (13, 10, 3)
☐ + ☐ = ☐   ☐ − ☐ = ☐
☐ + ☐ = ☐   ☐ − ☐ = ☐

**3** (16, 11, 5)
☐ + ☐ = ☐   ☐ − ☐ = ☐
☐ + ☐ = ☐   ☐ − ☐ = ☐

**4** (35, 20, 15)
☐ + ☐ = ☐   ☐ − ☐ = ☐
☐ + ☐ = ☐   ☐ − ☐ = ☐

Create your own fact families for each group of objects.

**1**

☐ + ☐ = ☐   ☐ − ☐ = ☐

☐ + ☐ = ☐   ☐ − ☐ = ☐

**2**

☐ + ☐ = ☐   ☐ − ☐ = ☐

☐ + ☐ = ☐   ☐ − ☐ = ☐

Circle the mistakes in the number sentences below.

**3**

2 + 8 = 10

10 − 4 = 2

**4**

16 − 5 = 11

11 + 6 = 16

**5**

7 + 7 = 12

12 − 5 = 7

**6**

18 − 11 = 7

11 + 9 = 18

Join the number bonds that add up to **10**.

1, 5, 0, 5, 8, 9, 2, 6, 3, 7, 4, 10

Join the number bonds that add up to **100**.

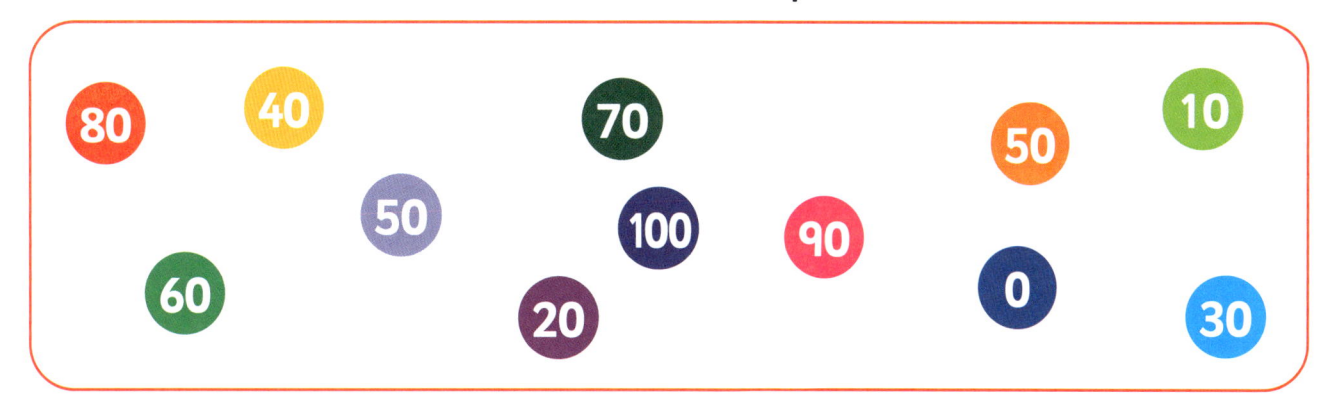

80, 40, 70, 50, 10, 60, 50, 100, 90, 0, 20, 30

Colour all the pairs that add up to **20**.

| 2 | 5 | 15 | 3 | 7 | 9 | 11 | 6 | 4 | 13 | 7 | 2 | 9 |
|---|---|---|---|---|---|---|---|---|---|---|---|---|
| 8 | 5 | 6 | 4 | 7 | 0 | 8 | 6 | 17 | 4 | 2 | 1 | 13 |
| 12 | 1 | 10 | 4 | 13 | 11 | 4 | 3 | 3 | 5 | 12 | 8 | 11 |
| 9 | 19 | 12 | 5 | 14 | 16 | 7 | 10 | 2 | 9 | 2 | 8 | 5 |
| 8 | 0 | 1 | 16 | 8 | 4 | 3 | 10 | 3 | 7 | 15 | 7 | 2 |
| 7 | 14 | 6 | 2 | 3 | 10 | 4 | 0 | 9 | 11 | 1 | 9 | 18 |
| 8 | 4 | 7 | 7 | 19 | 6 | 8 | 7 | 8 | 13 | 12 | 6 | 5 |
| 3 | 9 | 20 | 0 | 4 | 15 | 5 | 2 | 5 | 3 | 8 | 6 | 1 |

**ADDITION AND SUBTRACTION**

**1** Fill the ten-frames with the counters below.
Then complete the number sentences.

☐ + ☐ = ☐

☐ − ☐ = ☐

**2** Jack has 8 sweets. James has 4 more sweets than Jack. Fill the ten-frames to show the number of sweets. Then complete the number sentences.

☐ + ☐ = ☐

☐ − ☐ = ☐

**3** Pippa has 20 bows. All are purple or red. She has 6 more purple bows than red ones. Show how many she has of each colour on the ten-frames and complete the sums.

☐ + ☐ = ☐

☐ − ☐ = ☐

**4** The fancy dress shop has 20 silver and gold crowns.

How many gold crowns do they have if the number of silver crowns is 6 more than 5? ☐

Show how you worked the sum out: ☐ − ☐ = ☐

# more or less

Draw lines to match each number on the left with the number on the right that is **10 more**.

12   96
53   22
68   63
86   78
75   85

Draw lines to match each number on the left with the number on the right that is **10 less**.

91   49
59   54
47   13
64   81
23   37

ADDITION AND SUBTRACTION

167

Holly, Pat and Mo each win 10p on a slot machine. **Add 10p** to each purse and then write the new total amount.

☐ p

☐ p

☐ p

Abdul, Asha, and George each spend 10p. **Take 10p away** from each purse and then write the new total amount.

☐ p

☐ p

☐ p

**ADDITION AND SUBTRACTION**

**1** **Add 10ml** more to each test tube.
Write the new total in ml.

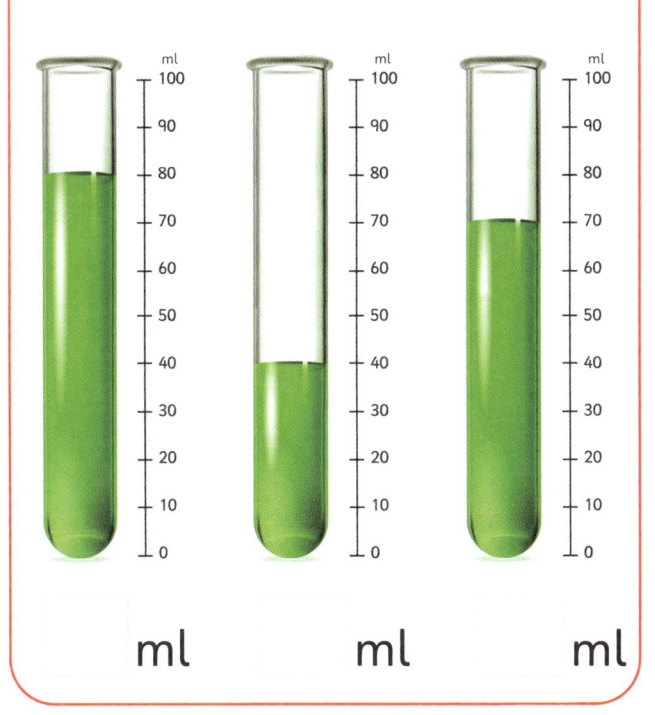

____ ml   ____ ml   ____ ml

**Take 10ml** from each test tube.
Write the new total in ml.

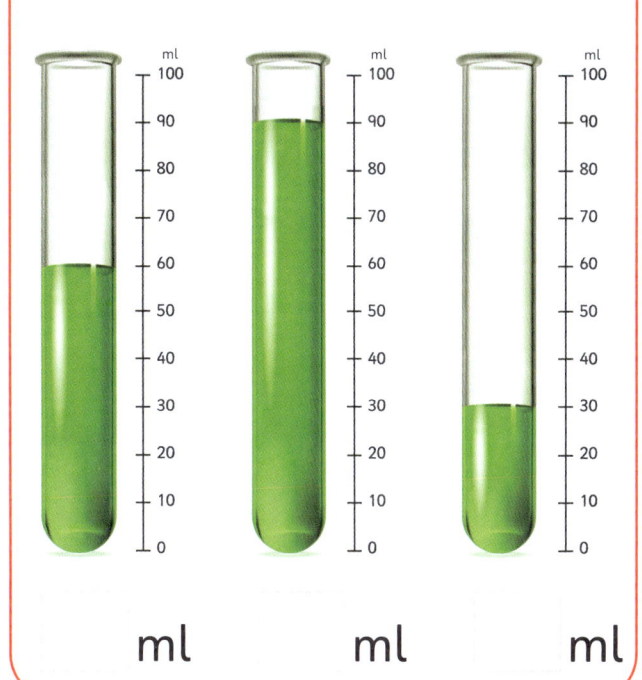

____ ml   ____ ml   ____ ml

**2** Jemima has 24 pieces of fudge. Hamish has 10 pieces more than Jemima.
How many does Hamish have?

Jordan has 10 pieces more than Hamish.
How many does Jordan have?

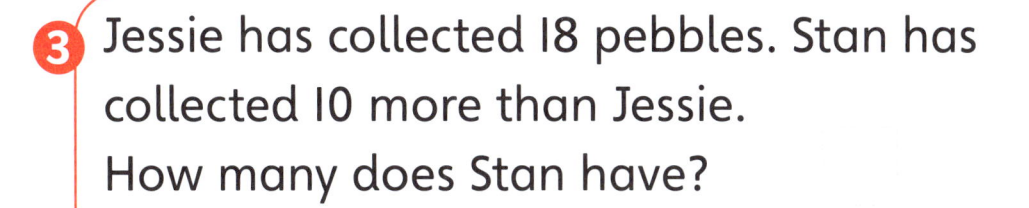

**3** Jessie has collected 18 pebbles. Stan has collected 10 more than Jessie.
How many does Stan have?

Lewis has collected 10 less than Jessie.
How many does Lewis have?

169

Help Milo and Mila find their way through the toy shop maze to their chosen toy. They can only travel to a square which is 10 more or 10 less than the one they are standing on. They can move horizontally, vertically or diagonally. Colour in their paths.

| 3 | 13 | 16 | 30 | 23 | 5 |
|---|---|---|---|---|---|
| 65 | 23 | 98 | 67 | 15 | 43 |

| 36 | 64 | 31 | 63 | 33 | 24 | 25 | 45 | 40 | 66 |
|---|---|---|---|---|---|---|---|---|---|
| 50 | 19 | 33 | 43 | 54 | 35 | 88 | 17 | 44 | 50 |
| 34 | 23 | 30 | 79 | 18 | 45 | 55 | 80 | 89 | 34 |
| 22 | 13 | 20 | 67 | 61 | 99 | 77 | 45 | 35 | 25 |
| 23 | 32 | 92 | 91 | 83 | 69 | 95 | 66 | 75 | 35 |
| 61 | 33 | 43 | 53 | 21 | 80 | 65 | 55 | 45 | 22 |
| 71 | 81 | 48 | 51 | 63 | 75 | 44 | 77 | 56 | 36 |
| | 33 | 79 | 73 | 82 | 85 | 23 | | | |
| | 93 | 83 | 64 | 58 | 99 | 95 | | | |

170

# adding 3 numbers

Write the total of each set of numbers. Check your answers by adding the numbers in a different order.

> Addition is **commutative**. You can add the numbers in any order.

**ADDITION AND SUBTRACTION**

Starfish: 6, 3, 4

☐ + ☐ + ☐ = ☐
☐ + ☐ + ☐ = ☐
☐ + ☐ + ☐ = ☐

Hats: 5, 9, 2

☐ + ☐ + ☐ = ☐
☐ + ☐ + ☐ = ☐
☐ + ☐ + ☐ = ☐

Star balloons: 8, 7, 9

☐ + ☐ + ☐ = ☐
☐ + ☐ + ☐ = ☐
☐ + ☐ + ☐ = ☐

Apples: 4, 0, 8

☐ + ☐ + ☐ = ☐
☐ + ☐ + ☐ = ☐
☐ + ☐ + ☐ = ☐

### Did you know?
Seastars are commonly known as starfish, but they are not fish. Most have five arms, but some can grow as many as 50. They can regrow their arms if they become damaged!

Add the numbers below. Each total matches a colour. Use the code to colour in the parrot.

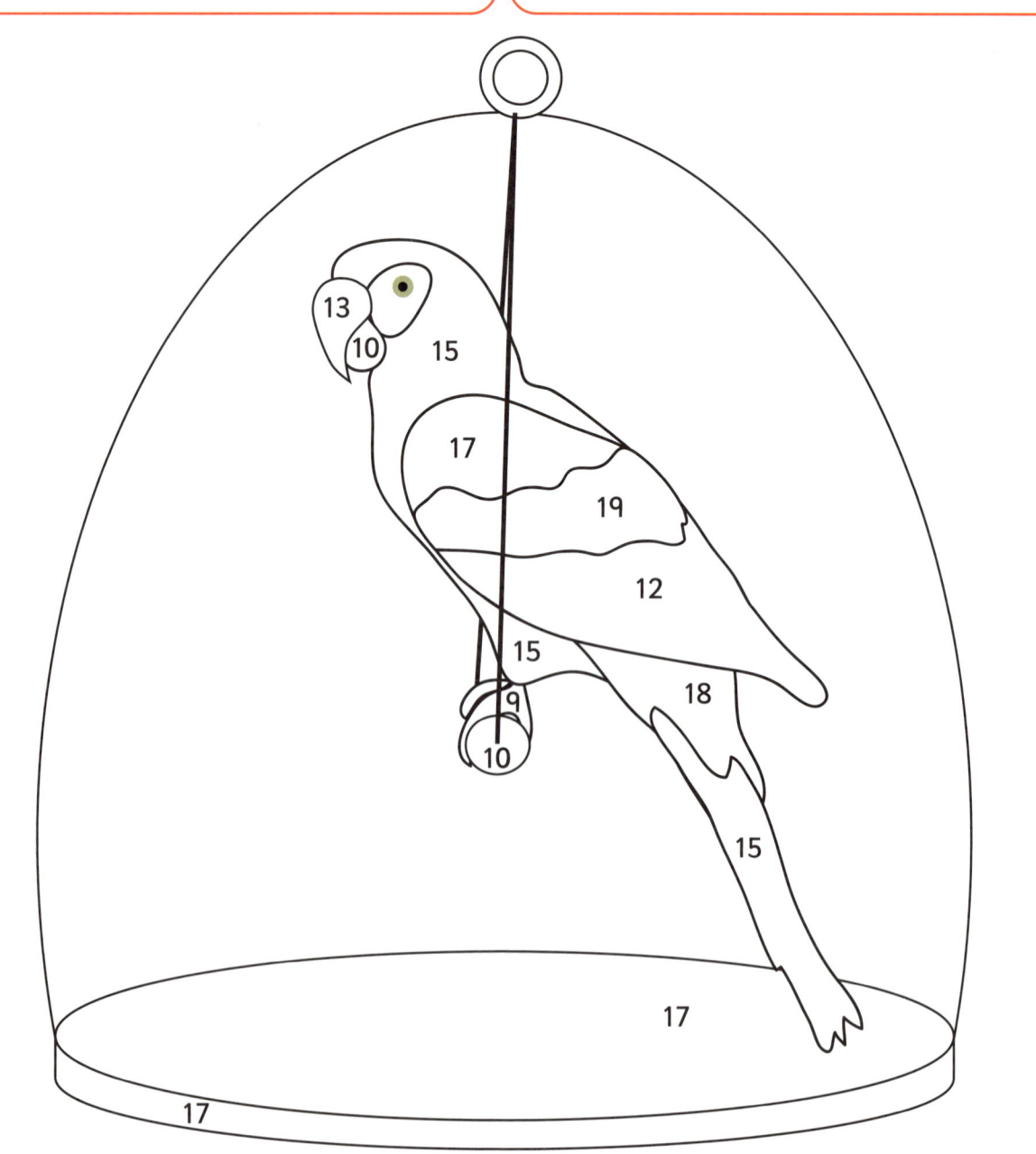

5 + 3 + 2 = ☐ (black)
4 + 6 + 9 = ☐ (green)
3 + 1 + 8 = ☐ (blue)
8 + 7 + 0 = ☐ (red)

2 + 4 + 3 = ☐ (black)
2 + 7 + 8 = ☐ (yellow)
6 + 5 + 7 = ☐ (blue)
9 + 1 + 3 = ☐ (orange)

Find the total of each row and column.

| 2 | 3 | 7 | |
|---|---|---|---|
| 9 | 4 | 6 | |
| 1 | 8 | 2 | |
| | | | |

| 6 | 7 | 5 | |
|---|---|---|---|
| 8 | 5 | 0 | |
| 3 | 7 | 9 | |
| | | | |

| 9 | 1 | 8 | |
|---|---|---|---|
| 3 | 6 | 4 | |
| 4 | 7 | 5 | |
| | | | |

Work out the missing numbers

| | 5 | 3 | 16 |
|---|---|---|---|
| 4 | | 9 | 14 |
| 6 | 7 | | 15 |
| 18 | 13 | 14 | |

| | 4 | 8 | 15 |
|---|---|---|---|
| 7 | | 1 | 13 |
| 2 | 9 | | 17 |
| 12 | 18 | 15 | |

| | 6 | 7 | 14 |
|---|---|---|---|
| 5 | | 8 | 15 |
| 9 | 4 | | 16 |
| 15 | 12 | 18 | |

Joshua has added up some numbers. Mark his answers.
Write ✓ for true or ✗ for false.

**a** 2 + 1 + 8 = 11

**b** 7 + 7 + 3 = 16

**c** 9 + 0 + 7 = 17

**d** 5 + 6 + 4 = 15

**e** 8 + 4 + 6 = 18

**f** 3 + 2 + 9 = 14

# hop on over

Help Frank the frog hop over the lily pads to the log. He must jump on **three** lily pads and the **sum** of those three lily pads must be **greater than 20**. Draw different coloured lines to show the different ways he can jump, then write two ways as number sentences.

☐ >20

Lily pads: 2, 4, 7, 9, 8, 6, 3, 6, 5

☐ + ☐ + ☐ = ☐      ☐ + ☐ + ☐ = ☐

# adding two 2-digit numbers

Solve the sums below.

*Add the ones. Then add the tens.*

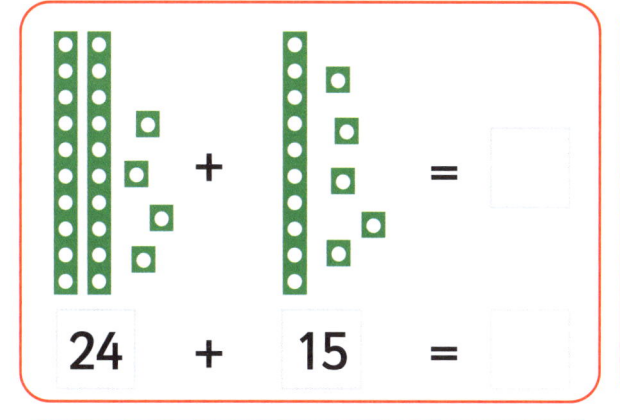

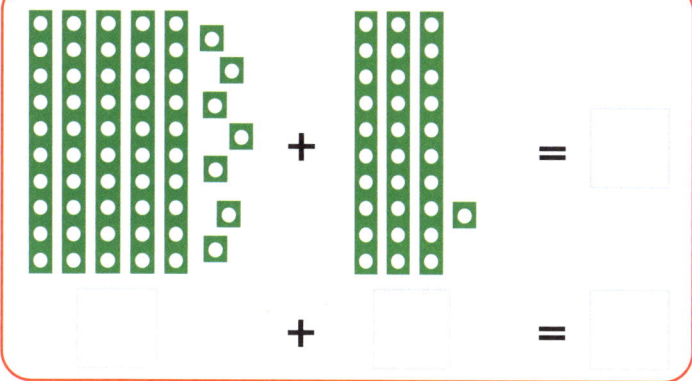

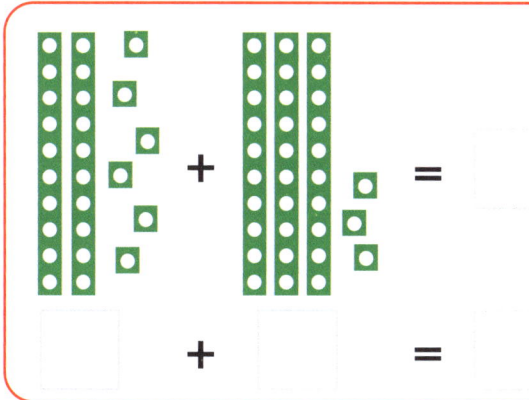

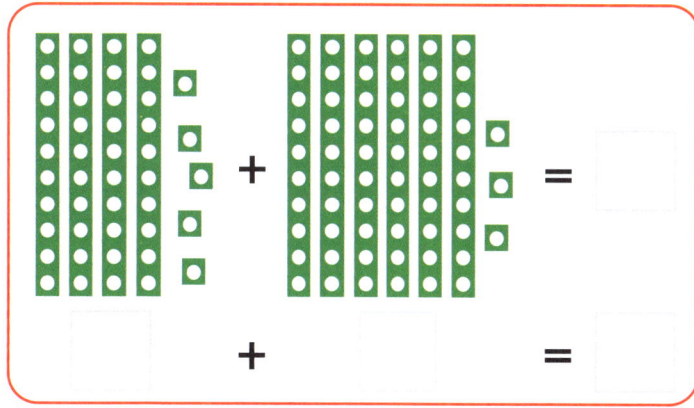

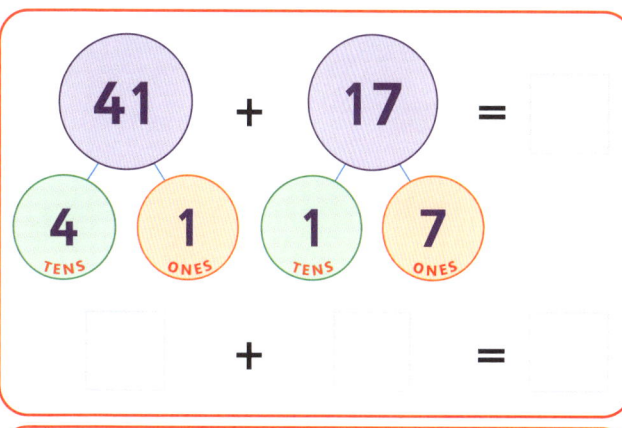

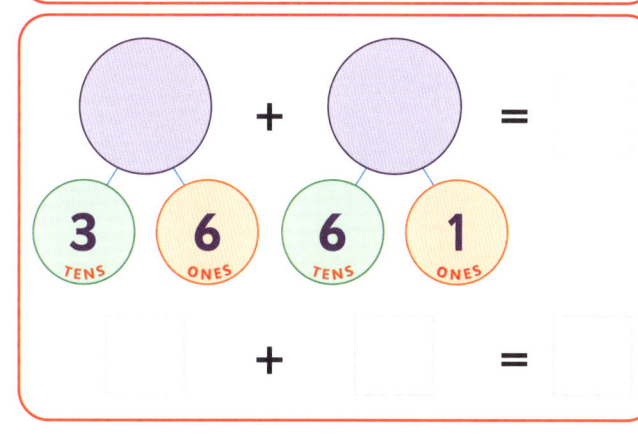

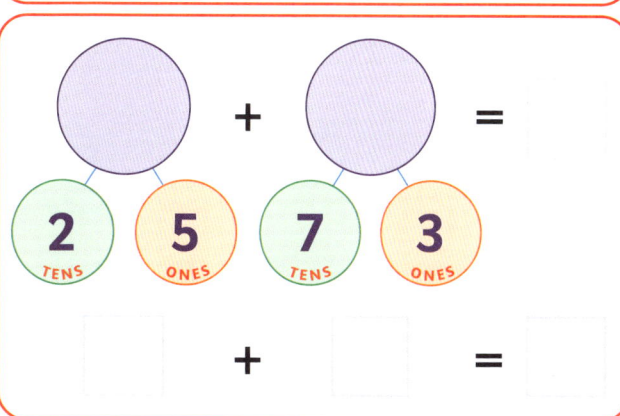

ADDITION AND SUBTRACTION

24 + 15 =

___ + ___ =

___ + ___ =

___ + ___ =

13 + 24 =
1 TENS   3 ONES   2 TENS   4 ONES
___ + ___ =

41 + 17 =
4 TENS   1 ONES   1 TENS   7 ONES
___ + ___ =

___ + ___ =
3 TENS   6 ONES   6 TENS   1 ONES
___ + ___ =

___ + ___ =
2 TENS   5 ONES   7 TENS   3 ONES
___ + ___ =

175

Which number card belongs to which child? Join them up.

43  55  61  34  22  16

Alice: My number has 4 tens.

Jinny: My number has 2 ones.

Oliver: My number is more than 50 but less than 60.

Jordan: My number is more than 30 but less than 40.

Ren: My number has 6 ones.

Layla: My number has 6 tens.

If Ren and Jinny team up, how much would their cards add up to?  ☐ + ☐ = ☐

Which children can team up to make a total of 77?

____ and ____    ☐ + ☐ = ☐

____ and ____    ☐ + ☐ = ☐

____ and ____    ☐ + ☐ = ☐

Katy goes on a bug hunt. She collects 13 bugs. After lunch she collects 21 more bugs. How many bugs does she have altogether? Write it as a number sentence.

☐ + ☐ = ☐

Graham makes cupcakes for the village fête. In his first batch he bakes 22 cupcakes. In his second batch he bakes 24 cupcakes. How many cupcakes does he make altogether? Write it as a number sentence.

☐ + ☐ = ☐

Circle the two numbers that you could add together to make the total. Write the calculation below.

12  64  71  93  25     83

___ + ___ = ___

22  16  23  65  46     69

___ + ___ = ___

40  32  21  43  64     75

___ + ___ = ___

**ADDITION AND SUBTRACTION**

Peter is at the fruit stall at the market. He has 60p to spend. Join the pairs of items he could buy if he wants to spend *all* his money.

- Pear 30p
- Mango 35p
- Banana 25p
- Strawberries 30p
- Watermelon 40p
- Grapes 45p
- Orange 20p
- Apple 15p

Selina has added up some numbers. Mark her answers. Write ✓ for true or ✗ for false.

a) 12 + 32 = 44
b) 62 + 17 = 79
c) 23 + 16 = 29
d) 25 + 34 = 69
e) 41 + 55 = 86
f) 51 + 42 = 93

Work out the sums below. Circle the *largest* total in blue, and the *smallest* total in green.

g) 25 + 41 =
h) 52 + 16 =
i) 43 + 22 =
j) 43 + 30 =
k) 11 + 58 =
l) 26 + 44 =

# adding in columns

Add the numbers. Write the sum below the line. Then draw a line to match the butterflies with the same sum.

2
+ 4
___

7
+ 2
___

5
+ 6
___

3
+ 4
___

2
+ 8
___

4
+ 5
___

6
+ 4
___

5
+ 2
___

3
+ 8
___

1
+ 5
___

We can also add in columns with 2-digit numbers. Write the sum in each box.

> First add the numbers in the *ones* column. Then add the numbers in the *tens* column.

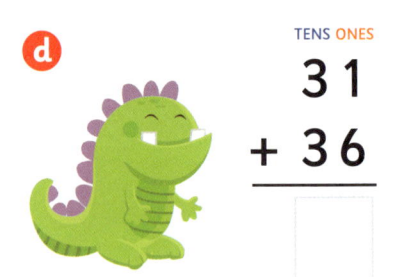

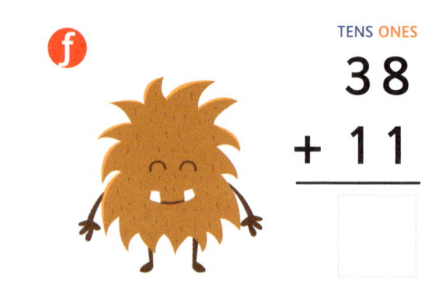

a) TENS ONES
   23
 + 46

b) TENS ONES
   17
 + 12

c) TENS ONES
   15
 + 62

d) TENS ONES
   31
 + 36

e) TENS ONES
   45
 + 41

f) TENS ONES
   38
 + 11

g) TENS ONES
   52
 + 34

h) TENS ONES
   73
 + 22

i) TENS ONES
   64
 + 12

j) TENS ONES
   13
 + 35

k) TENS ONES
   21
 + 77

l) TENS ONES
   48
 + 20

# subtracting

Solve the sums below.

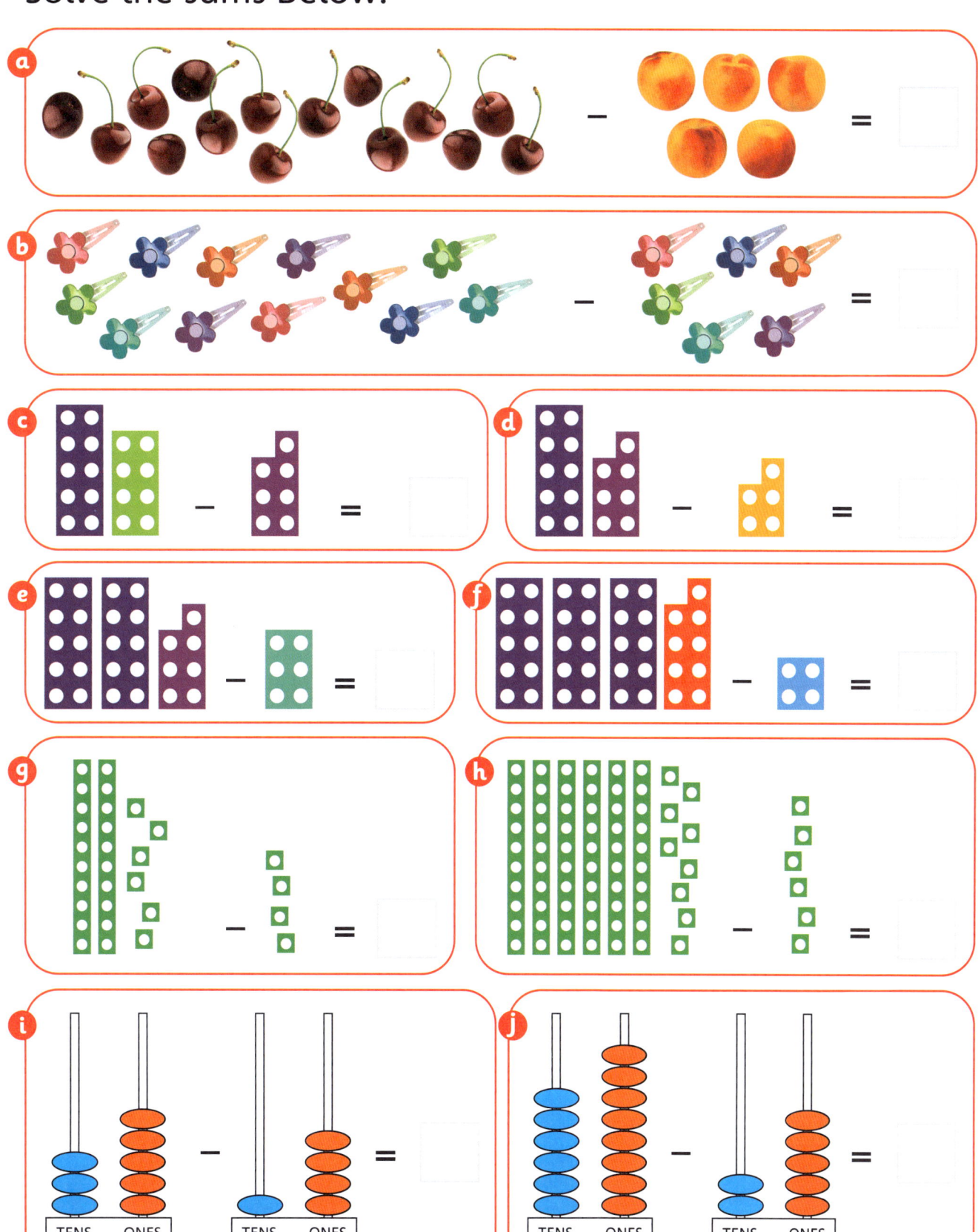

a) 🍒 − 🍑 =

b) 🌸 − 🌸 =

c) − =

d) − =

e) − =

f) − =

g) − =

h) − =

i) − =

j) − =

Cross out the sheep that escape each pen. Write how many are left.

If 7 sheep escape ...

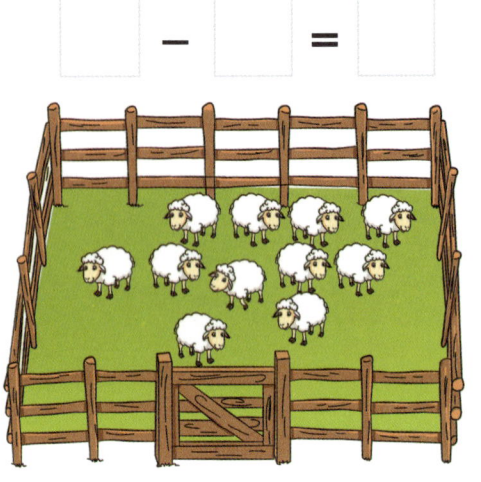

☐ − ☐ = ☐

If 5 sheep escape ...

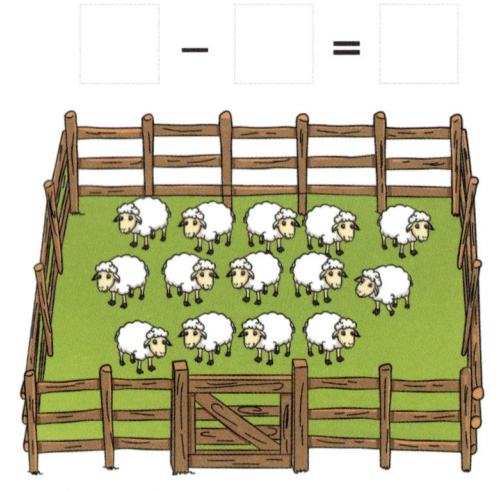

☐ − ☐ = ☐

If 6 sheep escape ...

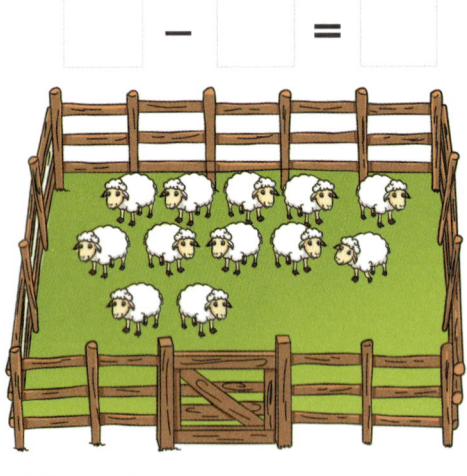

☐ − ☐ = ☐

If 8 sheep escape ...

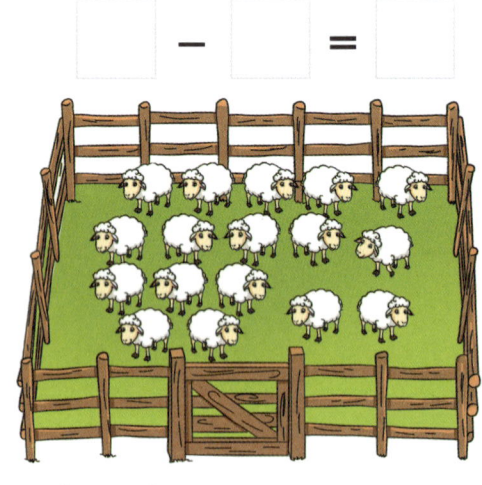

☐ − ☐ = ☐

If 3 sheep escape ...

☐ − ☐ = ☐

If 9 sheep escape ...

☐ − ☐ = ☐

Write 10 less than each number.

22 ☐   74 ☐   83 ☐   65 ☐   90 ☐

Write 5 less than each number.

77 ☐   68 ☐   35 ☐   41 ☐   24 ☐

Draw lines to match the sums with the same total.

18 − 12 = ☐      16 − 4 = ☐

13 − 8 = ☐      19 − 8 = ☐

19 − 10 = ☐      19 − 12 = ☐

16 − 5 = ☐      17 − 11 = ☐

20 − 8 = ☐      14 − 9 = ☐

14 − 7 = ☐      15 − 6 = ☐

Complete the sums to work out the riddle.

20 − 5 = ☐ A          20 − 11 = ☐ B

20 − 16 = ☐ C         20 − 8 = ☐ D

20 − 3 = ☐ E          20 − 15 = ☐ H

20 − 12 = ☐ I         20 − 7 = ☐ O

20 − 10 = ☐ R         20 − 4 = ☐ S

20 − 19 = ☐ T         20 − 6 = ☐ U

20 − 2 = ☐ W

20 − 13 = ☐ Y

Why can't bicycles stand up?

__ __ __  __ __ __ __         __ __ __ __
9  17  4  15 14 16 17         1  5  17  7

__ __ __  __ __ __         __  __ __ __ __
15 10 17  1  18 13         1   8 10 17 12

# more subtracting

Use the place value counters to work out the answers.

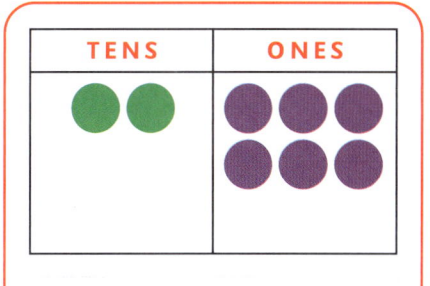

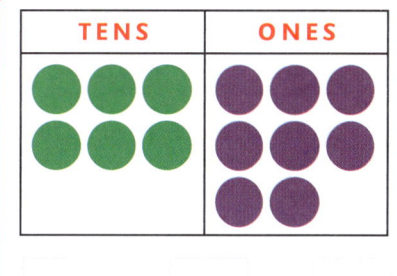

| TENS | ONES |
|---|---|

26 − 12 =

| TENS | ONES |
|---|---|

68 − 24 =

| TENS | ONES |
|---|---|

44 − 31 =

| TENS | ONES |
|---|---|

75 − 62 =

| TENS | ONES |
|---|---|

57 − 14 =

| TENS | ONES |
|---|---|

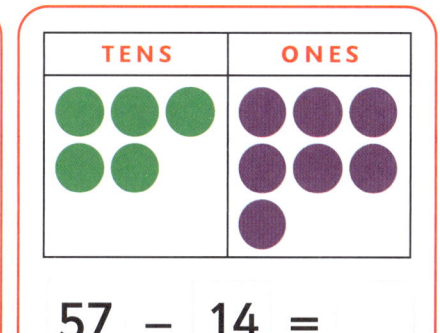

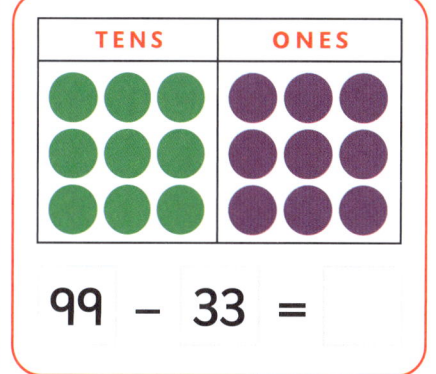

99 − 33 =

Work out these sums.

Tilly makes 45 cupcakes for a cake sale.
She sells 31.
How many does she have left?      □ − □ = □

Mum makes 24 sandwiches for the school picnic.
There are 12 sandwiches left over.
How many were eaten?      □ − □ = □

Mr Brown bakes 64 croissants. He sells 42.
How many does he have left?      □ − □ = □

Each child has £1 (100p) to spend. Work out the sums.

Frog 20p, Spinning top 40p, Dinosaur 70p, Knight 60p, Slinky 80p, Windmill 90p

**a)** Justin buys a toy dinosaur.
How much change will he have?  100 p − 70 p = ☐ p

**b)** Suzy buys a slinky.
How much change will she have?  ☐ p − ☐ p = ☐ p

**c)** Maya buys a windmill.
How much change will she have?  ☐ p − ☐ p = ☐ p

**d)** Tom buys a wind-up frog.
How much change will he have?  ☐ p − ☐ p = ☐ p

**e)** Jessica buys a spinning top.
How much change will she have?  ☐ p − ☐ p = ☐ p

**f)** Craig buys a toy knight.
How much change will he have?  ☐ p − ☐ p = ☐ p

**g)** Does Justin have enough money left over to buy a whistle? _____  (whistle 30p)

**h)** Does Jessica have enough money left over to buy a toy tiger? _____  (tiger 70p)

# subtracting – crossing ten

Use the number line to help you work out the answer.

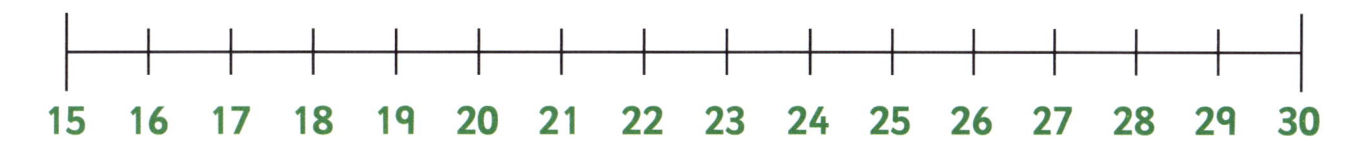

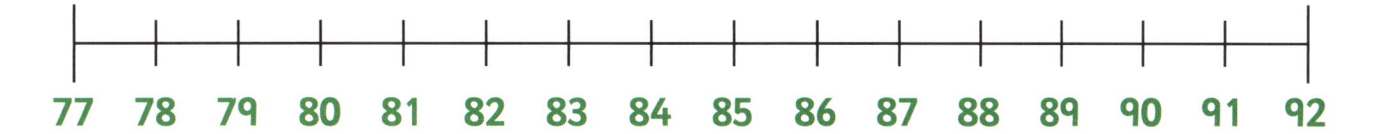

15  16  17  18  19  20  21  22  23  24  25  26  27  28  29  30

a) 24 – 8 =

b) 26 – 7 =

c) 22 – 6 =

d) 27 – 9 =

77  78  79  80  81  82  83  84  85  86  87  88  89  90  91  92

e) 82 – 4 =

f) 92 – 3 =

g) 88 – 9 =

h) 91 – 8 =

Complete these sums.

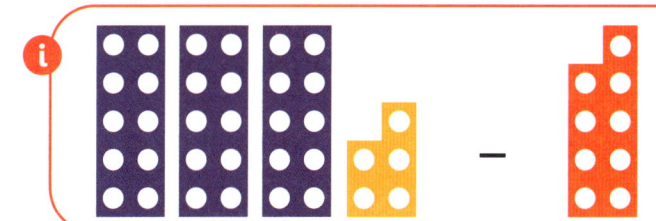

i) 35 – 9 =

j) 57 – 8 =

k) 44 – 6 =

Work out the sums. Use the number grid to help you. Then check your answer by adding.

for example   82 − 4 = 78    78 + 4 = 82

| 61 | 62 | 63 | 64 | 65 | 66 | 67 | 68 | 69 | 70 |
|---|---|---|---|---|---|---|---|---|---|
| 71 | 72 | 73 | 74 | 75 | 76 | 77 | 78 | 79 | 80 |
| 81 | 82 | 83 | 84 | 85 | 86 | 87 | 88 | 89 | 90 |
| 91 | 92 | 93 | 94 | 95 | 96 | 97 | 98 | 99 | 100 |
| 101 | 102 | 103 | 104 | 105 | 106 | 107 | 108 | 109 | 110 |

a) 72 − 3 =  ☐        ☐ + ☐ = ☐

b) 94 − 7 = ☐         ☐ + ☐ = ☐

c) 86 − 9 = ☐         ☐ + ☐ = ☐

Work out the sums below and look for patterns.

d)
93 − 5 = ☐
83 − 5 = ☐
73 − 5 = ☐

e)
105 − 6 = ☐
95 − 6 = ☐
85 − 6 = ☐

f)
91 − 8 = ☐
81 − 8 = ☐
71 − 8 = ☐

Now work out these sums and cross check your answers.

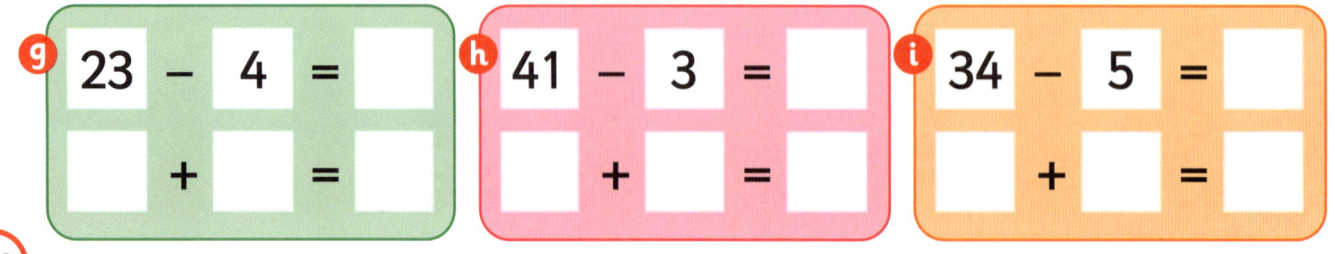

g) 23 − 4 = ☐
   ☐ + ☐ = ☐

h) 41 − 3 = ☐
   ☐ + ☐ = ☐

i) 34 − 5 = ☐
   ☐ + ☐ = ☐

# subtracting in columns

Complete the sums. Then colour the fruit and plate.

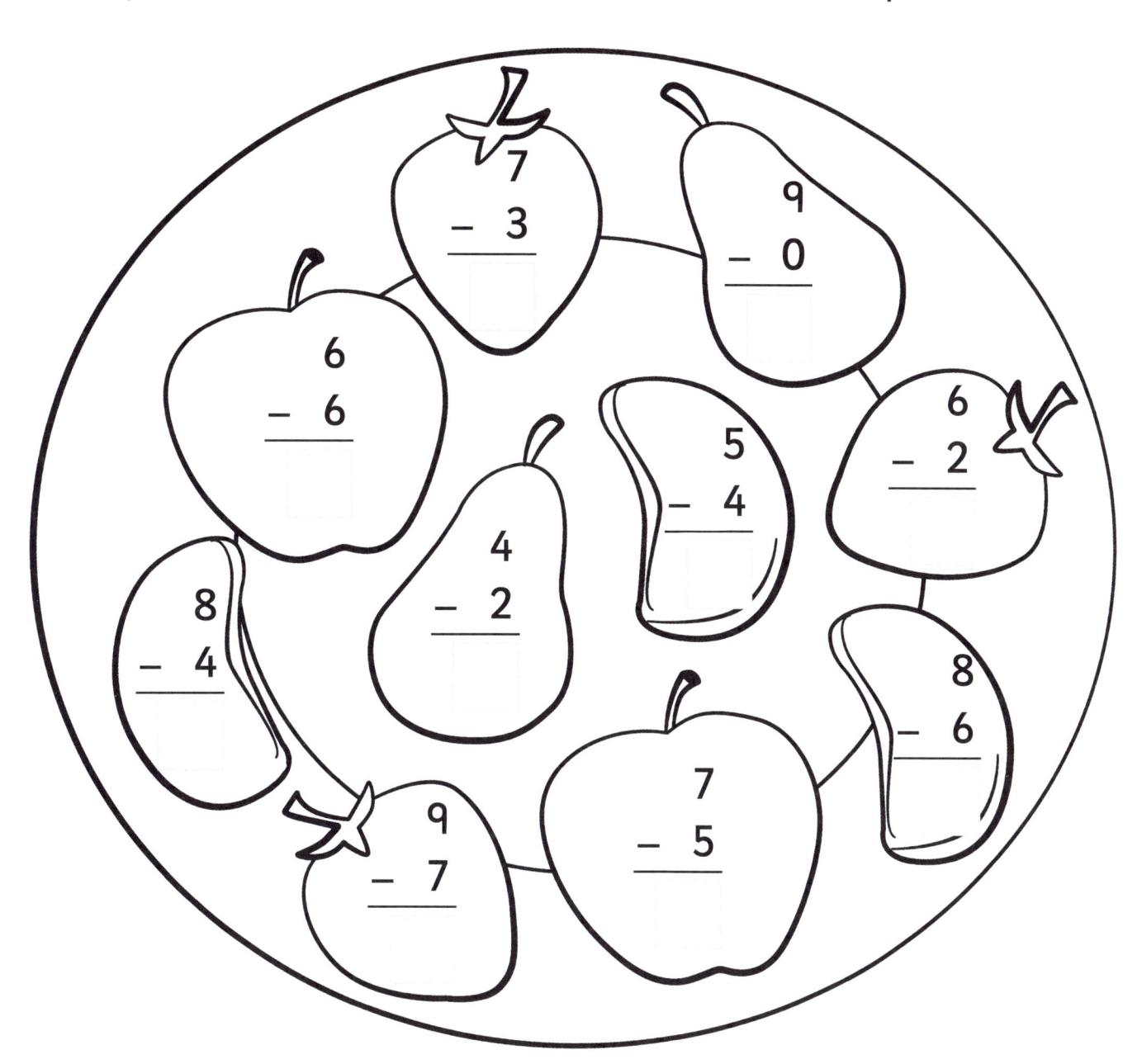

$$7 - 3 =$$
$$9 - 0 =$$
$$6 - 6 =$$
$$5 - 4 =$$
$$6 - 2 =$$
$$8 - 4 =$$
$$4 - 2 =$$
$$8 - 6 =$$
$$9 - 7 =$$
$$7 - 5 =$$

Complete some more monster subtractions.

$$8 - 2 =$$
$$12 - 4 =$$
$$11 - 3 =$$

# all relative

Look at the sum at the top of each box. Then work out the related sums below.

**a)**
- 5 − 2 = 3
- 50 − 20 =
- 15 − 2 =
- 25 − 2 =
- 35 − 2 =

**b)**
- 4 + 6 = 10
- 40 + 60 =
- 14 + 6 =
- 24 + 6 =
- 34 + 6 =

**c)**
- 7 + 1 = 8
- 70 + 10 =
- 17 + 1 =
- 27 + 1 =
- 37 + 1 =

**d)**
- 8 − 3 = 5
- 80 − 30 =
- 18 − 3 =
- 28 − 3 =
- 38 − 3 =

**e)**
- 2 + 7 = 9
- 20 + 70 =
- 12 + 7 =
- 22 + 7 =
- 32 + 7 =

**f)**
- 7 − 5 = 2
- 70 − 50 =
- 17 − 5 =
- 27 − 5 =
- 37 − 5 =

# pasta problems

**1** The supermarket has 64 packets of spaghetti and 23 packets of tagliatelle.

How many packages of spaghetti and tagliatelle are there altogether?

**2** Noni cooks her spaghetti sauce for 45 minutes. Then she cooks the spaghetti for 11 minutes.

How long does it take her to cook both the sauce and the pasta?

**3** One recipe needs 80g of pasta. Another recipe needs 60g of pasta.

What is the difference in the quantity of pasta needed?

g

**4** A packet of fusilli has 78 pieces of pasta. A packet of farfalle has 55 pieces of pasta.

How many more pieces of pasta are in a packet of fusilli?

**5** The cafeteria has 44 bowls of chicken noodle soup. People eat 32 bowls.

How many bowls are left?

# more number puzzles

**1** Read the clues to work out the missing number.

It is less than 18.   Half this number is 8.   It is an even number.

7 + ☐ > 20 – 8

What is the number? ☐

**2** In each of the number sentences below something is missing. Fill in the missing symbol: – or +.

- **a** 16 ☐ 5 = 11
- **b** 60 = 100 ☐ 40
- **c** 30 ☐ 70 = 100
- **d** 49 = 28 ☐ 21
- **e** 74 ☐ 21 = 53
- **f** 62 = 85 ☐ 23

**3** A jigsaw puzzle is on sale for 85p.

Toby has this much money:

Stella has this much money:

If they club together, can they buy the puzzle?

If so, how much change would they get? ☐ p

**4** Jasper and his friends were very thirsty. They drank 5 glasses of apple juice, 6 glasses of orange juice, and 8 glasses of water.

How many drinks did they have altogether?

**5** Jenny and Tony went to the tuckshop. Jenny bought a packet of crisps and a bottle of water. Tony bought a bar of chocolate and a can of cola.

Who spent the most money?

**6** Sammy sent out 20 invitations to his birthday party. He heard back from everybody. Three of his friends can't come.

How many can come to his party?

**7** There are 15 dogs in the kennel. Jack wants to give them each a bone. He has 9 bones.

How many more does he need?

**8** There are 31 children in Clever Cats Class and 28 in Brainy Badgers Class.

If the two classes go on a school trip, how many children will there be altogether?

**9** Grandad planted 7 tulips, 5 daffodils and 9 roses. How many flowers did he plant in total?

**10** Mr Smith went to the hardware store to buy paint. He spent £20 and was given £6 change.

How much did the paint cost?

£

**11** An aquarium has 85 tropical fish. It sends 22 of them to another aquarium.

How many are left?

**12** The fair has a stall where you can buy toys for tickets.

| party blower | whistle | bell | xylophone | drum |
|---|---|---|---|---|
| 5 | 8 | 9 | 25 | 40 |

How many tickets would you need to buy . . .

. . . a whistle, a bell and a party blower?

. . . a bell and a xylophone?

. . . a drum and a xylophone?

# Multiplication and Division

# equal groups

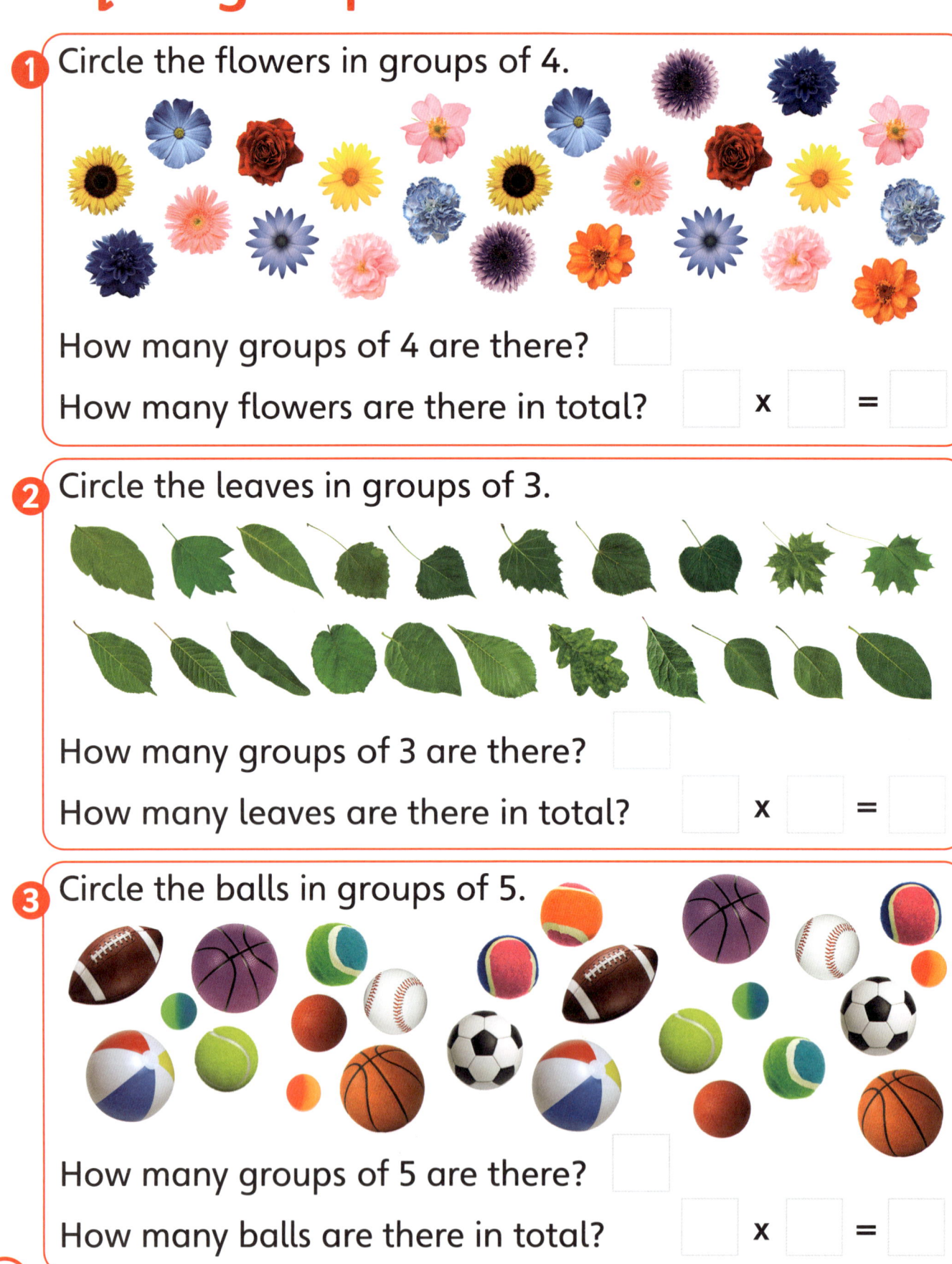

**1** Circle the flowers in groups of 4.

How many groups of 4 are there? ☐

How many flowers are there in total? ☐   ☐ x ☐ = ☐

**2** Circle the leaves in groups of 3.

How many groups of 3 are there? ☐

How many leaves are there in total? ☐   ☐ x ☐ = ☐

**3** Circle the balls in groups of 5.

How many groups of 5 are there? ☐

How many balls are there in total? ☐   ☐ x ☐ = ☐

Complete the number sentences below.

**4**

There are ☐ equal groups of ☐ bananas.

10 + 10 + 10 + 10 + 10 = ☐

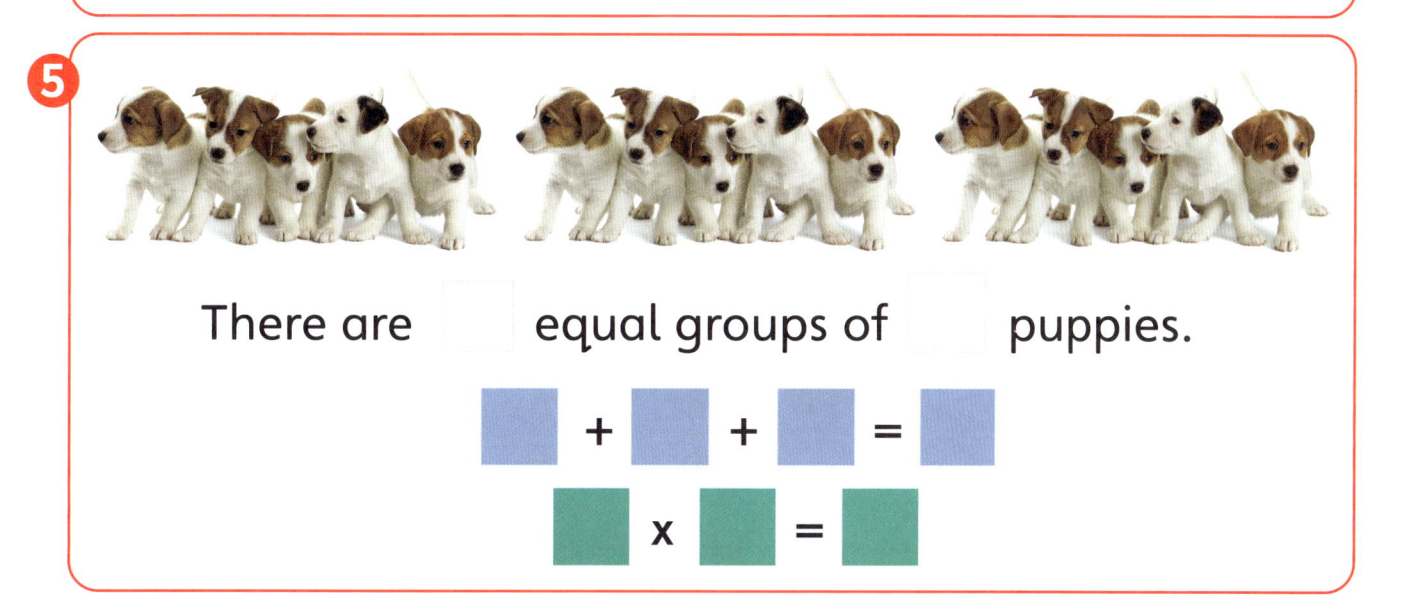

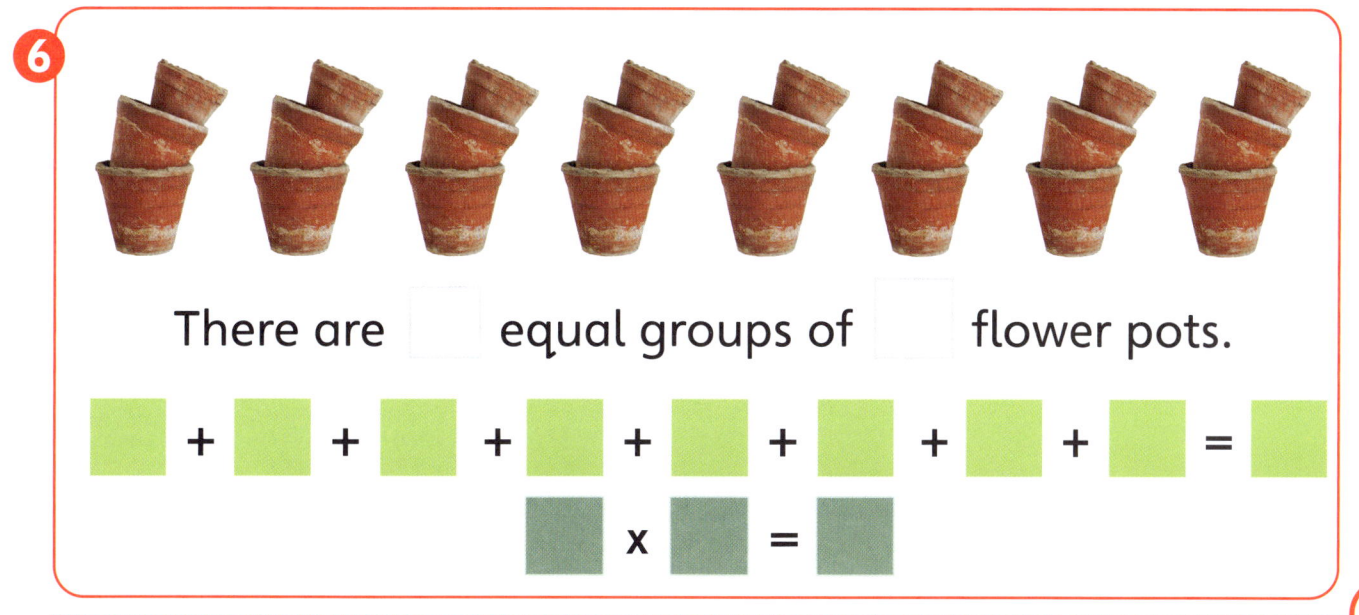

5 × 10 = ☐

**5**

There are ☐ equal groups of ☐ puppies.

☐ + ☐ + ☐ = ☐

☐ × ☐ = ☐

**6**

There are ☐ equal groups of ☐ flower pots.

☐ + ☐ + ☐ + ☐ + ☐ + ☐ + ☐ + ☐ = ☐

☐ × ☐ = ☐

Circle the group that is not equal to the others.

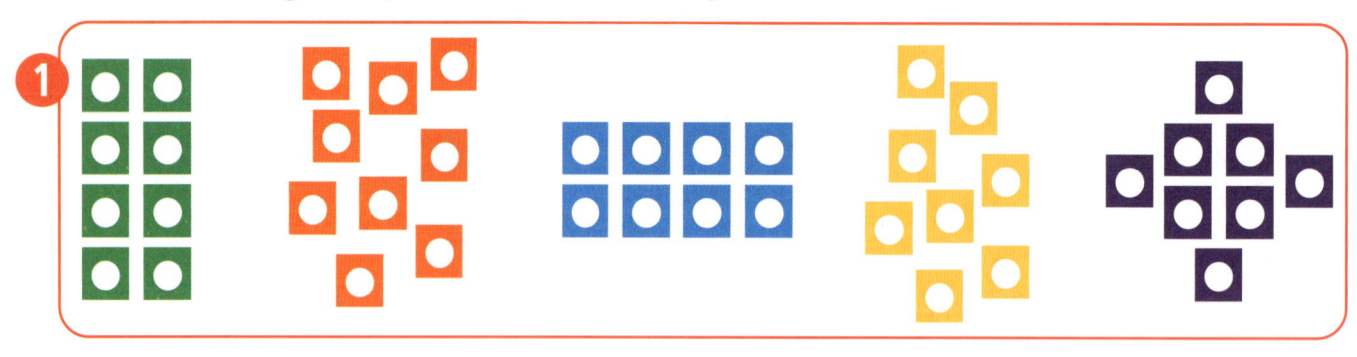

**1**

Join the equal groups.

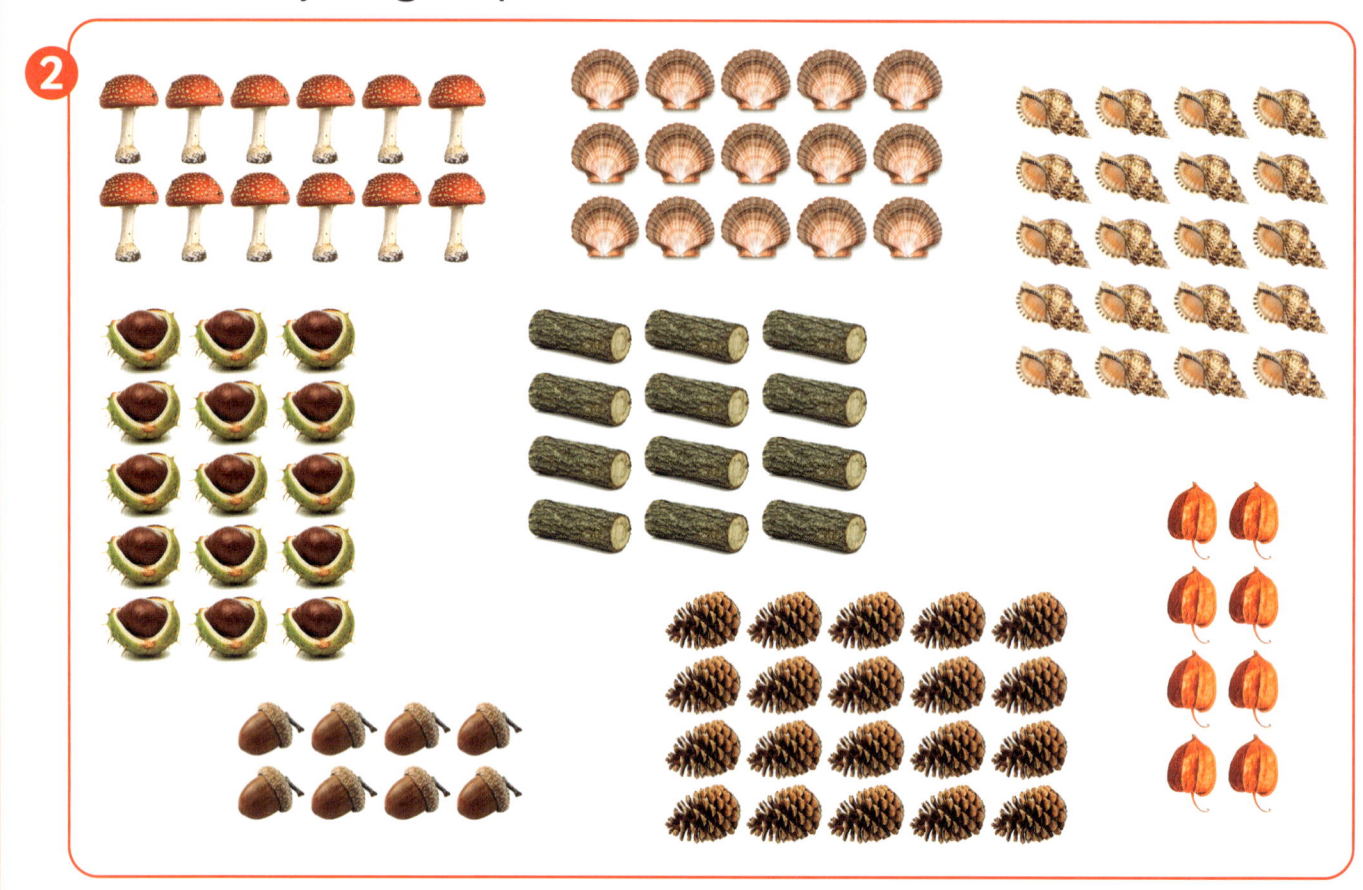

**2**

**3** Draw these counters in 2 equal groups.

**4** Draw these counters in 3 equal groups.

# arrays

Each array shows two multiplications. Write them.

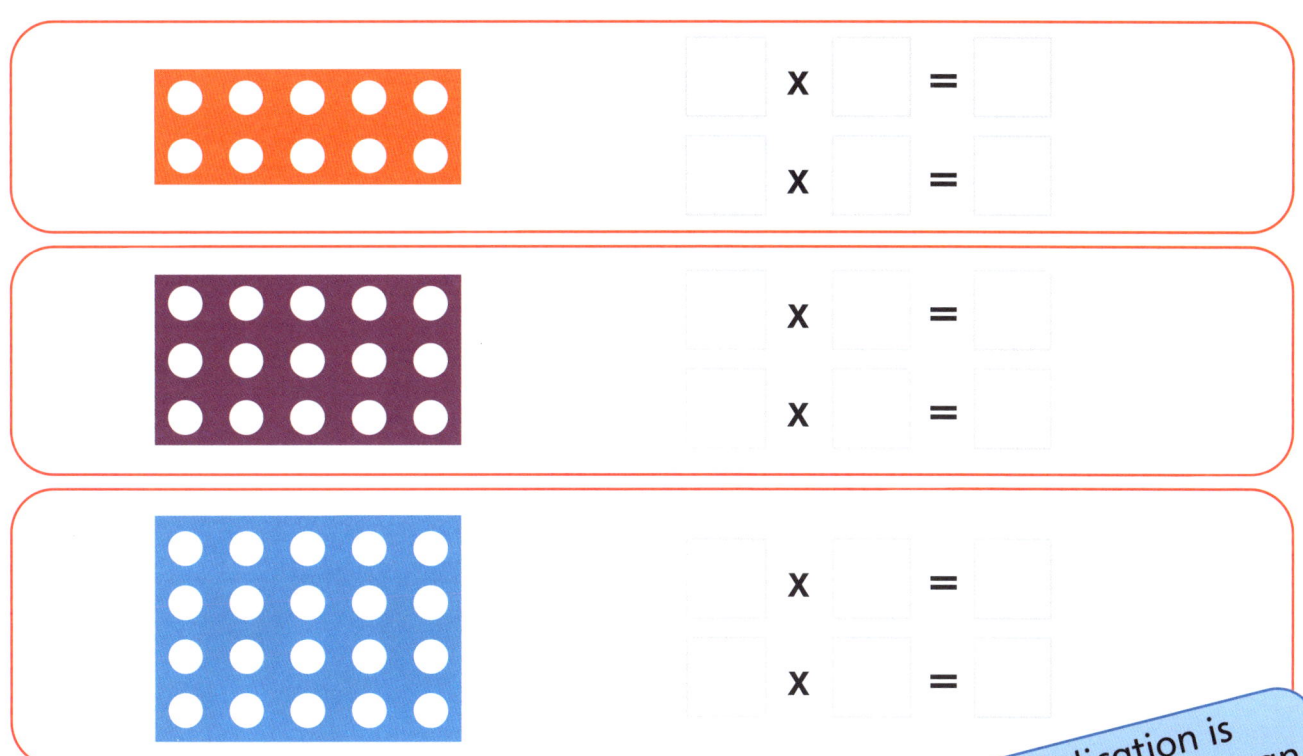

☐ x ☐ = ☐
☐ x ☐ = ☐

☐ x ☐ = ☐
☐ x ☐ = ☐

☐ x ☐ = ☐
☐ x ☐ = ☐

Draw lines to match two number sentences to each array.

**Multiplication is commutative.** You can multiply the numbers in any order.

3 x 4
2 x 5
3 x 6
4 x 2

6 x 3
4 x 3
2 x 4
5 x 2

Redraw the biscuits in an array, and complete the number sentences to match.

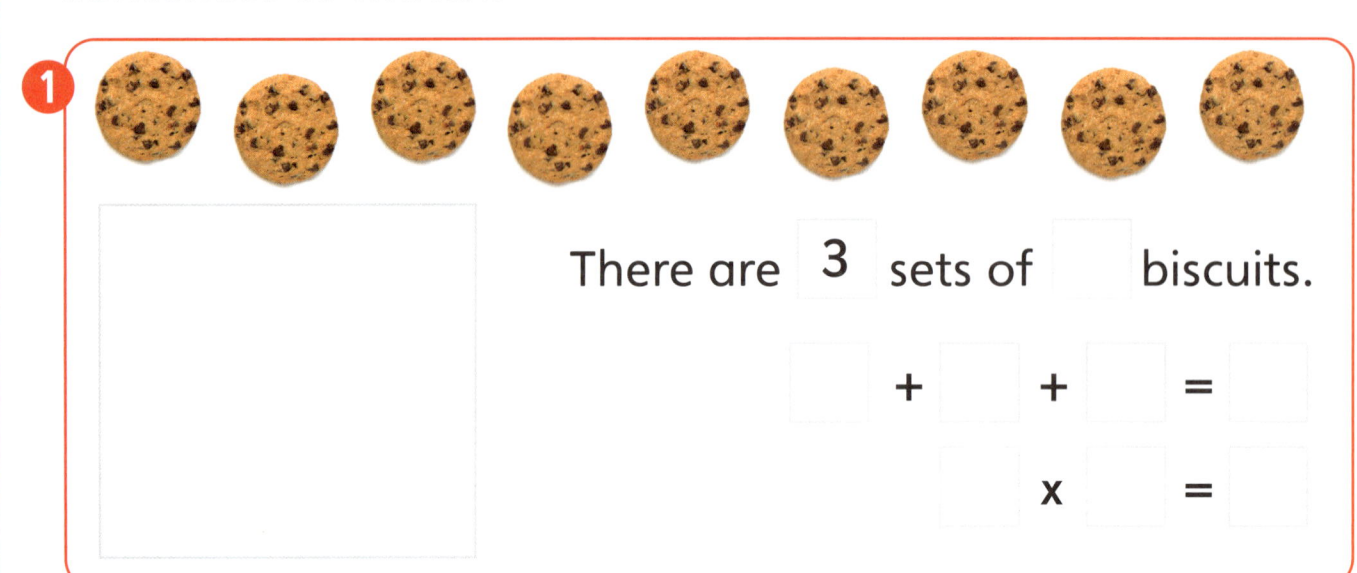

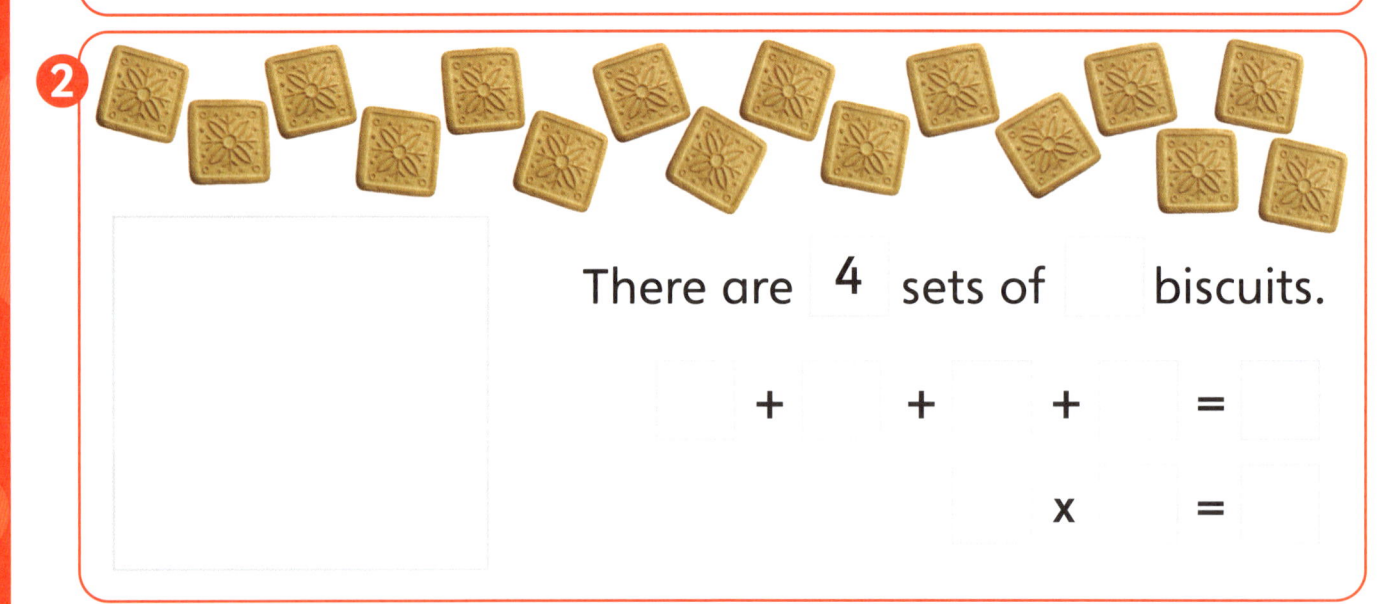

**1**

There are  3  sets of ☐ biscuits.

☐ + ☐ + ☐ = ☐

☐ × ☐ = ☐

**2**

There are  4  sets of ☐ biscuits.

☐ + ☐ + ☐ + ☐ = ☐

☐ × ☐ = ☐

Draw an array to show . . .

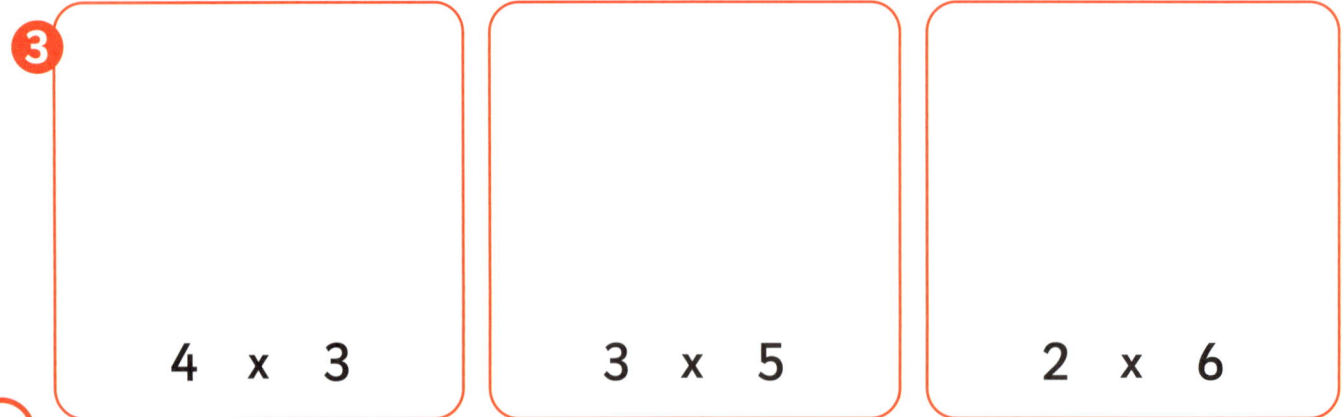

**3**

4 × 3

3 × 5

2 × 6

# puzzling it out

Cut out the number sentences on page 385 to complete the missing pieces below.

# doubling up

Double the numbers. Use the ladybirds to help you.

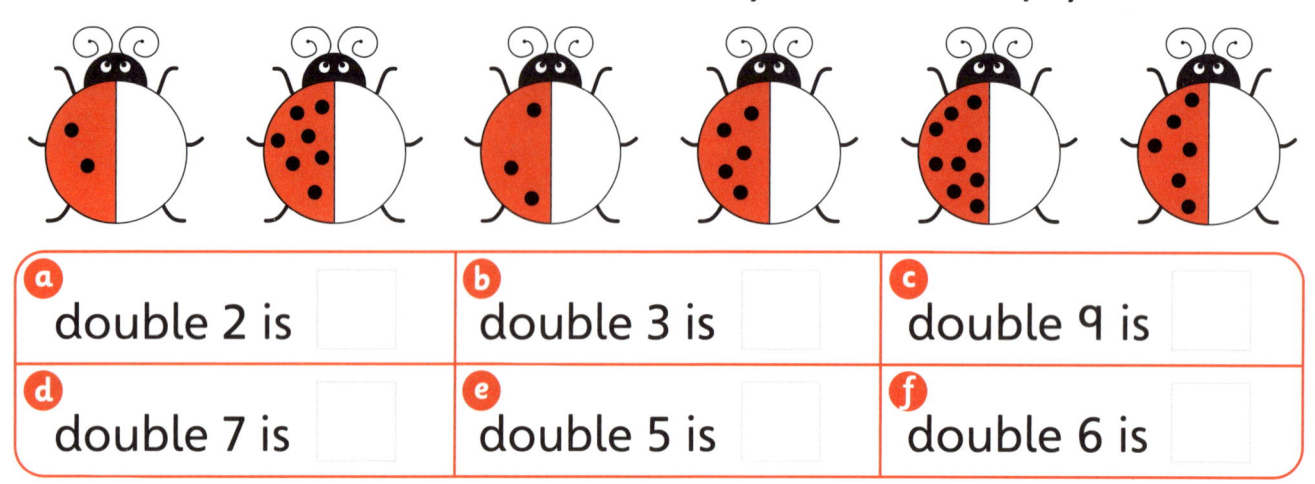

a. double 2 is ☐
b. double 3 is ☐
c. double 9 is ☐
d. double 7 is ☐
e. double 5 is ☐
f. double 6 is ☐

Work out the missing numbers.

g. double ☐ is 2
h. double ☐ is 22
i. double ☐ is 8
j. double ☐ is 20
k. double ☐ is 24
l. double ☐ is 16

Play the doubling game with a friend. Take turns to roll a dice. Double the number you roll and colour in a box with that number. If there are no boxes left with that number, miss a turn. The player with the most coloured boxes wins.

| 8 | 4 | 10 | 8 | 6 | 2 |
|---|---|----|---|---|---|
| 4 | 12 | 6 | 8 | 2 | 10 |
| 12 | 10 | 2 | 4 | 12 | 6 |
| 2 | 6 | 8 | 12 | 4 | 10 |

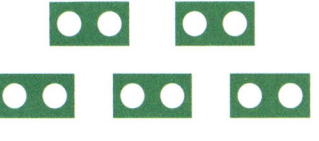

# 2 times table

Count in twos and colour in the grid. What do you notice?

| 1 | 2 | 3 | 4 | 5 | 6 |
|---|---|---|---|---|---|
| 7 | 8 | 9 | 10 | 11 | 12 |
| 13 | 14 | 15 | 16 | 17 | 18 |
| 19 | 20 | 21 | 22 | 23 | 24 |

*All multiples of 2 are **even**.*

**1** Write the answers to these sums.

a) 1 x 2 =

b) 2 x 2 =

c) 3 x 2 =

d) 4 x 2 =

e) 5 x 2 =

f) 6 x 2 =

g) 7 x 2 =

h) 8 x 2 =

i) 9 x 2 =

**MULTIPLICATION AND DIVISION**

j) 10 x 2 =

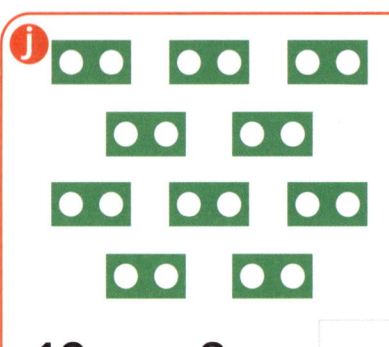

k) 11 x 2 =

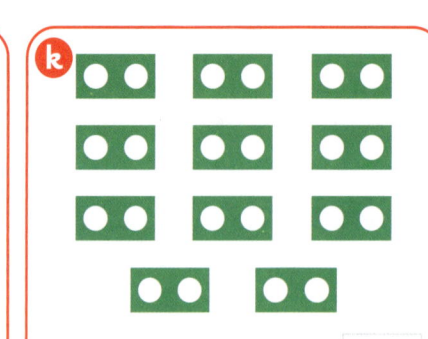

l) 12 x 2 =

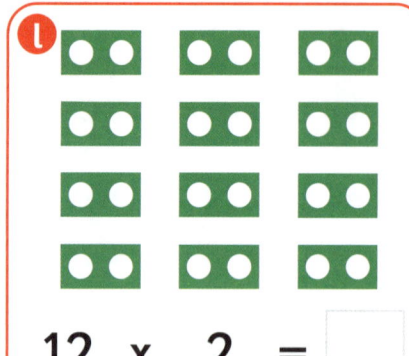

**2** Match the number questions to the right answer.

| 3 x 2 | 9 x 2 | 4 x 2 | 7 x 2 | 6 x 2 |

18   8   14   12   6

**3** Answer the questions below.

Each bird has 2 wings.
How many wings are there if there are 6 birds?

Each child has 2 shoes.
How many shoes are there if there are 10 children?

Each plate can hold 2 burgers.
How many burgers are there if there are 8 plates?

**Did you know?**
In America, around 50 billion burgers are eaten every year!

204

**4** Solve the sums below. Then find the numbers in the word search.

**a**
3 x 2 =
4 x 2 =
7 x 2 =
11 x 2 =

**b**
1 x 2 =
6 x 2 =
2 x 2 =
8 x 2 =

**c**
5 x 2 =
12 x 2 =
9 x 2 =
10 x 2 =

```
t w e n t y f o u r s
r s i x s q m l u o e
t n m t w e l v e s i
w i e w s q m l u o g
e n i p t e n n y y h
n b g s i x t e e n t
t r h s o l r p n t e
y y t t v b m n g w e
f o u r t e e n h o n
u m y k b f o u r w a
s t w e n t y t w o i
```

# 5 times table

Count in fives and colour in the grid.

| 1 | 2 | 3 | 4 | 5 | 6 | 7 | 8 | 9 | 10 |
|---|---|---|---|---|---|---|---|---|---|
| 11 | 12 | 13 | 14 | 15 | 16 | 17 | 18 | 19 | 20 |
| 21 | 22 | 23 | 24 | 25 | 26 | 27 | 28 | 29 | 30 |
| 31 | 32 | 33 | 34 | 35 | 36 | 37 | 38 | 39 | 40 |
| 41 | 42 | 43 | 44 | 45 | 46 | 47 | 48 | 49 | 50 |
| 51 | 52 | 53 | 54 | 55 | 56 | 57 | 58 | 59 | 60 |

**1** Count in fives to work out the answers to these sums.

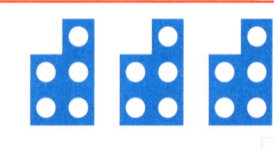

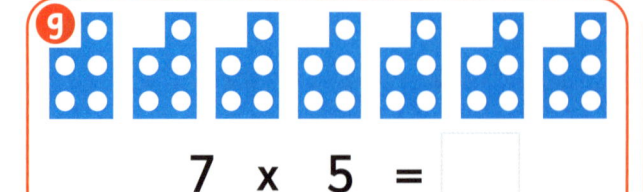

a) 1 × 5 =

b) 2 × 5 =

c) 3 × 5 =

d) 4 × 5 =

e) 5 × 5 =

f) 6 × 5 =

g) 7 × 5 =

h) 8 × 5 =

i) 9 x 5 =

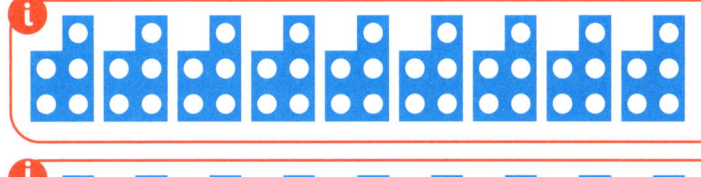

j) 10 x 5 =

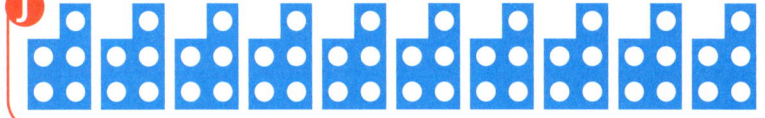

k) 11 x 5 =

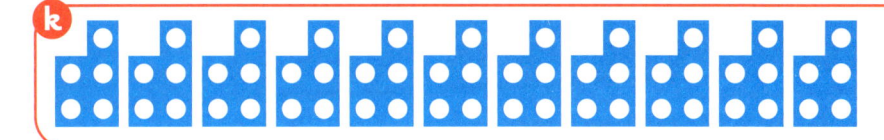

l) 12 x 5 =

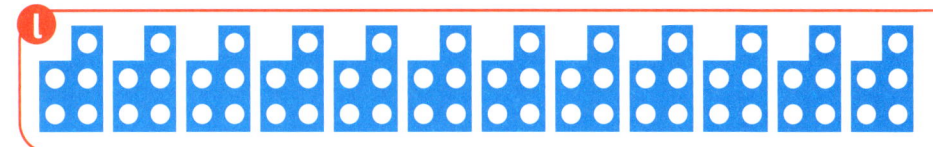

## 2 Answer the questions below.

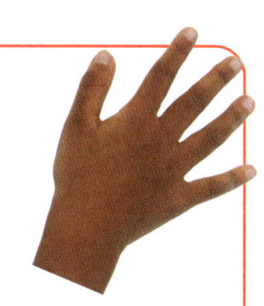

How many fingers are there on 2 hands?

How many fingers are there on 4 hands?

How many fingers are there on 8 hands?

If there are 30 fingers, how many hands are there?

If there are 45 fingers, how many hands are there?

If there are 60 fingers, how many hands are there?

## 3 Match the number questions to the right answer.

| 3 x 5 | 9 x 5 | 4 x 5 | 7 x 5 | 6 x 5 |

35    30    15    20    45

MULTIPLICATION AND DIVISION

**4** Answer the questions below.

Each flower has 5 petals.
How many petals are there if there are 5 flowers?

Each stack has 5 books.
How many books are there if there are 7 stacks?

Each group has 5 dogs.
How many dogs are there if there are 3 groups?

Each group has 5 eggs.
How many eggs are there if there are 11 groups?

Each starfish has 5 arms.
How many arms are there if there are 8 starfish?

**5** Fill in the missing numbers.

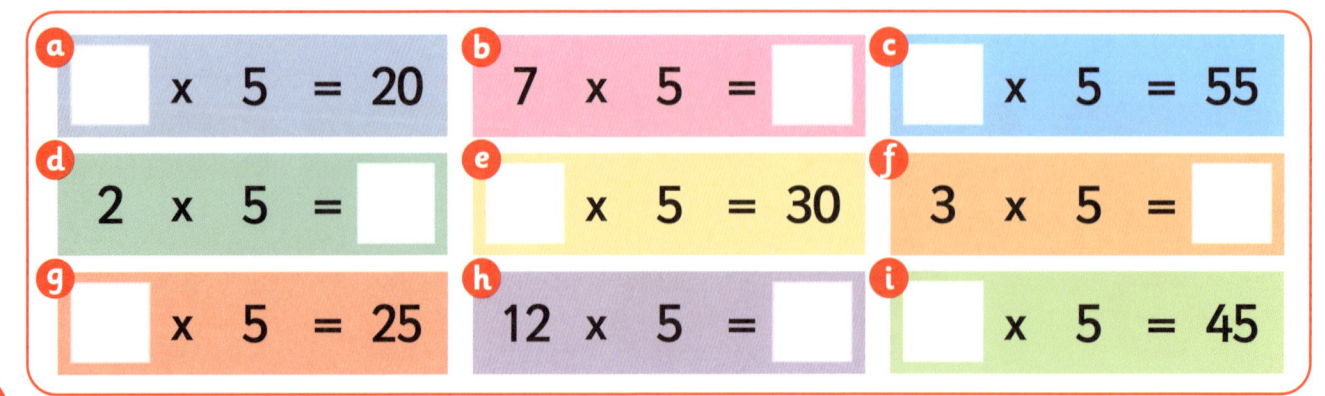

a) ☐ x 5 = 20
b) 7 x 5 = ☐
c) ☐ x 5 = 55
d) 2 x 5 = ☐
e) ☐ x 5 = 30
f) 3 x 5 = ☐
g) ☐ x 5 = 25
h) 12 x 5 = ☐
i) ☐ x 5 = 45

# 5 times table and telling the time

Use the 5 times table to fill in the missing numbers.

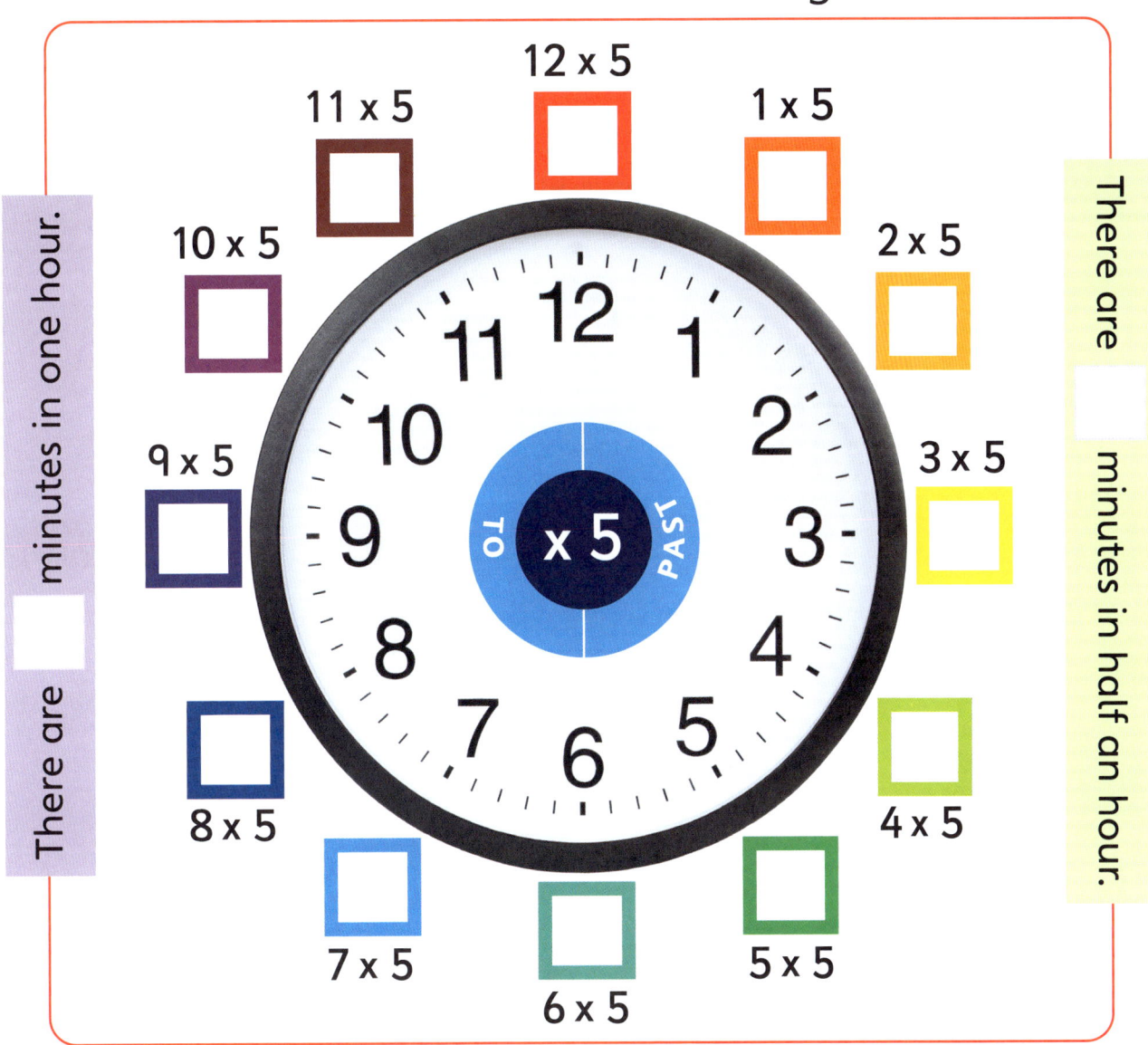

11 x 5 ☐
12 x 5 ☐
1 x 5 ☐
10 x 5 ☐
2 x 5 ☐
9 x 5 ☐
3 x 5 ☐
8 x 5 ☐
4 x 5 ☐
7 x 5 ☐
6 x 5 ☐
5 x 5 ☐

There are ☐ minutes in one hour.

There are ☐ minutes in half an hour.

Tell the time shown on each clock.

☐ minutes *past* ☐

☐ minutes *to* ☐

# 10 times table

Colour the apples with numbers that are in the 10 times table. What do you notice about the numbers?

105, 20, 38, 55, 30, 79, 51, 22, 50, 45, 102, 60, 25, 38, 90, 100, 98, 120, 5, 110, 35, 72

Numbers in the 10 times table always end in 0.

**1** Count in tens to work out the answers to these sums.

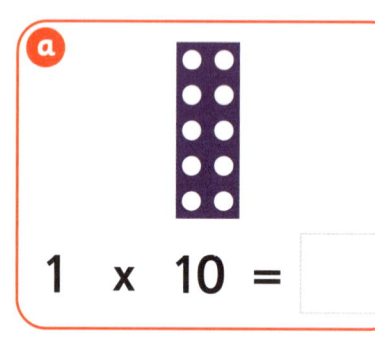

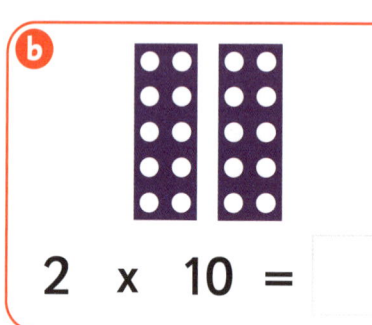

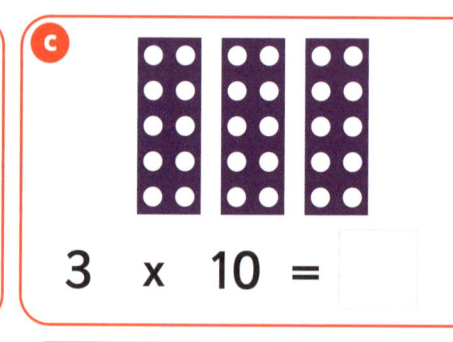

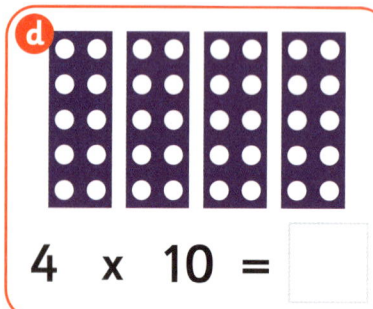

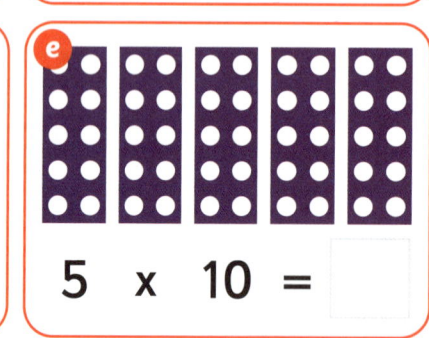

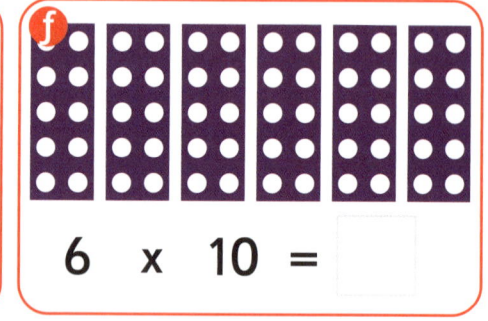

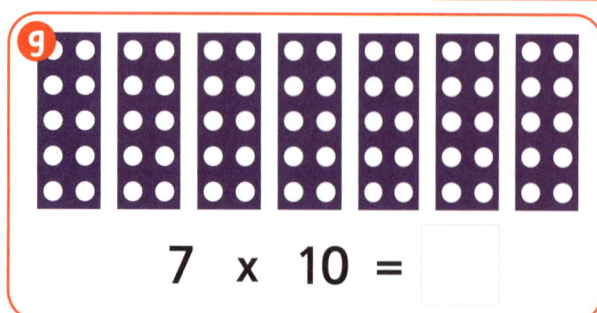

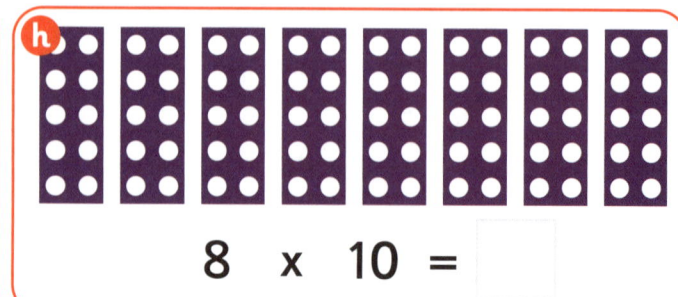

a) 1 × 10 =

b) 2 × 10 =

c) 3 × 10 =

d) 4 × 10 =

e) 5 × 10 =

f) 6 × 10 =

g) 7 × 10 =

h) 8 × 10 =

i. 9 x 10 = ☐

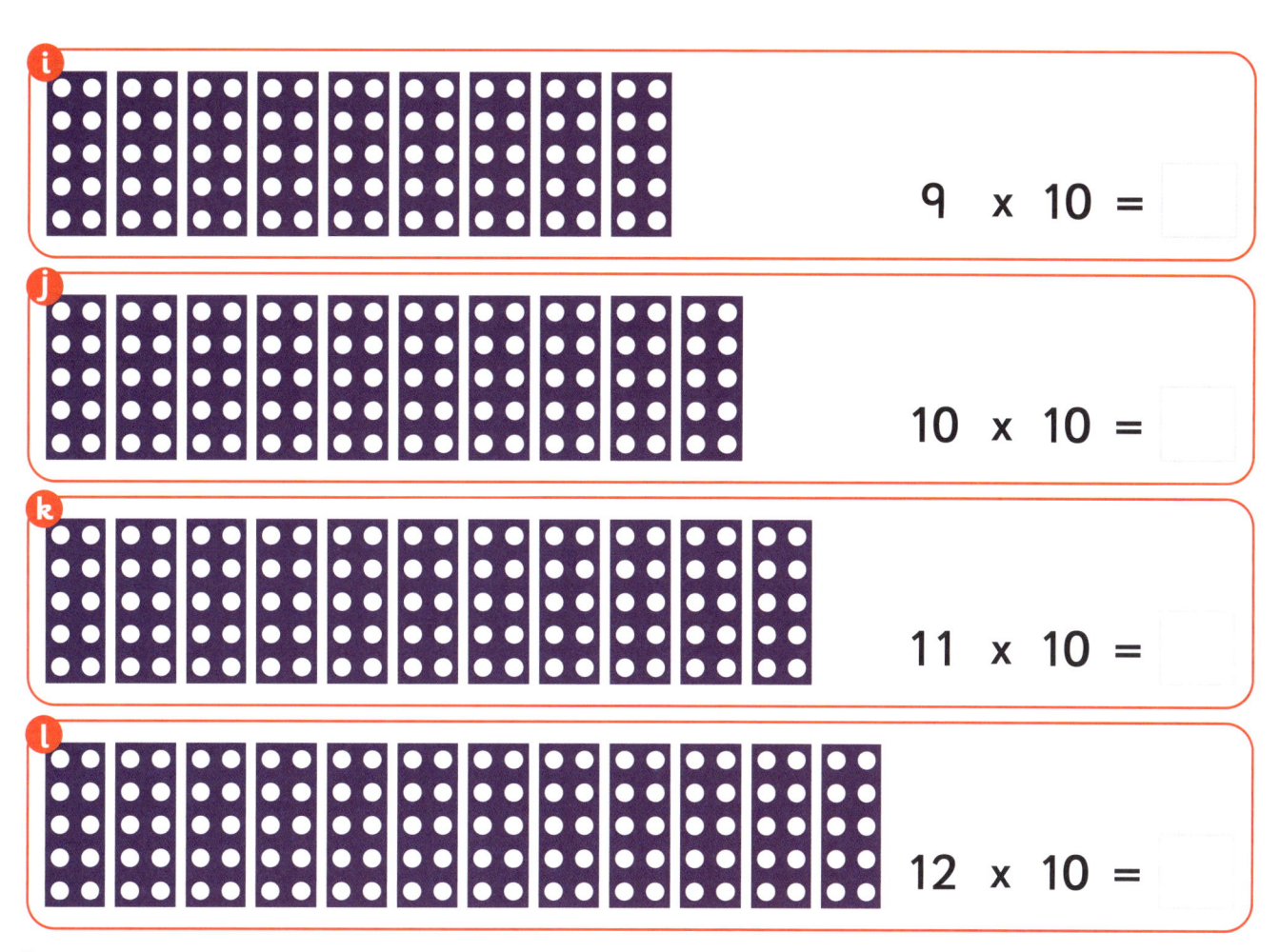

j. 10 x 10 = ☐

k. 11 x 10 = ☐

l. 12 x 10 = ☐

## 2 Complete the calculations below.

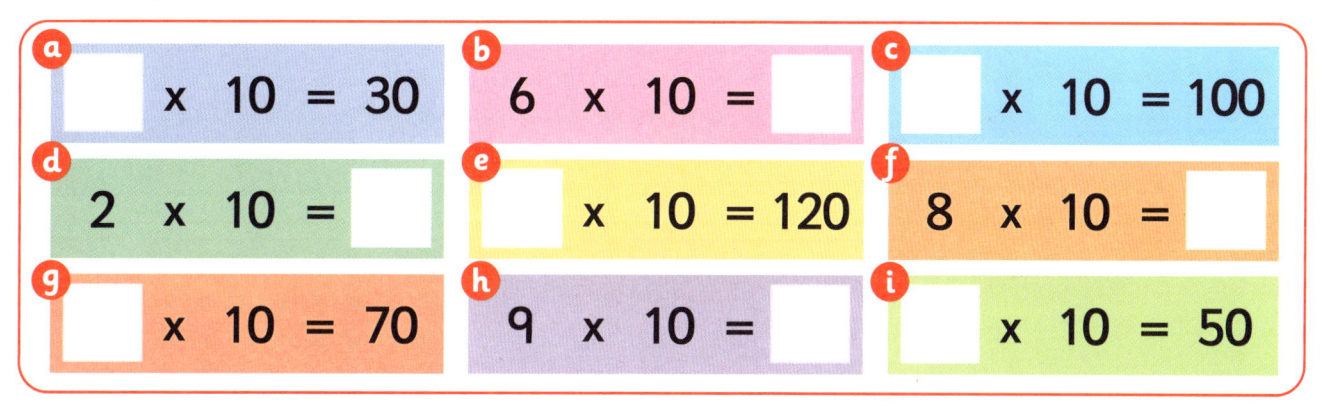

a. ☐ x 10 = 30
b. 6 x 10 = ☐
c. ☐ x 10 = 100
d. 2 x 10 = ☐
e. ☐ x 10 = 120
f. 8 x 10 = ☐
g. ☐ x 10 = 70
h. 9 x 10 = ☐
i. ☐ x 10 = 50

## 3 Match the number questions to the right answer.

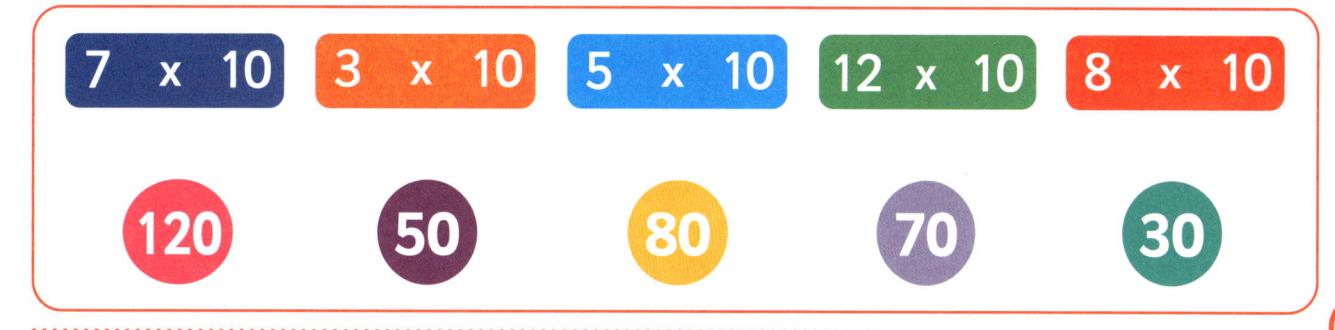

7 x 10     3 x 10     5 x 10     12 x 10     8 x 10

120     50     80     70     30

**4** There are 10 crayons in each packet. Answer the questions below.

How many crayons are there in 5 packets? ☐

How many crayons are there in 9 packets? ☐

How many crayons are there in 10 packets? ☐

If there are 20 crayons, how many packets are there? ☐

If there are 60 crayons, how many packets are there? ☐

If there are 30 crayons, how many packets are there? ☐

**5** Answer the questions below.

Each dumbbell bar has 10 weight plates.
How many weight plates are there if there are 6 dumbbell bars? ☐

Each chocolate bar has 10 squares.
How many squares are there if there are 8 bars of chocolate? ☐

Each conference table can fit 10 chairs.
How many chairs are there if there are 3 conference tables? ☐

# speedy calculations

Test yourself against the clock. See how many sums you can complete in 60 seconds!

**a**
- 3 x 2 = ☐
- ☐ x 5 = 30
- 11 x 5 = ☐
- 3 x ☐ = 30
- 9 x 2 = ☐
- 1 x ☐ = 5
- 11 x 10 = ☐
- ☐ x 2 = 14
- 9 x 10 = ☐
- 12 x 2 = ☐
- 5 x ☐ = 25
- ☐ x 10 = 20

**b**
- 7 x 5 = ☐
- 2 x 5 = ☐
- ☐ x 10 = 120
- 6 x ☐ = 60
- 8 x 5 = ☐
- 8 x ☐ = 16
- ☐ x 2 = 2
- 1 x 10 = ☐
- ☐ x 2 = 10
- 5 x 10 = ☐
- 9 x ☐ = 45
- 12 x 5 = ☐

**c**
- ☐ x 2 = 8
- 4 x 10 = ☐
- 2 x ☐ = 4
- 3 x 5 = ☐
- 10 x ☐ = 50
- 7 x 10 = ☐
- ☐ x 5 = 20
- 6 x 2 = ☐
- 8 x 10 = ☐
- 10 x ☐ = 20
- 10 x 10 = ☐
- ☐ x 2 = 22

Cut out the times tables bookmarks on page 387!

# sharing equally

Share these objects equally.

**1** 4 nuts between 2 chipmunks . . .

Each chipmunk will have ☐ nuts.

**2** 9 carrots between 3 rabbits . . .

Each rabbit will have ☐ carrots.

**3** 8 bones between 4 dogs . . .

Each dog will have ☐ bones.

**4** 8 flowers between 2 butterflies . . .

Each butterfly will have ☐ flowers.

**5** 3 bananas between 3 monkeys . . .

Each monkey will have ☐ banana(s).

**6** There are 12 coins. Divide the coins equally between the 2 piggy banks.

How many coins are in each piggy bank? ☐

12 ÷ 2 = ☐

**7** Count the marbles. Divide the marbles equally between the 3 jars. Draw the marbles in the jars.

How many marbles are in each jar? ☐

☐ ÷ 3 = ☐

**Did you know?**
Piggy banks have been around for hundreds of years, but they weren't always shaped like pigs. They were made from a type of clay called 'pygg'. At some point, someone decided to make a pig-shaped money bank from pygg!

**8** Count the eggs. Divide them equally between the 2 boxes. Draw the eggs in the boxes.

How many eggs are in each box?

☐ ÷ 2 = ☐

**9** Count the doughnuts. Divide them equally between the plates. Draw the doughnuts on the plates.

How many doughnuts are on each plate?

☐ ÷ 4 = ☐

If there are 20 doughnuts divided equally between the 4 plates, how many doughnuts are on each plate?

☐ ÷ 4 = ☐

# dividing by 2

Colour in the squares which can be divided by 2 to give equal shares. What do you notice?

| 10 | 16 | 31 | 26 | 12 | 19 | 28 | 13 | 36 | 23 |
|----|----|----|----|----|----|----|----|----|----|
| 27 | 17 | 39 | 11 | 38 | 34 | 37 | 22 | 29 | 15 |
| 24 | 33 | 18 | 21 | 32 | 20 | 14 | 35 | 30 | 25 |

All **even** numbers are divisible by 2.
**Odd** numbers cannot be exactly divided by 2.

Complete the calculations.

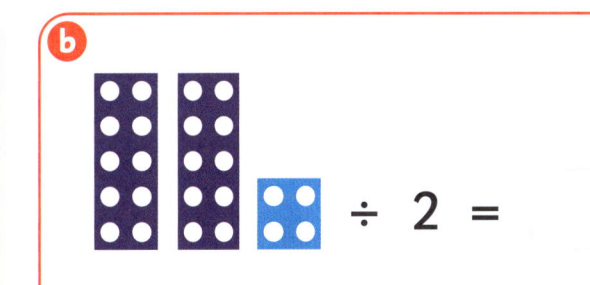

**a** ☐ ÷ 2 =

**b** ☐ ÷ 2 =

**c** 10 ÷ 2 =

**d** 16 ÷ 2 =

**e** 8 ÷ 2 =

**f** 34 ÷ 2 =

**g** 70 ÷ 2 =

**h** 28 ÷ 2 =

Dividing by 2 is the same as **halving** a number.

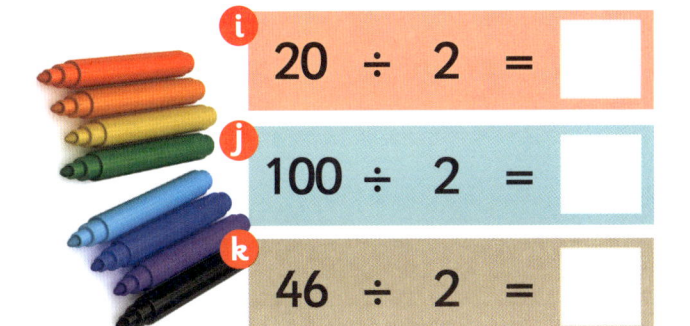

**i** 20 ÷ 2 =

half of 20 =

**j** 100 ÷ 2 =

half of 100 =

**k** 46 ÷ 2 =

half of 46 =

# dividing by 5

**1** Complete the calculations.

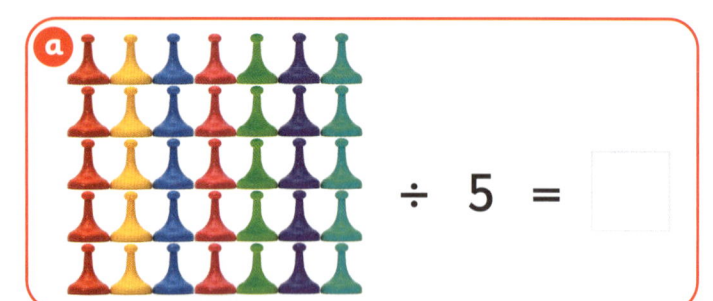

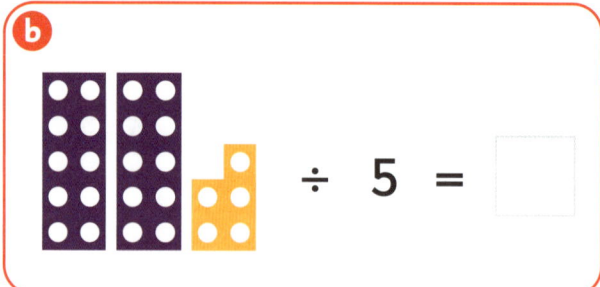

a) ☐ ÷ 5 =  ☐

b) ☐ ÷ 5 = ☐

**5 TIMES TABLE**
1 x 5 = 5
2 x 5 = 10
3 x 5 = 15
4 x 5 = 20
5 x 5 = 25
6 x 5 = 30
7 x 5 = 35
8 x 5 = 40
9 x 5 = 45
10 x 5 = 50
11 x 5 = 55
12 x 5 = 60

Use your knowledge of the 5 times table to help you complete the calculations.

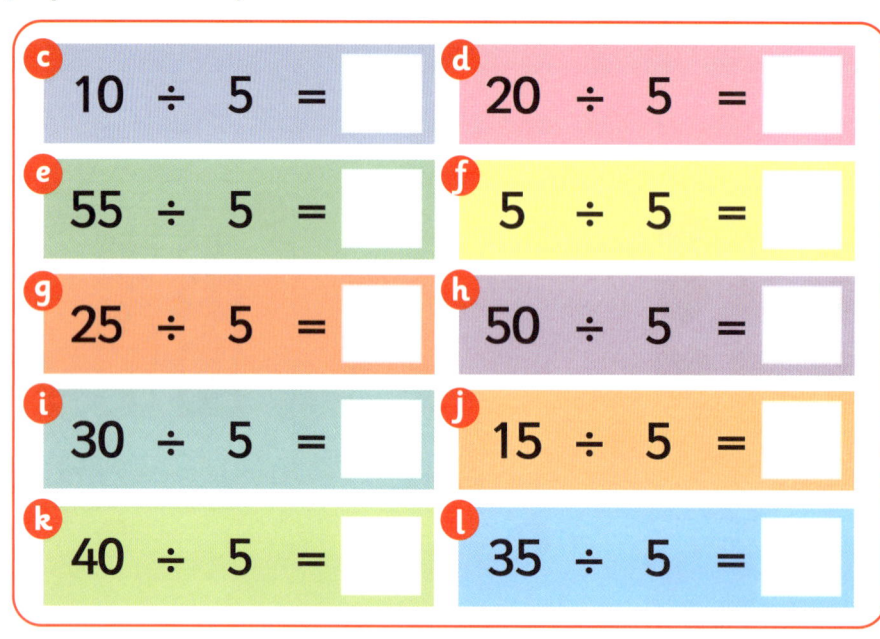

c) 10 ÷ 5 = ☐
d) 20 ÷ 5 = ☐
e) 55 ÷ 5 = ☐
f) 5 ÷ 5 = ☐
g) 25 ÷ 5 = ☐
h) 50 ÷ 5 = ☐
i) 30 ÷ 5 = ☐
j) 15 ÷ 5 = ☐
k) 40 ÷ 5 = ☐
l) 35 ÷ 5 = ☐

**2** Use the *multiplication* calculation below to complete 2 related *division* calculations.

9 x 5 = 45

☐ ÷ ☐ = ☐
☐ ÷ ☐ = ☐

**3** Use the *division* calculation below to complete 2 related *multiplication* calculations.

60 ÷ 5 = 12

☐ x ☐ = ☐
☐ x ☐ = ☐

# dividing by 10

**1** Complete the calculations.

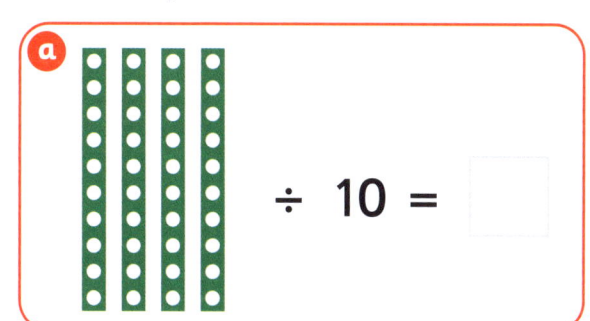

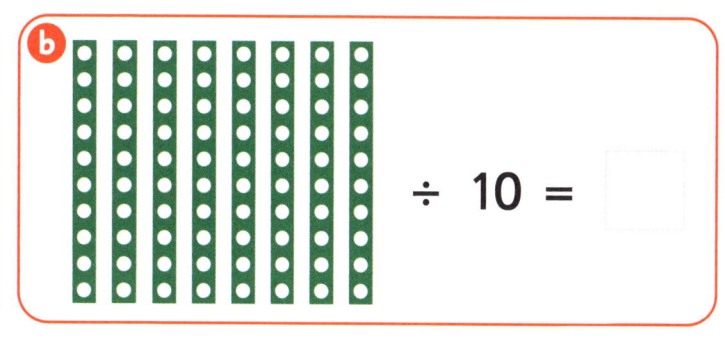

**a** ☐ ÷ 10 =  ☐

**b** ☐ ÷ 10 = ☐

**c** seventy ÷ 10 = ☐

**d** one hundred ÷ 10 = ☐

Divide each of these numbers by 10. What do you notice?

**e** 10 ÷ 10 = ☐
**f** 20 ÷ 10 = ☐
**g** 30 ÷ 10 = ☐
**h** 40 ÷ 10 = ☐
**i** 50 ÷ 10 = ☐
**j** 60 ÷ 10 = ☐
**k** 70 ÷ 10 = ☐
**l** 80 ÷ 10 = ☐
**m** 90 ÷ 10 = ☐
**n** 100 ÷ 10 = ☐
**o** 110 ÷ 10 = ☐
**p** 120 ÷ 10 = ☐

**2** Use the *multiplication* calculation below to complete 2 related *division* calculations.

9 x 10 = 90

☐ ÷ ☐ = ☐

☐ ÷ ☐ = ☐

**3** Use the *division* calculation below to complete 2 related *multiplication* calculations.

60 ÷ 10 = 6

☐ x ☐ = ☐

☐ x ☐ = ☐

MULTIPLICATION AND DIVISION

# more division

**1** Divide this array into sets of 4.

12 ÷ 4 = ☐

Divide this array into sets of 2.

☐ ÷ ☐ = ☐

Divide this array into sets of 3.

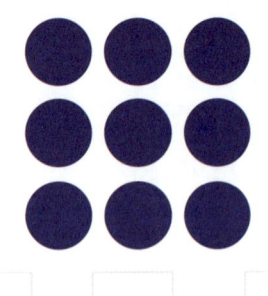

☐ ÷ ☐ = ☐

Divide this array into sets of 3.

27 ÷ 3 = ☐

**2** Draw an array to show this calculation.

15 ÷ 5 = ☐

**3** Draw an array to show this calculation.

30 ÷ 5 = ☐

Match the calculations to the correct answer.

**4**

20 ÷ 2    6    7    30 ÷ 5

60 ÷ 5              45 ÷ 5

        9    4    10

80 ÷ 10              12 ÷ 6

        5    2    12

15 ÷ 3              22 ÷ 2

35 ÷ 5    8    11    16 ÷ 4

**5** Write a division statement for the following problems.

There are 20 balloons and 5 children. How many balloons will each child get if they are divided equally?       ÷     =

There are 35 pencils and 5 pots. How many pencils will fit in each pot if they are divided equally?       ÷     =

**6** Circle the mistake.

100 ÷ 10 = 10
45 ÷ 9 = 5
10 ÷ 10 = 10
24 ÷ 2 = 12

Circle the mistake.

35 ÷ 5 = 7
60 ÷ 10 = 6
22 ÷ 11 = 2
18 ÷ 2 = 8

# colour by division

Solve the calculations in the picture to work out which colour to use.

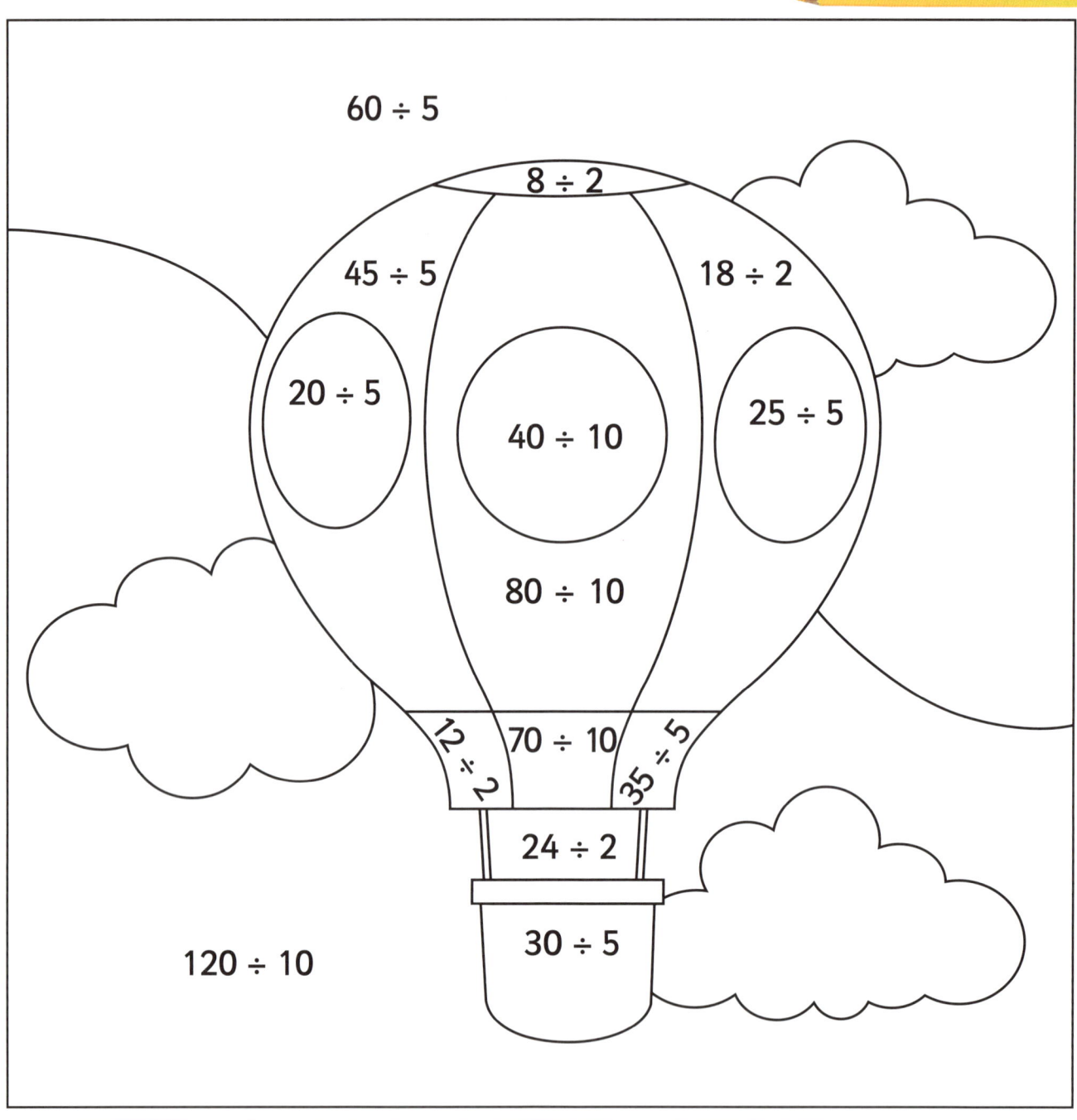

- 60 ÷ 5
- 8 ÷ 2
- 45 ÷ 5
- 18 ÷ 2
- 20 ÷ 5
- 40 ÷ 10
- 25 ÷ 5
- 80 ÷ 10
- 12 ÷ 2
- 70 ÷ 10
- 35 ÷ 5
- 24 ÷ 2
- 30 ÷ 5
- 120 ÷ 10

| 4-5 yellow | 6-7 green | 8 red | 9 purple | 12 blue |

# race to divide

Move around the race track below by dividing the numbers. Divide the numbers on blue squares by 2, on orange squares by 5 and on green squares by 10. Time yourself to see how long it takes you to finish the race!

# number puzzles

**1** There are 20 children in the class. The teacher asks them to stand in groups of 4.
How many groups will there be? ☐

**2** Mo has 12 marbles. Leo has double the number of marbles that Mo has.
How many marbles does Leo have? ☐
How many marbles do they have altogether? ☐

**3** Use the multiplication calculation below to complete 2 division calculations.

5 x 7 = 35

☐ ÷ ☐ = ☐
☐ ÷ ☐ = ☐

**4** Each cone has 3 scoops of ice cream.
How many scoops are there if there are 4 cones? ☐
How many are there if there are 10 cones? ☐

**5** Jake, Tom, Molly and Alex have 20 apples between them. They want to share them equally. Write a calculation to show how many they get each.

☐ ÷ ☐ = ☐

**6** Pippa wants to give her friends 4 pieces of fudge each. She has 6 friends.

How many pieces of fudge does she need? ☐

**7** Tia runs 10 metres five times.

Circle the number statements that do *not* describe this.

| 10 + 5 | 10 x 5 | 5 + 5 + 5 + 5 + 5 |

| 10 + 10 + 10 + 10 + 10 | 5 x 10 |

**8** Jasper bakes 36 biscuits. Half the biscuits are heart-shaped and half the biscuits are round.

How many round biscuits are there? ☐

**9** There are 6 groups of 5 eggs. True or false? Circle the answer.

TRUE          FALSE

**10** Use the number cards to make multiplication and division sentences.

40  8  10  5  4

How many can you make?

**11** How many strawberries would you need for 5 children to get 5 each? ☐

**12** Each cake needs 2 eggs. How many eggs do you need to make 4 cakes? ☐

**13** There are 36 bottles of water. They are divided equally and each athlete gets 2 bottles.
How many athletes are there? ☐

**14** There are 20 people and 2 buses. An equal number get on each bus.
How many are on each bus? ☐

**15** What is the time shown on the clock?
☐ minutes *past* ☐

**16** Each ant carries 5 leaves to the nest. There are 8 ants.
How many leaves do they carry altogether? ☐

# Fractions

# equal parts

**1** How many equal parts has each shape been divided into?

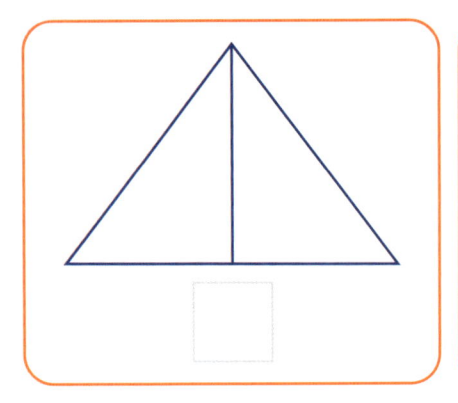

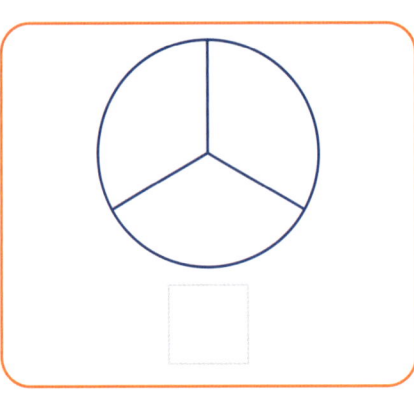

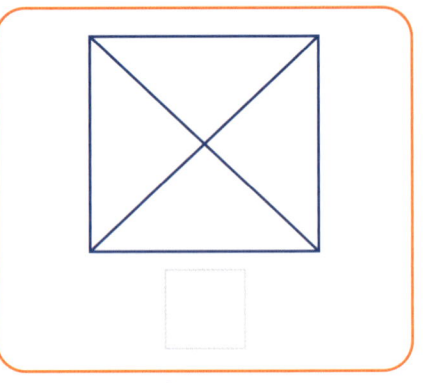

**2** Are these foods divided into equal parts? ✓ or ✗

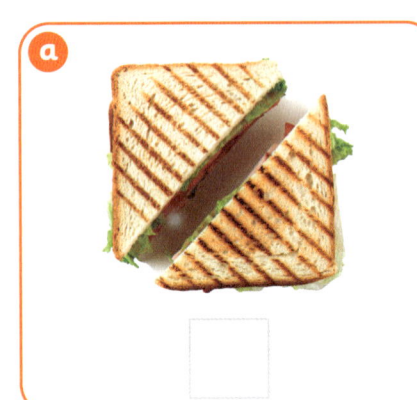

a  b  c

d  e  f

**3** Divide these foods into the given number of equal parts.

2  3  4

**4** Cut out the shapes on page 389 and put them under the correct heading.

| Equal Parts | Not Equal Parts |
|---|---|
|  |  |

**5** Draw a line on each shape to show **2 equal** parts.

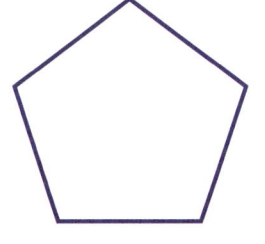

**6** Draw lines on each shape to show **4 equal** parts.

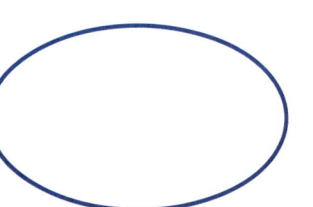

# identifying fractions

**1** Colour the fractions.

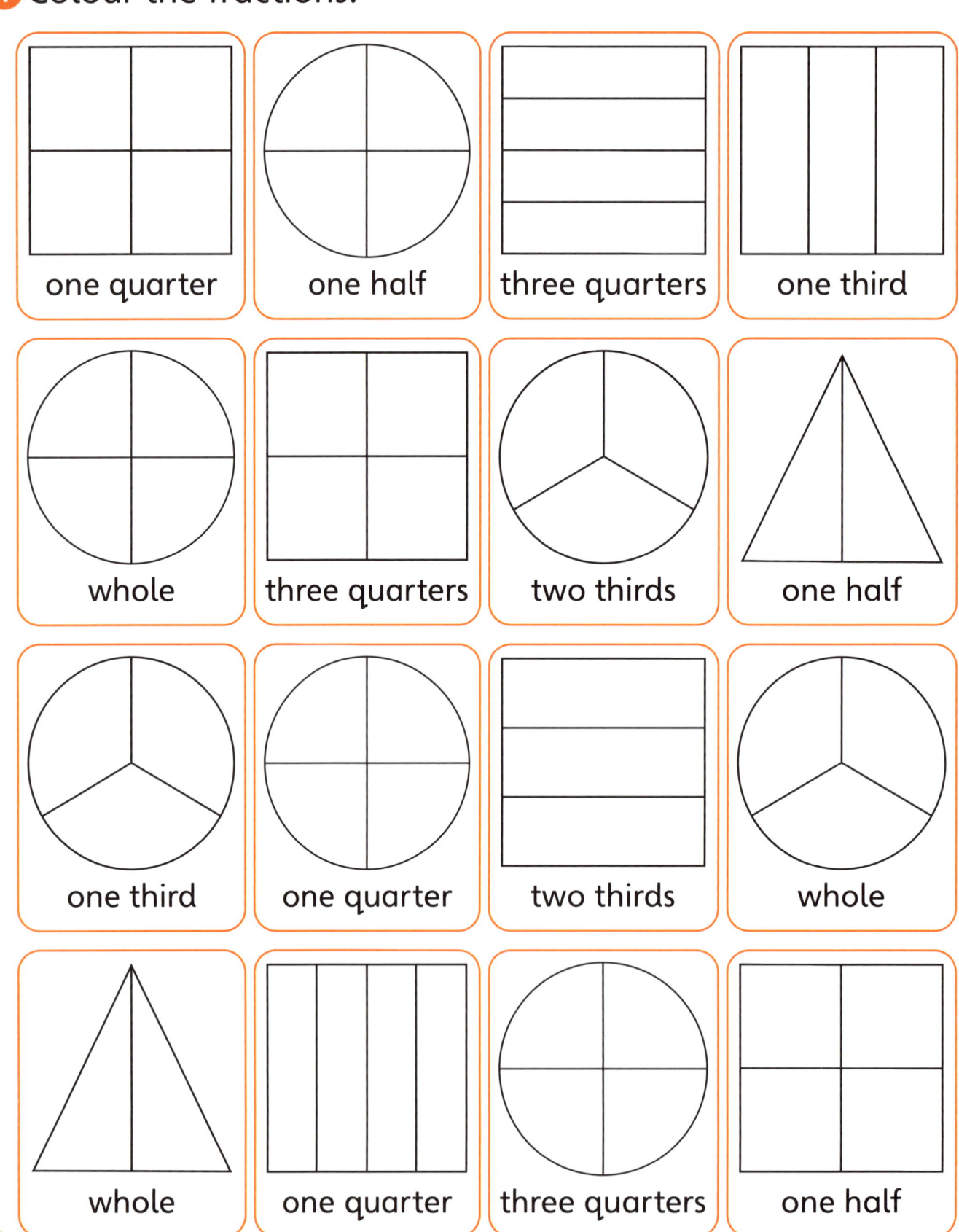

| one quarter | one half | three quarters | one third |
| whole | three quarters | two thirds | one half |
| one third | one quarter | two thirds | whole |
| whole | one quarter | three quarters | one half |

**2** What fraction of each shape is coloured? Match the shape to the fraction.

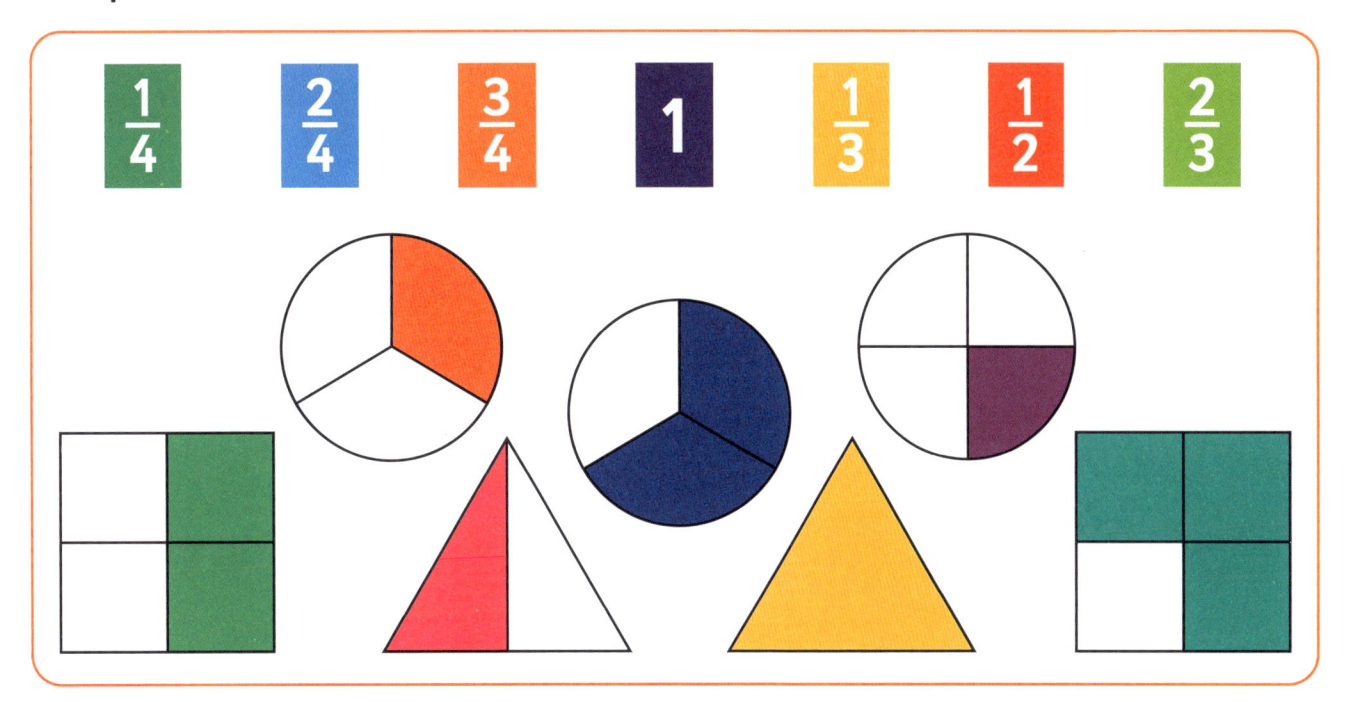

| 1/4 | 2/4 | 3/4 | 1 | 1/3 | 1/2 | 2/3 |

**3** Draw lines to match the equal fractions.

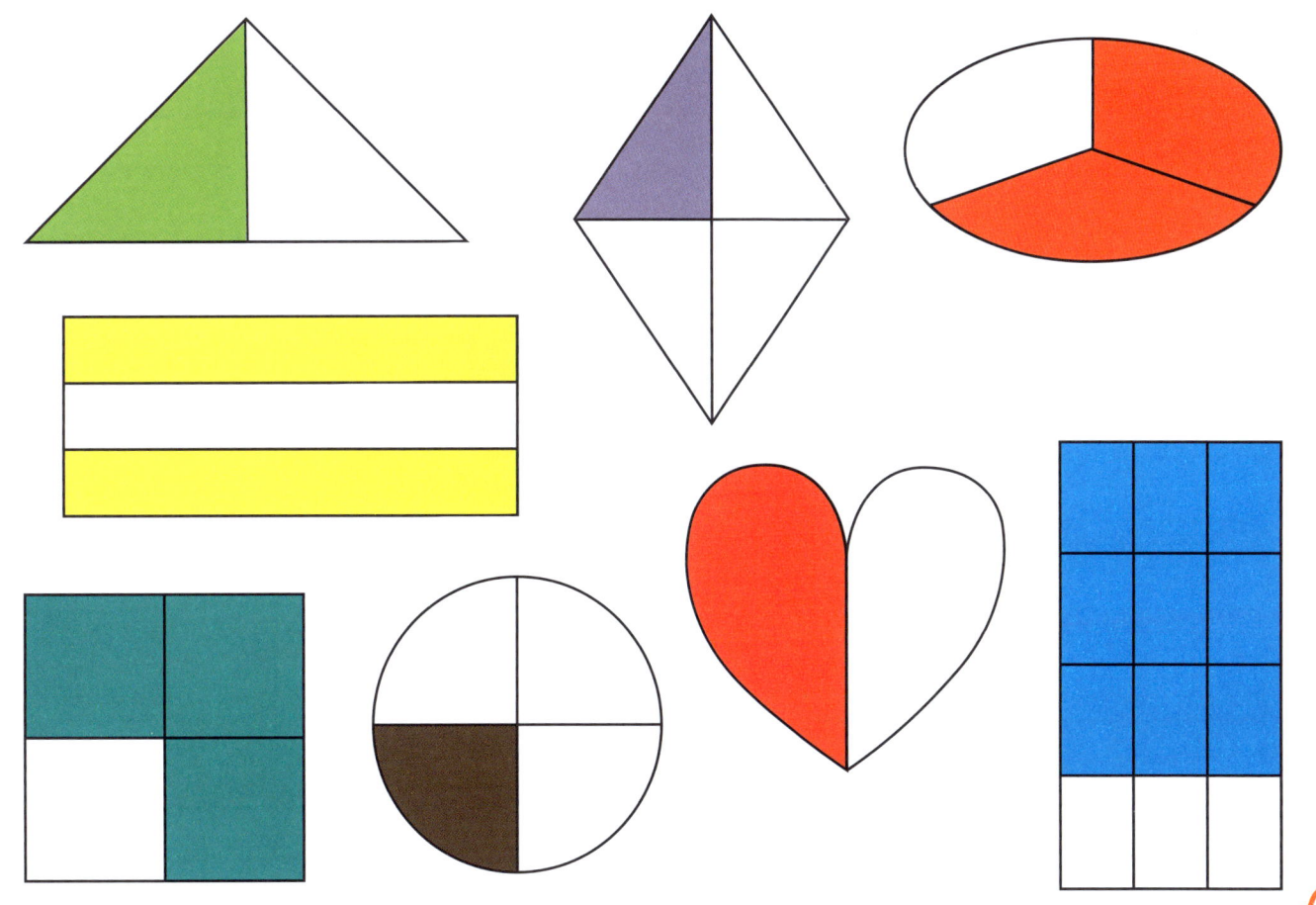

FRACTIONS

## fraction pairs game

Cut out the cards on page 391, and lay them face down. Take it in turns to turn over two cards. If the fractions match, keep them. Otherwise turn them back over. The player who ends the game with the most pairs is the winner!

$\frac{3}{4}$

Find different ways to colour one **half** of each shape.

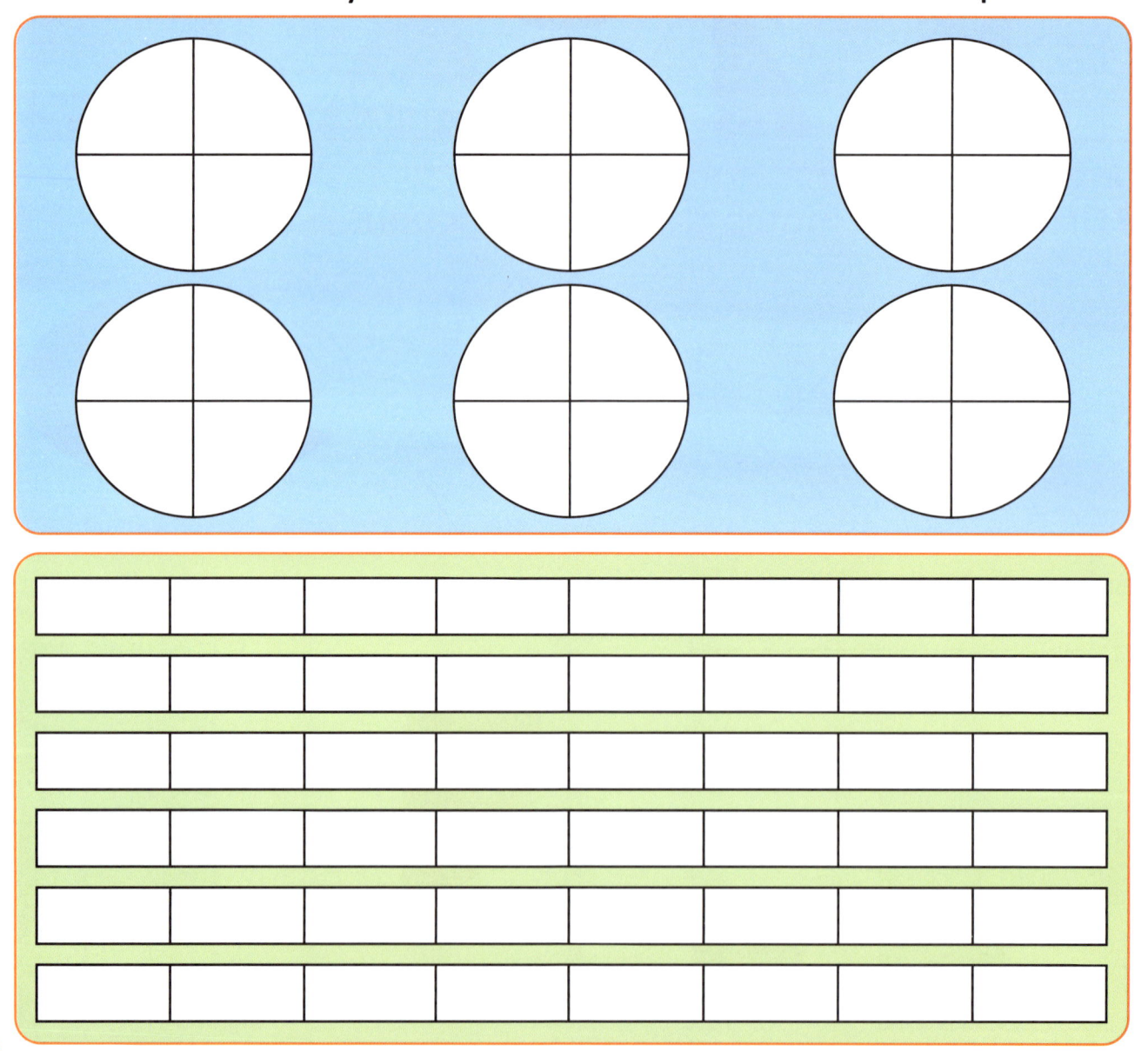

Find different ways to colour one **quarter** of each shape.

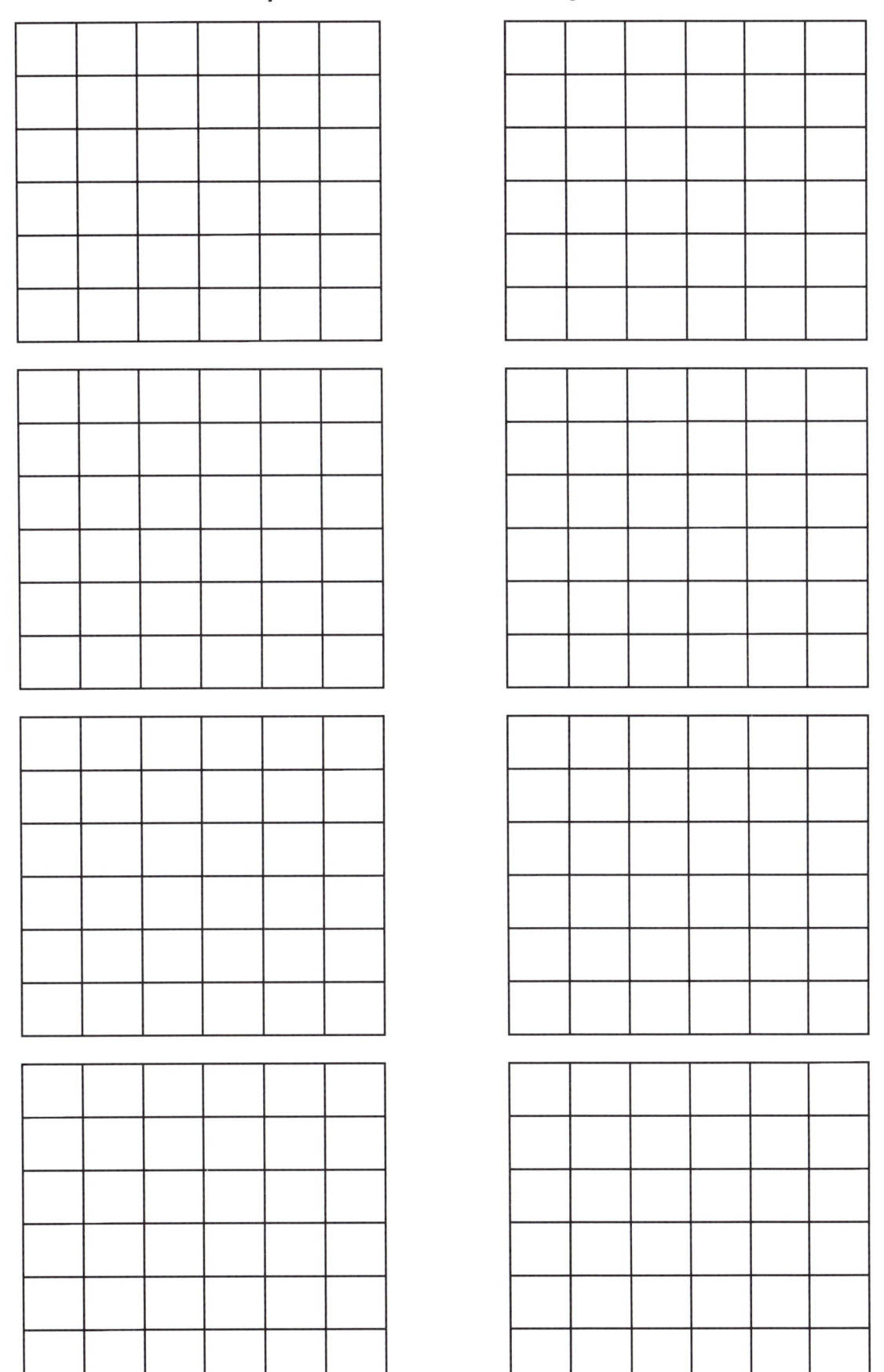

Colour $\frac{1}{2}$ of each shape.

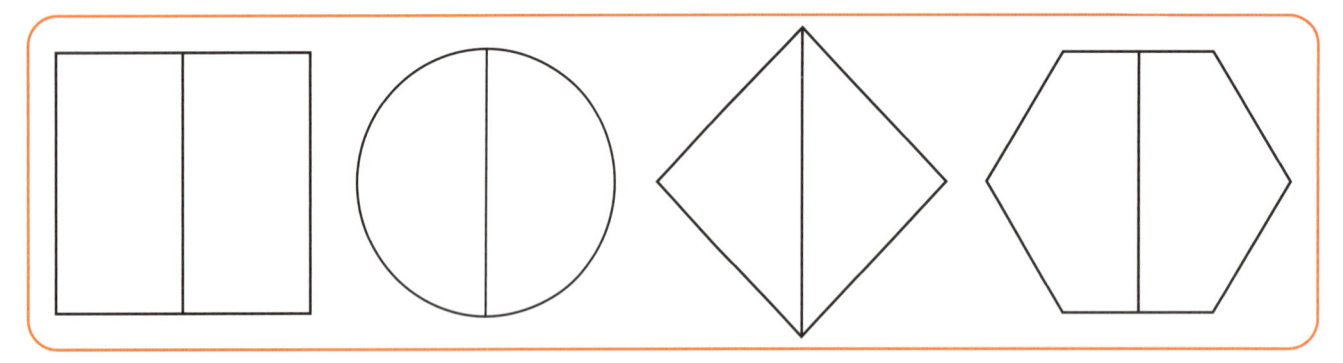

Colour $\frac{2}{4}$ of each shape.

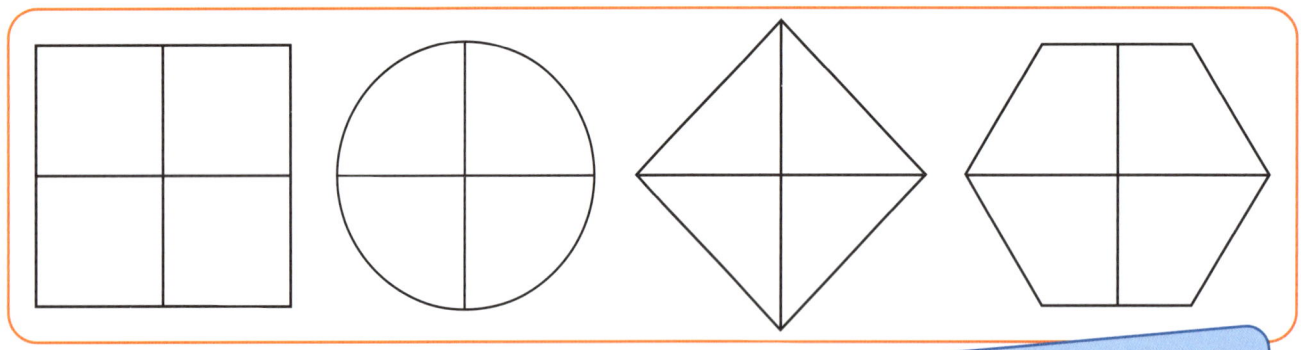

What do you notice?

$\frac{1}{2}$ and $\frac{2}{4}$ are **equivalent**.

Write the fraction of the coloured part of each shape.

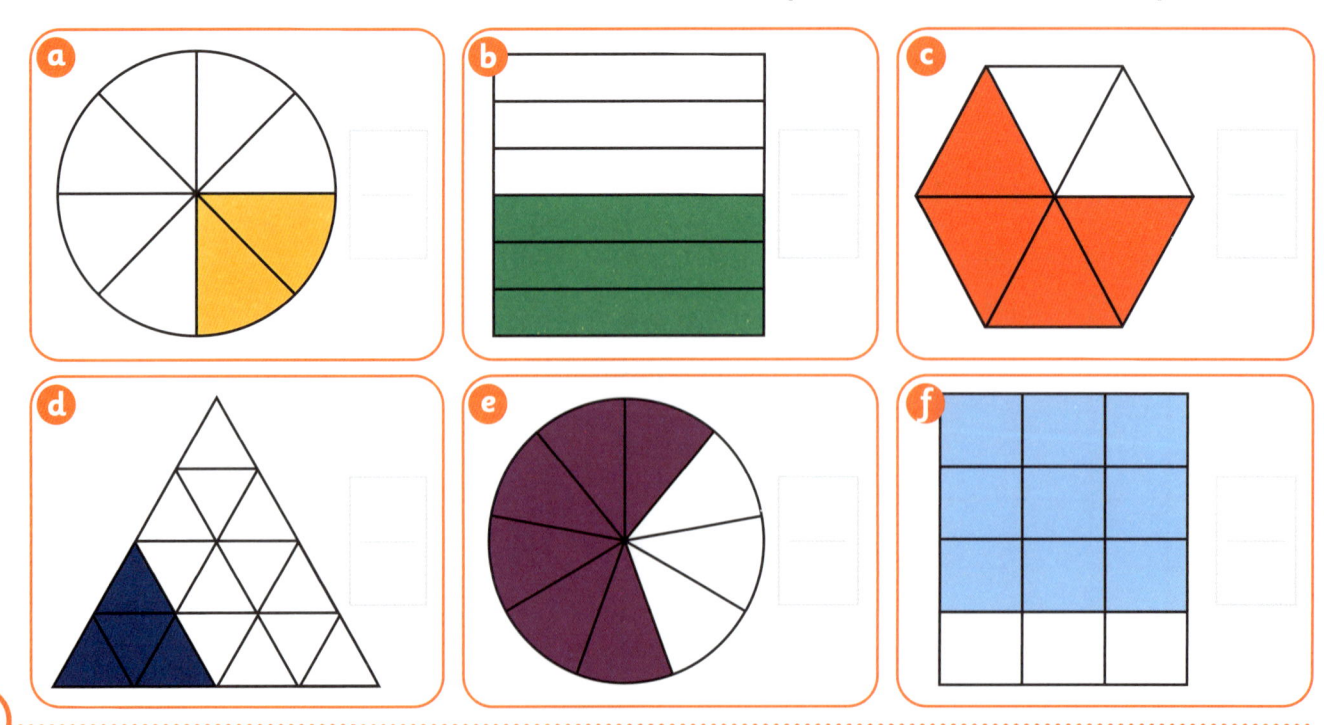

a
b
c
d
e
f

# fractions of amounts

Circle one **half** of each group.

**1** How many pencils are there in total?

How many is half of that number?

**2** How many gems are there in total?

How many is half of that number?

**3** What is one half of 8?

**4** What is one half of 14?

**5** What is one half of 18?

# FRACTIONS

Circle one **quarter** of each group.

**1** How many pears are there in total?

How many is quarter of that number?

**2** How many guitars are there in total?

How many is quarter of that number?

**3** What is one quarter of 12?

**4** What is one quarter of 24?

**5** What is one quarter of 48?

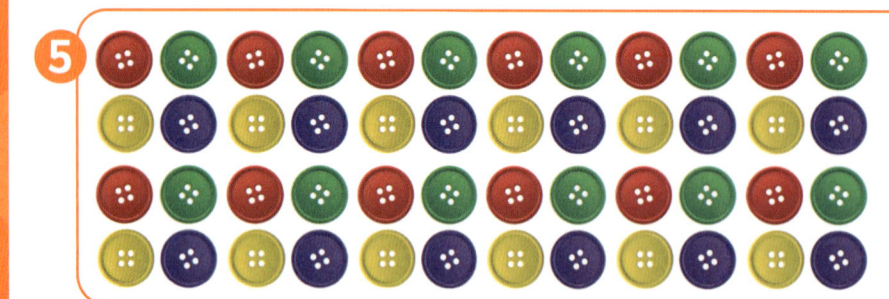

**6** What is one quarter of 100?

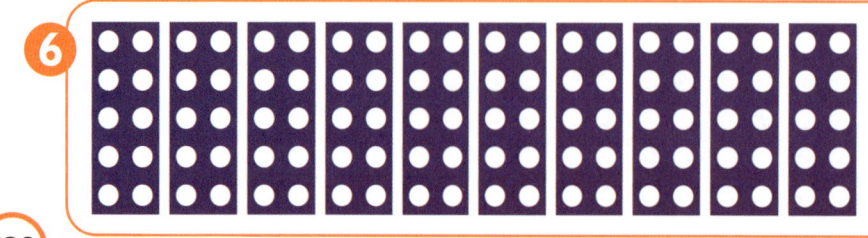

Circle one **third** of each group.

1. How many coins are there in total?
   
   How many is a third of that number?

2. How many stones are there in total?
   
   How many is a third of that number?

3. What is one third of 30?

4. What is one third of 18?

5. What is one third of 24?

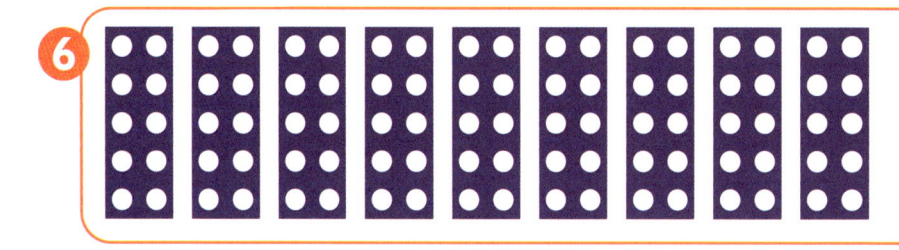

6. What is one third of 90?

FRACTIONS

Find **three quarters** of each group.

**1**

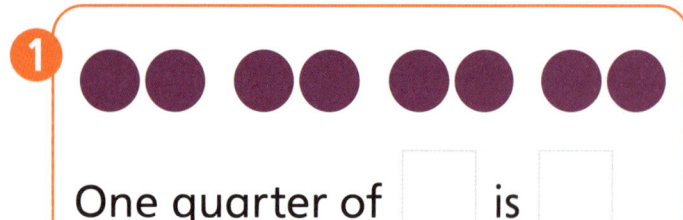

One quarter of ☐ is ☐
Two quarters of ☐ is ☐
Three quarters of ☐ is ☐
Four quarters of ☐ is ☐

**2**

One quarter of ☐ is ☐
Two quarters of ☐ is ☐
Three quarters of ☐ is ☐
Four quarters of ☐ is ☐

**3**

One quarter of ☐ is ☐
Two quarters of ☐ is ☐
Three quarters of ☐ is ☐
Four quarters of ☐ is ☐

**4** Write the total for each fraction.

a) $\frac{1}{4}$ of 40 = ☐

b) $\frac{1}{2}$ of 28 = ☐

c) $\frac{1}{3}$ of 36 = ☐

d) $\frac{1}{2}$ of 90 = ☐

e) $\frac{2}{3}$ of 30 = ☐

f) $\frac{3}{4}$ of 12 = ☐

g) $\frac{3}{4}$ of 16 = ☐

h) $\frac{2}{4}$ of 80 = ☐

i) $\frac{2}{3}$ of 60 = ☐

j) $\frac{2}{4}$ of 32 = ☐

k) $\frac{1}{3}$ of 27 = ☐

l) $\frac{1}{2}$ of 44 = ☐

**1** Follow the clues to work out the number each child has chosen.

**Tomo:** My number is half of 5 × 8.

**Emilia:** My number is $\frac{1}{3}$ of 15.

**Jamila:** My number is $\frac{1}{4}$ of 100.

**Ade:** My number is half of 60 ÷ 2.

Place their names and numbers on the line below in order of lowest to highest.

low ←——————————————————→ high

**2** Which is greater? Use <, >, or = to compare the fractions.

a) $\frac{1}{4}$ of 12 ☐ $\frac{1}{2}$ of 12

b) $\frac{1}{3}$ of 27 ☐ $\frac{1}{4}$ of 36

c) $\frac{2}{3}$ of 90 ☐ $\frac{1}{2}$ of 50

d) $\frac{1}{2}$ of 26 ☐ $\frac{3}{4}$ of 16

e) $\frac{1}{3}$ of 18 ☐ $\frac{1}{4}$ of 24

f) $\frac{3}{4}$ of 20 ☐ $\frac{1}{3}$ of 60

## colour by fractions

Solve the calculations in the picture to work out which colour to use.

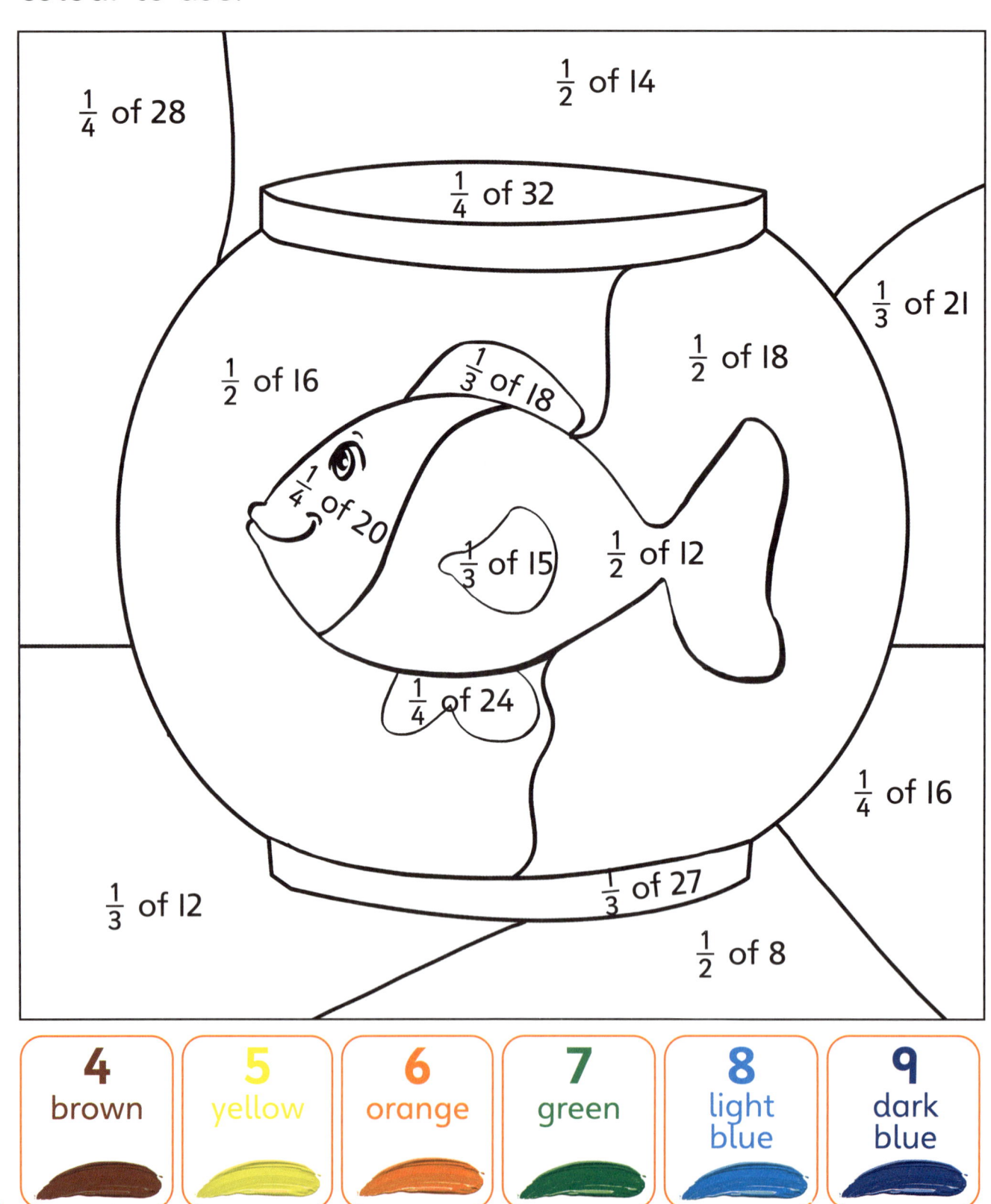

$\frac{1}{4}$ of 28

$\frac{1}{2}$ of 14

$\frac{1}{4}$ of 32

$\frac{1}{3}$ of 21

$\frac{1}{2}$ of 16

$\frac{1}{3}$ of 18

$\frac{1}{2}$ of 18

$\frac{1}{4}$ of 20

$\frac{1}{3}$ of 15

$\frac{1}{2}$ of 12

$\frac{1}{4}$ of 24

$\frac{1}{4}$ of 16

$\frac{1}{3}$ of 12

$\frac{1}{3}$ of 27

$\frac{1}{2}$ of 8

**4** brown
**5** yellow
**6** orange
**7** green
**8** light blue
**9** dark blue

# fractions and measuring

Compare the pencil lengths below.

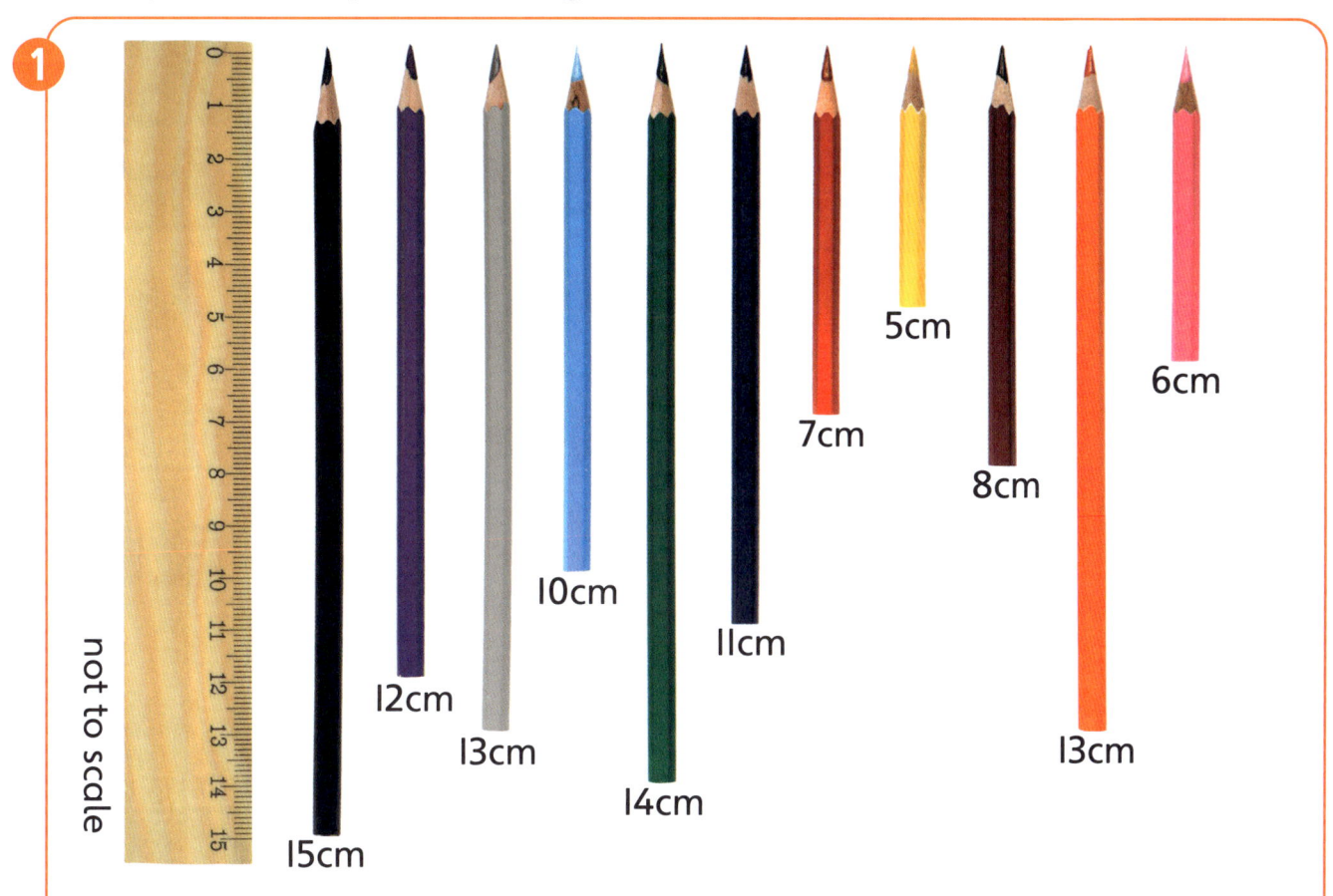

**1**

Pencils shown (not to scale): 15cm (black), 12cm (purple), 13cm (grey), 10cm (blue), 14cm (green), 11cm (dark blue), 7cm (orange), 5cm (yellow), 8cm (brown), 13cm (orange), 6cm (pink).

Which pencil is $\frac{1}{2}$ the length of the green pencil? _____

Which pencil is $\frac{1}{2}$ the length of the purple pencil? _____

Which pencil is $\frac{1}{3}$ the length of the black pencil? _____

Compare the weights below.

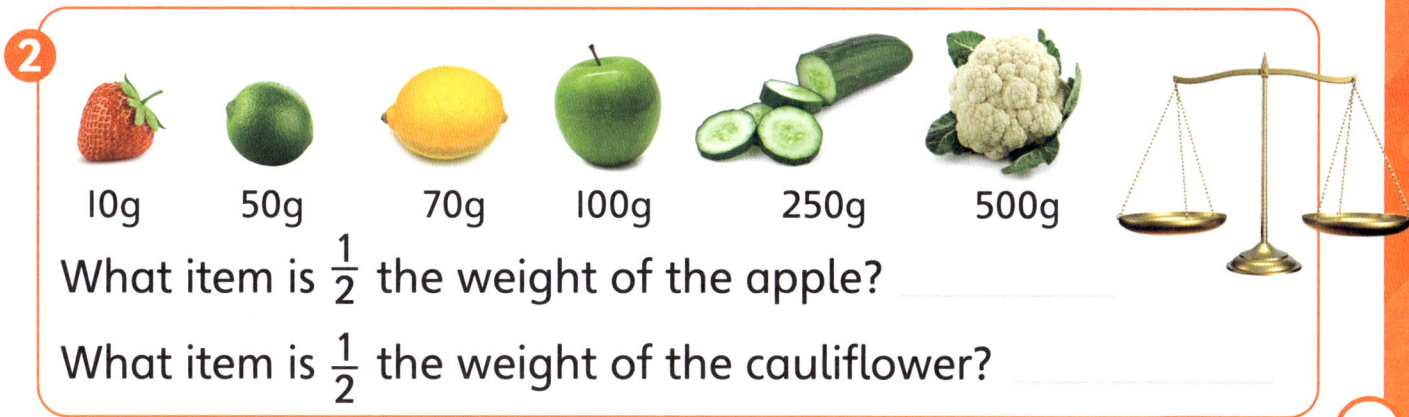

**2**

Strawberry 10g, Lime 50g, Lemon 70g, Apple 100g, Cucumber 250g, Cauliflower 500g

What item is $\frac{1}{2}$ the weight of the apple? _____

What item is $\frac{1}{2}$ the weight of the cauliflower? _____

**FRACTIONS**

**3** A recipe calls for **half** as much flour as butter.

The recipe requires 400g butter.
How much flour is needed? ☐ g

**4** Circle the bottle that is **half full**.

**5** What is **half** the quantity shown in each jug?

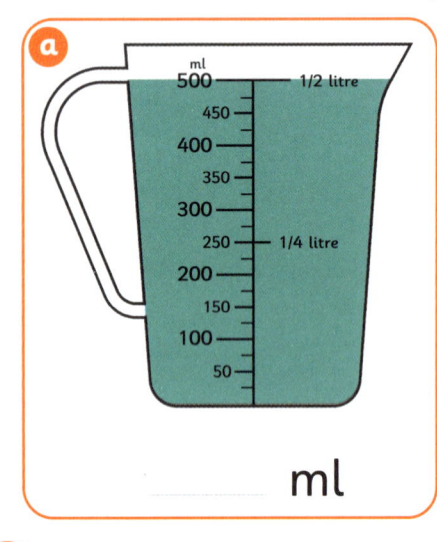

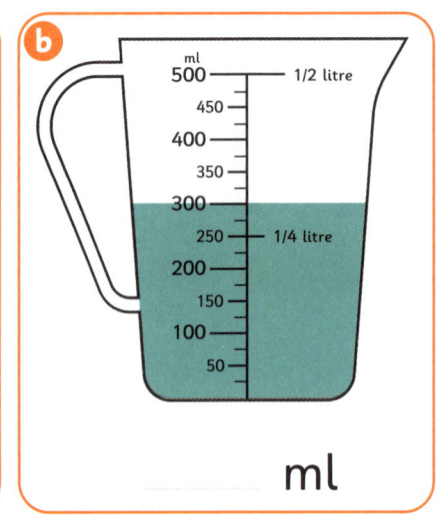

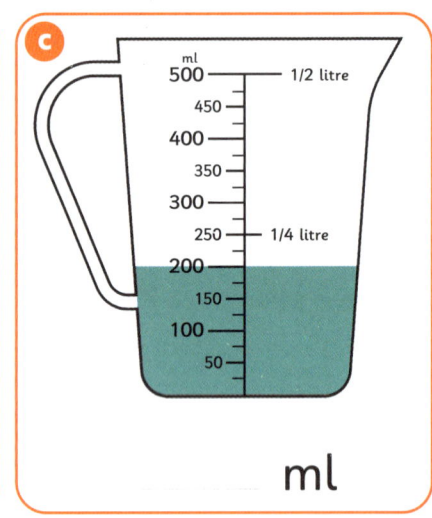

a) _____ ml

b) _____ ml

c) _____ ml

**6** Colour each jug to match the quantity shown.

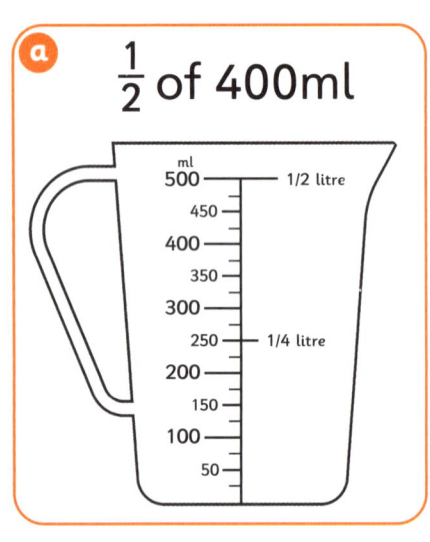

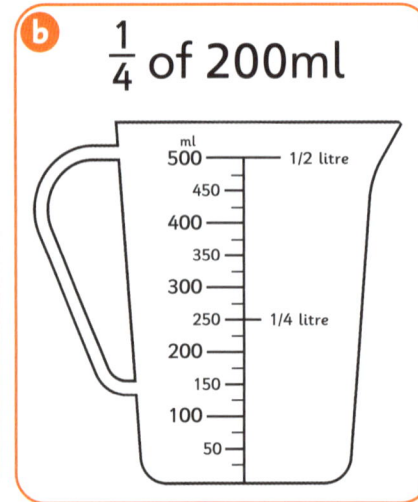

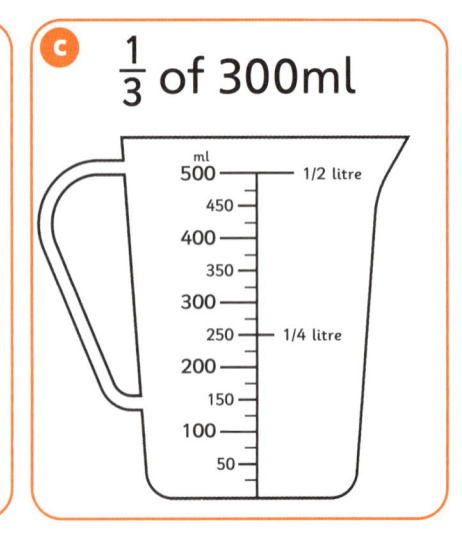

a) $\frac{1}{2}$ of 400ml

b) $\frac{1}{4}$ of 200ml

c) $\frac{1}{3}$ of 300ml

# counting in fractions

Complete the number line by colouring in the right number of **halves**.

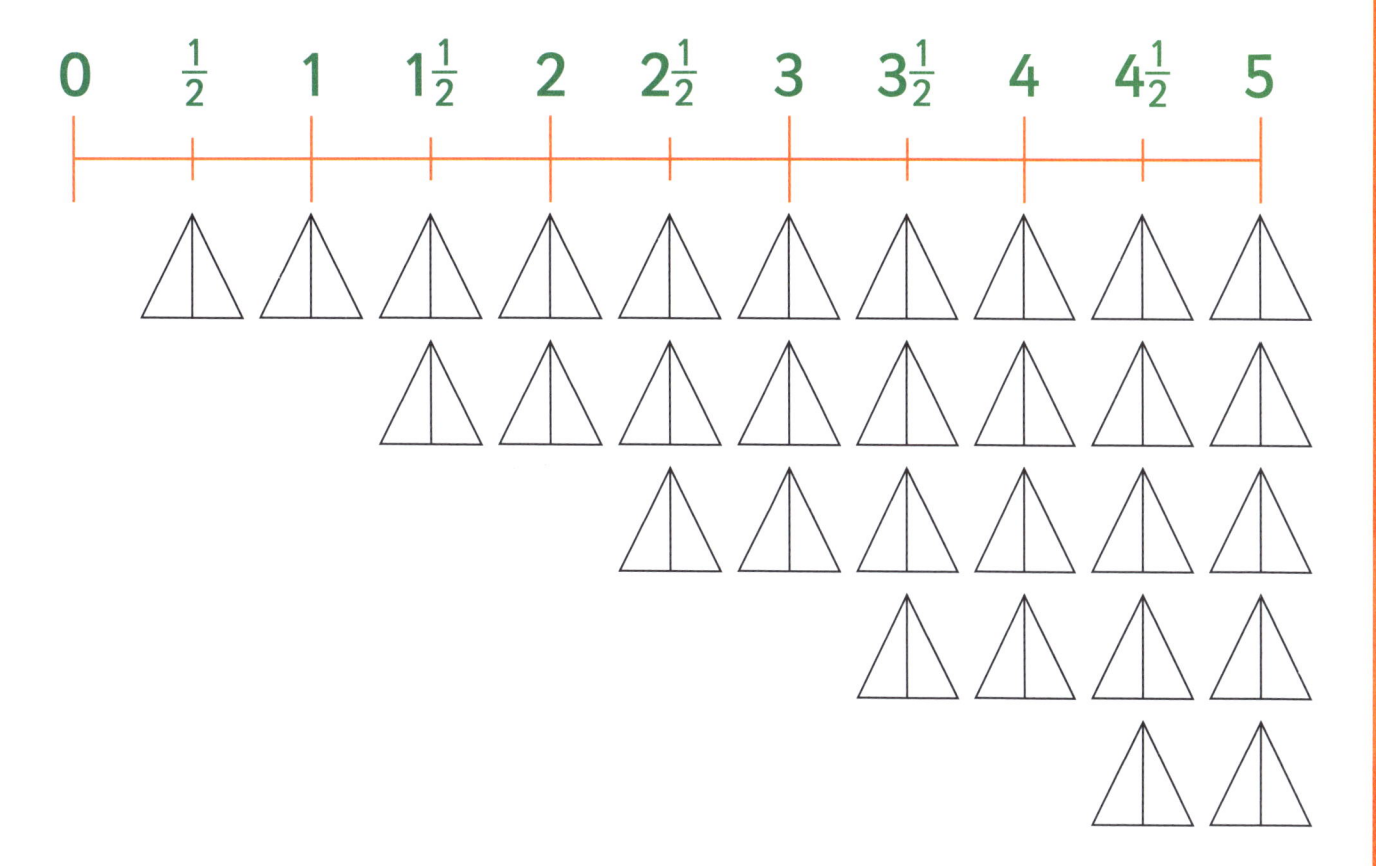

0   $\frac{1}{2}$   1   $1\frac{1}{2}$   2   $2\frac{1}{2}$   3   $3\frac{1}{2}$   4   $4\frac{1}{2}$   5

Complete the number line by colouring in the right number of **thirds**.

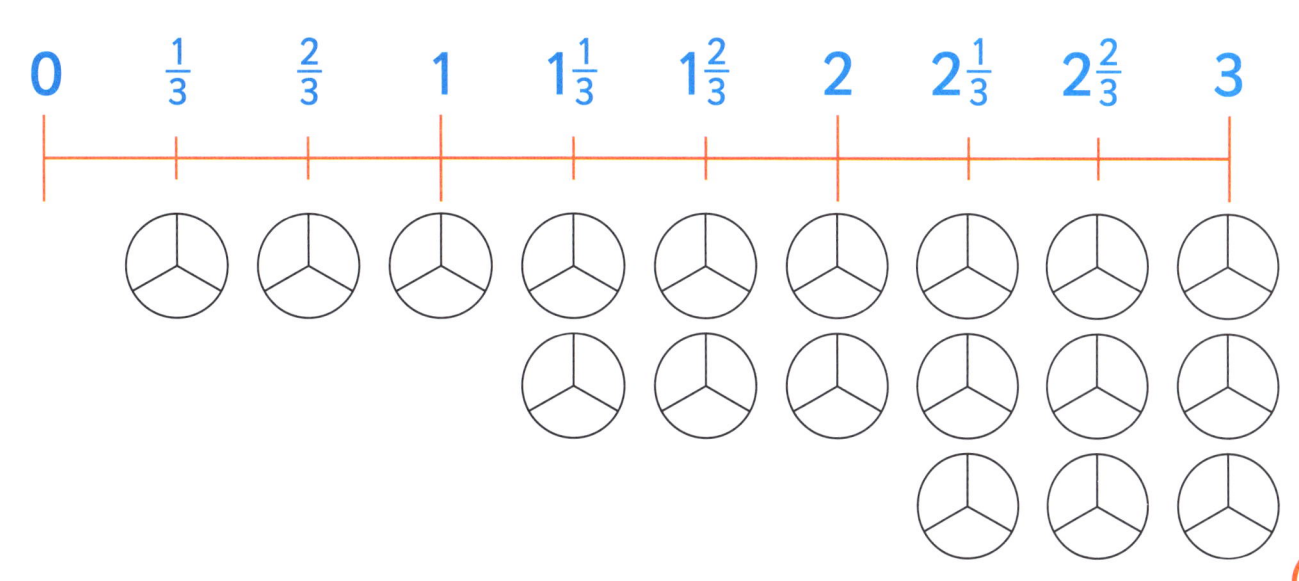

0   $\frac{1}{3}$   $\frac{2}{3}$   1   $1\frac{1}{3}$   $1\frac{2}{3}$   2   $2\frac{1}{3}$   $2\frac{2}{3}$   3

Complete the number line by colouring in the right number of **quarters**.

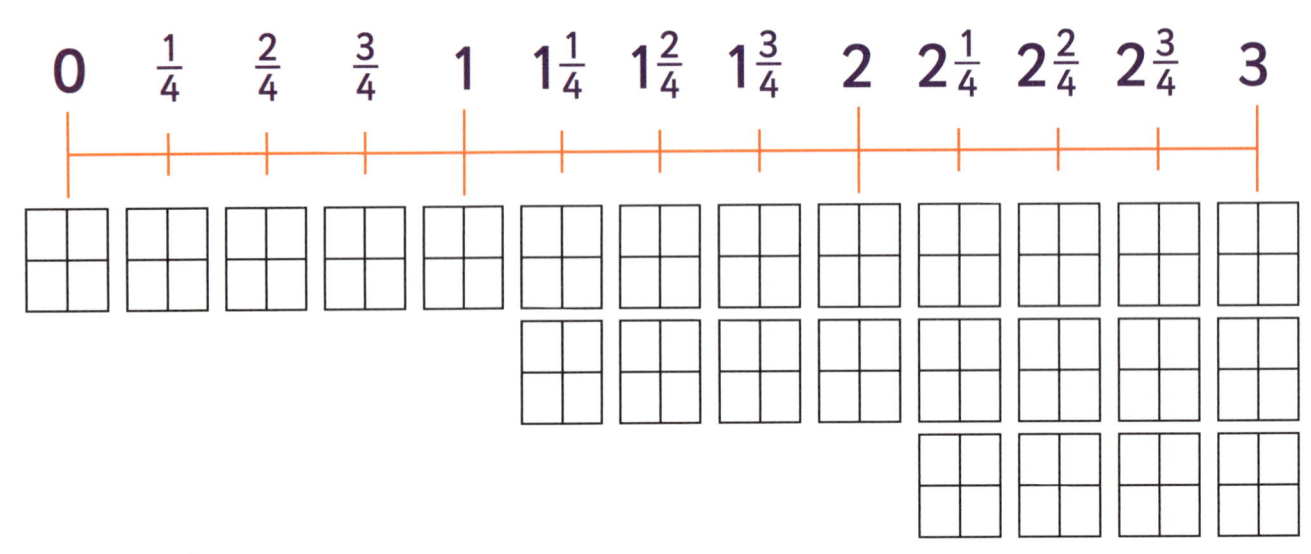

0   $\frac{1}{4}$   $\frac{2}{4}$   $\frac{3}{4}$   1   $1\frac{1}{4}$   $1\frac{2}{4}$   $1\frac{3}{4}$   2   $2\frac{1}{4}$   $2\frac{2}{4}$   $2\frac{3}{4}$   3

Fill in the gaps.

| $2\frac{3}{4}$ | | $3\frac{1}{4}$ | | | |

| $1\frac{1}{2}$ | | | 3 | |

| $5\frac{1}{3}$ | $5\frac{2}{3}$ | | | |

| | | $9\frac{1}{4}$ | | $9\frac{3}{4}$ |

| | $4\frac{1}{3}$ | | | $5\frac{1}{3}$ |

| $7\frac{1}{2}$ | | $8\frac{1}{2}$ | |

Draw shapes to represent this number line.

$1\frac{3}{4}$ — 2 — $2\frac{1}{4}$ — $2\frac{2}{4}$ — $2\frac{3}{4}$

# fraction puzzles

**1** There are an equal number of boys and girls in a class.

If there are 15 boys, how many girls are there? ☐

How many children are there in total? ☐

**2** Molly has half of £24.
Oscar has one third of £30.

Who has the most? _____

How much do they have together? ☐

**3** How many teddies have a bow? Write the answer as a fraction.

☐

**4** The weight limit for the airplane is 15kg. Aunt Ivy's suitcase weighs 20kg. She reduces the weight of her suitcase by one quarter by unpacking some items.

Will she be able to take it on the plane now? ✓ or ✗ ☐

**FRACTIONS**

**5** Charlie's uncle is 2 metres tall. Charlie is exactly half the height of his uncle.

How tall is Charlie? ☐ m

Charlie's dog is exactly half the height of Charlie.

How tall is Charlie's dog? ☐ cm

*There are 100cm in 1 metre.*

**6** Jamie ate three quarters of his pizza. Jessica ate two thirds of her pizza. Charlie ate half of his pizza.

Match the leftover pizza to each person.

Jamie   Jessica   Charlie

**7**  There are 24 leaves.

If half the leaves blow away, how many are left? ☐

One third of the remaining leaves blow away.

How many are left now? ☐

# Measurement

# measuring length & height

**1** Circle the correct positioning for measuring the carrot.

What is wrong with the other positioning?

_____

**2** Draw a line to complete each shape. Then measure the length of the line.

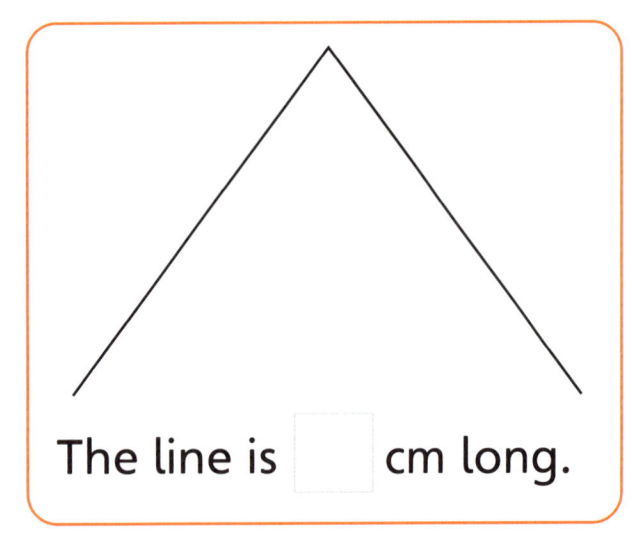

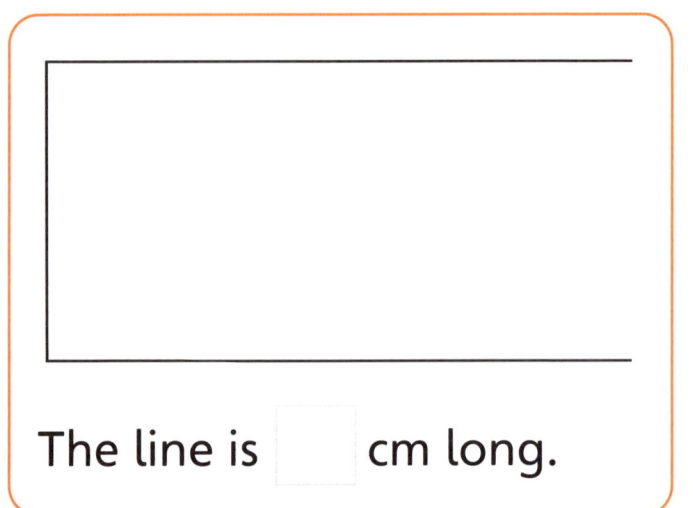

The line is ☐ cm long.

The line is ☐ cm long.

**3** Using a ruler, draw lines to match the length in each box.

14cm

6cm

9cm

**4** Measure the length of each toy car to the nearest half centimetre.

If you don't have a ruler, use the cutout ruler on page 383.

☐ cm

☐ cm

☐ cm

☐ cm

☐ cm ☐ cm ☐ cm

☐ cm ☐ cm

How long is the shortest car? ☐ cm

Which is the longest car?

Which cars are the same length?

Which car is double the length of the black car?

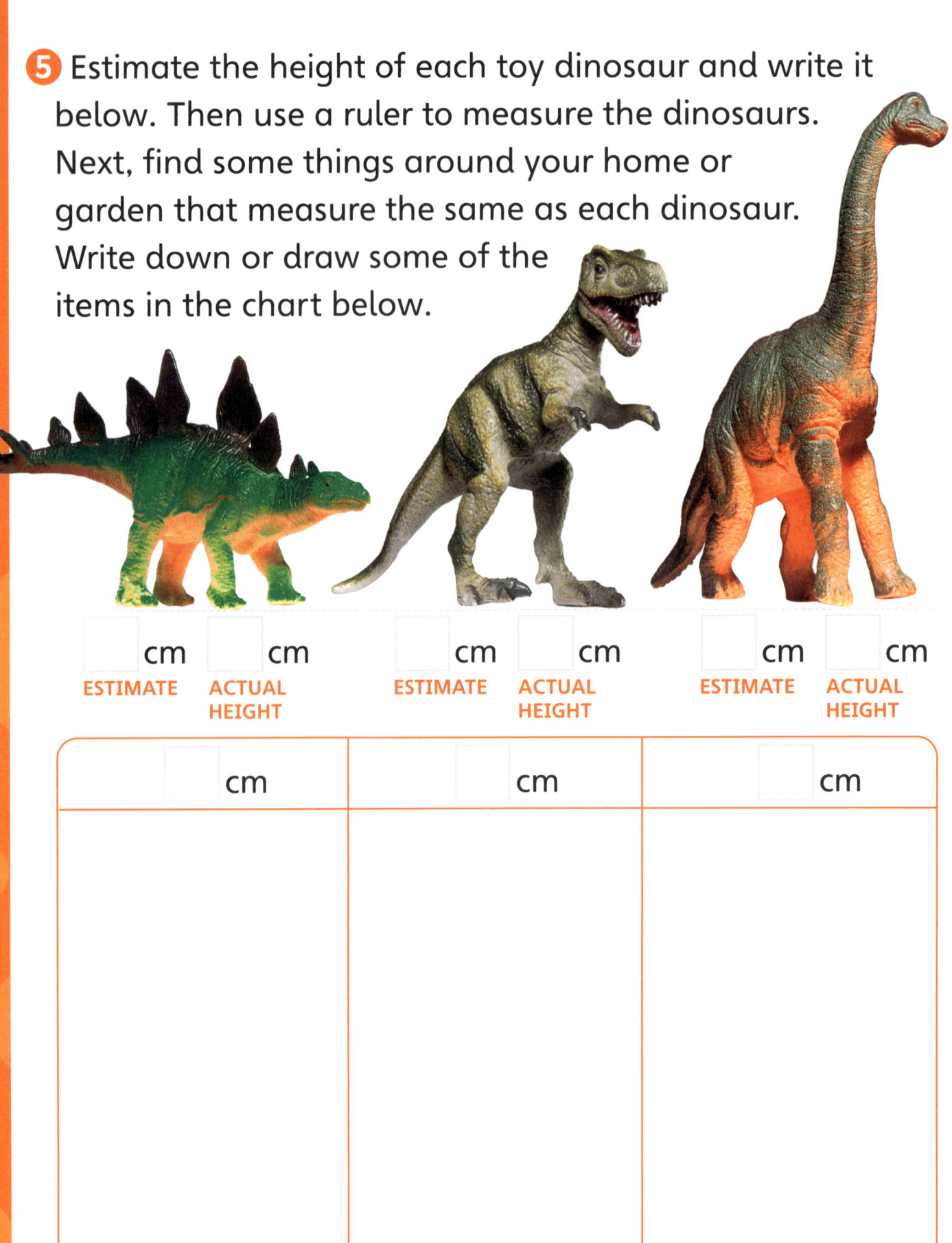

**5** Estimate the height of each toy dinosaur and write it below. Then use a ruler to measure the dinosaurs. Next, find some things around your home or garden that measure the same as each dinosaur. Write down or draw some of the items in the chart below.

| ☐ cm | ☐ cm | ☐ cm | ☐ cm | ☐ cm | ☐ cm |
|---|---|---|---|---|---|
| ESTIMATE | ACTUAL HEIGHT | ESTIMATE | ACTUAL HEIGHT | ESTIMATE | ACTUAL HEIGHT |

| ☐ cm | ☐ cm | ☐ cm |
|---|---|---|
|  |  |  |

**6** Circle the items you would **not** measure with a ruler.

**7** How tall do you think the items below are? Circle the most likely answer.

Door: 2cm  20cm  2m  20m

Light bulb: 1cm  10cm  1m  10m

Paint brush: 2cm  20cm  2m  20m

**8** How long do you think the items below are? Circle the most likely answer.

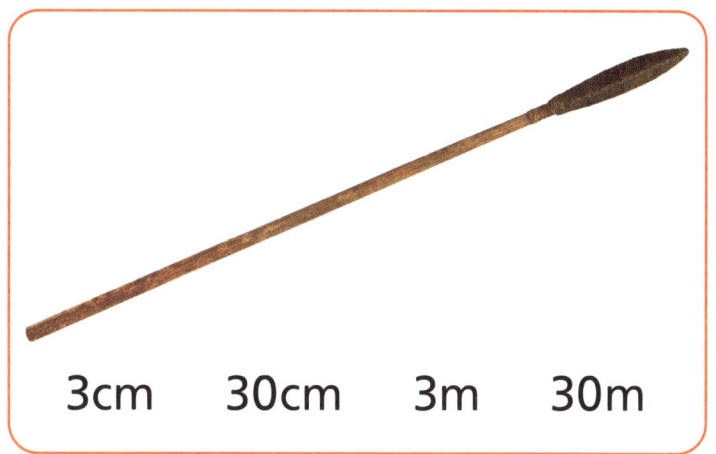

Spear: 3cm  30cm  3m  30m

Bread: 3cm  30cm  3m  30m

# comparing length & height

**1** Order the trees from tallest [1] to shortest [5].

| A | B | C | D | E |
|---|---|---|---|---|
| 35m | 25m | 20m | 40m | 60m |

**a** TALLEST ☐ ☐ ☐ ☐ ☐ SHORTEST

**b** Which tree is double the height of tree C? ☐

**c** Compare the heights of tree B and tree C. Complete the equation below using >, <, or =.

TREE B ☐ TREE C

**d** Tree F is half the height of tree C. How tall is it? ☐ m

**e** If tree A and tree B are placed on top of one another, how tall would they be? ☐ m

**f** If 10m is cut from tree E, how tall would it be? ☐ m

**g** Tree G is 15m taller than tree A. Is it taller or shorter than tree D? Use >, <, or = to complete the equation.

TREE G ☐ TREE D

**2** Five children see how far they can throw a tennis ball. The results are shown below.

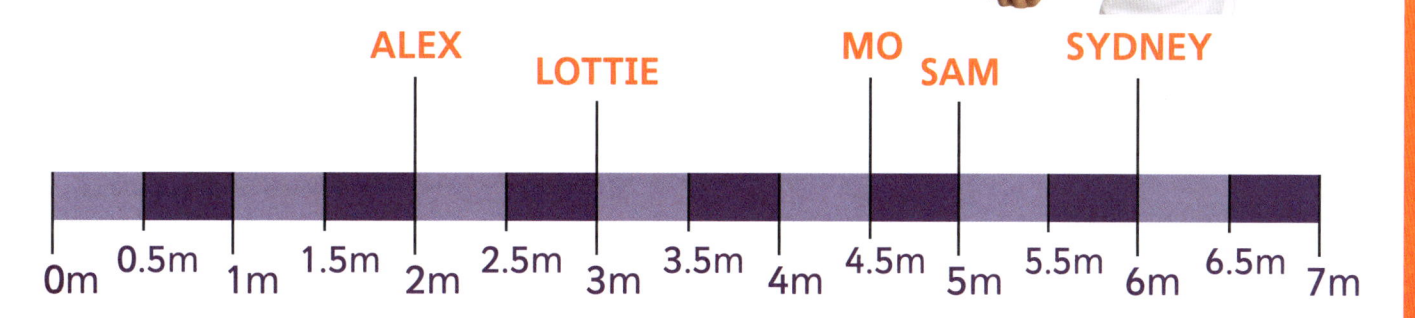

Alex: 1.75m, Lottie: 2.5m, Mo: 4m, Sam: 4.5m, Sydney: 6m (positions on number line from 0m to 7m)

**a** Who threw the ball half as far as Sydney?

**b** Who threw the ball one third of 6m?

**c** Who threw the ball 2m further than Lottie?

**d** Who threw the ball twice as far as 3m?

**3** Compare these lengths using >, <, or =.

| | | |
|---|---|---|
| 25cm + 20cm | ☐ | 50cm − 4cm |
| half of 50 metres | ☐ | 8m + 15m |
| one third of 30cm | ☐ | 7cm + 5cm + 3cm |
| 49cm − 19cm | ☐ | double 15cm |
| 30cm ÷ 2cm | ☐ | 5cm x 4cm |
| double 12 metres | ☐ | 15m + 6m |

# weight and volume

**1** Circle the unit that would be best to measure each item.

| | | |
|---|---|---|
| g / kg | g / kg | g / kg |

**2** Cut out the objects on page 389, then stick them into the correct box below. For guidance, an average apple weighs 100g.

100g

| weighs less than 100g | weighs more than 100g |
|---|---|
| | |

If you have some kitchen scales at home, weigh some small household objects or items of food.

**3** Write the mass shown on the scales.

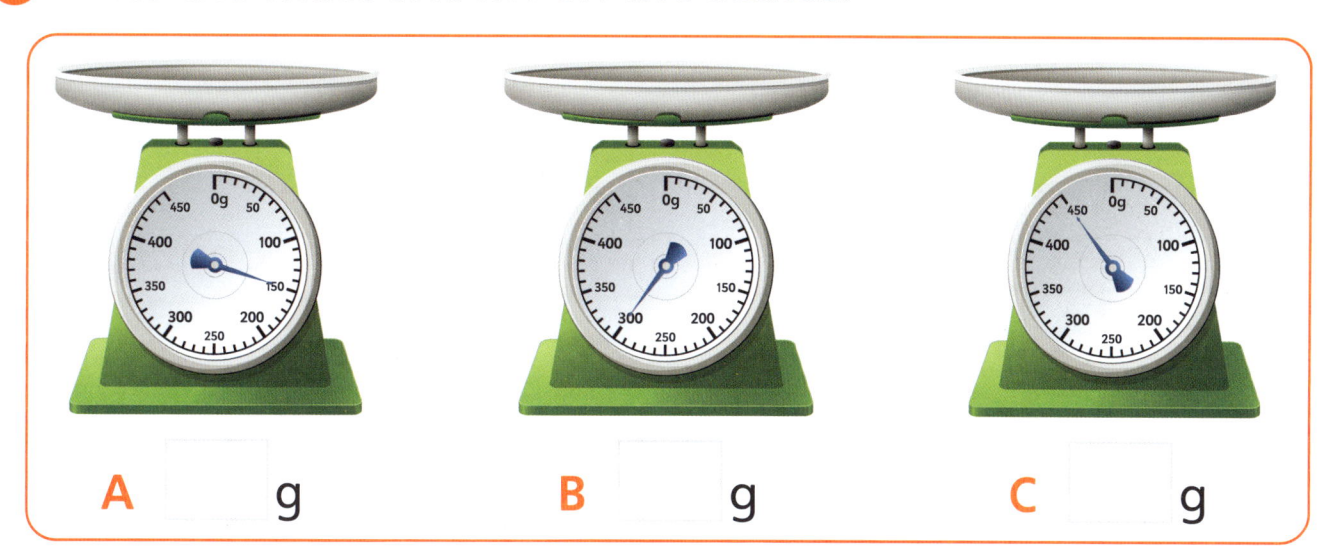

A ☐ g    B ☐ g    C ☐ g

What is the difference in mass between scales A and B? ☐ g

If scales A and C are added together, what is the total mass? ☐ g

**4** Write the mass shown on the scales.

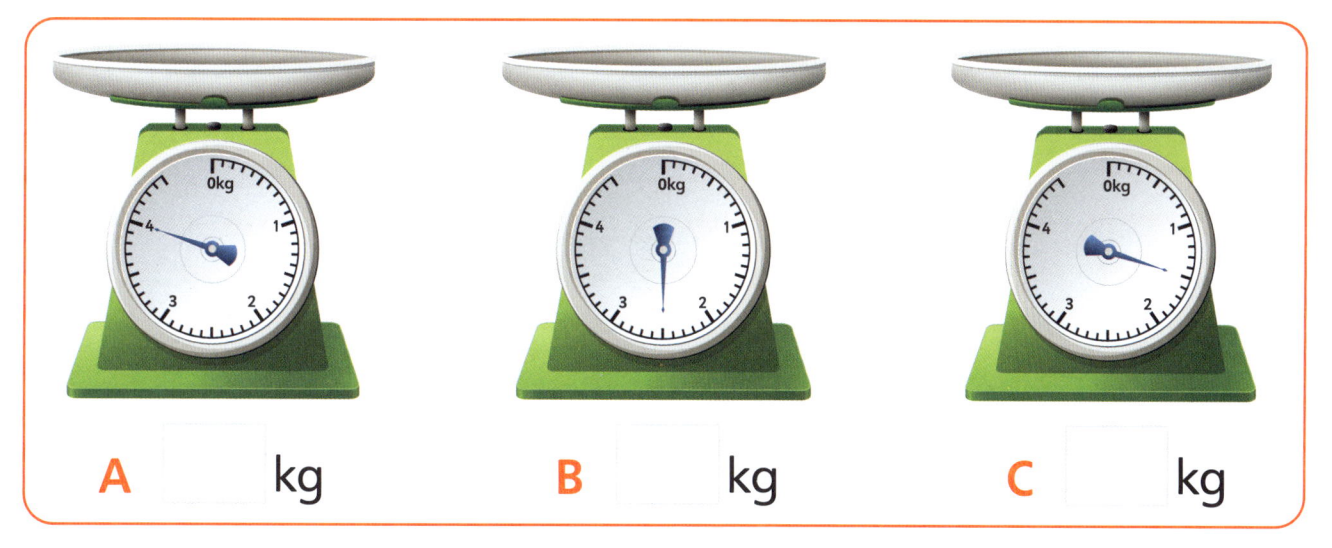

A ☐ kg    B ☐ kg    C ☐ kg

What is the difference in mass between scales A and C? ☐ kg

If scales B and C are added together, what is the total mass? ☐ kg

**5** How heavy do you think the items below are? Circle the most likely answer.

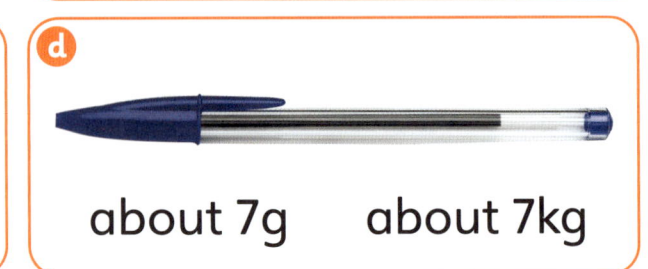

a) about 10kg / about 100kg

b) about 120g / about 12g

c) about 150g / about 15kg

d) about 7g / about 7kg

e) about 280g / about 280kg

f) about 1g / about 100g

**6** Look at the scales below.

Which is **heavier**, an orange or a lime?

Explain your answer.

# volume

**1** Circle the unit that would be best to measure each item.

| | | |
|---|---|---|
| ml / l | ml / l | ml / l |

**2** Circle the better estimate for each amount of liquid.

| | |
|---|---|
| about 2ml / about 2l | about 60ml / about 60l |
| about 350ml / about 3.5l | about 50ml / about 5l |
| 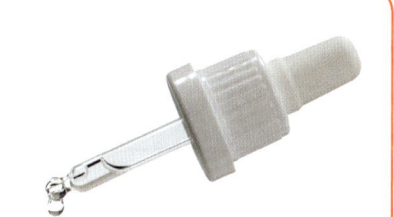 | about 1ml / about 1l |

**3** Compare the volume of liquid in each glass. Then complete the sentences using **more** or **less**.

A    B    C    D

| | |
|---|---|
| A has _____ than B. | D has _____ than A. |
| B has _____ than C. | C has _____ than A. |
| C has _____ than D. | B has _____ than D. |

257

**MEASUREMENT**

**4** Colour each jug to show where the level line would be if the water was poured into it from the smaller container.

250ml

450ml

150ml

330ml

**5** How many millilitres have to be **added** to **fill** each jug?

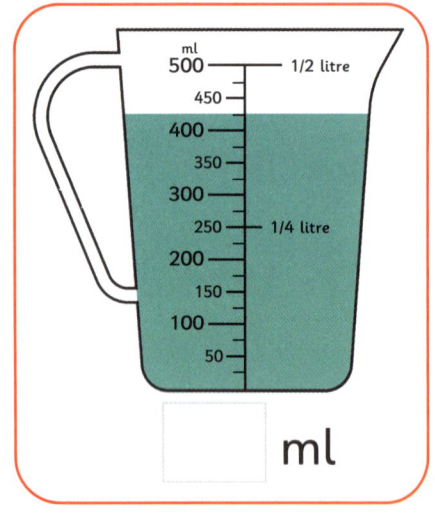

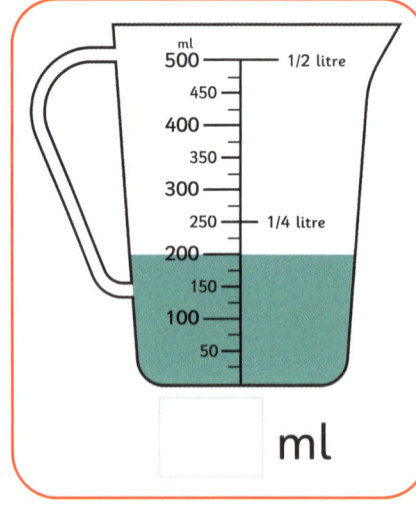

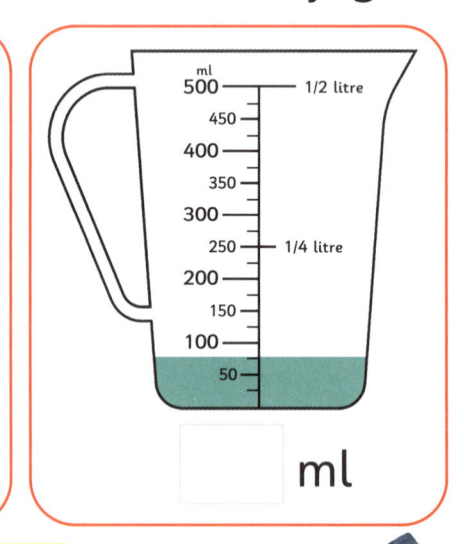

____ ml

____ ml

____ ml

**Did you know?**
Metric capacity also uses kilolitres (1,000 litres) and centilitres (10 millilitres). A 500ml water bottle contains 50 centilitres or 0.0005 kilolitres!

**6** Compare the capacity of the items below.

teaspoon 5ml
pot 10l
mug 250ml
teacup 150ml
tablespoon 15ml
bottle 500ml

How many teaspoons would it take to fill a tablespoon?

How many tablespoons would it take to fill a teacup?

How many mugs would it take to fill a bottle?

How many bottles would it take to fill a pot?

**7** Compare these measures using >, < , or =.

| | | |
|---|---|---|
| 80g + 40g | | double 60g |
| 35ml – 22ml | | one third of 30ml |
| two thirds of 90g | | 3 x 25g |
| double 20l | | 12l + 25l |
| 29kg – 15kg | | 5kg + 3kg + 8kg |
| half of 36ml | | 44ml – 23ml |

## animal analysis

Compare the animal fact files, then answer the questions.

**hippo**
Height: 1.5m
Weight: 3000kg
Top Speed: 45km/h

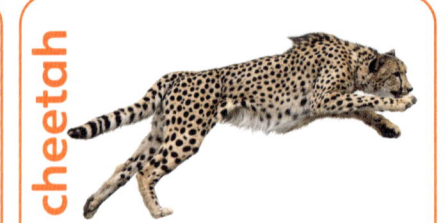

**cheetah**
Height: 90cm
Weight: 60kg
Top Speed: 120km/h

**elephant**
Height: 4m
Weight: 7000kg
Top Speed: 40km/h

**lion**
Height: 1.2m
Weight: 200kg
Top Speed: 80km/h

**rhino**
Height: 1.8m
Weight: 2500kg
Top Speed: 55km/h

**zebra**
Height: 1.4m
Weight: 350kg
Top Speed: 65km/h

Which animal is shorter than the elephant but taller than the hippo?

How much would the cheetah and the zebra weigh together? ☐ kg

Which is the slowest animal?

What is the difference in weight between the hippo and the rhino? ☐ kg

Which animal is faster than the lion?

Which animal is half the rhino's height?

# measuring temperature

**1** Join each picture to the correct temperature.

Cold    Hot

**2** Write the temperature shown on each thermometer in degrees Celsius. Look out for different scales.

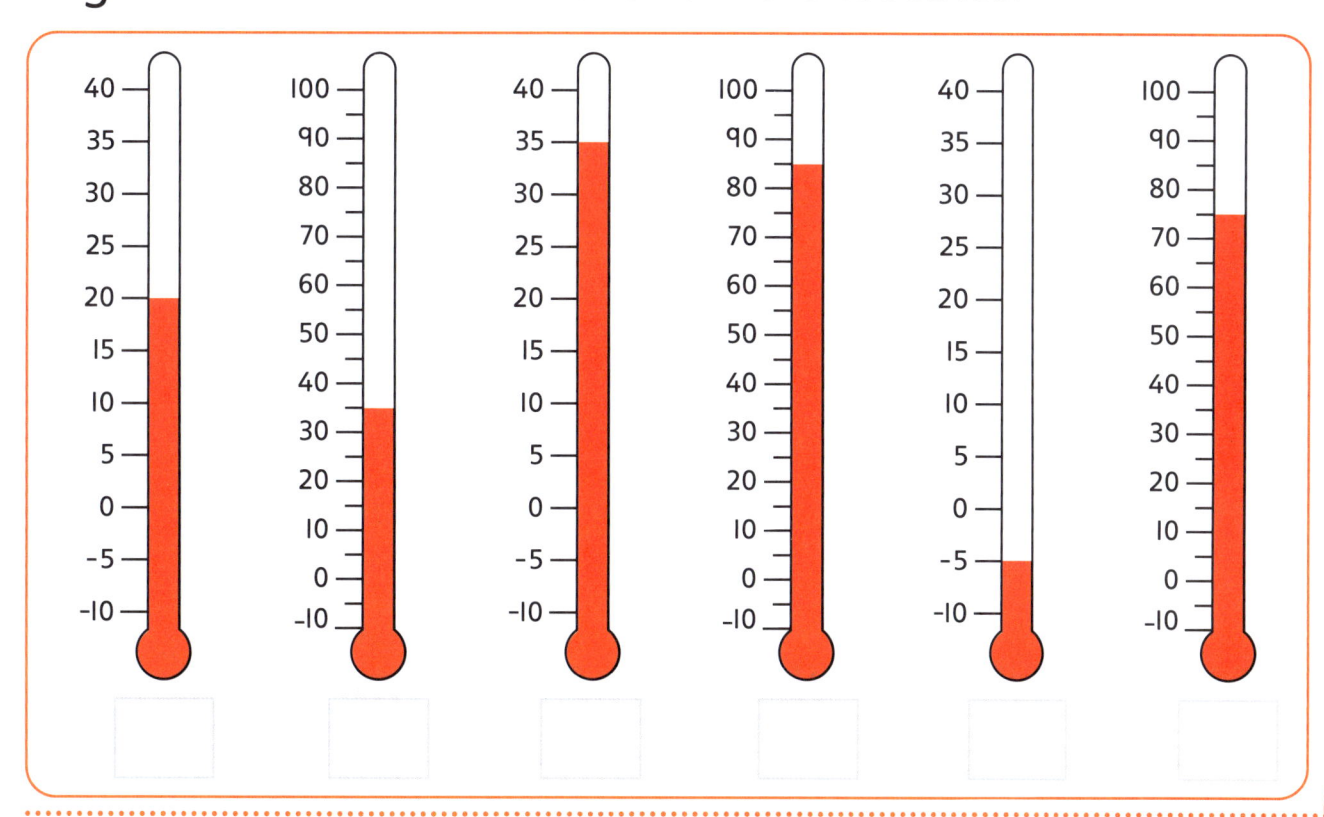

**3** Colour in the thermometers to show the correct temperature for each city. Then answer the questions.

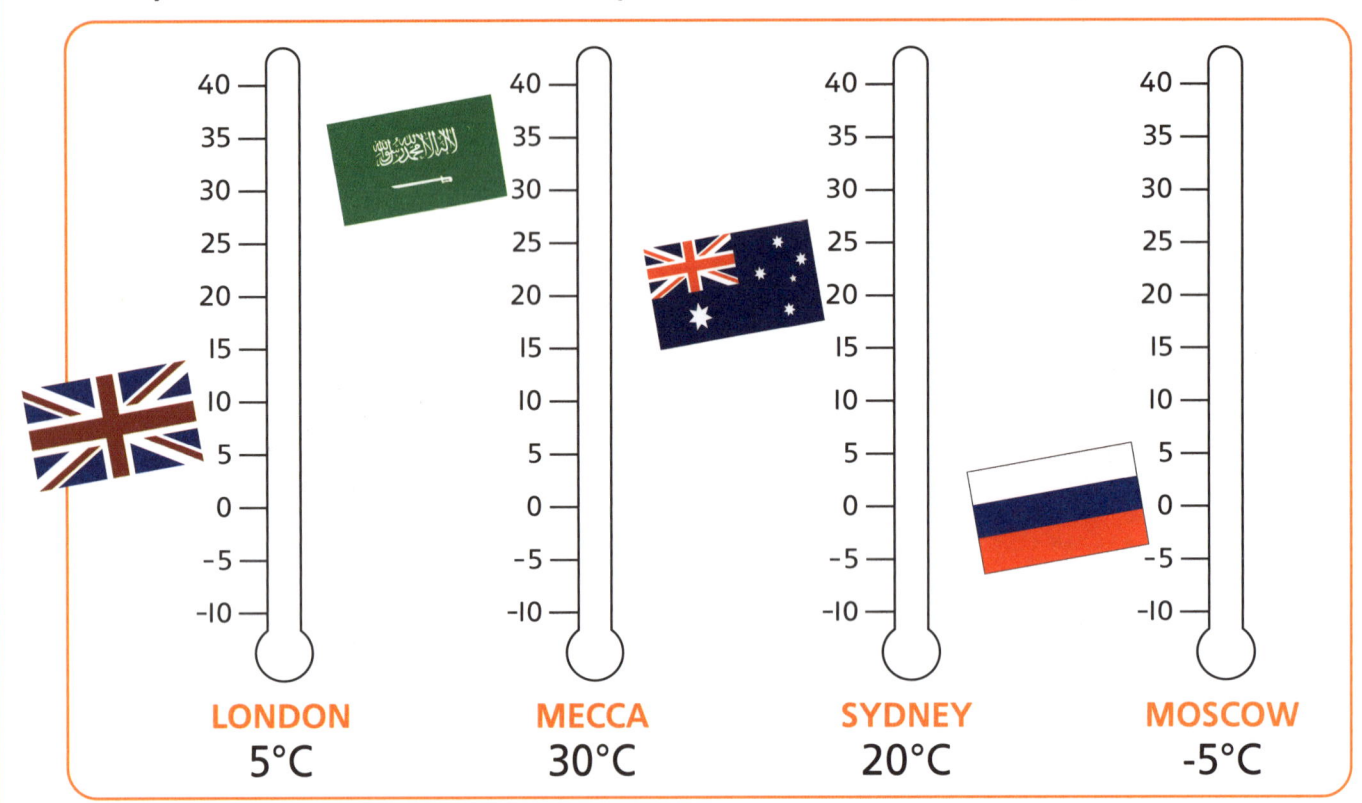

|  | | | |
|---|---|---|---|
| LONDON 5°C | MECCA 30°C | SYDNEY 20°C | MOSCOW -5°C |

Which is the coldest city?

What is the difference in temperature between Sydney and London?

Yesterday it was 5° hotter in Sydney. What was the temperature?

At night the temperature in Mecca dropped by 9°C. What was the temperature at night?

How much warmer was London than Moscow?

**Did you know?**
The Celsius scale is the most common scale used throughout the world, but you might also see temperatures measured in degrees Fahrenheit.

money matters

1. Match the totals with the coins.

£3    63p    72p    35p

£2    24p    51p    £1

2. Solve the equations.

☐ p

☐ p

☐ p

3. Compare these amounts using >, <, or =.

**3** How much money is in each purse or wallet?

Alonso's wallet: ☐ p

Gina's purse: ☐ p

Ahmed's wallet: £ ☐

Aisha's purse: £ ☐ and ☐ p

Zach's wallet: £ ☐ and ☐ p

Becky's purse: £ ☐ and ☐ p

4 Compare the totals on the previous page.

Order the totals from **least** to **most** by writing each child's name in the right box.

LEAST ☐ ☐ ☐ ☐ ☐ MOST

Complete the sentences below using **more** or **less**.

Ahmed has _____ money than Becky.

Gina has _____ money than Aisha.

5 Calculate the change you would get if you buy the following items with the money shown.

50p     ☐ p

35p     ☐ p

75p     ☐ p

89p     ☐ p

**6** Draw lines between the matching amounts.

**7** Circle coins to make the amount shown.

53p

82p

£1 and 25p

**8** Compare the prices below.

Pear 40p, Grapes 95p, Apple 25p, Lemon 30p, Lime 19p, Banana 15p, Pineapple 85p

What is the difference between the cost of . . .

    **a**  a pineapple and a pear? ☐ p

    **b**  a bunch of grapes and a banana? ☐ p

Add the following items together and write the total.

**c**  pear + pear = ☐ p

**d**  apple + apple + banana = ☐ p

**e**  lemon + lime = ☐ p

**f** An orange costs the same as an apple. Write the total for the sum below.

orange + orange + apple = ☐ p

**g** A peach costs 5p more than a lemon. How much does it cost? ☐ p

**h** How much change would you get from £1 if you bought a pineapple? ☐ p

**9** Draw four different ways to make £2 using these coins. You can use each coin more than once.

**10** Count the money and write the total.

£ ☐ and ☐ p    £ ☐ and ☐ p

**money pairs game**

Cut out the cards on page 395, and lay them face down. Take it in turns to turn over two cards. If the values match, keep them. Otherwise turn them back over. The player who ends the game with the most pairs is the winner!

# telling the time

> ❗ The hour hand moves along with the minute hand—when the time is *quarter past* the hour, the hour hand will be just *past* the hour, and when the time is *quarter to*, the hour hand will be just *before* the hour.

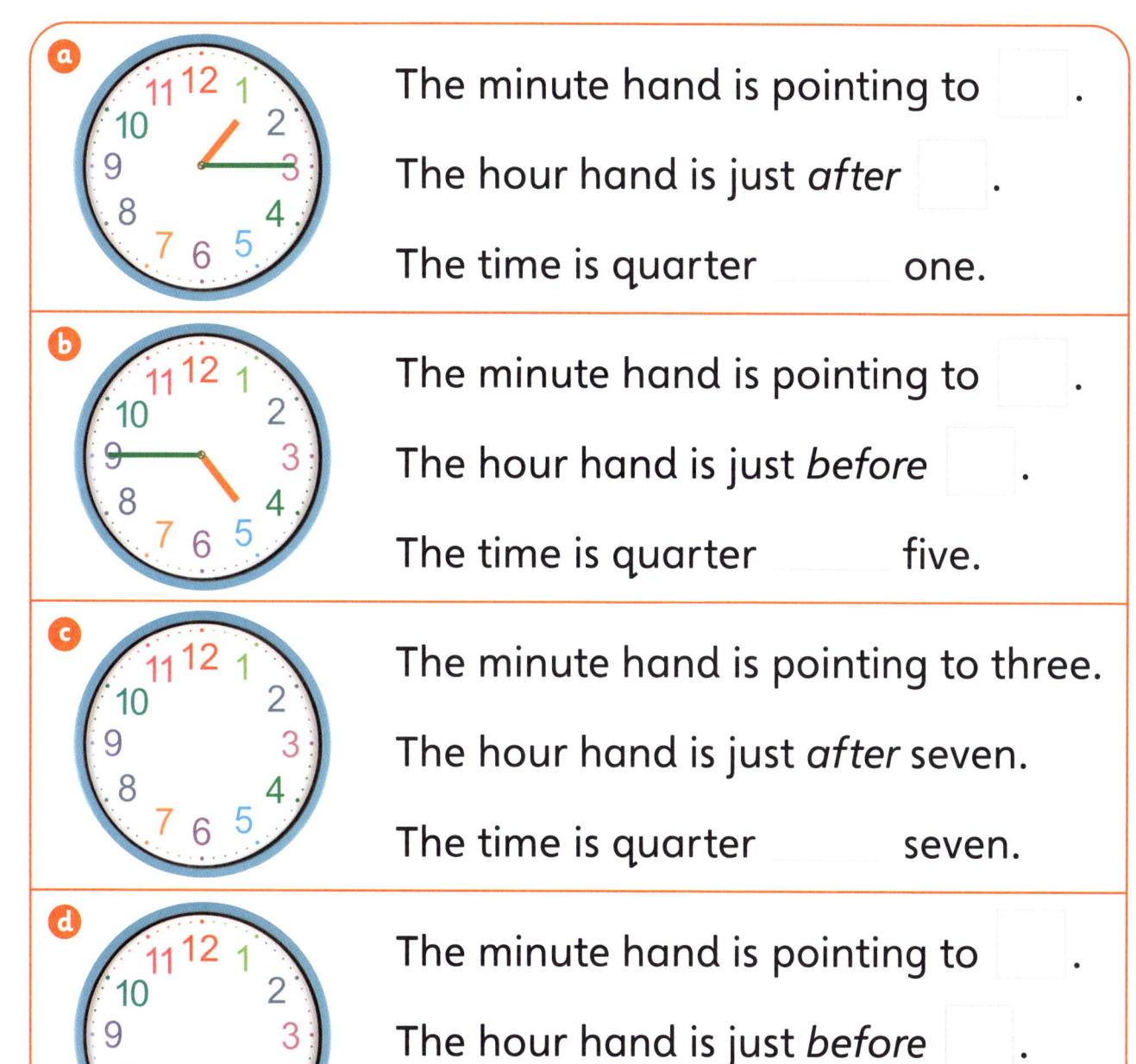

**1** Complete the table.

| | |
|---|---|
| **a** | The minute hand is pointing to ☐. |
| | The hour hand is just *after* ☐. |
| | The time is quarter _____ one. |
| **b** | The minute hand is pointing to ☐. |
| | The hour hand is just *before* ☐. |
| | The time is quarter _____ five. |
| **c** | The minute hand is pointing to three. |
| | The hour hand is just *after* seven. |
| | The time is quarter _____ seven. |
| **d** | The minute hand is pointing to ☐. |
| | The hour hand is just *before* ☐. |
| | The time is quarter to twelve. |

MEASUREMENT

**2** Write the time shown on each clock.

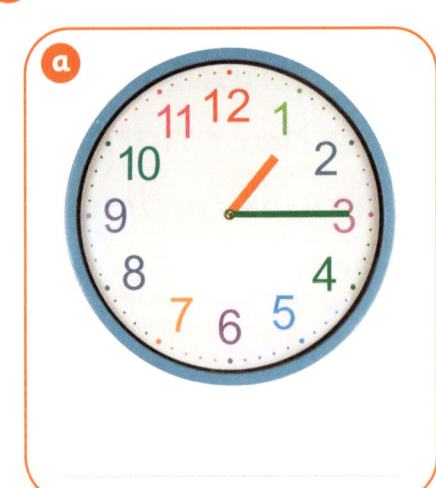

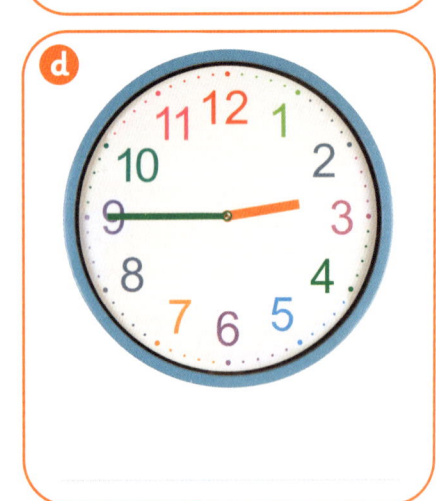

a.

b.

c.

d.

e.

f.

**3** Draw the correct time on each clock.

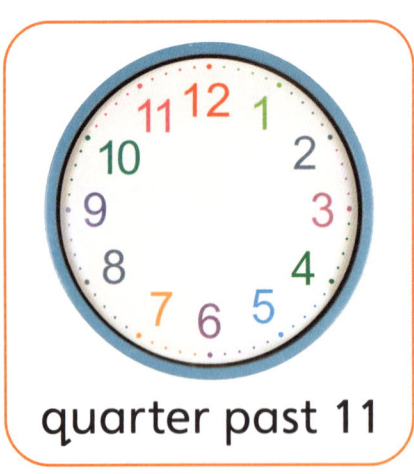

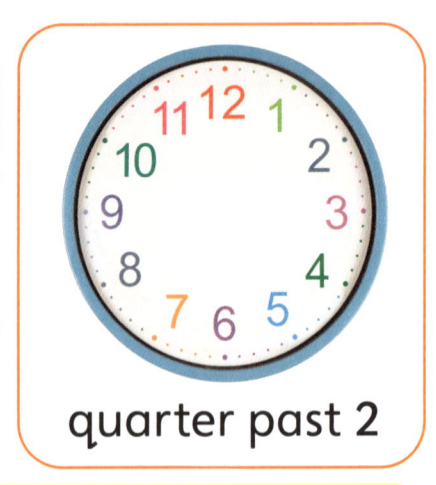

quarter past 11

quarter to 7

quarter past 2

**Did you know?**
In the past, people used burning candles, dripping water or sand to measure time. People still use sand clocks and hourglasses.

**4** Complete the table.

| Minute hand pointing to | 1 | 2 | 3 | 4 | 5 | | | | | | |
|---|---|---|---|---|---|---|---|---|---|---|---|
| Minutes past the hour | 5 | 10 | 15 | 20 | | | | | | | |

**5** Match the times to the correct clock.

20 past 5

10 past 9

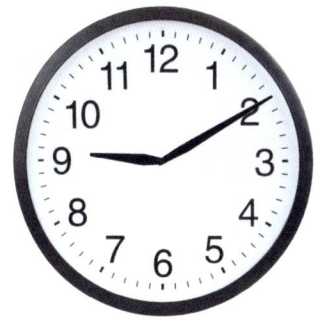

5 to 4

25 to 3

5 past 8

25 past 2

20 to 12

10 to 7

MEASUREMENT

271

# intervals of time

**1** Order these activities from the shortest length of time [1] to the longest [6].

a football match

eating lunch

washing hands

a family holiday

a day at school

making a bed

**2** Make a list of some activities that take *less than* or *more than* an hour.

| Less Than an Hour | More Than an Hour |
|---|---|
|  |  |

**3** Circle the longest time.

| 55 minutes | three quarters of an hour | 48 minutes | 1 hour | half an hour |

**4** Join the number to the correct description.

7    12    24    60    60

| minutes in an hour | months in a year | hours in a day | days in a week | seconds in a minute |

**5** Compare these measures of time using >, < , or =.

| an hour and a half | ☐ | 80 minutes |
| 48 hours | ☐ | two days |
| two weeks | ☐ | 12 days |
| 40 seconds | ☐ | half a minute |
| 100 minutes | ☐ | two hours |
| two years | ☐ | 22 months |

**6** Read the rhyme, then answer the questions.

How many days are in July? ☐

How many days are in April? ☐

Which is the shortest month?

*30 days have September,
April, June and November.
All the rest have 31,
Except for February,
Which has but 28 days clear,
And 29 days each leap year.*

**7** Complete the table.

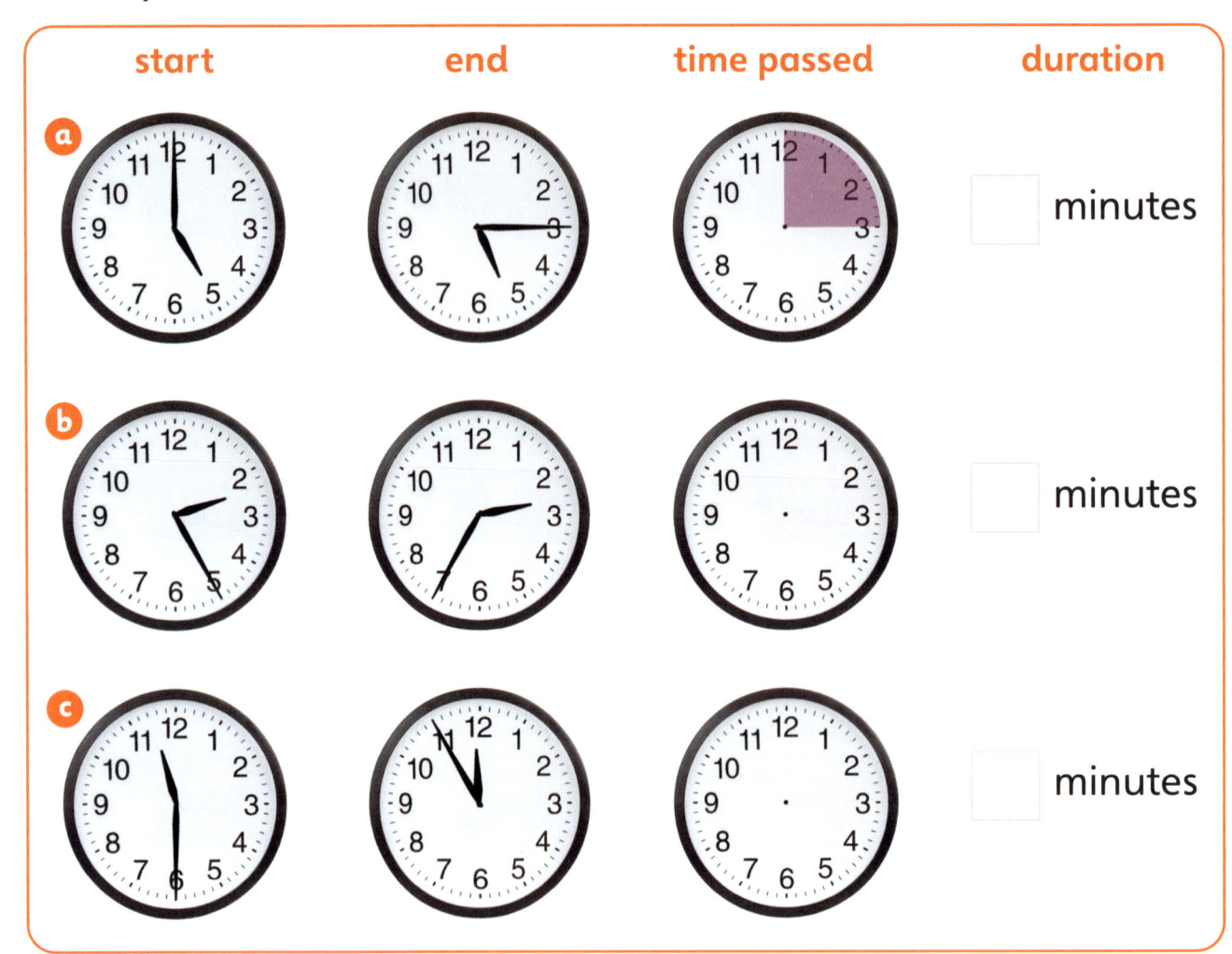

| start | end | time passed | duration |
|---|---|---|---|
| a | | | ☐ minutes |
| b | | | ☐ minutes |
| c | | | ☐ minutes |

**8** Compare the durations of the films below. All the films *finish* at **6 o'clock**. Draw the *start* times on each clock.

Superheroes on Holiday — 120 MINUTES

Mystery on the Mountain — 100 MINUTES

Manic Monster Mission — 95 MINUTES

Below the Waves — 150 MINUTES

**9** Look at the following information from a running time trial. Then answer the questions.

| runner | start time | end time | runner | start time | end time |
|---|---|---|---|---|---|
| Benji | | | Pippa | | |
| Jo | | | Gina | | |
| Ahmed | | | Sam | | |

**a** Who is the slowest to complete the trial?

**b** Who is the fastest to complete the trial and how long did it take them? ☐ minutes

**c** How long did it take Benji to complete it? ☐ minutes

**d** How many minutes slower than Pippa was Gina?

**e** Who was 5 minutes quicker than Jo?

**f** Charlotte started 5 minutes after Sam. It took her 35 minutes to complete the trial. Draw her start time and end time on the clocks.

start time     end time

# measurement puzzles

**1** Malika has a set of big books about animals. There are 8 books in the set. Each book has a mass of 2 kilograms.

What is the mass of the whole set? ☐ kg

**2** Mum buys three juice cartons.

Each carton holds 200 millilitres. How much juice is there in all? ☐ ml

**3**

25p
50p
35p
30p

What is the difference in price between a pencil and a biro? ☐ p

Andy has £1. How much change will he get if he buys a pencil, a rubber and a sharpener? ☐ p

**4** Uncle Harry is buying toy mice for his cat. Each toy mouse is 9 grams.

How many grams will a pack of 6 toy mice measure? ☐ g

**5** Marcus sells bundles of wood during the summer. He has 500 kilograms of wood to sell. So far, he has sold 320 kilograms.

How much wood does he have left to sell? ☐ kg

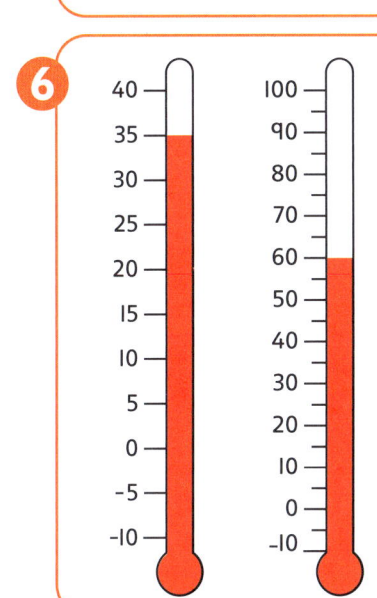

**6** Jack says that thermometer A shows a greater temperature than thermometer B.

Is he right? _____

Explain your answer.

_____

**7** A vet feeds a kitten 60 millilitres of formula in a day. There are 6 equal feedings per day.

How many millilitres does the kitten get at each feeding? ☐ ml

**8** The McCarthy family has two dogs. The Great Dane has a mass of 89 kilograms, and the French Bulldog has a mass of 13 kilograms.

What is the total mass of the dogs? ☐ kg

**9** The show starts at 3.30. It finishes at 5.15.

How long does it last?

☐ minutes

**10** Kim takes 15ml of medicine in the morning, after lunch, and before she goes to bed.

How many millilitres of medicine does she take in a day? ☐ ml

If she takes it for 2 days, how much will she have taken? ☐ ml

**11** Sam is running the last leg of the 4 x 100m relay race. His three team mates complete their legs successfully, but Sam falls over half way through his 100m leg.

How far does Sam's team run in total? ☐ m

How much further did they need to run to complete the race? ☐ m

**12** A teacup holds 150ml. A kettle holds 1.5l.

How many cups can be filled using a full kettle? ☐

If the teacup is a third full, how much more liquid can be added? ☐ ml

**13** Alexi and Amhar have been counting their money.

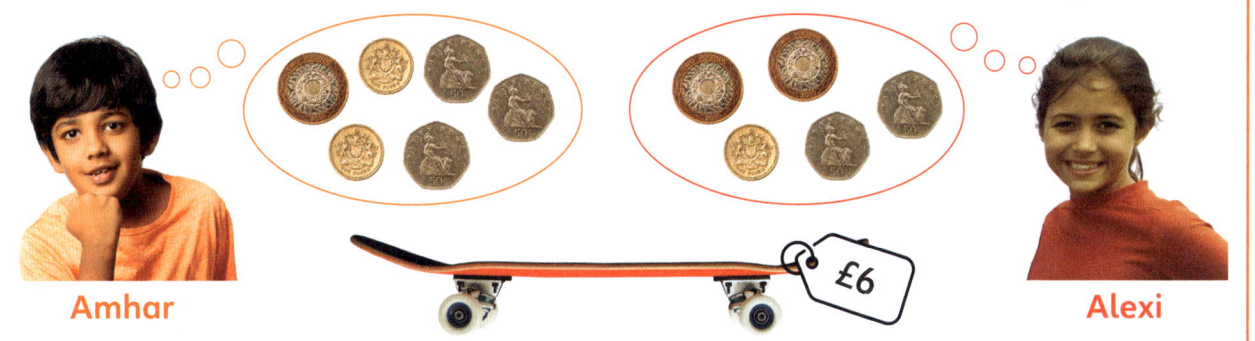

Amhar

Alexi

£6

Who has enough money to buy the skateboard?
Circle the correct answer.    **Amhar**    **Alexi**

**14** Colour in the clock face that shows *ten past twelve*.

**15** A bucket holds 10 litres of water.

How many litres will there be in 7 buckets? ☐ l

The capacity of Alex's new paddling pool is 140 litres.

How many buckets will it take to fill it? ☐

**16** Tristan takes a packed lunch to school. It weighs 350g. He eats his apple at breaktime.

If his packed lunch now weighs 260g, how much did the apple weigh? ☐ g

MEASUREMENT

279

**17** A glass has a capacity of 150ml.

How much liquid will be in it when it is half full? ☐ ml

**18** Harry has 4 books in his backpack. Each book weighs 500g.

How much do the books weigh? ☐ kg

**19** Jenna has this much money in her purse.

She spends £1 and 20p at the fair.

How much does she have left? £ ☐ and ☐ p

Fudge is 90p for 100g.

If Jenna buys 200g of fudge, how much money will she have left? £ ☐ and ☐ p

**20** Nadia can make 3 heart-shaped candles from 1 kilogram of wax.

How many candles can she make from 9 kilograms of wax? ☐

**Did you know?**
Have you ever made a ball from rubber bands? A world-record rubber-band ball was made from 700,000 rubber bands of all sizes. It took Joel Waul of Florida 4 years to make the 4,079-kilogram ball!

# Geometry

GEOMETRY

# 2D shapes

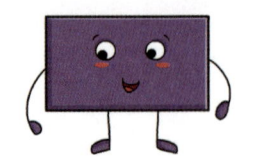

! You can name a shape by its numbers of **sides** and **corners** or **angles**. A corner is the point where the edges of a solid figure meet. It is also called a **vertex**.

**1** Name each shape and complete the information for the fact files. Then colour in the shapes.

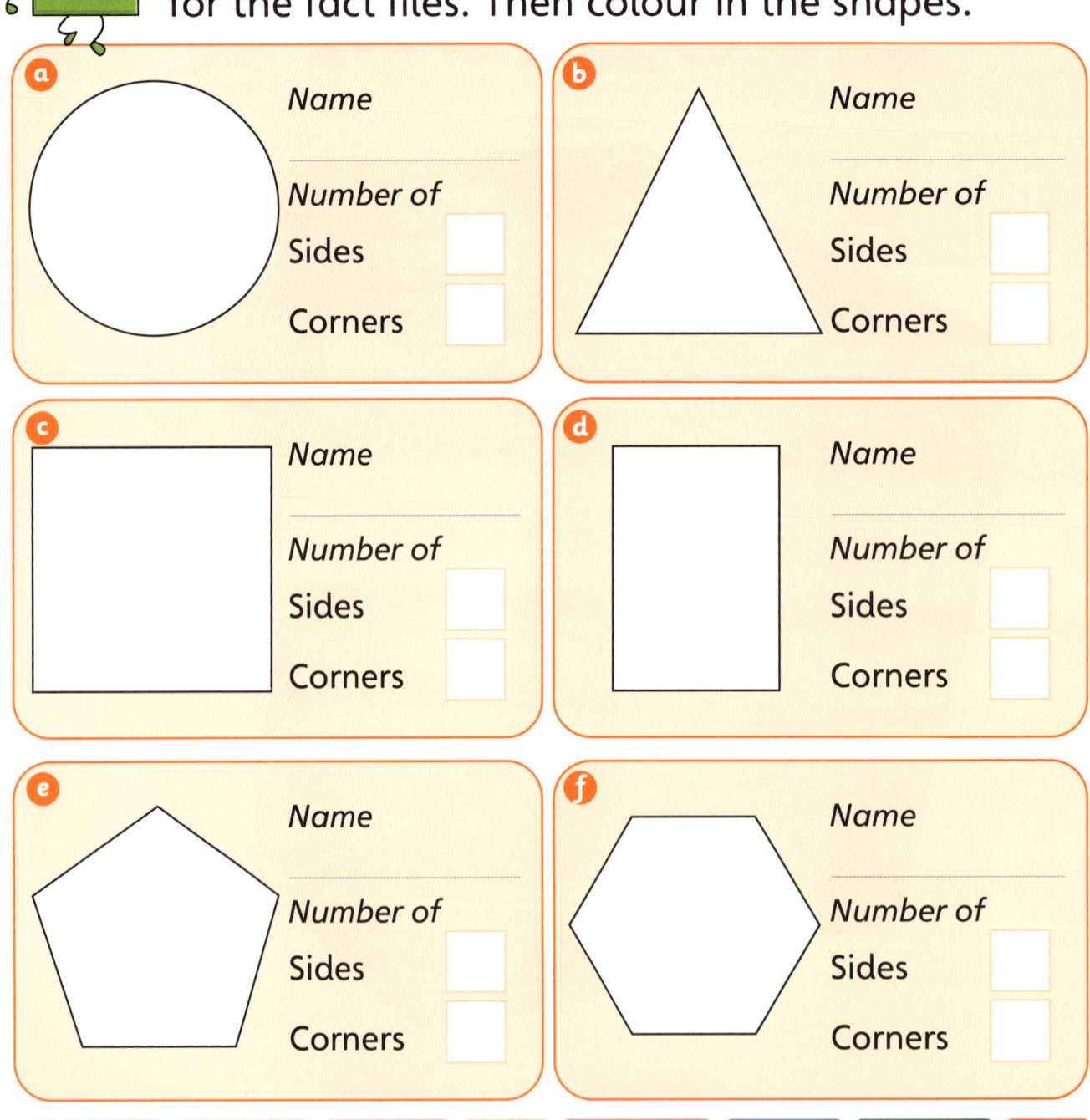

**a**
Name _____
Number of
Sides ☐
Corners ☐

**b**
Name _____
Number of
Sides ☐
Corners ☐

**c**
Name _____
Number of
Sides ☐
Corners ☐

**d**
Name _____
Number of
Sides ☐
Corners ☐

**e**
Name _____
Number of
Sides ☐
Corners ☐

**f**
Name _____
Number of
Sides ☐
Corners ☐

rectangle | hexagon | triangle | circle | pentagon | square | rhombus | oval

**g)** Name _____

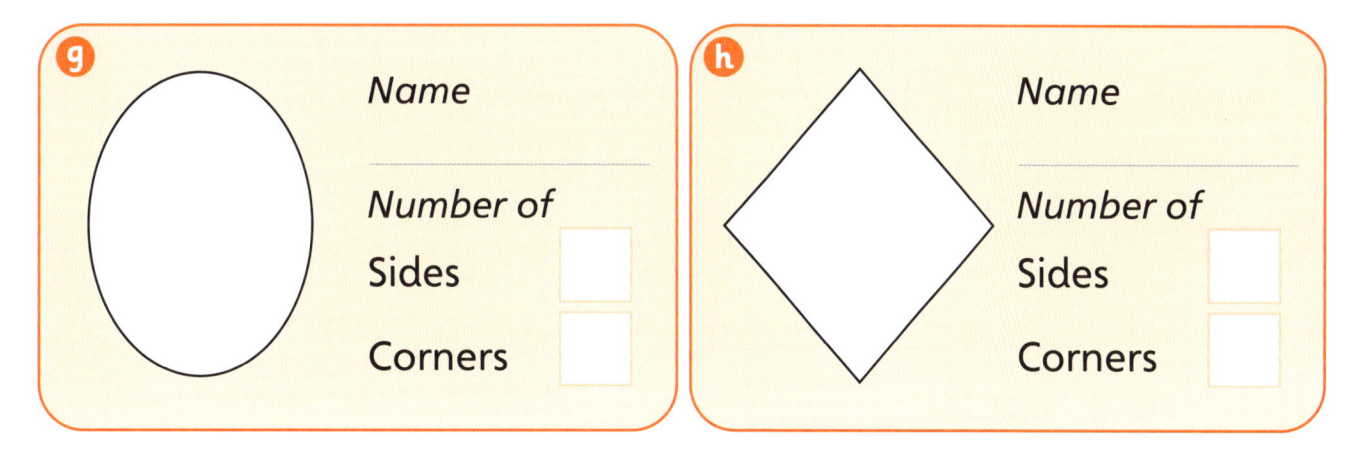

Number of

Sides ☐

Corners ☐

**h)** Name _____

Number of

Sides ☐

Corners ☐

**2** Using a pencil and ruler, draw the following shapes on the grid below and name them.

> A shape with 4 straight sides of equal length and 4 right angled corners.

> A shape with 3 straight sides and 3 corners.

> A shape with 4 straight sides and 4 right angled corners. Pairs of opposite sides are the same length.

GEOMETRY

> A **polygon** is a 2D shape with any number of straight sides. If all the sides are equal length, the polygon is **regular**. If not, it is **irregular**.

*Regular shapes have equal sides and equal angles.*

**3** Are these polygons **regular** or **irregular**? Colour the **regular** polygons green, and the **irregular** polygons yellow.

*A shape with 4 sides is called a **quadrilateral**. The sides can be equal or unequal.*

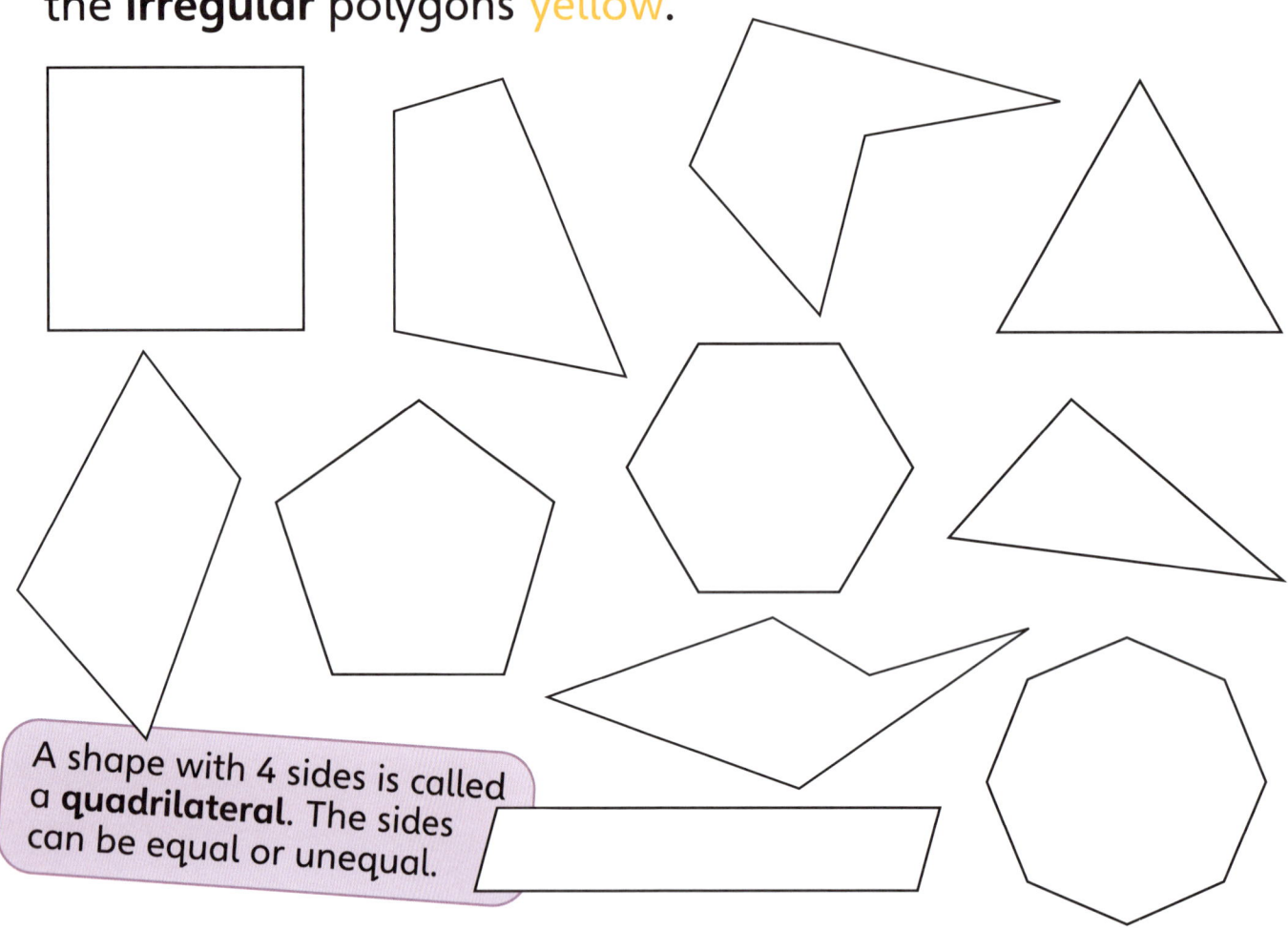

**4** Mark the **corners** on these shapes.

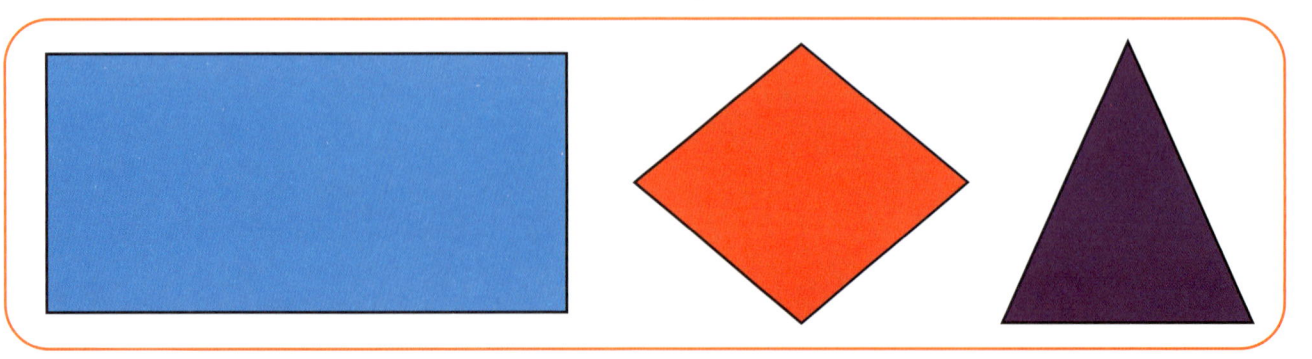

**5** Colour in the odd one out in each set of shapes.

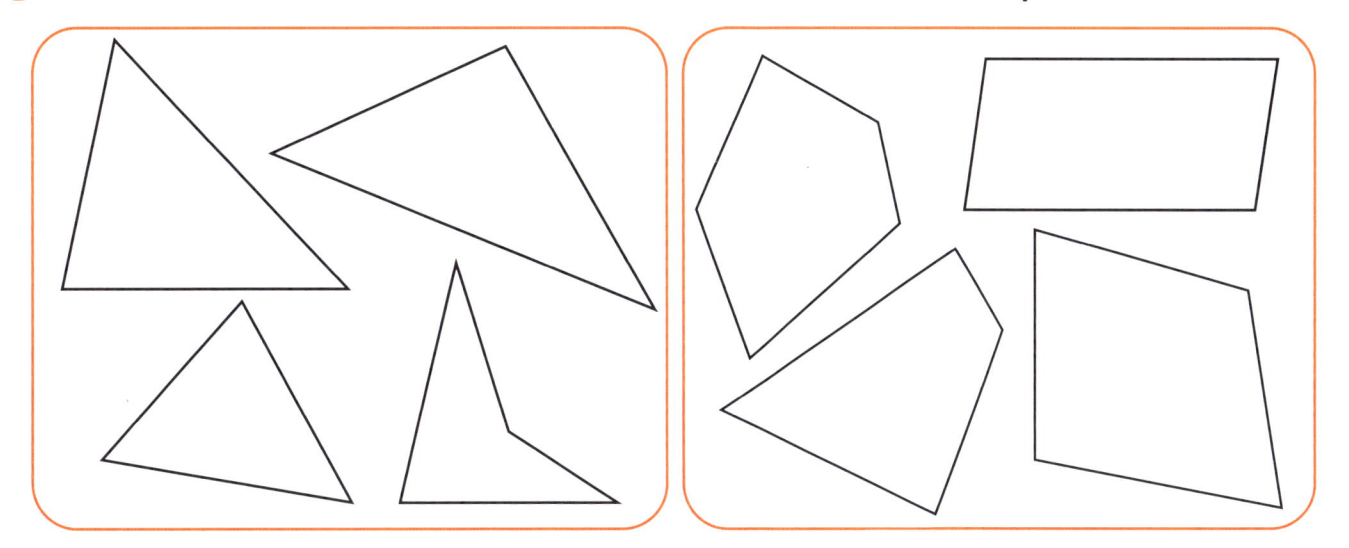

**6** Put these shapes in order [1–5] from the one with the least number of sides to the shape with the greatest number of sides.

**7** Compare the total number of sides using >, < , or =.

| | | |
|---|---|---|
| 2 rectangles | | 1 hexagon |
| 3 triangles | | 2 squares |
| 2 hexagons | | 4 triangles |
| 1 pentagon | | 2 triangles |

# 2D colouring

Use the colour chart below to colour the shapes in this picture.

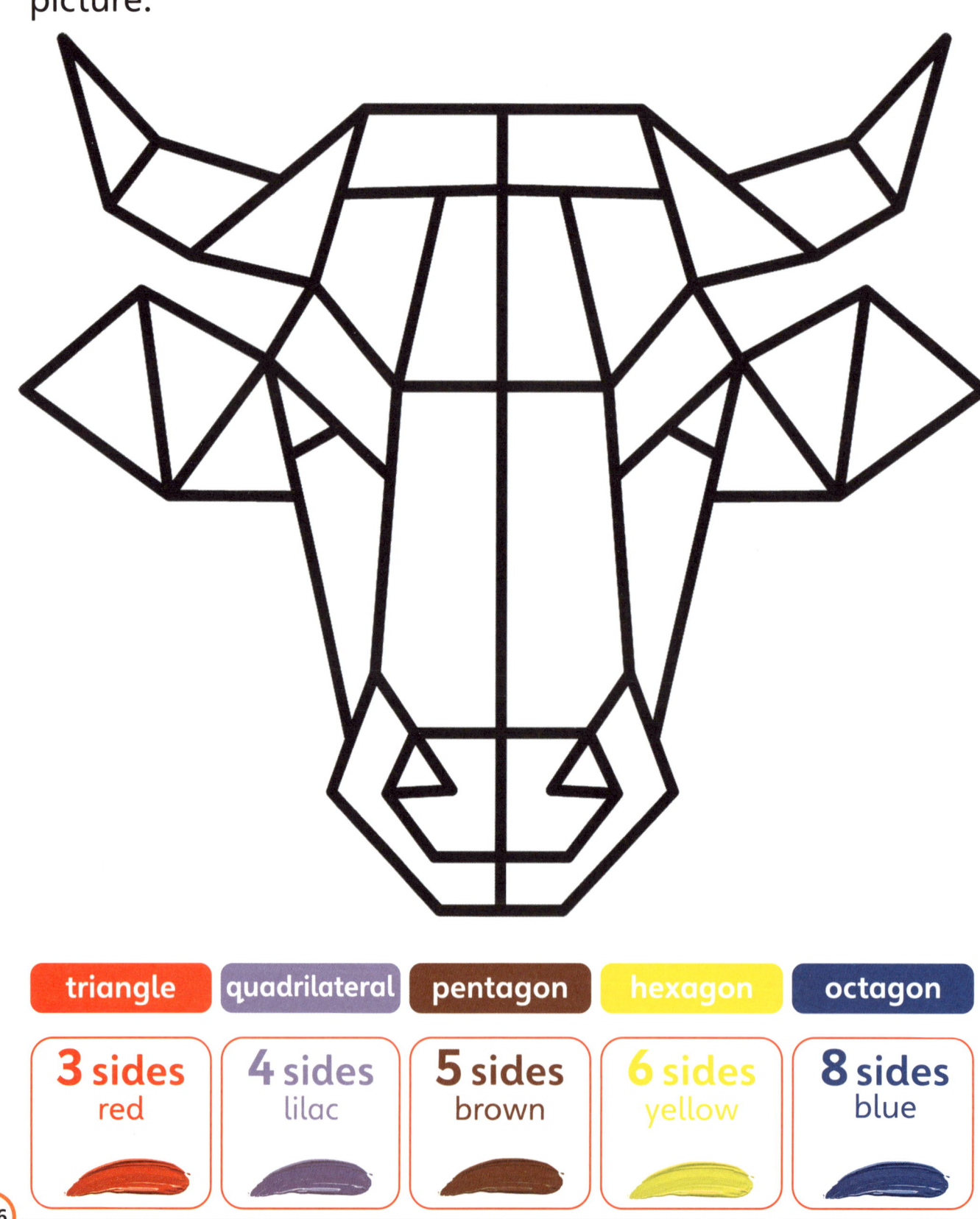

| triangle | quadrilateral | pentagon | hexagon | octagon |
|---|---|---|---|---|
| **3** sides red | **4** sides lilac | **5** sides brown | **6** sides yellow | **8** sides blue |

# lines of symmetry

**1** Colour in the shapes that have a *correct* line of symmetry.

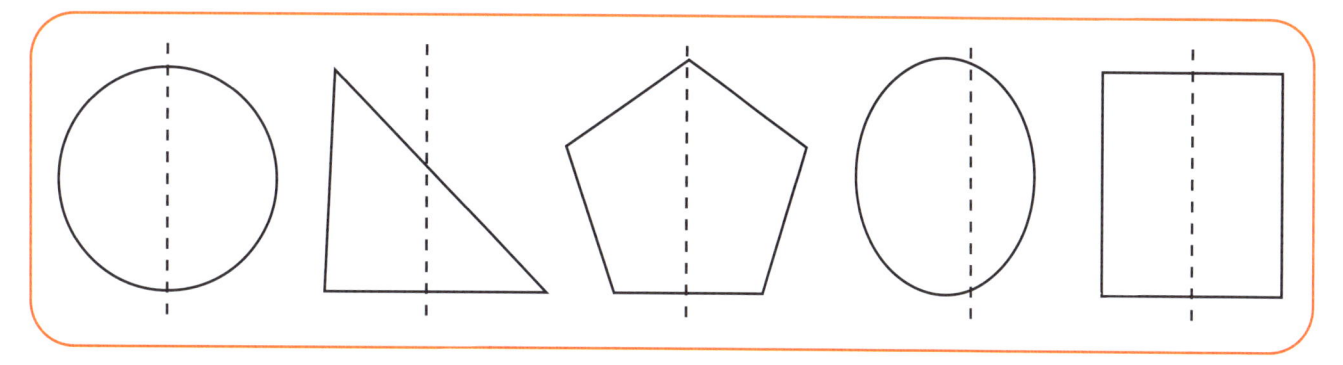

**2** Tick the shapes that have a *vertical* line of symmetry.

**3** Draw a *vertical* line of symmetry on the shapes below.

**4** Look at the 2D shapes below. Draw them in the correct place in the Venn diagram below.

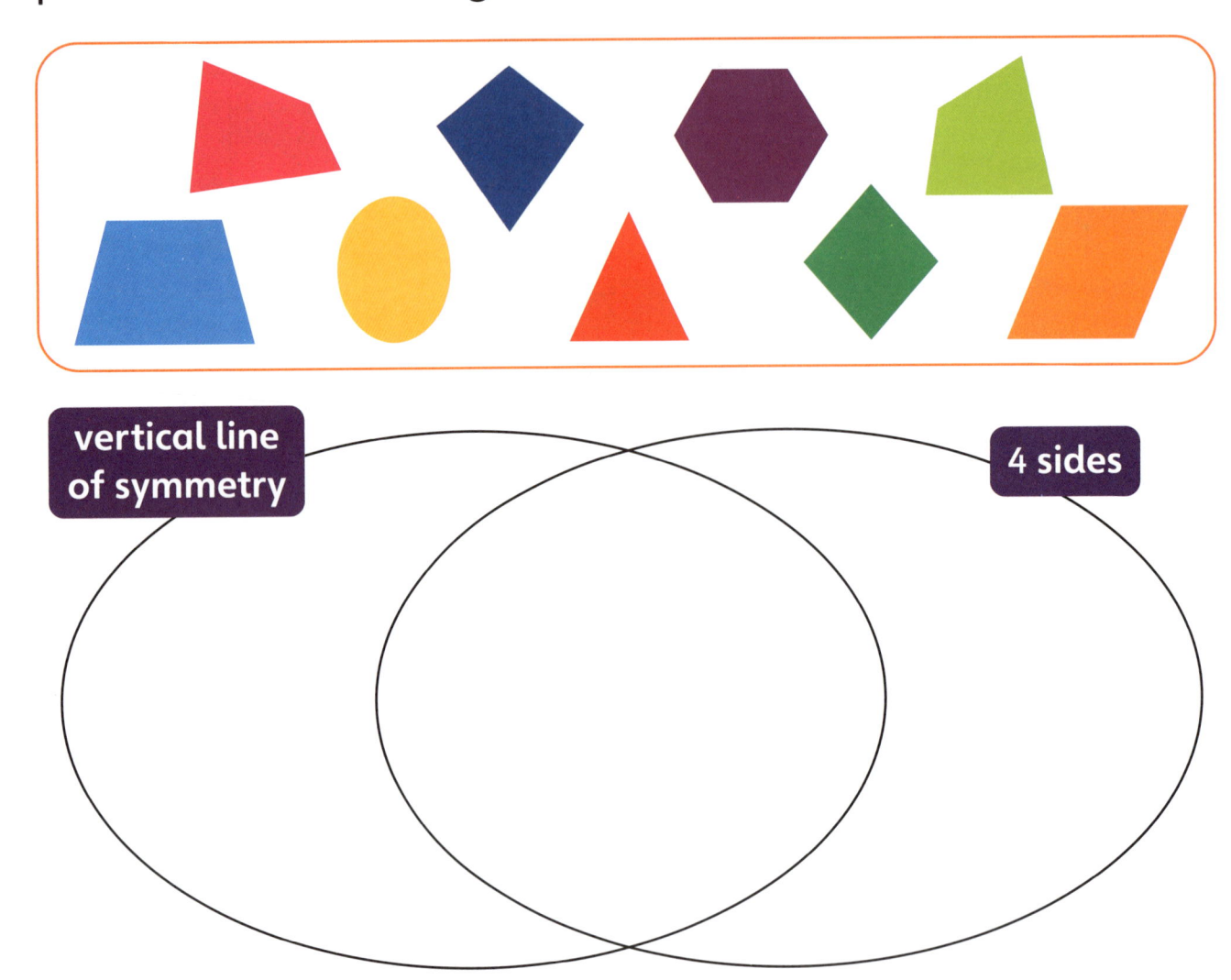

vertical line of symmetry | 4 sides

**5** Can you draw a vertical line of symmetry on any of these road signs? Do so if you can.

**6** Using a ruler, draw as many lines of symmetry on these letters as you can find.

A B C D E
H I M O T
U V W X Y

**7** Cut out the shapes on page 393. Match the other half of each shape based on its vertical line of symmetry. Then colour them in.

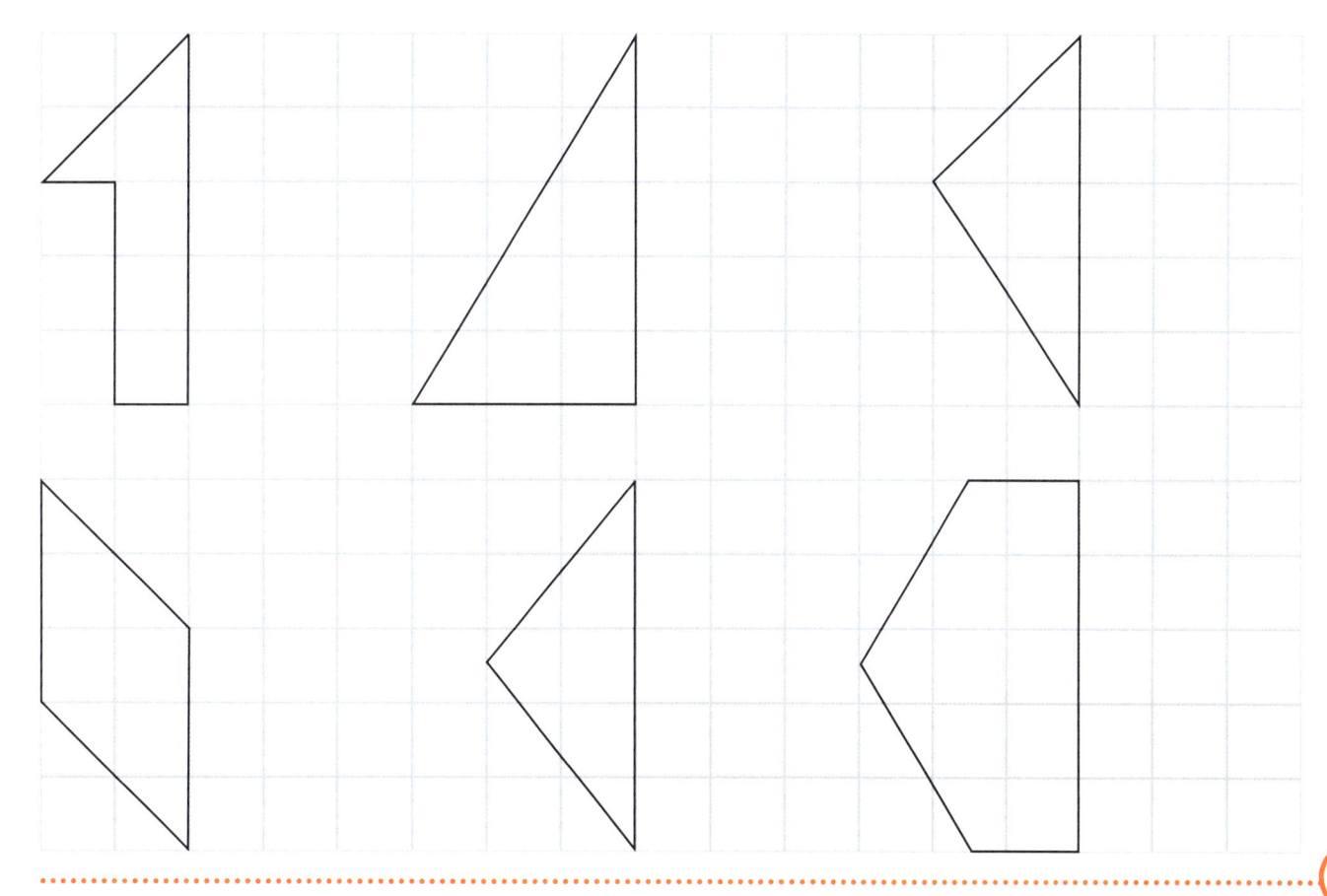

# properties of 3D shapes

**1** Match the shape to its name. Complete the information for each shape.

> A **vertex** is where two lines or edges meet to make a corner.

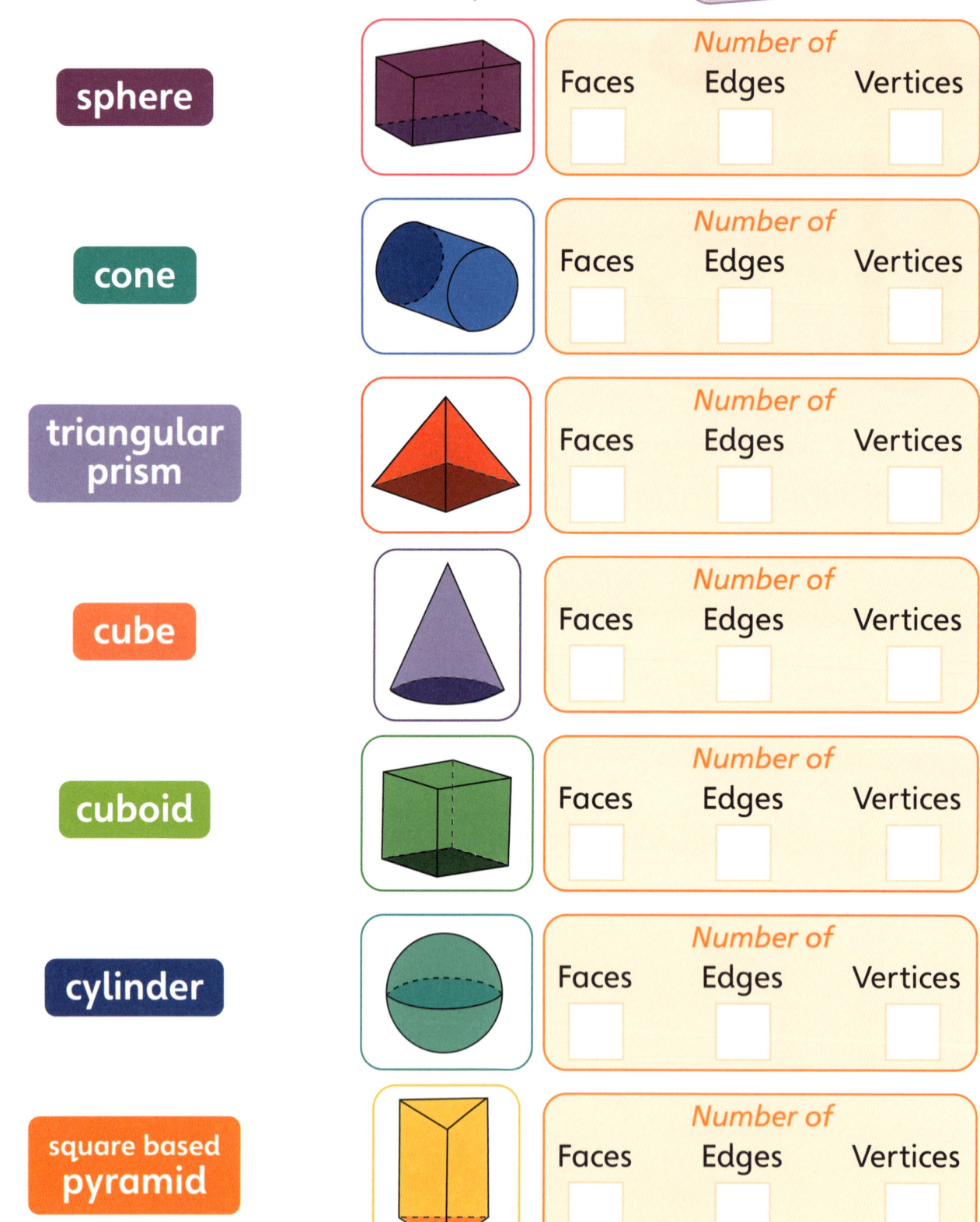

- sphere
- cone
- triangular prism
- cube
- cuboid
- cylinder
- square based pyramid

For each shape:
Number of Faces ☐ Edges ☐ Vertices ☐

**2** Read the clues. Write the name of the 3D shape.
Trace the drawing of that shape in the colour of the clue.

> I have 6 square faces that are all the same size and shape. Each face is a square. I am a _____.

> I have 6 faces. Opposite faces are the same size and shape. I am a _____.

> I have a point. I sit on a circle. I am a _____.

> A circle on the opposite faces make me special. I am a _____.

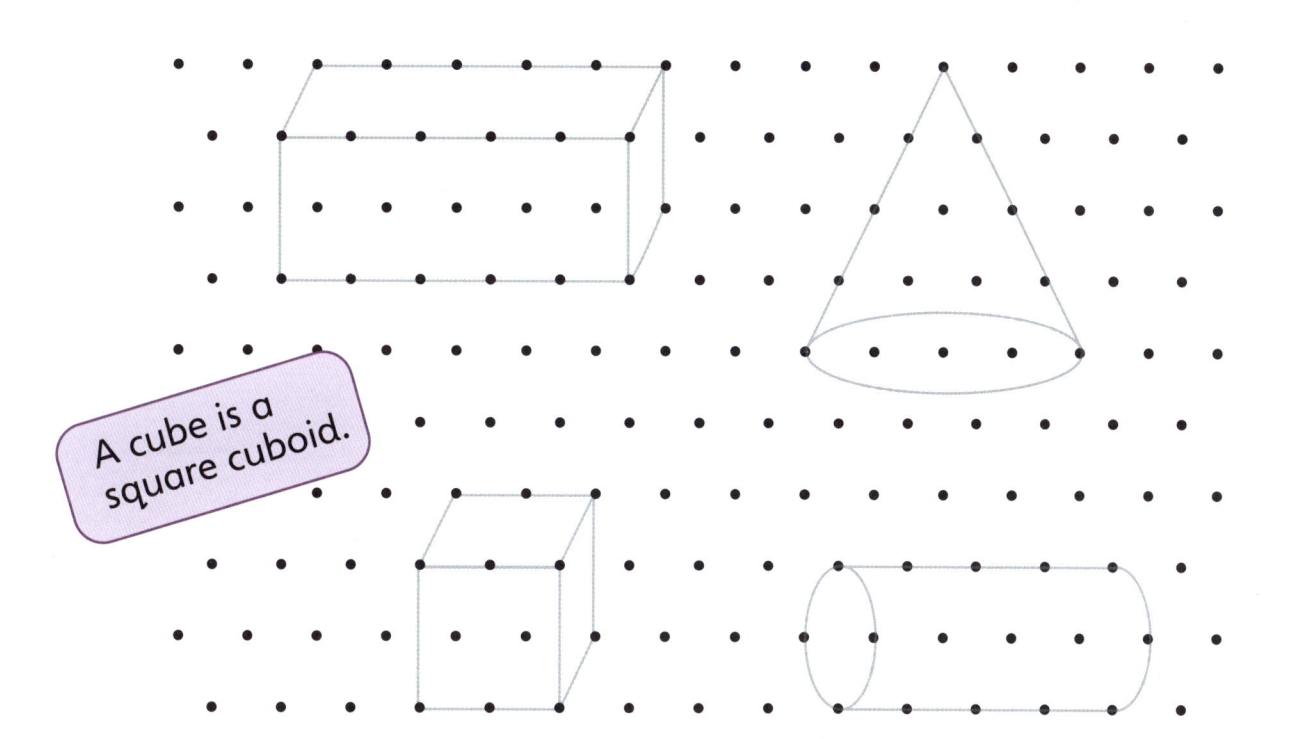

*A cube is a square cuboid.*

**3** What shape is the purple face of each shape below?

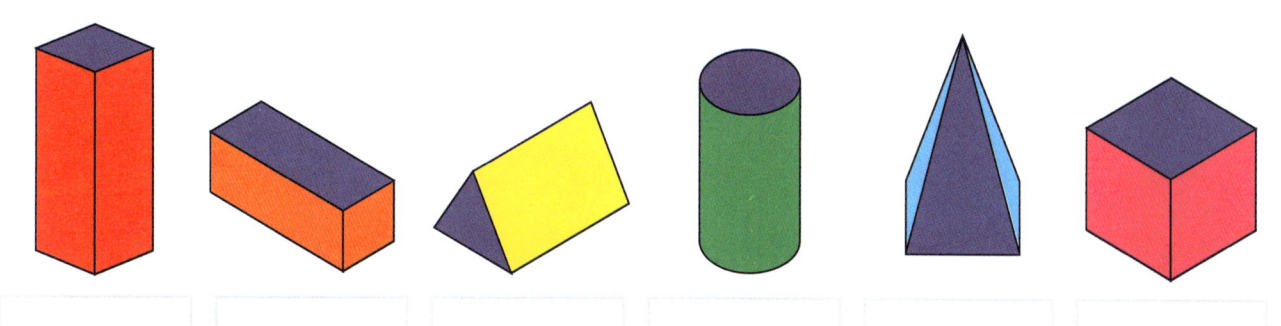

**4** Everyday objects can resemble 3D shapes. Draw a line from each object to the shape that best matches them. Use pink for the **cuboid** shapes, blue for **cylinders**, yellow for **cones**, red for **pyramids**, purple for **triangular prisms**, and green for **spheres**.

**ⓐ** Which shape did you draw **most** lines to?

**ⓑ** Which shape did you draw **fewest** lines to?

**ⓒ** How many cone shapes did you find?

**ⓓ** How many cylinder shapes did you find?

**5** Sort these shapes into the Venn diagram below.

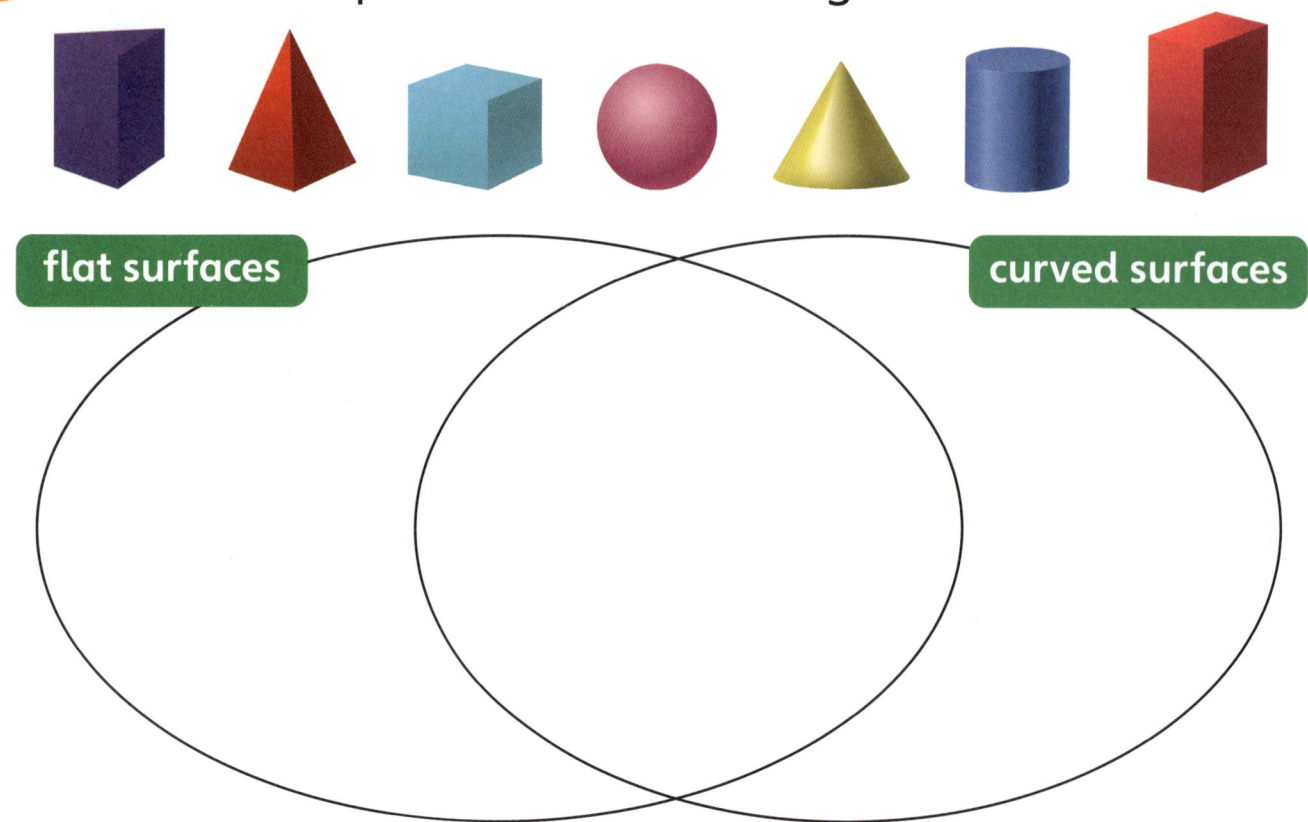

flat surfaces

curved surfaces

**6** Look for these 3D shapes around your house and garden. Draw some of the objects you find.

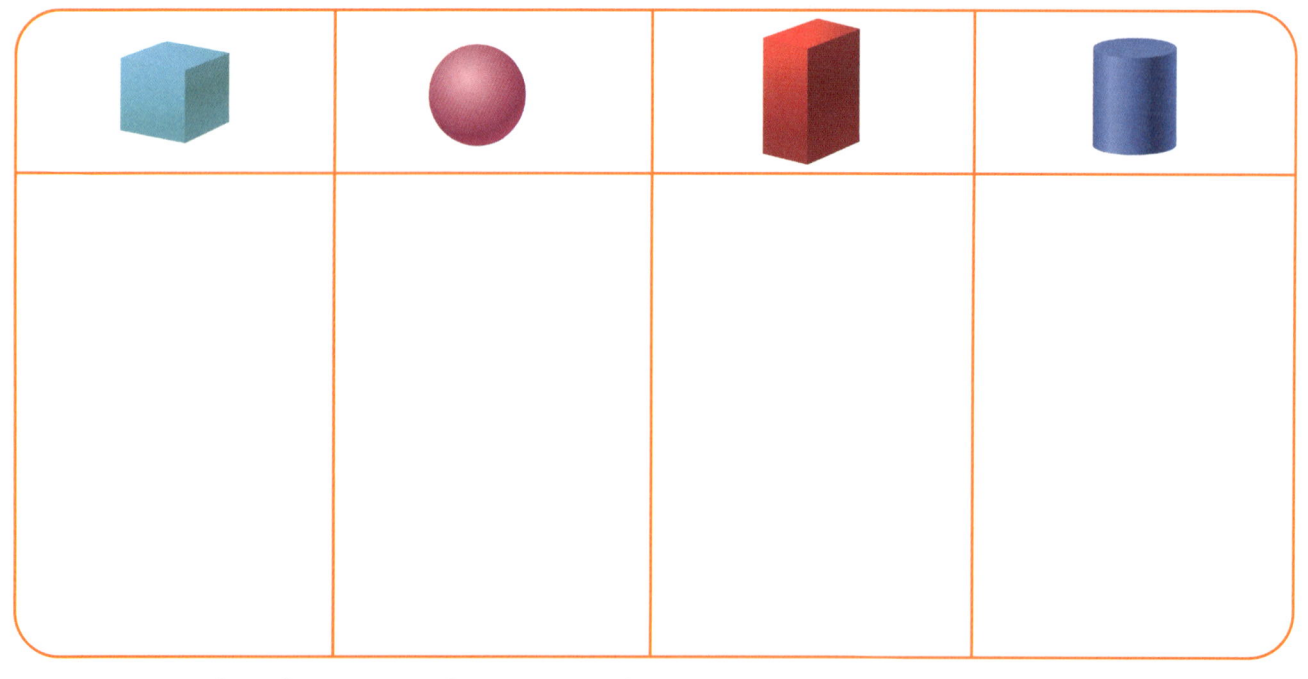

Can you find any other 3D shapes?

**7** Put these shapes in order [1–5] from the one with the *least* number of **vertices** to the one with the *greatest* number of **vertices**.

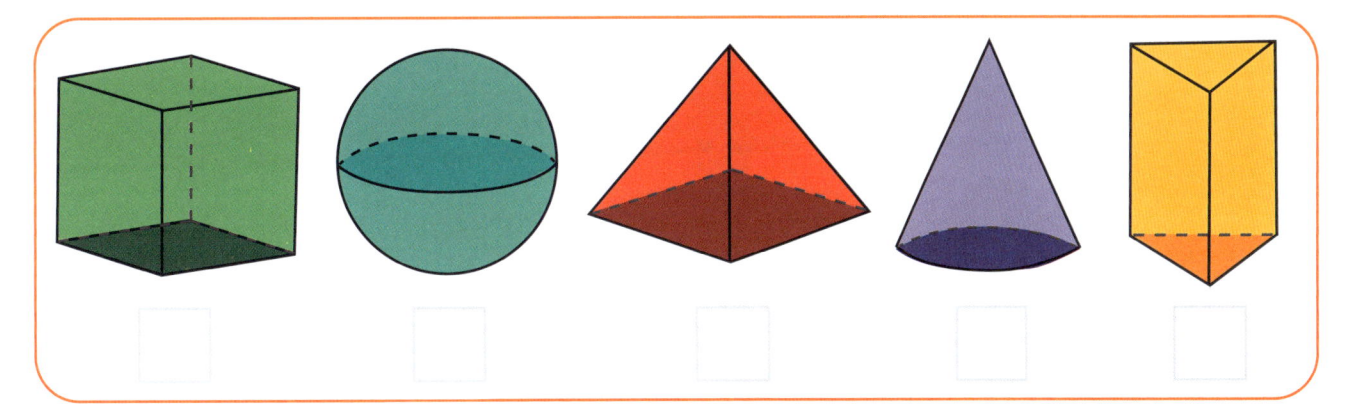

**8** Match these shapes to the number of **edges**.

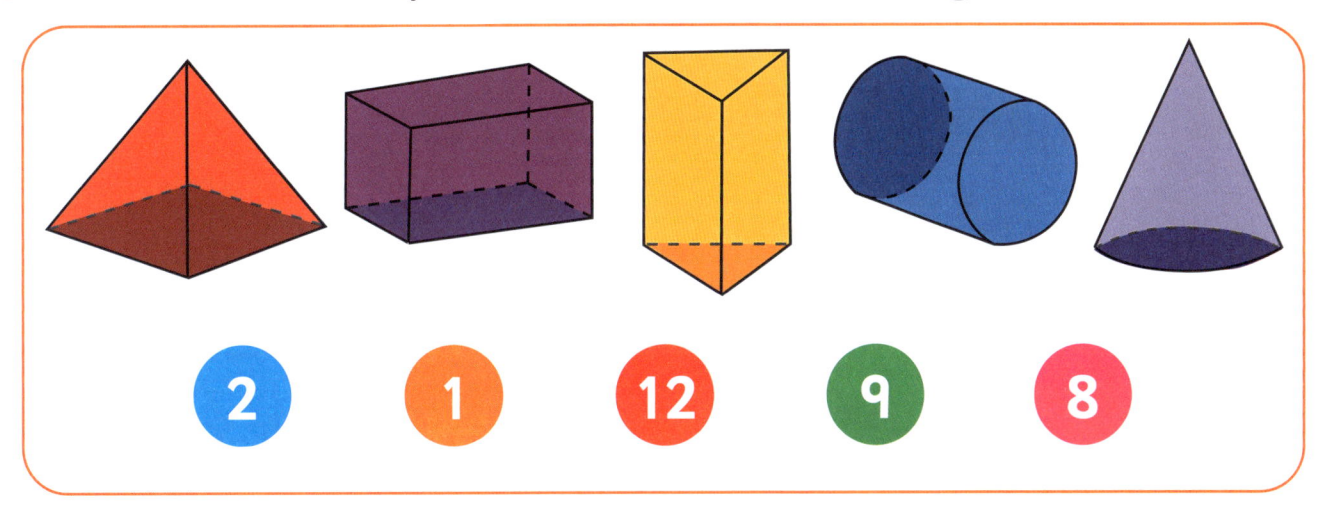

2   1   12   9   8

**9** Complete the calculation based on the number of **edges**.

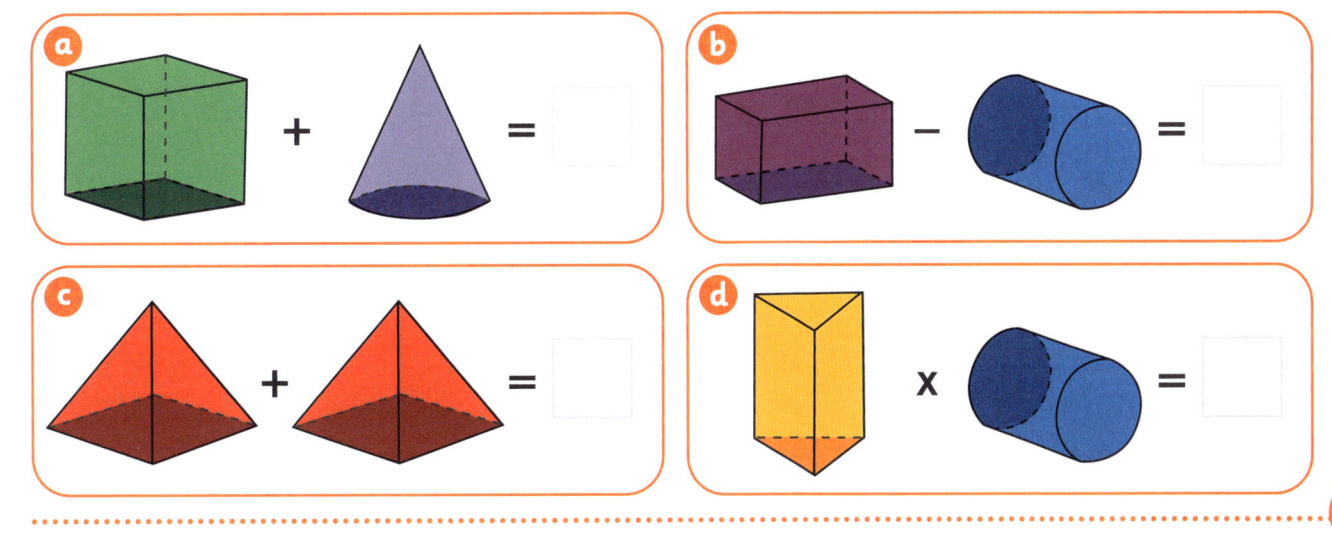

a) ⬛ + △ =

b) ⬛ − ⬤ =

c) △ + △ =

d) △ × ⬤ =

## patterns and sequences

**1** Continue each pattern.

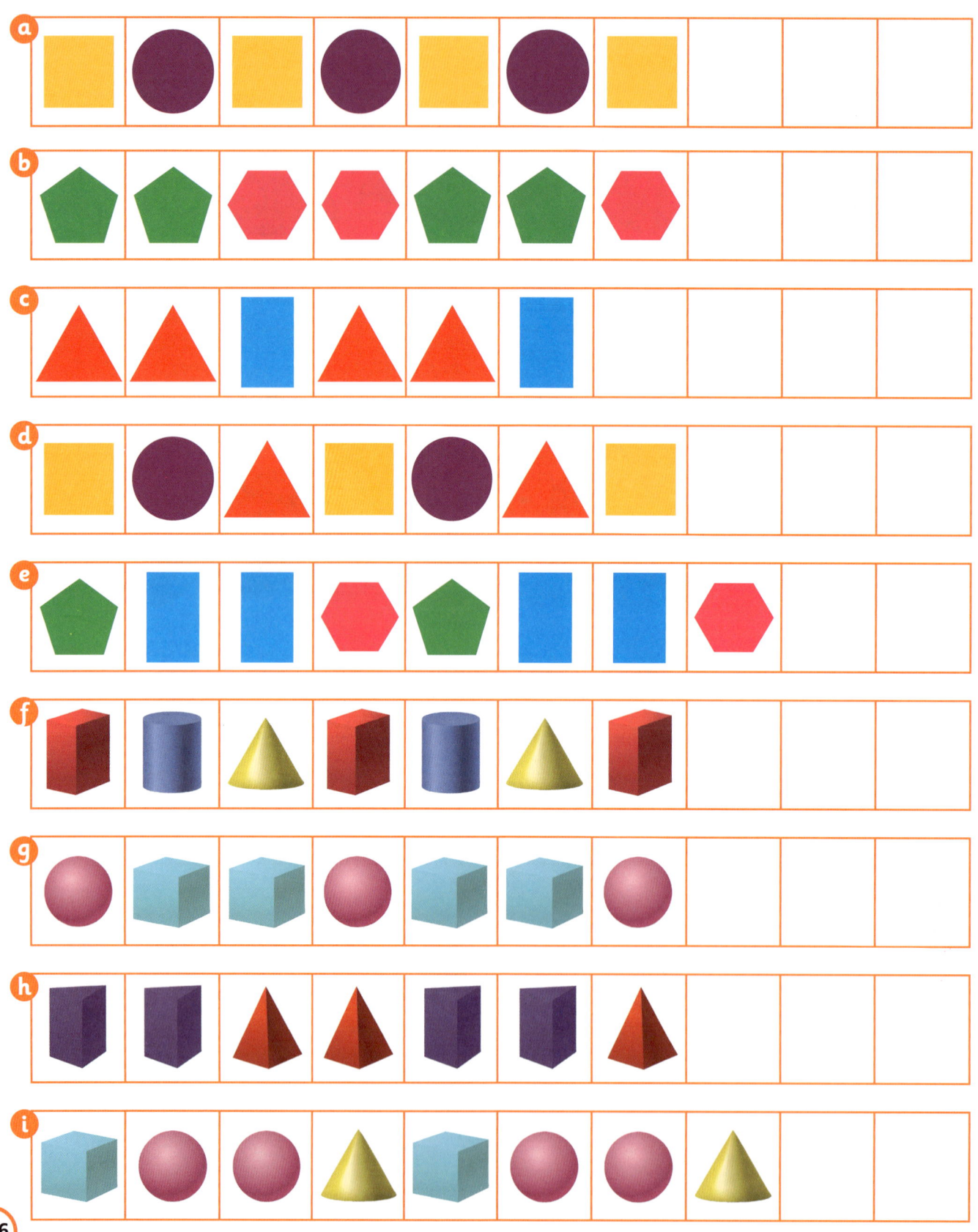

❷ Draw the missing shapes to complete each pattern.

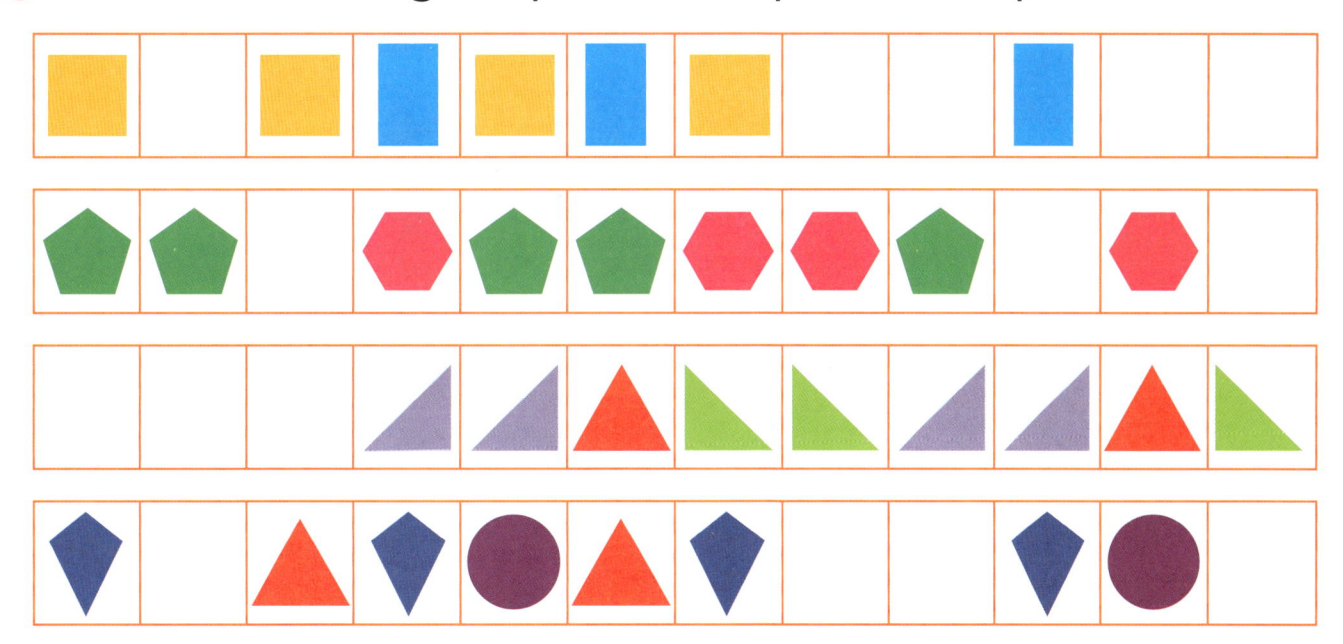

❸ What will be the **12th** shape in this sequence? Draw it.

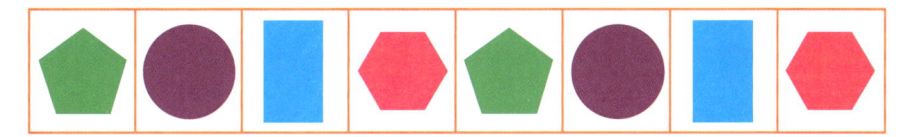

❹ What will be the **15th** shape in this sequence? Draw it.

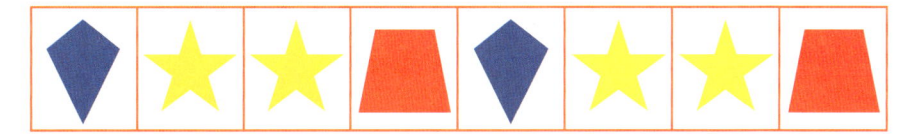

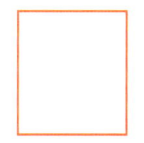

❺ Circle the mistake in each sequence.

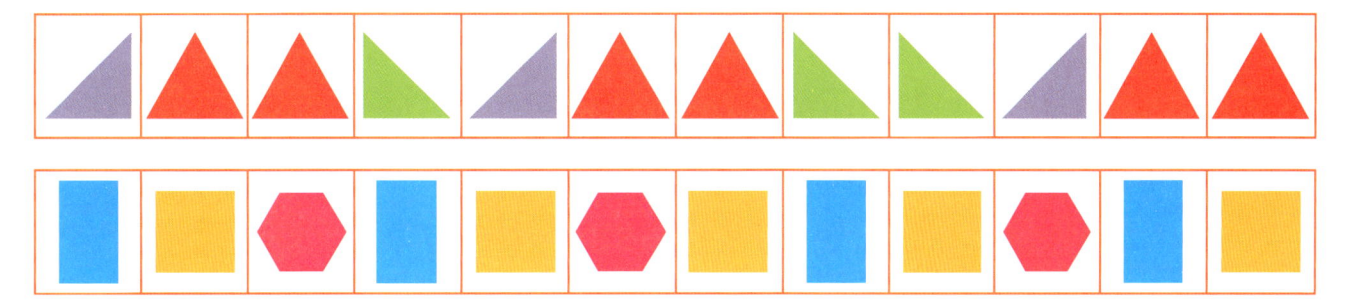

**Did you know?**
Patterns occur widely in nature. The colourful stripes of the royal angelfish may help provide camouflage.

GEOMETRY

# position and direction

**1** Write labels to show the correct directions.

forwards
backwards
left
right

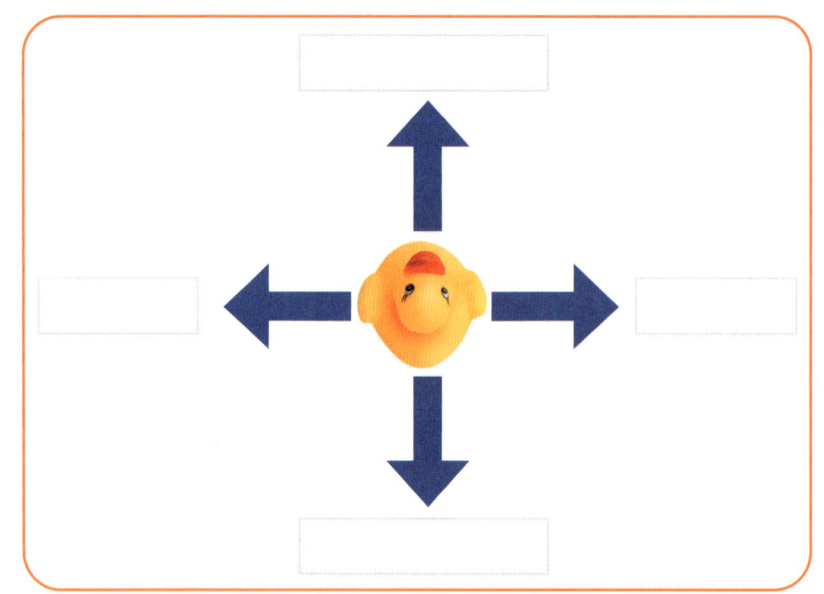

**2** Cut out the fruit on page 393. Then stick each item in the correct square by following the clues.

The orange is directly **above** the lime.
The strawberry is 2 squares **below** the orange.
The pear is to the **right** of the lime.
The grapes are to the **left** of the strawberry.
The cherries are directly **above** the grapes.
The banana is directly **below** the pear.
The lemon is 2 squares **above** the banana.
The apple is to the **left** of the orange.

**3** Circle *all* the instructions that will take the rubber duck to the bathtub.

Three steps forwards.
One step to the left.

Three steps forwards.
One step to the right.

Two steps to the right.
Three steps forwards.

One step to the right.
Three steps forwards.

**4** Write instructions to take the footprints to the towel.

**5** Complete the sentences below.

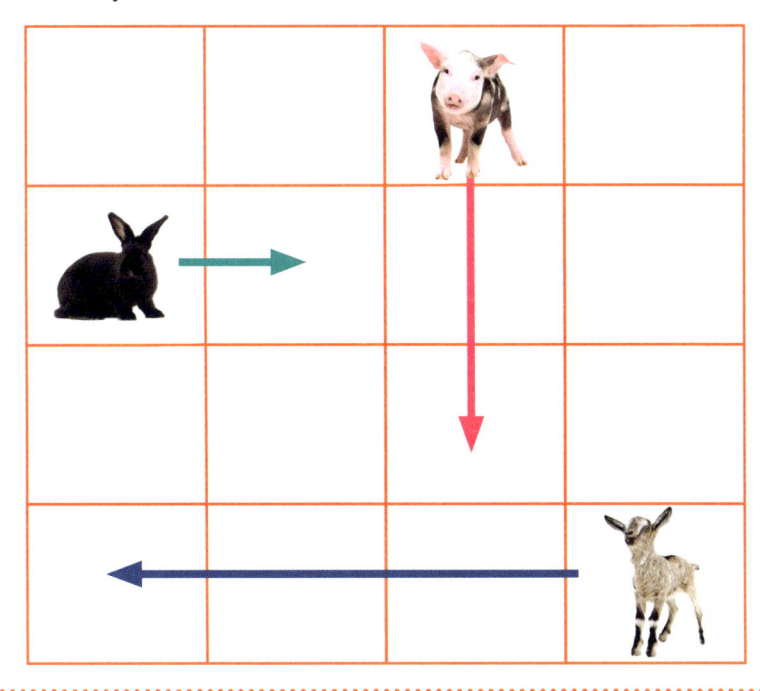

The rabbit has moved ☐ square to the _____ .

The pig has moved ☐ squares _____ .

The goat has moved ☐ squares to the _____ .

GEOMETRY

**6** Follow the instructions and mark each move with an arrow to record the journey. Draw an 'x' to show the correct new position.

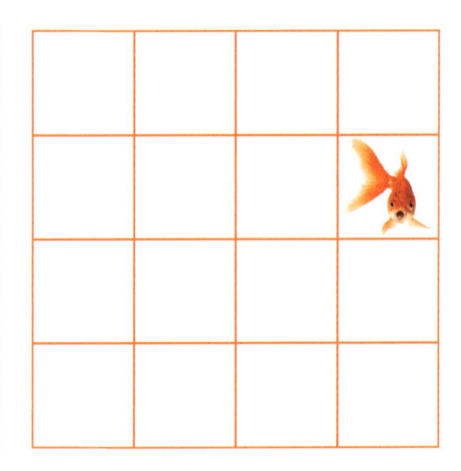

**The mouse moves:**

2 squares backwards.

2 squares left.

3 squares down.

1 square right.

**The puppy moves:**

2 squares right.

3 squares down.

1 square right.

2 squares backwards.

**The fish moves:**

2 squares left.

2 squares forwards.

1 square left.

2 squares backwards.

**7** Follow the instructions and draw each shape in its new position.

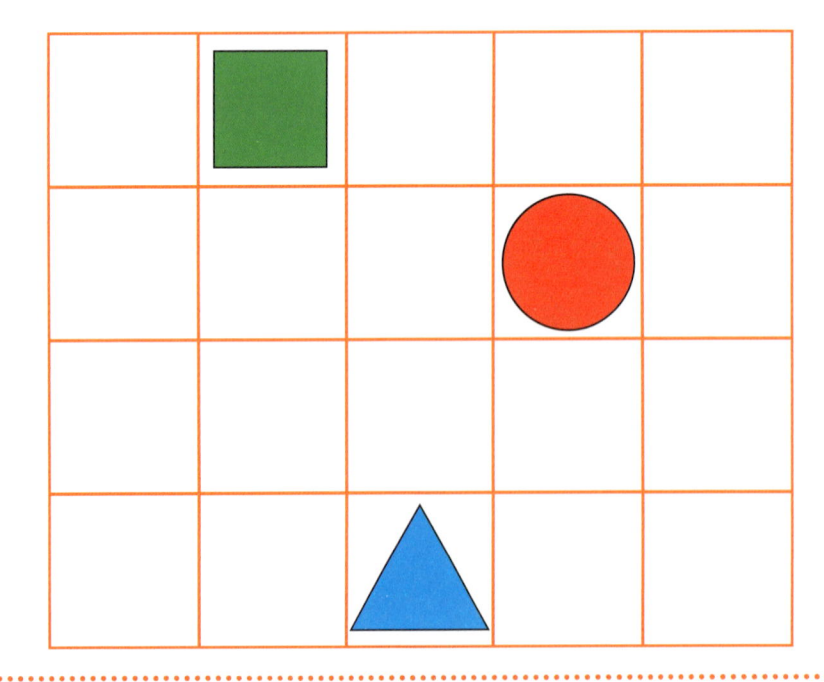

**The square moves:**

Three squares right and two squares down.

**The circle moves:**

Three squares left, two squares down and one square right.

**The triangle moves:**

Two squares up and two squares left.

# rotation

anticlockwise   clockwise

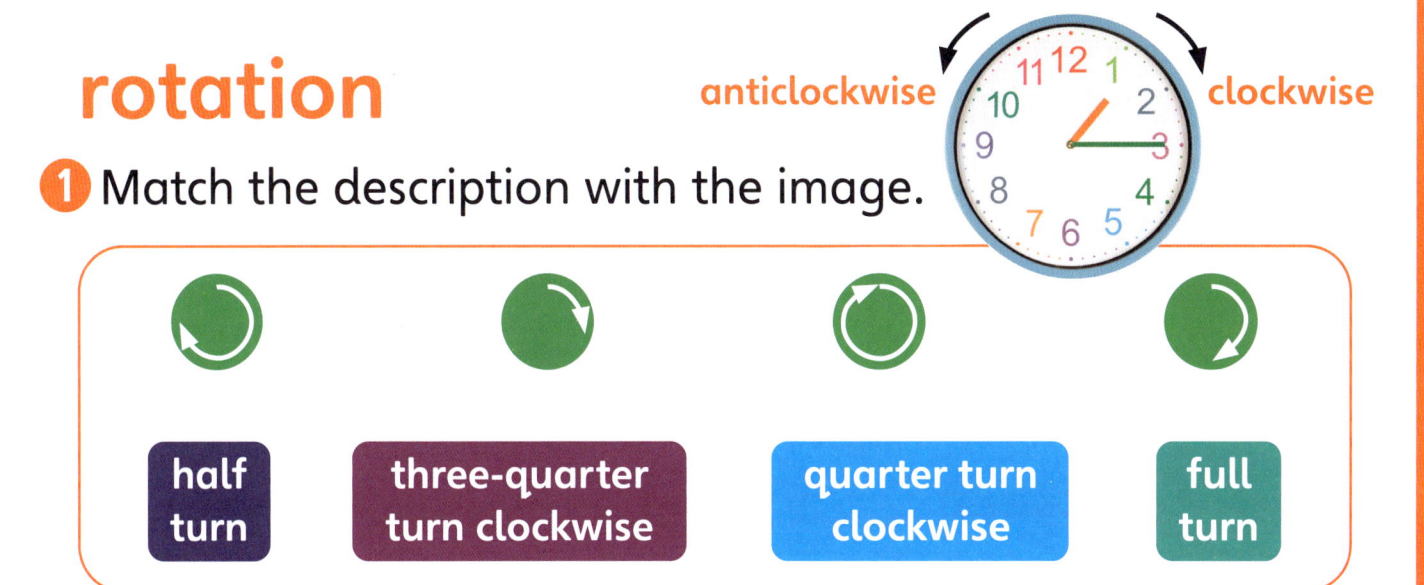

**1** Match the description with the image.

| half turn | three-quarter turn clockwise | quarter turn clockwise | full turn |

**2** Continue the patterns. Describe each pattern using the terms *half turn*, *quarter turn*, *clockwise* and *anticlockwise*.

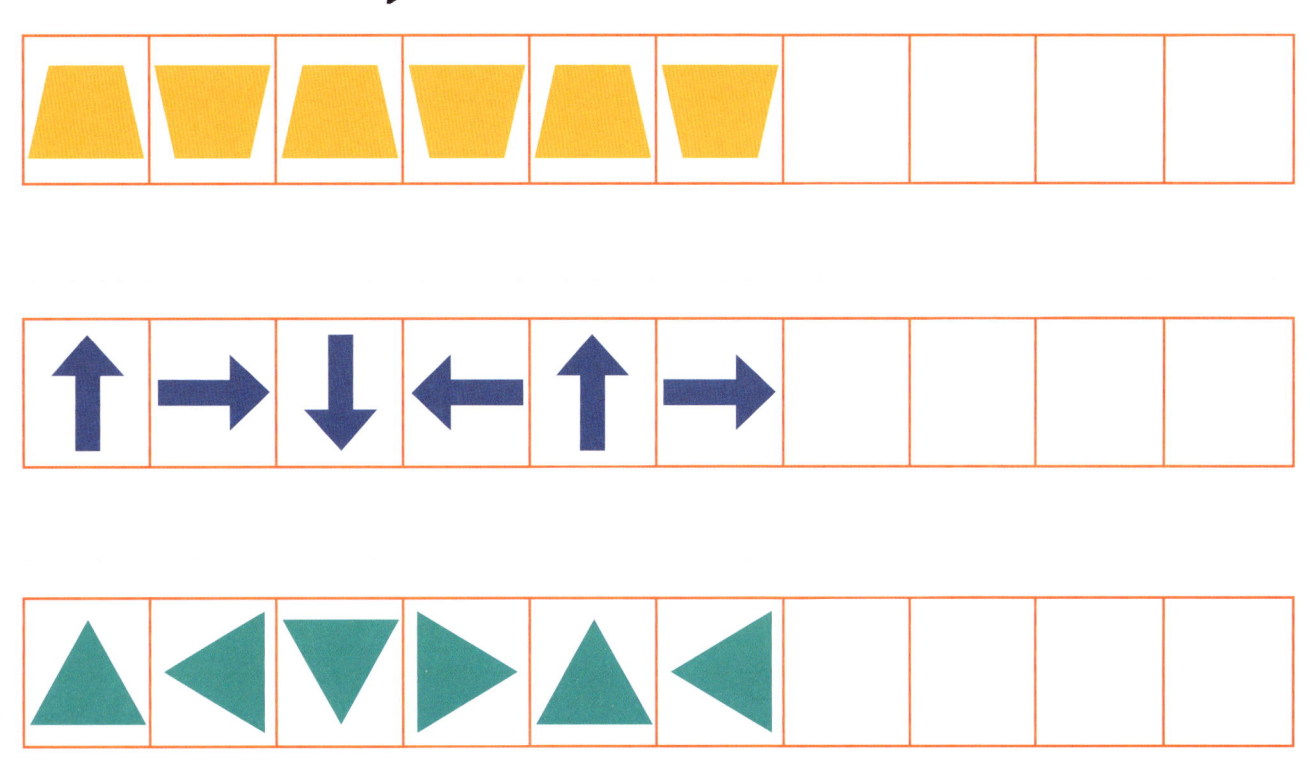

**3** Circle the mistake in the pattern. What *should* the shape be?

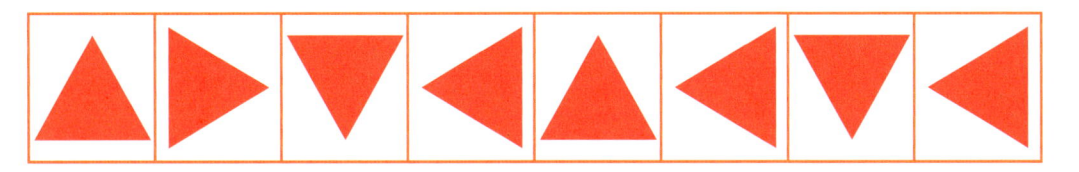

**4** Rotate each shape as instructed. Draw the rotated shape.

| | |
|---|---|
| A threequarters turn clockwise. | Three half turns anticlockwise. |
| A full turn anticlockwise. | Two threequarters turn clockwise. |
|  | A threequarters turn clockwise, followed by a half turn anticlockwise |

**5** Describe the turn each shape has made.

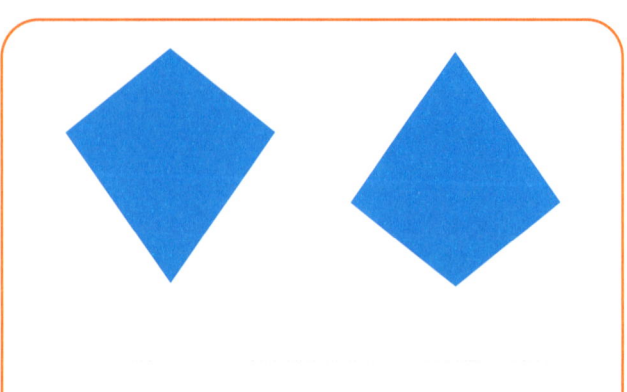

**6** Help the tortoise to find its way through the maze to the lettuce by following the directions.

1. Go forwards 1 square.
2. Take a quarter turn clockwise. Go forwards 2 squares.
3. Take a quarter turn anticlockwise. Go forwards 2 squares.
4. Take a quarter turn anticlockwise. Go forwards 1 square.
5. Take a quarter turn clockwise. Go forwards 2 squares.
6. Take a quarter turn clockwise. Go forwards 4 squares.
7. Take a quarter turn anticlockwise. Go forwards 2 squares.
8. Take a quarter turn anticlockwise. Go forwards 2 squares.
9. Take a quarter turn clockwise. Go forwards 1 square.

**Did you know?**
A tortoise is a turtle, but a turtle isn't a tortoise. Tortoises spend most of their time on land and turtles are adapted for life spent in water. A group of tortoises is called a creep!

**7** Draw the new time after the movement described.

**a** A full turn clockwise.

**b** A half turn clockwise.

**c** A quarter turn clockwise.

**d** A threequarters turn clockwise.

**8** The hen is facing West.

In which direction will it be facing after **3 clockwise half turns**?

In which direction will it be facing after **6 anticlockwise quarter turns**?

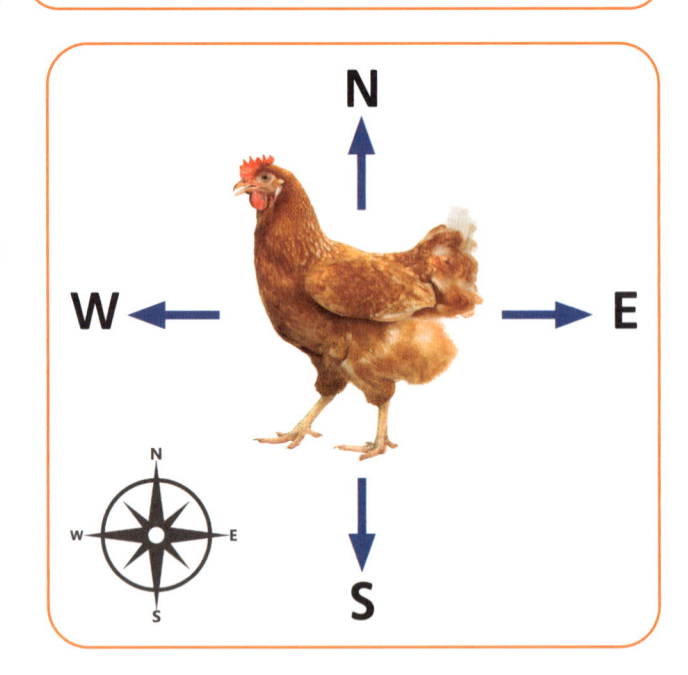

**Did you know?**
Most maps today show North at the top, but this idea is relatively new. For hundreds of years, map-makers put whatever they thought most important at the top. How might an upside-down map change your view of the world?

# Statistics

## recording and analysing data

**1** Count the different kinds of pets owned by the children in Mrs Robinson's class.

Complete the tally chart.

Then complete the pictogram below.

| Pet | Tally | Total |
|---|---|---|
| Dog | ||||  |||| | |
| Cat | | |
| Rabbit | | |
| Fish | | |

| Pet | Number of Pets |
|---|---|
| 🐕 | ● ● ● ● ● ● ● ● |
| 🐈 | |
| 🐇 | |
| 🐟 | |

**2** The children in Year 2 were asked how they travelled to school. They made a tally chart of the results.

| Transport | | Tally | Total |
|---|---|---|---|
| Walking | | ||||  ||||  || | |
| Bus | | ||||  | | |
| Car | | ||||  |||| | |
| Bike | | ||||  ||| | |

Fill in the totals.

Use this information to complete the pictogram. Then answer the questions.

| Transport | Number of Children Using This Transport |
|---|---|
| (walking) | |
| (bus) | |
| (car) | |
| (bike) | |

**a** How many children took the bus to school?

**b** How many more children travelled to school by car than by bus?

**c** How many children either walked or cycled to school?

**d** How many children travelled to school altogether?

**3** One hundred children were asked what was their favourite colour from a selection of five colours. The information is shown in the pictogram below.

Complete the pictogram with totals, paying special attention to the **key**. Then answer the questions.

> A **key** on a pictogram tells us how many each picture stands for.

| Colour | Number Who Chose Colour | Total |
|---|---|---|
| red | ★ ★ ★ ★ ★ | |
| green | ★ ★ | |
| orange | ★ ★ ★ | |
| blue | ★ ★ ★ ★ ★ ★ | |
| purple | ★ ★ ★ ★ | |

key: ★ = 5 children

**a** Which colour was the most popular?

**b** Which colour was the least popular?

**c** How many children chose red?

**d** How many more children chose pink than purple?

**e** How many fewer children chose green than blue?

**Did you know?**
According to scientists, red is the first colour that a baby sees. Gradually their colour vision develops and by the time they reach five months they see the full spectrum of colours.

**4** Louis recorded the number of different trees in a nearby park in a table.

| Tree | Total |
|---|---|
| Oak | 35 |
| Birch | 45 |
| Horse Chestnut | 25 |
| Ash | 15 |

Use the information from Louis' table to complete the pictogram below. Pay special attention to the key—each icon represents 5 trees.

| Tree | Number of Trees |
|---|---|
| Oak | |
| Birch | 🌲🌲🌲🌲🌲🌲🌲🌲🌲 |
| Horse Chestnut | |
| Ash | |

key 🌲 = 5 trees

**a** Which type of tree did Louis count most of?

**b** How many more birch trees than ash trees were there?

**c** How many oak and birch trees were there altogether?

**d** How many trees did Louis count altogether?

# bird bonanza

**1** Travis asked his friends which of these birds were their favourites. Complete the table he has made.

| Bird | Tally | Total |
|---|---|---|
| Puffin | ||||| | |  |
| Emu | | |  |
| Peacock | ||| |  |
| Snowy Owl | |||| |  |
| Toucan | ||| |  |
| Flamingo | || |  |

Use the information to complete the **block diagram** on the next page. Colour in one square for each bird.

Then answer the questions below.

- **a** Which was the most popular bird?

- **b** How many of his friends preferred the peacock?

- **c** How many more friends chose the snowy owl than the flamingo?

- **d** How many fewer friends chose the toucan than the puffin?

- **e** How many friends did Travis ask altogether?

**Number of Children** (y-axis: 1–8)

**Type of Bird** (x-axis): Puffin, Emu, Peacock, Owl, Toucan, Flamingo

---

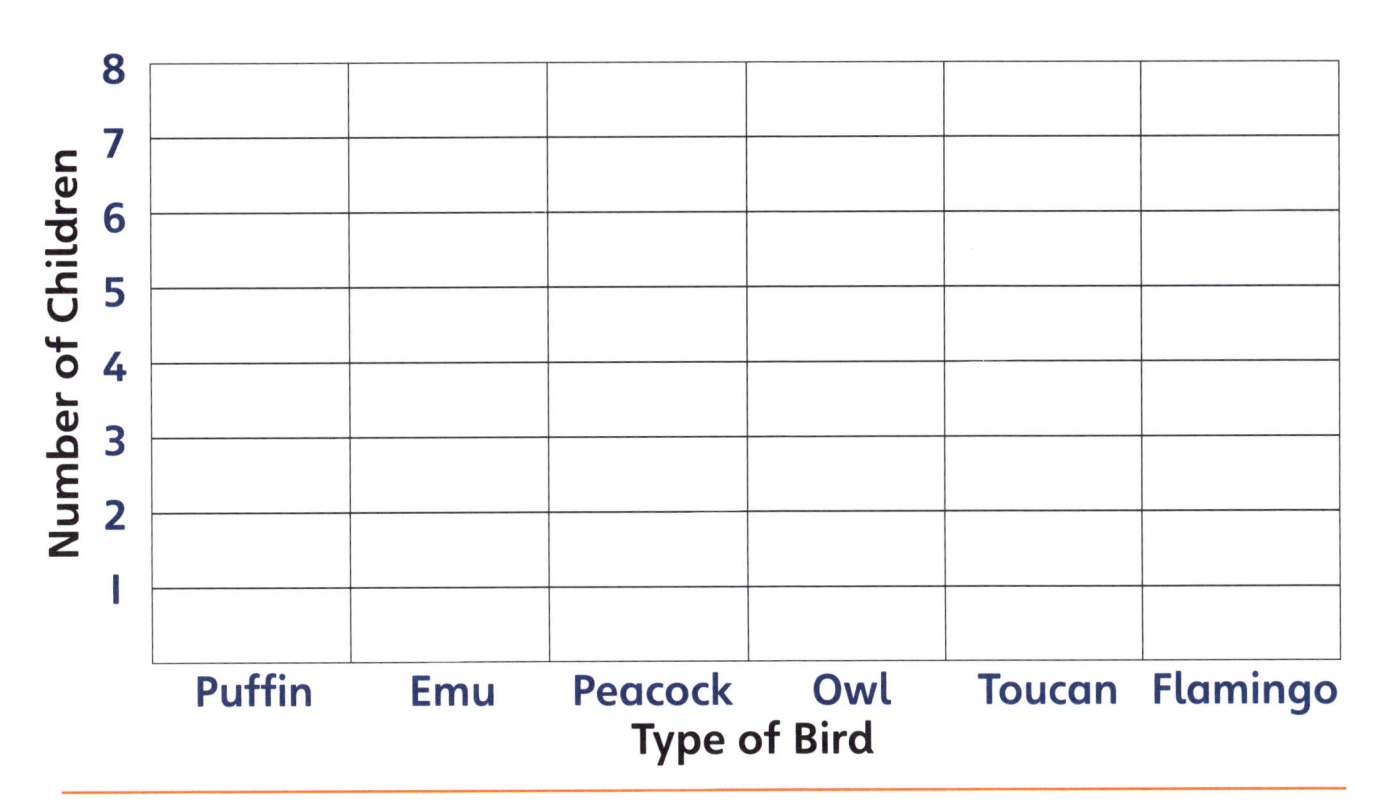

**2** Ilana, Gwen, and Clara went to the park. The block diagram shows the number of pigeons each girl saw.

**Pigeons**

Number of Pigeons (1–9)
- Ilana: 9
- Gwen: 7
- Clara: 5

**Girl**

- **a** Who saw the fewest pigeons?
- **b** How many pigeons did Gwen see?
- **c** Who saw 4 more pigeons than Clara?
- **d** How many pigeons did Gwen **and** Clara see?

311

# water work

Jessica and Emily kept a record of how many glasses of water they drank each day from Monday to Friday. They recorded the information in a table.

|         | Monday | Tuesday | Wednesday | Thursday | Friday |
|---------|--------|---------|-----------|----------|--------|
| Jessica | 4      | 5       | 3         | 4        | 4      |
| Emily   | 5      | 4       | 2         | 5        | 3      |

**a** Who drank the most water on Thursday?

**b** On which day did Jessica drink the most water?

**c** On which day did Emily drink the least water?

**d** How many glasses of water did they drink between them on Friday?

**e** Which girl drank the most water in total and how many glasses did she drink?

Carry out an investigation and draw your own pictogram!

# Science

# living things

All living things share certain characteristics. They all:

- move
- need food
- sense things around them
- get rid of waste
- make babies or new seeds
- need air
- grow

If something *stops doing* these things, it is *no longer alive*.
If something *never did* these things, it has *never lived*.

Join each object to the correct description.

**once living**

**living**

**never lived**

# habitats

> A **habitat** is a place where plants and animals live. There are many different habitats. Each provides the water, food, and shelter the animals and plants need to survive.

Complete the fact sheets for each of the habitats below. Use the word banks at the bottom of the page to help.

**a**

habitat
animal
plant

**b**

habitat
animal
plant

**c**

habitat
animal
plant

**d**

habitat
animal
plant

ocean   deer   reeds   desert   woodland   otter
palm tree   seaweed   river   whale   camel   moss

**1** Cut out the plants and animals on page 393. Stick them above the correct description. Draw a line to join them to the correct habitat.

Thick layers of fat and fur help keep me warm, and my white coat helps camouflage me.

I have long fuzzy hairs and grow close to the ground to protect me from the cold.

Wind passes through my leaves to cool me so that I don't lose water easily.

desert

I store water in my fleshy stems. My spikes protect me from animals.

I move from side to side so only a small part of my body touches the hot ground at any time.

polar

I can survive a long time without water and food by using the energy and moisture in my fat-filled humps.

I live in cracks between rocks. I need very little moisture and can absorb it from the air.

I have a thick layer of fat to keep me warm, and I use my strong tusks to break ice or to pull myself out of the ice.

❷ Draw a line to join each animal to its habitat.

mountains   coast   savannah   grasslands

❗ A **microhabitat** is a small area within a larger one which provides the perfect home for **minibeasts**, for example, a fallen log, a flowerbed, or even a rotting apple.

❸ Go on a minibeast hunt. Below are some examples of microhabitats you might search. Circle the ones you find.

under a stone   compost heap   grass   under leaves

old log   pond   rockpool   puddle

On the following page are some examples of minibeasts.

Circle the minibeasts that you find on your hunt.

ant, beetle, caterpillar, earwig, fly, worm, grasshopper, mussel, water boatman, millipede, limpet, bee, slug, moth, ladybird, butterfly, spider, hermit crab, crane fly, woodlouse, snail, wasp

Record your results below in a tally chart or pictogram. Think about how each beast survives in its habitat.

# habitat changes

Humans alter the world's habitats in a variety of ways. But some animals also make changes to their environment.

Beavers are animal engineers! They make big changes to their habitat by cutting down trees, building dams, creating ponds and building lodges.

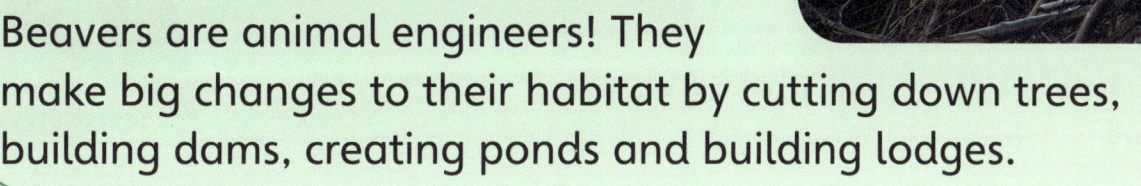

Look at these animals. What changes have they made?

woodpecker

termite

prairie dog

**Did you know?**
Other creatures use these homes, too. Owls and wrens live in abandoned woodpecker holes, snakes and jackrabbits shelter in prairie dog burrows, and leopards and cheetahs use termite mounds to scan for prey!

# habitat profile: the rainforest

It is almost always raining in rainforests. There are so many trees in the Amazon rain forest that they form several habitats. The habitats are in layers all the way from the forest floor to the treetops.

Rainforests are warm places where trees grow all year round. Tall trees with thick leaves and branches shelter and produce food for all kinds of animals.

**toucan**

Many animals, such as the toucan, live in the trees. There is so much food there that some animals never go to the ground! Others, such as the jaguar, find food on the forest floor.

**jaguar**

The forest floor is dark as little sunlight can get through the leaves above. Dark-loving plants such as ferns, moss and mushrooms and fungi grow there, along with many insects.

Read the passage above and look at the picture on the next page. Then write the answers to these questions.

a) Name two animals that spend time on the forest floor.

b) Name two plants that live on the forest floor.

c) In which layer does the eagle live?

d) In which layer can you see the sloth?

e) Name an animal in the understory layer.

harpy eagle

macaw parrot

**emergent layer**

sloth

spider monkey

**canopy layer**

quetzal

woodpecker

**understory layer**

anaconda

jaguar

tapir

**forest floor**

# make a mini rainforest

**What you need:**

- glass/plastic jar or container with a lid or top that can be sealed
- soil
- sand 
- small pebbles
- small plants, such as ferns or clover
- moss (optional) 
- water

**What you do:**

1. Clean the jar.
2. Pour sand on the bottom.
3. Cover with pebbles for drainage.
4. Cover with soil.
5. Set your plants (and moss) in the soil.
6. Water until the soil is soaked.
7. Seal the top.
8. Place in sunlight, but not direct sun or your plants will cook!

**What happens next:**

Observe your mini rainforest daily. Open the top once a week to let in air so that the inside doesn't get mouldy.

Keep a **record** of the changes you see. Are there droplets of water on the sides? Is the soil moist or dry? What other changes do you see?

# working together

! The living things in a habitat **depend** on each other. Trees and plants provide shelter and food for animals. Animals help plants by spreading their pollen and seeds.

How do each of these living things depend on each other? Complete the sentences using words from the word bank.

The bee needs _____ from the flower. It helps the flower by spreading _____ .

Woodpeckers eat _____ which are damaging trees from under the bark. They also make _____ in the tree trunks.

Bears eat large quantities of _____ and then disperse their _____ through their scat.

The anemone provides _____ for the clownfish. The clownfish _____ off other fish, and its waste is food for the anemone.

| insects | scares | seeds | nests |
| pollen | berries | nectar | shelter |

# who eats what

**1** These animals are all **herbivores**—they only eat plants. Join the animal to the food it would eat.

**2** These animals are all **carnivores**—they only eat meat. Join the animal to the food it would eat.

**Did you know?**
Plants can be carnivores, too. The Venus Flytrap traps and eats insects, snapping its leaves shut in milliseconds!

**3** Some animals are **omnivores**—they eat both plants and meat. Circle two things that each animal might eat.

# food chains

> A **food chain** is a series of living things which are linked to one another because each one feeds on the next one to it in the series. Energy passes along the food chain.

energy → producer → consumer → consumer

**1** Circle the living thing that could go at the end of the food chain below, and draw it in the box.

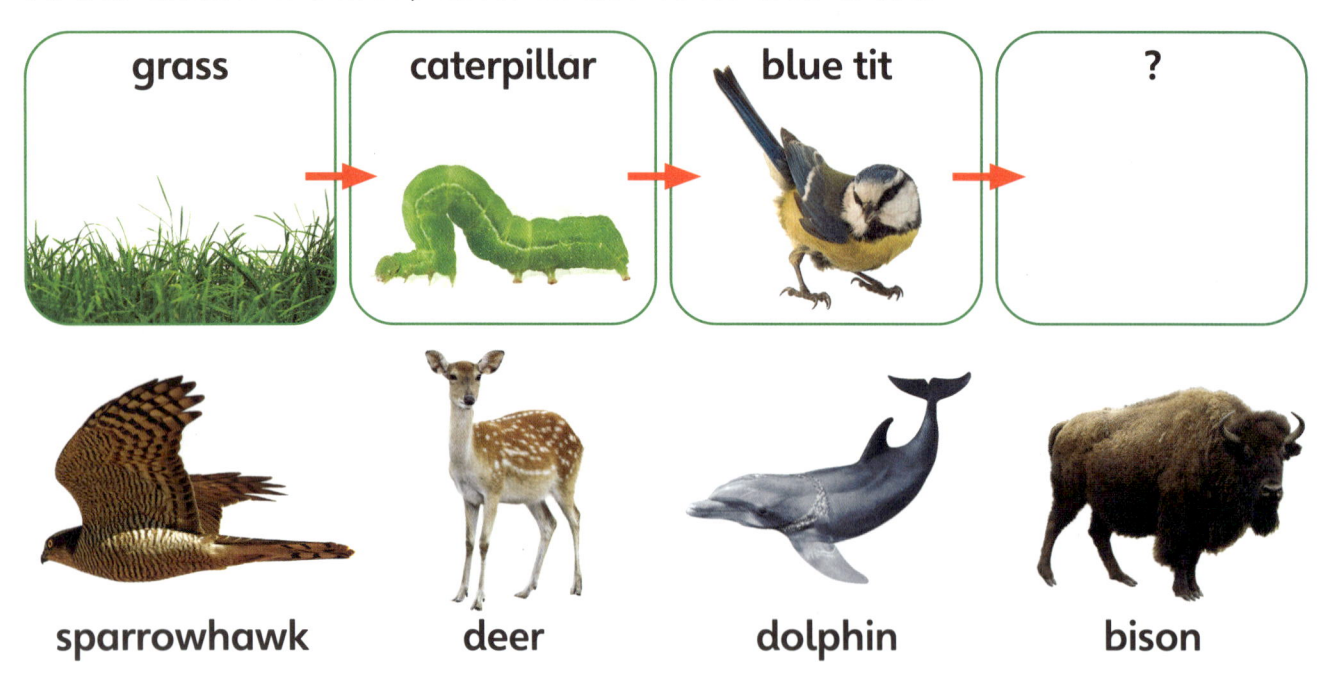

grass → caterpillar → blue tit → ?

sparrowhawk    deer    dolphin    bison

**2** In the food chain above, is the caterpillar a **producer** or a **consumer**? Circle the correct answer.

producer    consumer

The arrows in a food chain show the direction in which energy is flowing, not what eats what!

**3** Circle the living thing that could go at the start of the food chain below, and draw it in the box.

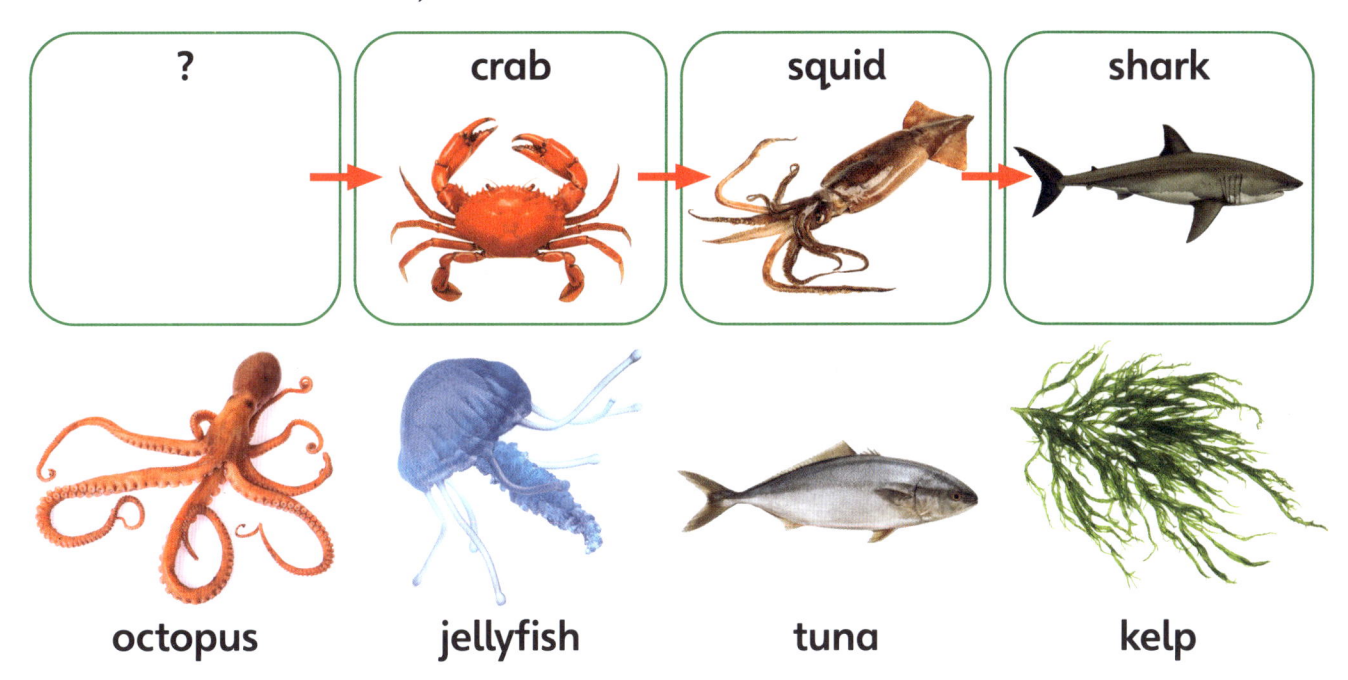

| ? | → | crab | → | squid | → | shark |

octopus    jellyfish    tuna    kelp

**4** Put these living things in the order they would be in a food chain.

**a** hedgehog    lettuce    badger    slug

☐ ☐ ☐ ☐

**b** rabbit    eagle    fox    grass

☐ ☐ ☐ ☐

# plants and what they need

**1** Most plants grow from **seeds**. If the seed is in the right environment, a small **seedling** will grow from it. This will grow into a full-grown **plant**, which will make **new seeds**.

Put the steps into order [1–4].

Each part of the plant has a function. **Roots** take in water and nutrients and anchor the plant in the ground. **Leaves** help the plant make food for itself. The **stem** supports the plant and transports water and nutrients. **Flowers** attract insects to help with pollination. The **fruit** contains the new **seeds**.

a tomato plant

**2** Label this tomato plant from the choices below.

- flower
- fruit
- seeds
- roots
- leaves
- stem

**3** To grow and be healthy all plants need certain things. Circle the **five** things that they need.

sand   air   wind   water   cereal

nutrients   light   rocks   warmth

Complete the sentences below.

Plants need _____ and _____ from the sun.

Plants need _____ or they will dry out and die.

Many plants get the _____ they need from soil.

Plants need _____ to breathe and to make food.

**4** Some plants need more water than others. Circle the plant that needs the *least* water.

**5** Some plants get most of their nutrients from water, not soil. Circle the plant that gets its nutrients from *water*.

**6** What might happen if you try to grow a plant in the dark?

# thirsty work

*Carry out this fun experiment to see how plants 'drink' water.*

! Plants cannot drink water like animals can. Water and nutrients enter through the the roots, then travel upwards along the stem to other parts of the plant.

**What you need:**

- a few white carnations
- food colouring
- glasses or jars
- water

**What you do:**

1. Fill each glass half full with water.
2. Carefully cut the end of each flower's stem diagonally, and place each flower in a separate glass.
3. Add 10 drops of food colouring to each glass – a different colour in each glass.
4. Watch what happens over the next hours and days.

**What happens next:**

Keep a record of the changes you see. Draw your results below.

# seeds and bulbs

> **Seeds** and **bulbs** have a store of food inside them. They need water to *germinate* (start growing), but most do *not* need light, as they already have a store of energy.

### The life cycle of the sunflower

The seed is inside a hard shell. A tiny green shoot—the seedling—pops out of the ground, and under the soil, roots grow downward. The seedling grows upward, and more leaves grow out from the stem. The plant produces a flower bud. Within the sunflower, hundreds of pods appear. Each will mature into a sunflower seed. The plant withers and dies, but the seeds are ready to start the cycle again.

Seeds can start to grow in the dark, but to grow into healthy plants the seedlings need light.

The following pictures show the life cycle of the sunflower. Place them in order [1–6].

## The life cycle of the daffodil

In late winter or early spring, daffodil sprouts appear, sending up leaves and buds using the stored energy in the bulb. After flowering, the leaves also die back. The bulbs become dormant during the summer. In the autumn, they produce roots. As spring approaches, the stored energy in the bulb provides food for the next year's daffodil growth.

**1** Add labels to show the life cycle of the daffodil.

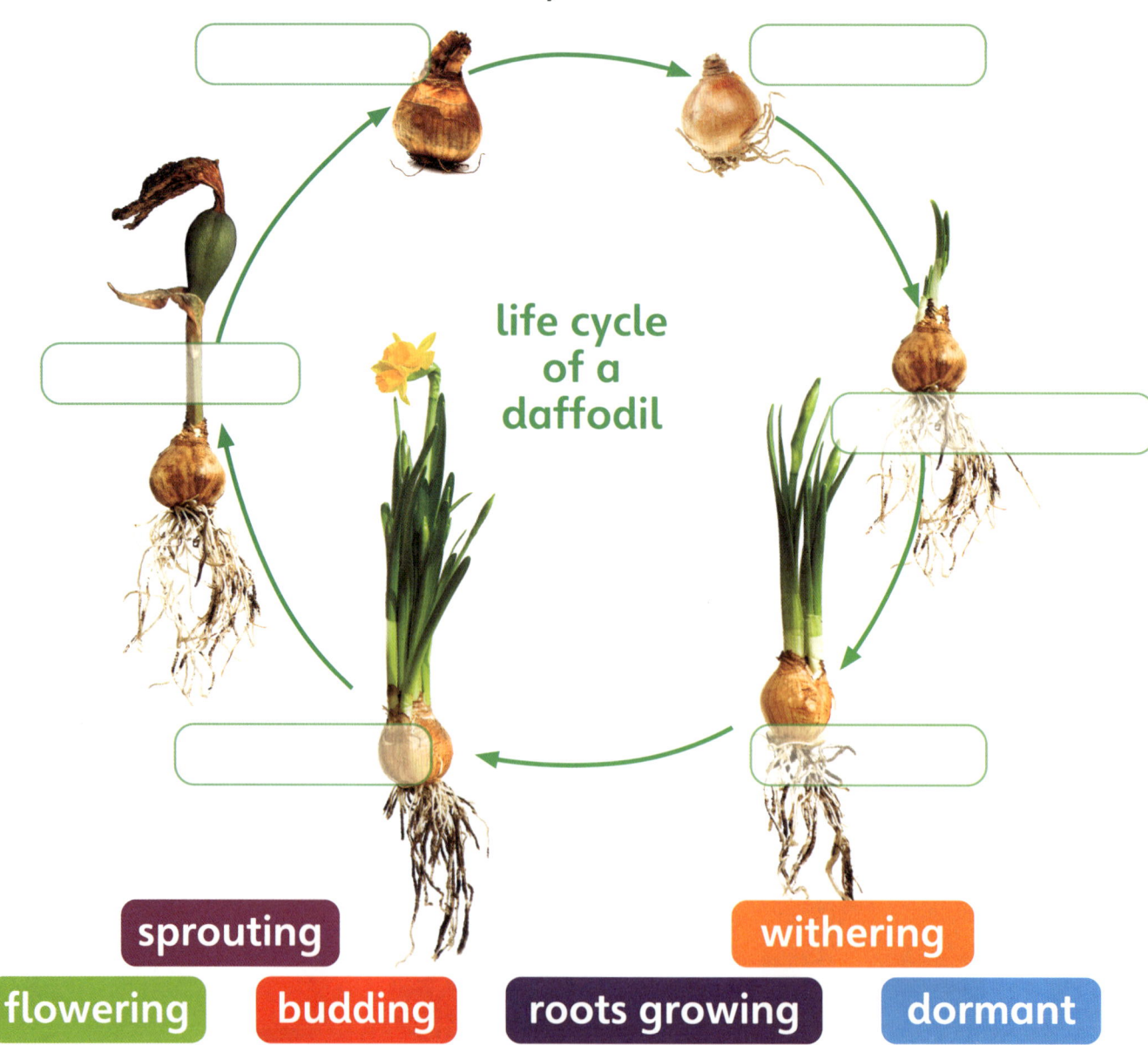

life cycle of a daffodil

sprouting  withering
flowering  budding  roots growing  dormant

**2** Match the word to the correct definition.

| | |
|---|---|
| life cycle | when a seed soaks up water and a new plant begins to grow |
| germination | a substance that is needed for healthy growth |
| nutrients | the journey of a living thing from beginning to end |

**3** What do seeds and bulbs need to start growing? Circle the correct answer.

light and air          water and warmth          cold and dry

**4** An alien wants to know how to grow its own plant. Use the following pictures to help you write instructions.

Why not grow your own seed or bulb? Keep a record of its growth.

# animal life cycles

Animals start off as babies and grow into adults. Some animals give birth to live young which look like a small version of the adult. Other animals, such as reptiles and birds, lay eggs. Their babies hatch from the eggs. Still others, such as amphibians and fish, give birth to offspring which look very different.

**1** Draw a line to match the baby to the adult.

**2** Do the same for this set of animals.

❸ Add labels to show the human life cycle.

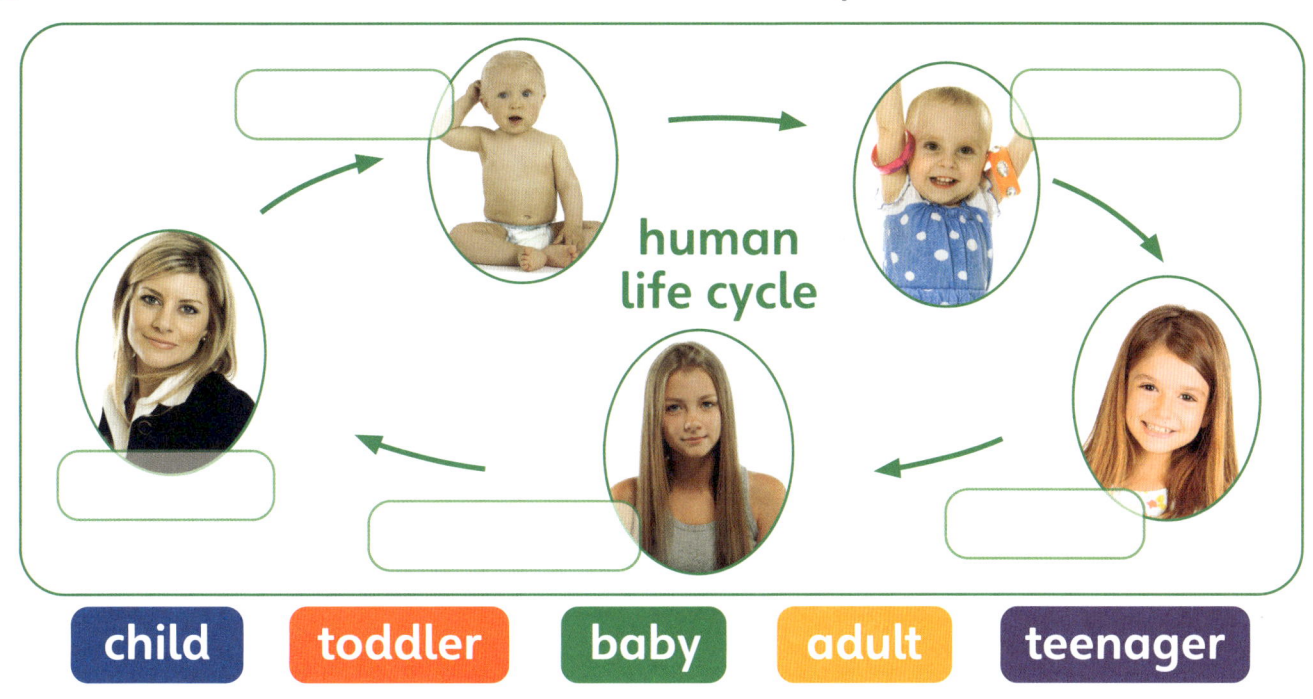

**human life cycle**

| child | toddler | baby | adult | teenager |

❹ Look at the diagram of the life cycle of a sea turtle. Then answer the questions.

**egg**
Sea turtles lay their eggs in the sand.

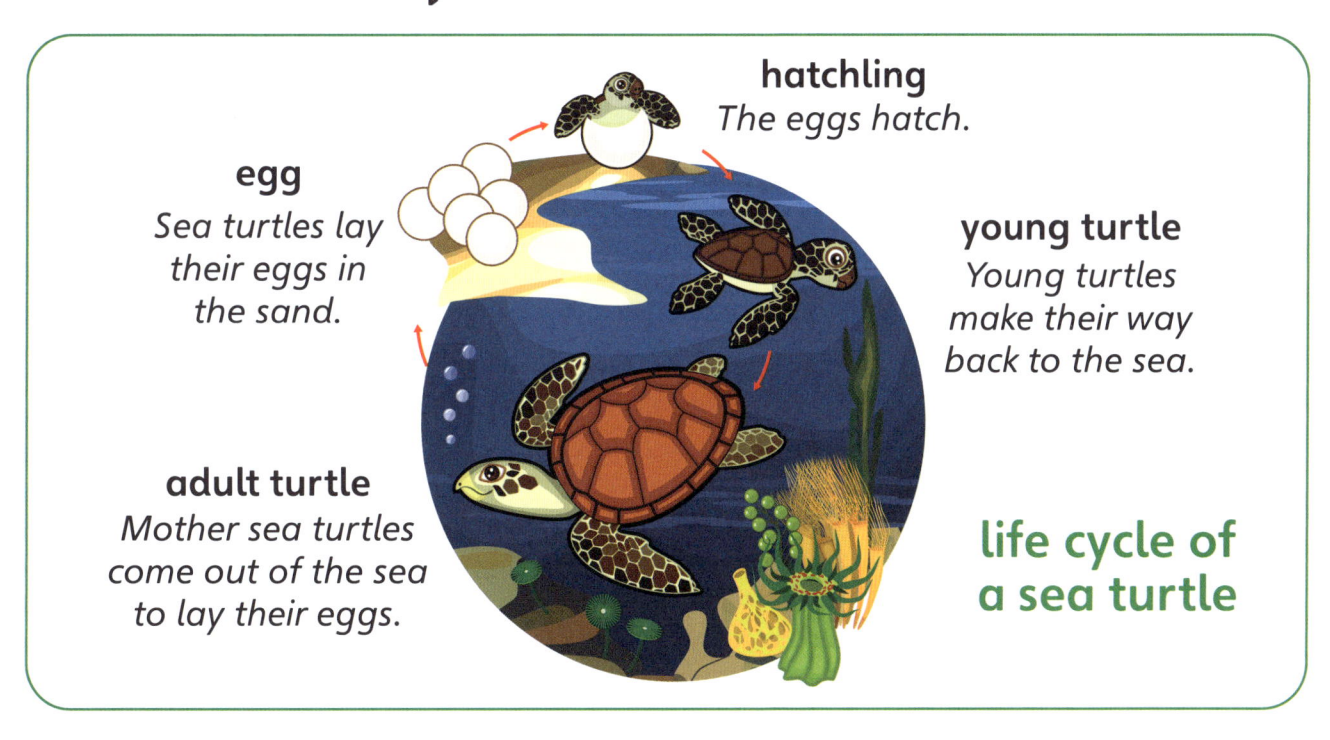

**hatchling**
The eggs hatch.

**young turtle**
Young turtles make their way back to the sea.

**adult turtle**
Mother sea turtles come out of the sea to lay their eggs.

**life cycle of a sea turtle**

Where do sea turtles lay their eggs?

How many stages are there in its life cycle?

**5** Draw arrows to complete the diagram of the life cycle of a frog. Make sure they point the right way.

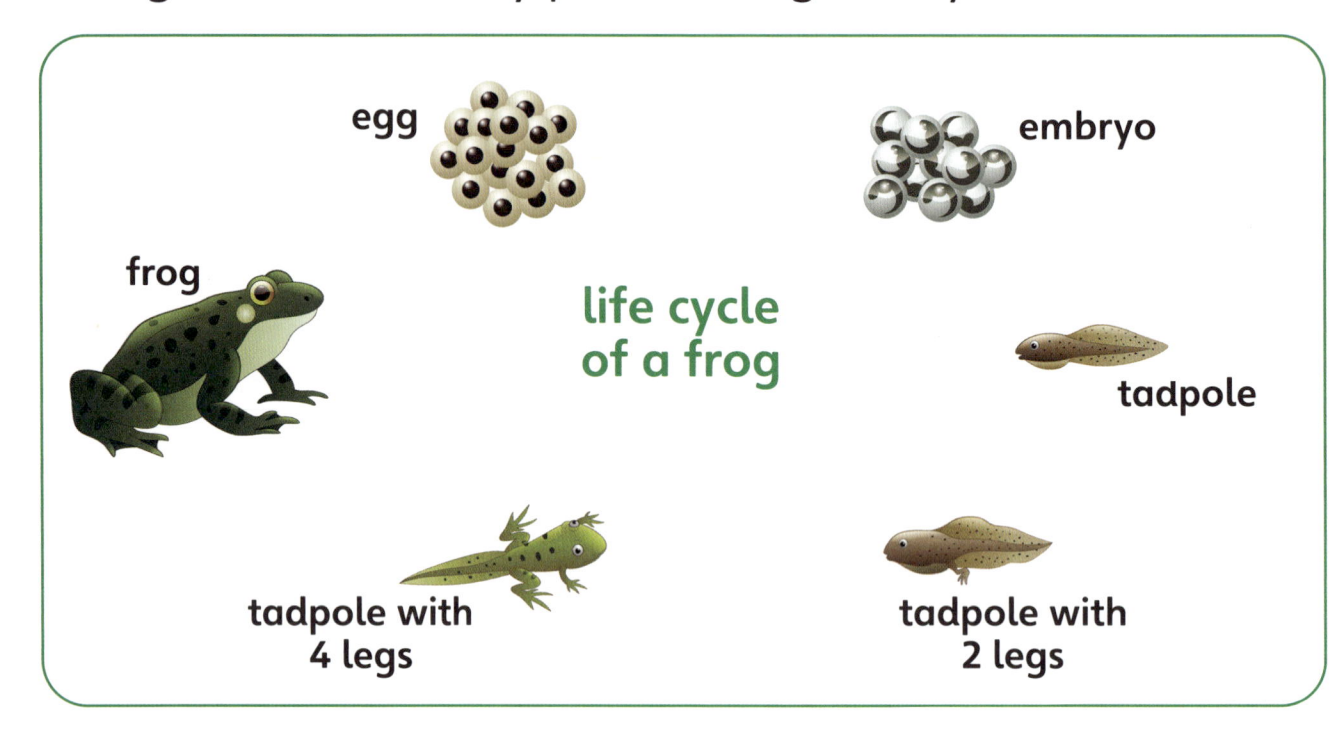

egg

embryo

frog

life cycle of a frog

tadpole

tadpole with 4 legs

tadpole with 2 legs

**6** Draw the right animal to fill in the gaps in the life cycles.

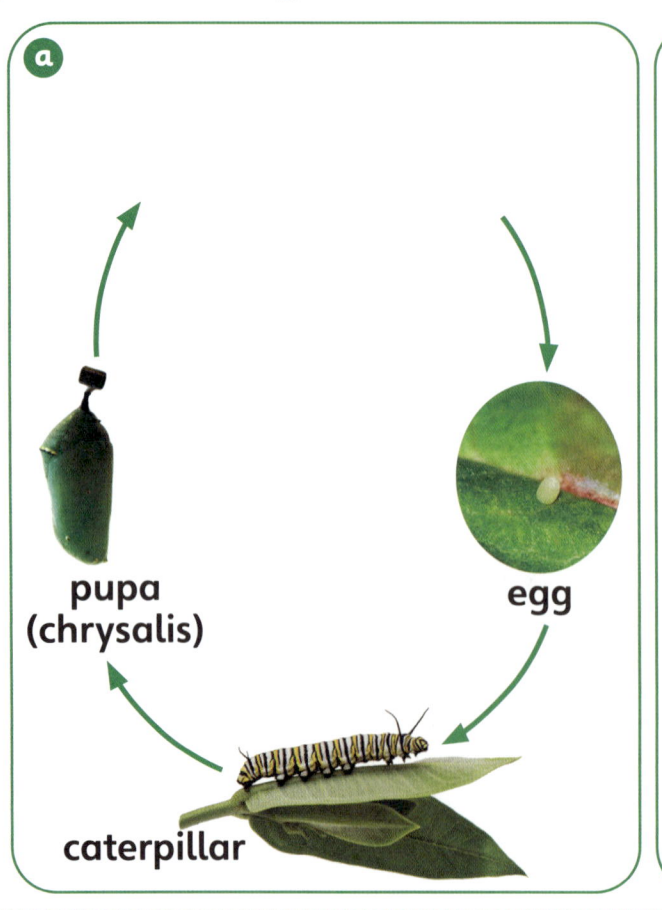

a

pupa (chrysalis)

egg

caterpillar

b

chick

hen

# what animals need

**1** All animals need certain things to stay alive. Circle the things below in blue that you **want**. Circle in red the things that you **need** to survive.

- shelter
- bed
- electricity
- air (oxygen)
- clothes
- bath
- money
- juice
- chocolate
- car
- water
- television
- toys
- food

**2** What are the basic needs of *all* animals? Unscramble the letters and write the words.

| tlsehre | | taerw | |
| dofo | | rai | |

Animals also need **space** to live. Some need a lot of space. Others need only a small space.

**3** Circle the animal that gets the **oxygen** it needs from *water* rather than breathing air.

**4** Match the animal to the **food**.

**5** Match the animal to the **shelter**.

338

**6** Circle the animal that *doesn't* need a lot of **water**.

**7** Circle the animal that needs the *most* **space**.

**8** Your cousin has promised to look after your dog while you go on holiday for two weeks. Write some detailed instructions, saying exactly what your dog needs to stay happy and healthy.

## staying healthy

**1** In order to stay healthy, some things are very important. Unscramble the letters to identify each thing.

cserixee

gyeenih

labandec ietd

What types of exercise do you do?

How do you keep yourself clean?

You should do at least one hour of exercise each day. It helps keep you healthy both physically and mentally.

Keeping clean helps to stop germs spreading.

! Food is commonly divided into five **food groups**.

- fruit and vegetables
- carbohydrates
- protein
- dairy
- fats and sugars

In a **balanced diet** we eat the right amount of foods from the different food groups.

❷ Add labels to the diagram.

*These foods give us energy.*

*These foods are good sources of fibre, vitamins and minerals*

*These foods help our bodies to repair themselves.*

*These foods give us calcium for strong bones.*

*These foods help help store energy for our bodies.*

Some sections are bigger than others. What do you think that means?

It is also essential to drink plenty of **water**.

**3** Circle in green the food you should eat plenty of in a balanced diet. Circle in red the food you should only eat a little of.

**4** Draw a meal on the plate below that would fit with a balanced diet.

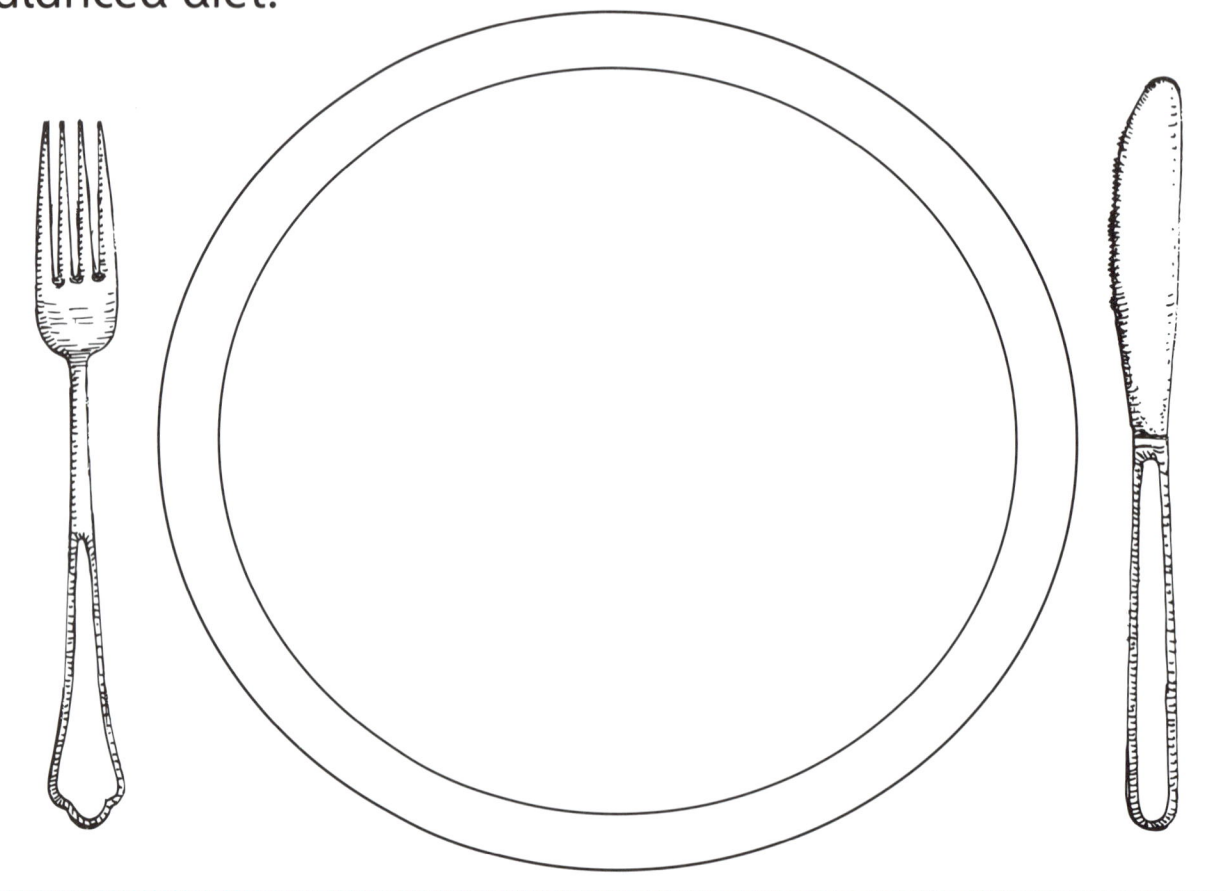

342

**5** Make your own health plan. Think of five things that you could do each day to keep yourself healthy, and either write them below, or draw pictures of yourself doing them. Look at the pictures on previous pages for ideas.

# materials and their uses

> **Natural materials**, such as wood or cotton, are found in the world around us. **Man-made materials**, such as glass or paper, are materials that have been changed through chemical processes.

**1** Circle the natural materials in green, and the man-made materials in purple.

- gold
- wool
- brass
- paper
- clay
- leather
- polyester
- cotton
- glass
- plastic
- wood

**2** Match each property to its **opposite**.

- transparent
- heavy
- waterproof
- rigid
- absorbent
- lightweight
- flexible
- opaque

Which of the above properties would be useful for a:

window ............................................  sponge ............................................

raincoat ..........................................  rope ...............................................

**3** Join the object to the material it is made out of.

brick   plastic   rubber   clay   fabric

**properties of materials**

lightweight  strong  waterproof  flexible  smooth  rough
hard  weatherproof  rigid  transparent  durable  soft

**4** Using the word bank, answer the following questions about the items above. Suggest two properties for each item. You can use words more than once.

What makes **bricks** suitable for building walls?

What makes **plastic** suitable for water bottles?

What makes **rubber** suitable for tyres?

What makes **fabric** suitable for clothes?

What makes **clay** suitable for mugs?

**5** Add labels to the car below, saying what material each part is made of, and what makes that material suitable.

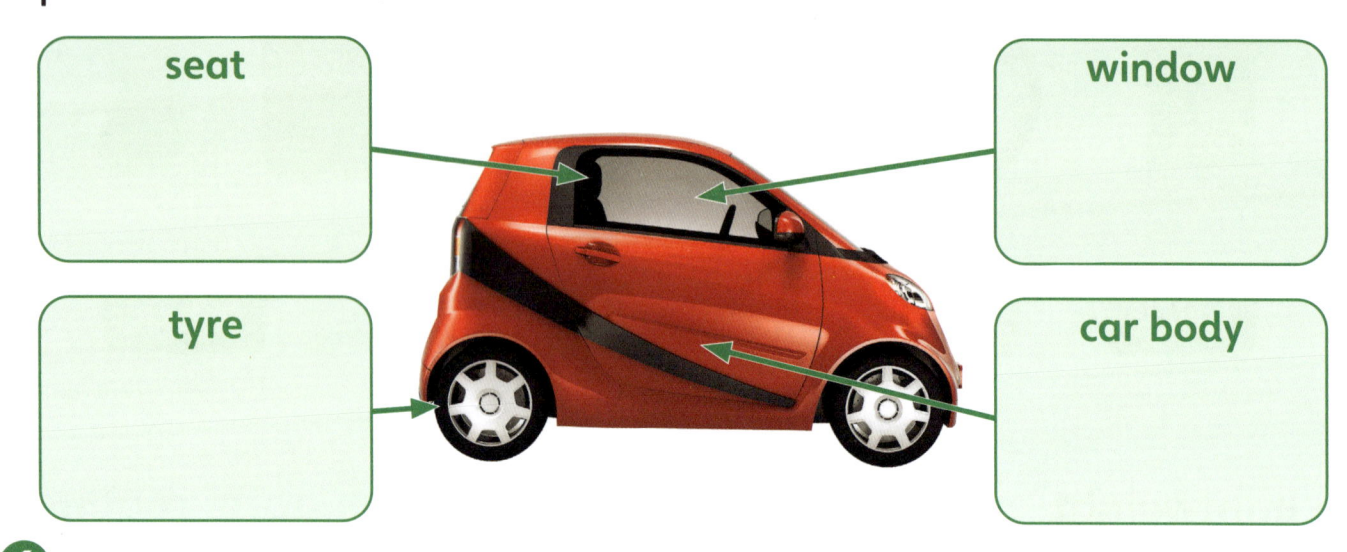

- seat
- window
- tyre
- car body

**6**

**a** Sometimes more than one material would be suitable. Name three materials you could use to make a spoon.

**b** What do they have in common?

**c** Materials can be used for more than one thing. Write down three uses for glass.

**7** What would be wrong with the following?

**a** a raincoat made of paper

**b** a window made of brick

**c** a kettle made of fabric

# changing materials

Materials can be changed in different ways. Draw a line to match the picture with the description.

| folded | twisted | stretched | bent | squashed |

Can you change the following? Carry out your own investigation. Complete the table below, using ✓ or ✗.

|  | fold | twist | stretch | bend | squash |
|---|---|---|---|---|---|
|   |  |  |  |  |  |
| 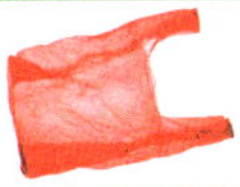  |  |  |  |  |  |
|  |  |  |  |  |  |
|   |  |  |  |  |  |
|   |  |  |  |  |  |
|   |  |  |  |  |  |
|   |  |  |  |  |  |
|   |  |  |  |  |  |
|   |  |  |  |  |  |

# inventors and inventions

**waterproof clothing**

**air-filled rubber tyre**

**'invisible' glass**

**industrial fibres**

**Charles Macintosh**
(1766 – 1843)
Invention: Waterproof clothing by sandwiching a layer of liquid rubber (made with naphtha) between two layers of cloth.

**John Dunlop**
(1840 – 1921)
Invention: The pneumatic (air-filled) rubber tire, originally used for bicycles, but subsequently used in cars and other motor vehicles.

**Katharine Burr Blodgett**
(1898 – 1979)
Invention: 'Invisible' or non-reflecting glass, which is used in spectacles, windscreens, camera lenses and picture frames.

**Stephanie Kwolek**
(1923 – 2014)
Invention: Lightweight but extremely tough industrial fibres used in bulletproof vests, spacecrafts, helmets and tennis racquets!

Write two properties for each of the inventions above.

Invent your own new material. What would it be used for? Draw it below and explain how it works.

# Geography

# seven continents

**1** The planet we live on, planet Earth, is a huge sphere! The **North Pole** is at the top and the **South Pole** is at the bottom. The **Equator** is like a belt around the middle.

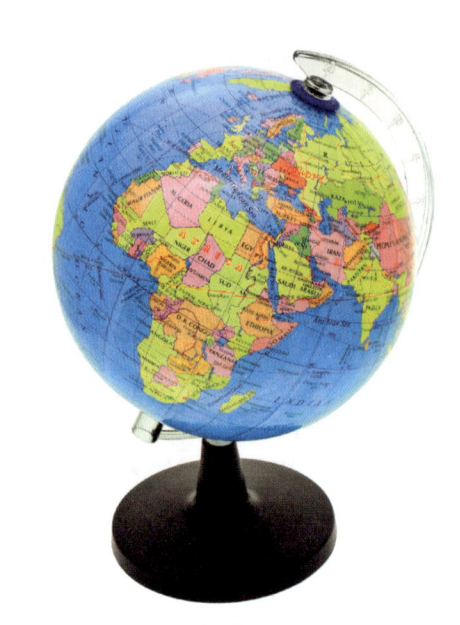

We divide it into seven **continents**:

> North America    South America    Africa
> Europe    Asia    Antarctica    Australia

Fill the continent names in on the map below.

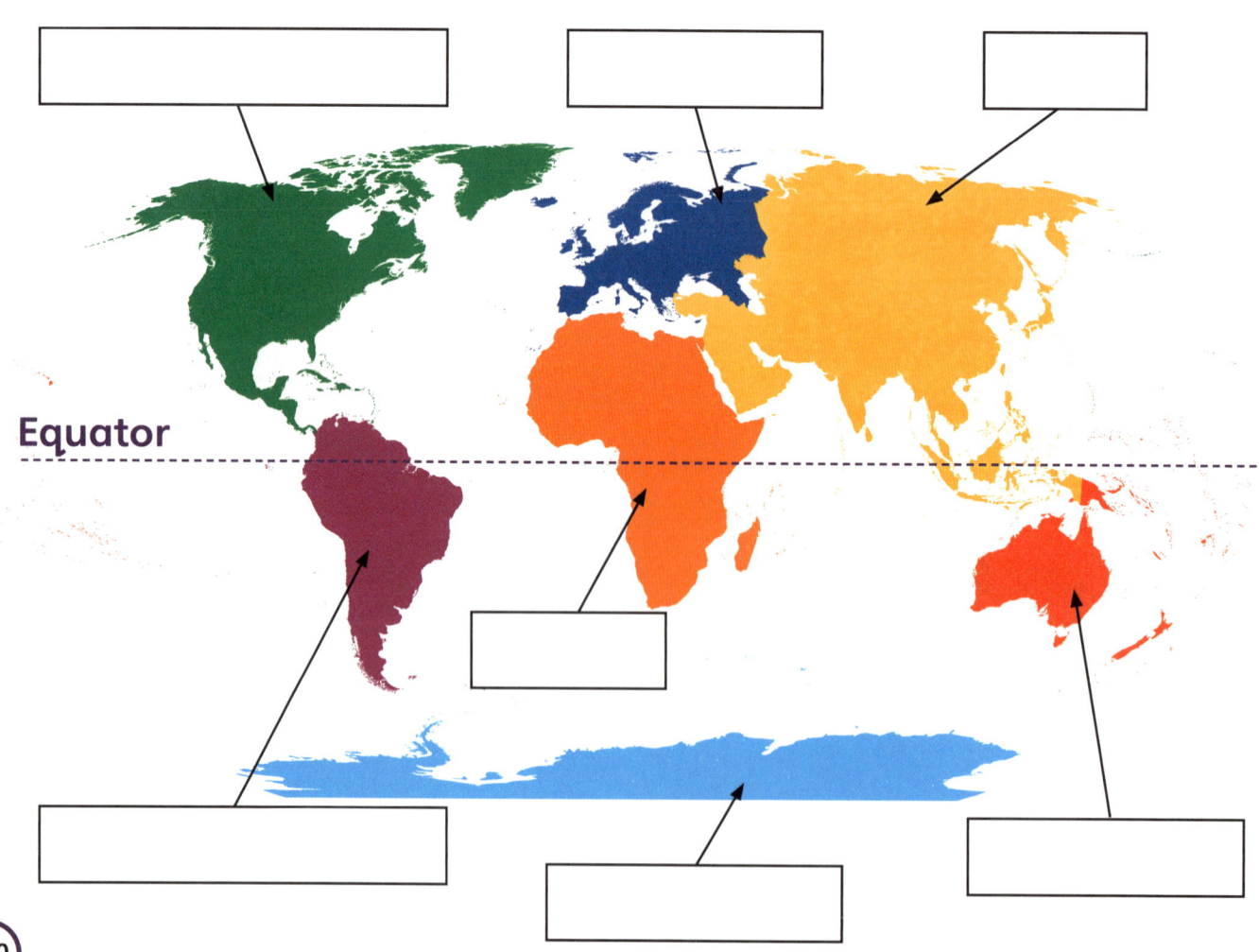

Equator

**2** Look at the map, then answer the questions below.

GEOGRAPHY

a  Which ocean lies between South America and Africa?

b  Which ocean is named after a country?

c  Which ocean lies between North America and Asia?

d  Which continents are mainly below the Equator?

e  Which continent is entirely below the Equator?

f  Which ocean is nearest to where *you* live?

**GEOGRAPHY**

> ❗ The **Equator** is **hot** all year round, and the **North** and **South Poles** are always **cold**. Everywhere else, the weather changes according to the time of year.

❸ Imagine you are packing for a trip. Circle in blue the clothes you would pack to visit the **North Pole**. Circle in red those you would pack to visit the **Equator**.

❹ Within each **continent** there are big differences in geography and climate. Below are pictures from one place in each continent. Write a description of each picture.

**North America**

**South America**

352

Europe

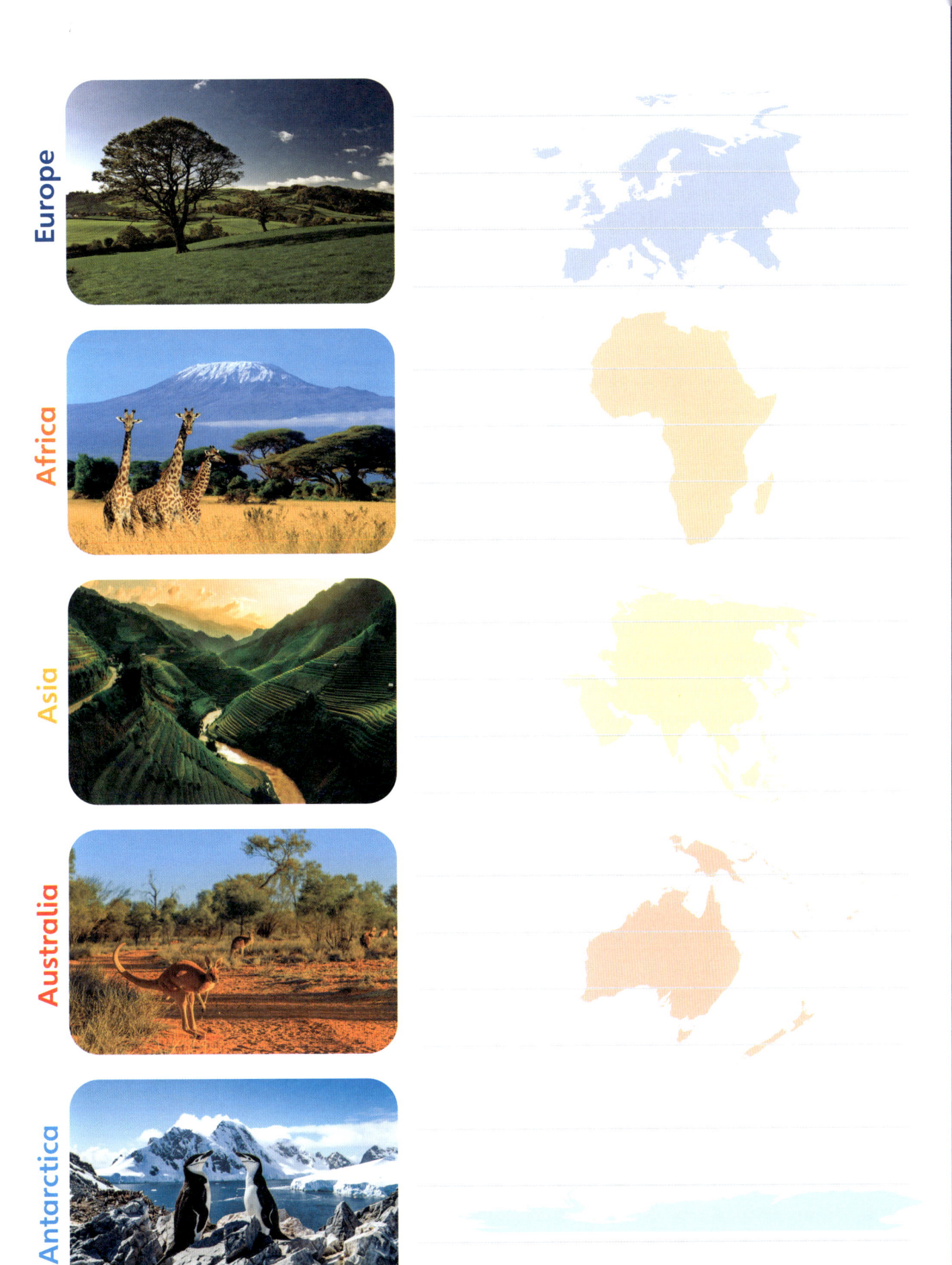

Africa

Asia

Australia

Antarctica

GEOGRAPHY

# north, south, east or west?

> This symbol is a **compass rose**. It points to the directions **N**orth, **S**outh, **E**ast and **W**est on a map. This one also shows intermediate directions such as Northwest **(NW)**.

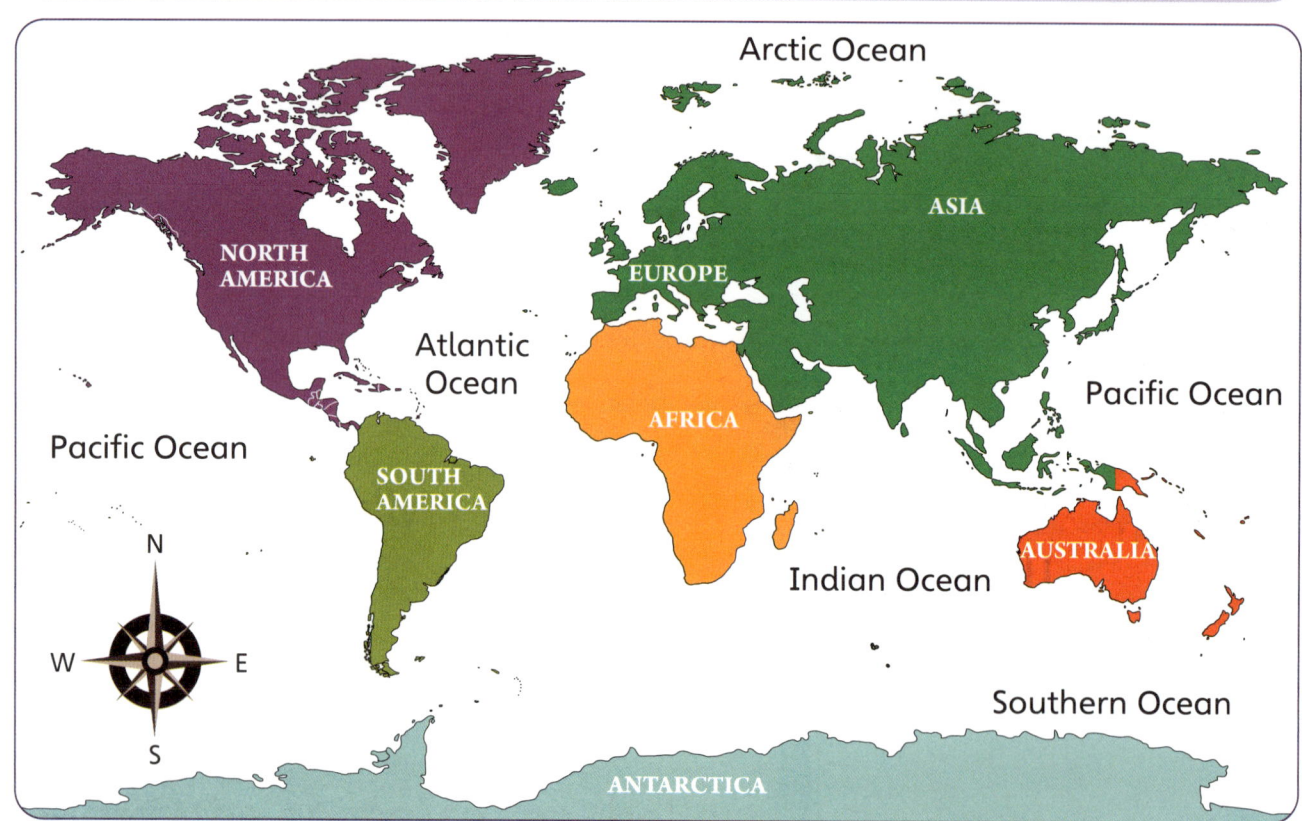

**1** Look at the map above. Complete each sentence.

The Indian Ocean is located to the _____ of Asia.

Europe is located to the _____ of Africa.

North America is located to the _____ of Europe.

Australia is located to the _____ of Africa.

The southernmost continent is _____.

The northernmost ocean is the _____.

**2** Look at the map below. Then complete each sentence.

**a** The lake is _____ of the factory.

The supermarket is _____ of the hospital.

The tyre centre is _____ of the petrol station.

The school is _____ of the circus.

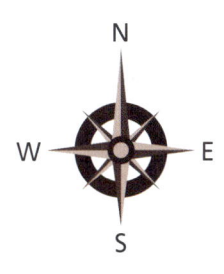

**b** Circle the correct answer.

The tyre centre is   near to   far from   the petrol station.

The school is   near to   far from   the factory.

The hospital is   near to   far from   the supermarket.

# around town

Look at the map below. Then answer the questions on the next page.

✓ or ✗

**a** Where is the ice cream shop?
- By the fire station. ☐
- In the park. ☐

**b** What would you pass on your way from the cinema to the hotel?
- The pharmacy. ☐
- The fire station. ☐

**c** What is next to the supermarket?
- The school. ☐
- The theatre. ☐

Follow the directions. Where do they take you?

**d** Stand at the entrance to the church on Church Street, facing the road. Go to the end of the road and turn right. Take the first left. What is on your left?

**e** Exit the stadium on West Street. Turn right. Take the first road immediately on your left. Take the next right. What building is on your right?

**f** Your granny has arrived at the bus station and wants to go to the church. Put the directions below in order [1–3].

| Take the first left, and the church is on your left. | Turn left out of the bus station. | Turn right at the end of the road. |

☐ ☐ ☐

# map symbols

> Some maps use **symbols**. The **key** explains what they mean.

Look at the symbols on the map below.

Draw the missing symbols to complete the map key. Draw two more symbols of your own. Add them to the map.

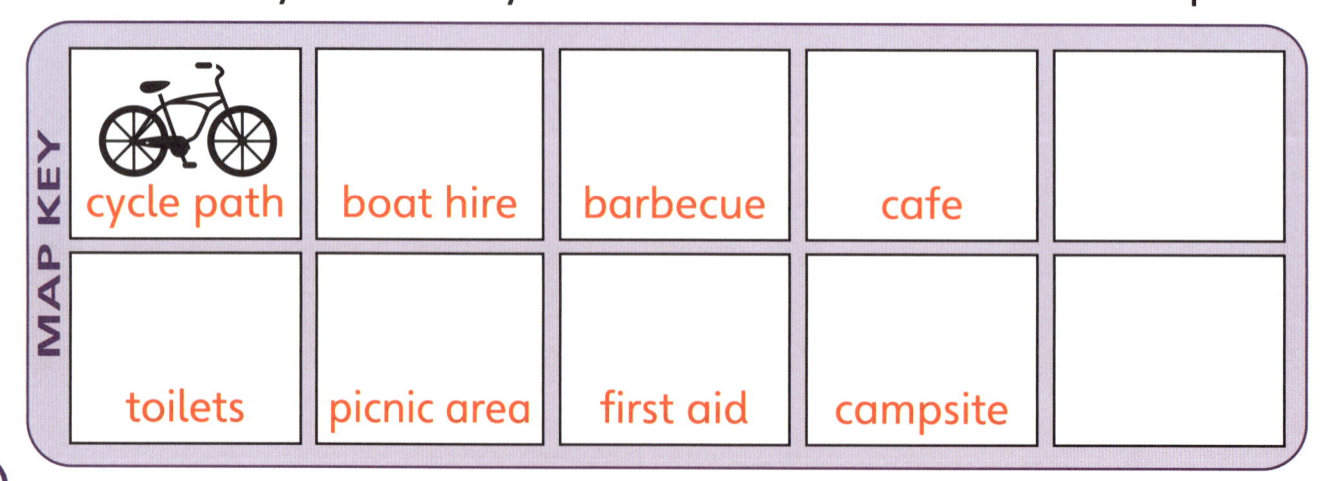

| MAP KEY | | | | |
|---|---|---|---|---|
| cycle path | boat hire | barbecue | cafe | |
| toilets | picnic area | first aid | campsite | |

Complete the map key below by adding a label for each symbol.

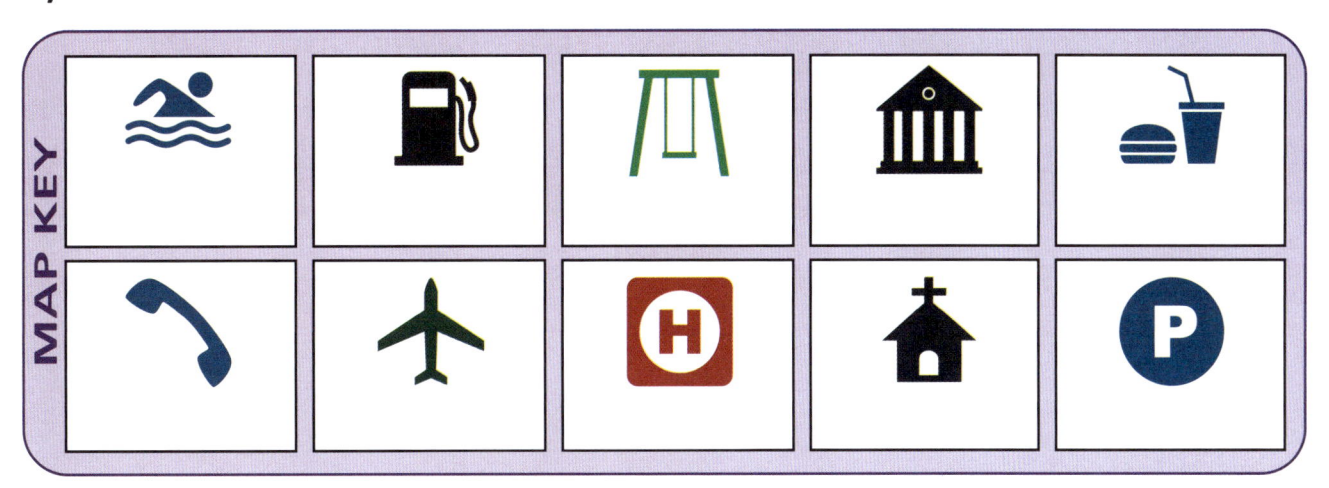

| MAP KEY | | | | |
|---|---|---|---|---|
| swimming | petrol station | playground | museum | fast food |
| telephone | airport | hospital | church | parking |

Draw your own map of a town. Choose some of the symbols above and add them to your map. Think carefully about where each place should be.

# a bird's-eye view

GEOGRAPHY

Look carefully at the photo below. See if you can spot the following things:

church    industrial park    main road    river

Draw arrows and labels to point them out.

Draw a bird's-eye view of your bedroom, showing your bed and any furniture.

# History

# keeping in touch

**1** Ways of communicating have changed greatly over time. Join each picture to its description. Then place the pictures in **chronological** order, starting with the oldest [1] to the most recent [5].

| telephone | printing press | cave paintings | email | telegraph messages |
|---|---|---|---|---|
| People could talk to others far away. | Books could be printed quickly and cheaply. | Cave pictures might have been messages. | People can access information online. | People could send messages through wires. |

**2** kings of communication

| William Caxton | Samuel Morse | Alexander Graham Bell | Tim Berners-Lee |
|---|---|---|---|
| (c. 1422 – 1491) Invention: He is thought to be the first person to introduce a printing press into England. | (1791 – 1872) Invention: He helped to invent the telegraph system, and Morse code to send messages. | (1847 – 1922) Invention: He was the first inventor to patent a working telephone. | (1955 – ) Invention: He invented the World Wide Web so information can be shared on the Internet. |

What did the first printing presses do?

What code was used to send messages by telegraph?

**3** Write about some ways of communicating *you* use.

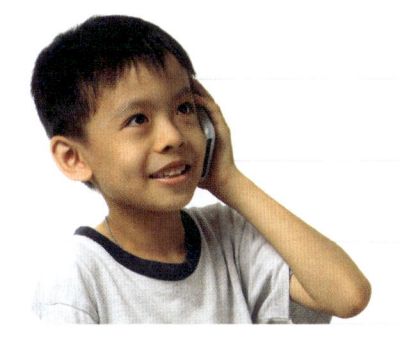

**4** You have won a competition. Your friend lives on the other side of the world. How might you tell them?

Imagine you live in the days of Samuel Morse. How could you tell your friend the news?

Draw a picture of you winning the competition to go on a cave wall!

**Did you know?**
January 1, 1983 is considered the official birthday of the Internet, but the online world took on the form we know in 1989, when Tim Berners-Lee invented the World Wide Web.

# spotlight on the past: The Great Fire of London

The Great Fire of London took place over 350 years ago, in 1666. It started in a bakery on Pudding Lane, and quickly spread through the wooden buildings and narrow lanes. Soon flames were raging and smoke covered the city. Wind fanned the flames. Before the fire began, there had been a long drought, so the city was very dry. There were no fire engines or hosepipes – only leather buckets, metal hooks and fire squirts, and it was difficult to fetch water from the river.

The fire lasted four days, and destroyed over 13,000 homes. Much of London was burnt to the ground. After the fire, new buildings were built out of brick and stone, with more space between them. It took ten years to rebuild the city.

People at the time wrote about the fire in letters and newspapers, and Samuel Pepys, who worked for the Navy, famously wrote about it in his diary, which is why we know what happened.

**1** Read the passage, then answer the questions.

**a** What year did the fire start?

**b** Where did the fire start?

**c** What was used to fight the fire?

**d** How long did the fire last?

**2** Why did the fire spread so fast and so far? Circle some of the reasons below.

- There had been no rain so it was very dry
- Water had to be fetched from the river
- The buildings were mainly made of wood
- The buildings were made of brick
- The buildings were close together
- Fire fighting equipment was poor
- The streets were very wide

**Did you know?**
With its narrow streets and wooden houses, London in 1666 would have looked rather like this picture of the Shambles in York.

**3** Nowadays, we have modern equipment to fight fires. Describe some of the differences between fire fighting at the time of the Great Fire, and today.

### Did you know?
Some people think this rhyme is about the Great Fire of London.

### London's Burning
London's burning, London's burning.
Fetch the engines, fetch the engines.
Fire, fire! Fire, fire!
Pour on water, pour on water.

**4** Write your own poem about a fire. Use some of the words below.

crackling  blazing
fierce  roaring
flickering  smoky
scorching  glowing
violent  wild

**5** Imagine you were present at the Great Fire of London. What would it have been like? Use the boxes below to write about it.

Things you would have **seen**.

Things you would have **heard**.

Things you would have **smelt**.

Things you would have **felt**.

Things you would have **tasted**.

# history near you

Write about an event that happened where you lived – something that changed the place. It might have happened long ago, or it could be more recent.

What happened?

When did it happen?

What changed?

Draw a picture of what happened, or what changed.

# nurses through time

**Florence Nightingale** was born in Italy in 1820, but grew up in England in a rich family. She trained to be a nurse in Germany, and afterwards worked at a hospital in London. When Britain went to war with Russia on the Crimean Peninsula, Florence gathered a group of nurses and travelled to Scutari Hospital in Turkey in 1854 to take care of injured soldiers.

When she arrived, the hospital was understaffed, overcrowded, smelly and dirty, and some of the soldiers had to lie on the ground. Most soldiers were dying due to infection or disease because of the conditions. Florence made sure the hospital was thoroughly cleaned, and made many improvements. She became famous as "the lady with the lamp" as she walked around caring for the soldiers at night. Her work saved many lives.

On her return to England she set up a training school for nurses, which was the beginning of modern nursing. She died at home in 1910 at the age of 90, and is still remembered today.

**1** Make your own fact file for Florence Nightingale.

### Florence Nightingale

Year of birth:

Year of death:

Significant achievements:

Interesting fact:

❷ What happened first? Put the following sentences in the correct order from first [1] to last [4].

| Florence trained to be a nurse in Germany | Florence was born in Italy | Florence set up a nursing school in London | Florence helped improve the hospital in Scutari |
|---|---|---|---|
| ☐ | ☐ | ☐ | ☐ |

❸ Imagine you are Florence Nightingale. Write a letter to Queen Victoria telling her how bad conditions are in the hospital, and explaining what is needed for things to improve.

**Edith Cavell** was born in England in 1865. Edith decided to be a nurse after caring for her sick father. She spent time working in a nursing school in Belgium where she trained many nurses and greatly improved the standard of nursing.

During World War I, she saved the lives of many soldiers on both sides of the fighting, but she was eventually arrested for treason by the Germans for helping British, French and Belgian soldiers to escape to the Netherlands. On 12th October 1915, she was executed by firing squad.

On the night of her death, Edith told a vicar, "I realise that patriotism is not enough. I must have no hatred or bitterness towards anyone."

**4** Make your own fact file for Edith Cavell.

### Edith Cavell

Year of birth: _____    Year of death: _____

Significant achievements:

Interesting fact:

**Did you know?**
A mountain in the Canadian Rockies was renamed Mount Edith Cavell in 1916 in honour of the British nurse.

## HISTORY

**5** Connect the fact to the right nurse.

**Florence Nightingale**

**Edith Cavell**

She trained as a nurse in Germany.

She saved soldiers during WWI.

She worked in a nursing school in Belgium.

She saved soldiers during the Crimean War.

She was arrested and executed for treason.

She was known as "the lady with the lamp".

**6** Compare the illustration of a nurse in Victorian times with a modern nurse. How different do you think it would be to be a nurse today? What similarities would there be?

_____

_____

_____

_____

_____

_____

_____

**7** How has health care changed over the years? What differences are there between hospitals at the time of Florence Nightingale and Edith Cavell and today? Use the word and picture bank below for ideas.

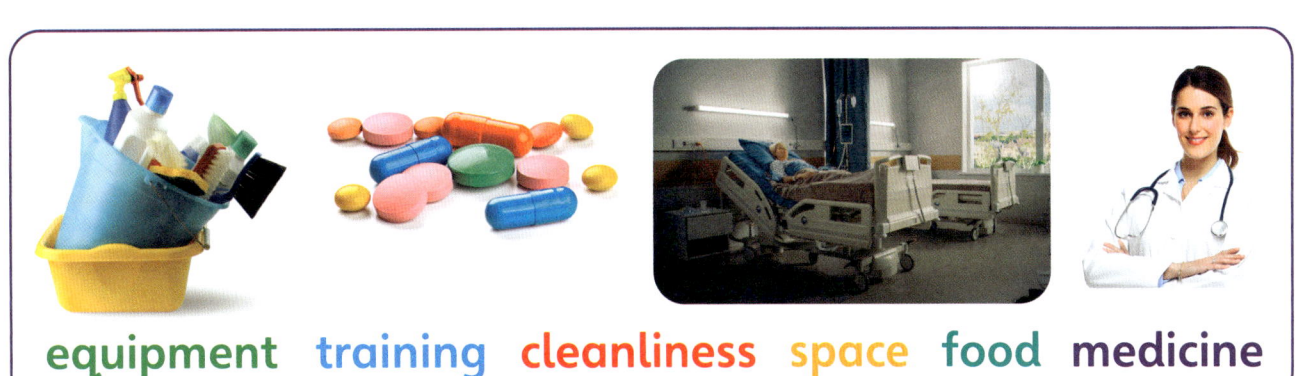

equipment   training   cleanliness   space   food   medicine

**HISTORY**

# close to home

Write about a famous person who is from where you live. What did they do? How did they shape history? Did they change your local area?

Name:

Date of birth:

Date of death:

Where they are from:

Draw a picture of them here:

What are they famous for?

An interesting fact about them:

# Hands-on

HANDS ON

# homophone bingo

Cut out these words for the activity on page 38.

| | | | |
|---|---|---|---|
| blew | tail | here | week |
| sea | flew | won | boy |
| flour | wail | saw | way |
| bare | dough | plain | male |

HANDS ON

## tense sorter

Cut out these sentences for the activity on page 67.

- They were laughing.
- Lilah plays the violin.
- He smiled happily.
- The plane was landing.
- The ship is sailing today.
- She dropped her cup.
- The children cheer loudly.
- I am eating my lunch.
- The bus broke down.
- My dog barks a lot.
- Sam is playing tennis.
- She was sitting quietly.

## recipe for a story

Cut out these ingredients for the activity on page 127.

- someone gets lost
- a talking goldfish
- a book goes missing
- a kitchen
- Lily and Liam
- Mrs Simonds
- someone gets a new pet
- a sunny beach
- a cave in the forest

HANDS ON

## ordering numbers

Cut out these numbers for the activity on page 137.

| | | |
|---|---|---|
| seventy-seven |  (25 smiley faces) | 6 tens and 8 ones |
| 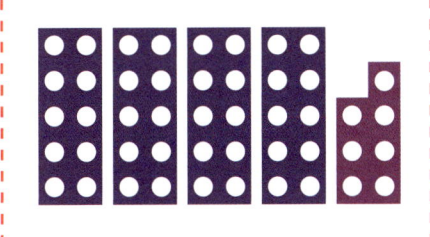 (8 tens and 6 ones shown with dot blocks) |  (86 shown with base-ten blocks) | **86** |
| fifty-three |  (3 tens and 8 ones shown with dot blocks) | 4 tens and 3 ones |

## counting in threes

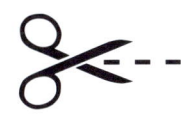

Cut out these numbers for the activity on page 141.

| 21 | 30 | 48 | 27 | 12 |
|---|---|---|---|---|
| 6 | 24 | 51 | 15 | 45 |
| 42 | 39 | 9 | 33 | |

HANDS ON

## place value bingo

Cut out these numbers for the activity on page 151.

| fifty-five | | | |
|---|---|---|---|
| | | **72** | 6 tens + 7 ones |
| **19** | 7 tens + 8 ones | | |
| | | | thirty-four |

## measuring

Cut out this ruler to use for activites on pages 248-249.

# multiplication matching

Cut out these number sentences for the activity on page 201.

| | |
|---|---|
| 5 + 5 + 5 + 5 | 3 + 3 + 3 |
| 4 × 2 | 2 + 2 + 2 + 2 |
| 3 × 4 | 4 + 4 |
| 2 × 4 | 4 + 4 + 4 |
| 2 × 5 | 5 + 5 |
| 4 × 5 | |
| 3 × 3 | |

# times tables bookmarks

Cut out these bookmarks to keep your 2, 5 and 10 times tables close to hand.

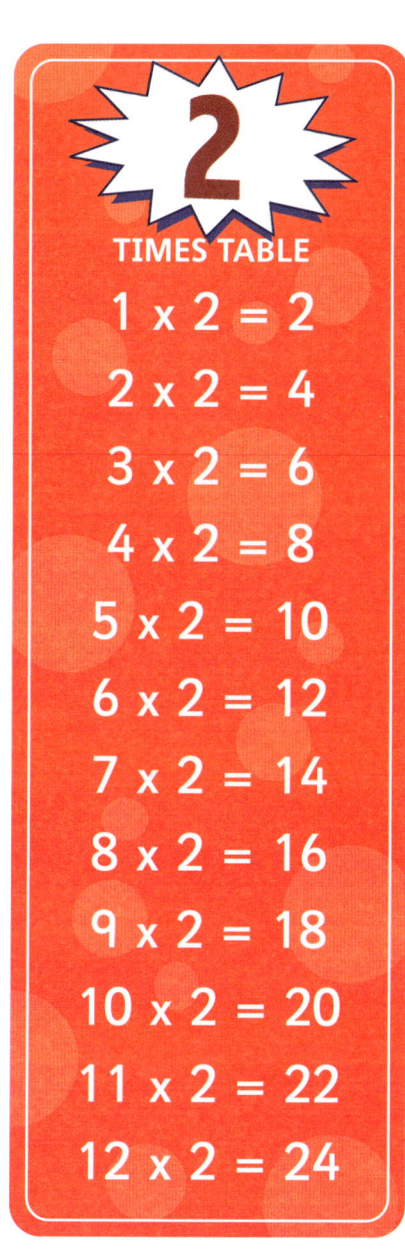

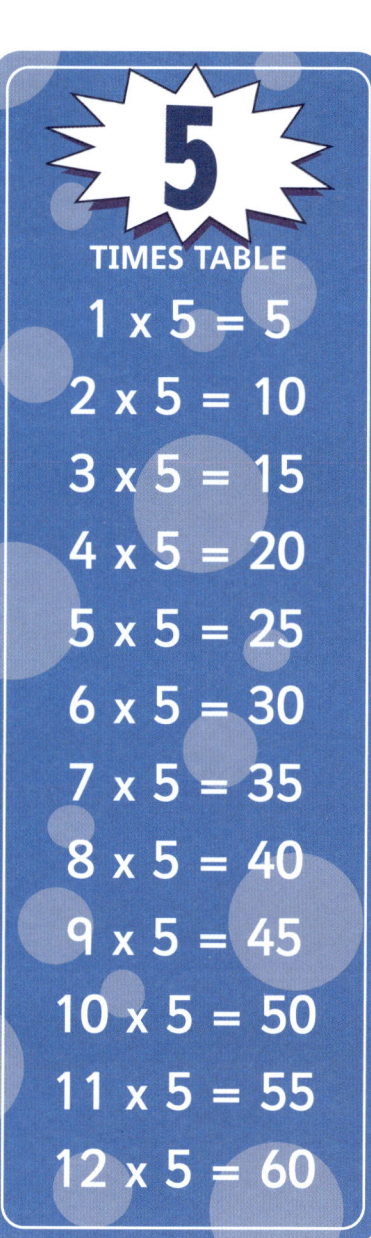

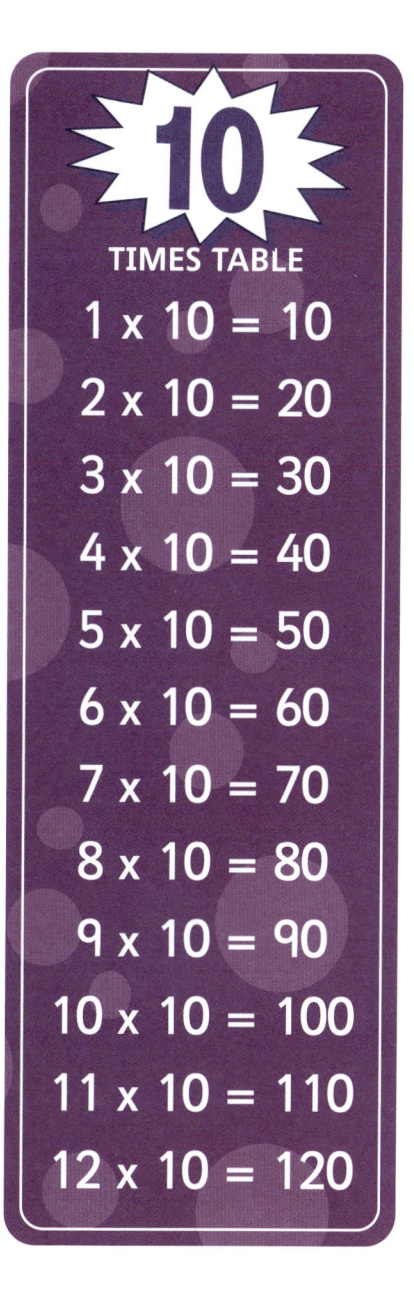

**2 TIMES TABLE**

1 x 2 = 2
2 x 2 = 4
3 x 2 = 6
4 x 2 = 8
5 x 2 = 10
6 x 2 = 12
7 x 2 = 14
8 x 2 = 16
9 x 2 = 18
10 x 2 = 20
11 x 2 = 22
12 x 2 = 24

**5 TIMES TABLE**

1 x 5 = 5
2 x 5 = 10
3 x 5 = 15
4 x 5 = 20
5 x 5 = 25
6 x 5 = 30
7 x 5 = 35
8 x 5 = 40
9 x 5 = 45
10 x 5 = 50
11 x 5 = 55
12 x 5 = 60

**10 TIMES TABLE**

1 x 10 = 10
2 x 10 = 20
3 x 10 = 30
4 x 10 = 40
5 x 10 = 50
6 x 10 = 60
7 x 10 = 70
8 x 10 = 80
9 x 10 = 90
10 x 10 = 100
11 x 10 = 110
12 x 10 = 120

HANDS ON

# equal parts?

Cut out these shapes for the activity on page 229.

# weighing things up

Cut out these items for the activity on page 254.

HANDS ON

# fraction matching ✂---

Cut out these cards for the activity on page 232.

| | | | |
|---|---|---|---|
| $\frac{1}{4}$ | 1 | $\frac{2}{4}$ | $\frac{3}{4}$ |
| $\frac{1}{2}$ | $\frac{1}{3}$ | $\frac{2}{3}$ | $\frac{1}{4}$ |
| $\frac{2}{3}$ | $\frac{1}{4}$ | 1 | $\frac{1}{2}$ |

HANDS ON

# lines of symmetry ✂---

Cut out these shapes for the activity on page 289.

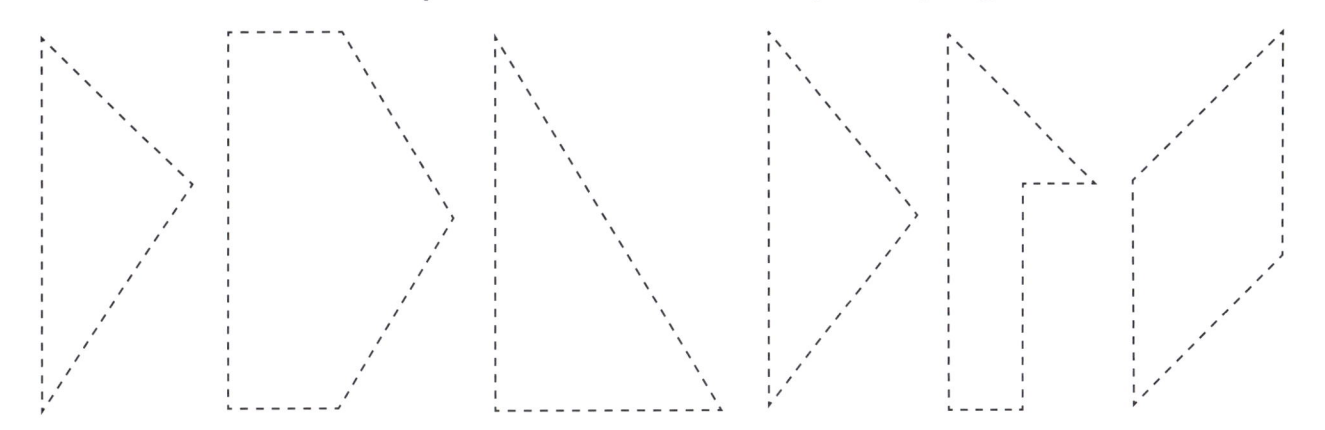

# fruit frames ✂---

Cut out the fruit for the activity on page 298.

# habitats ✂---

Cut out the images for the activity on page 316.

dwarf willow

lichen

cactus

palm tree

walrus

sidewinder rattlesnake

camel

polar bear

HANDS ON

## money match

Cut out these cards for the activity on page 268.

| 78p | £1 | £5 | £4 |
| 99p | £2 | 27p | 26p |
| 15p | £3 | 45p | 81p |

HANDS ON

# Answers

## Spelling

### page 14
snowman [2], toothbrush [2], lighthouse [2], skateboard [2], grasshopper [3], lawnmower [3]; phone, photo, dolphin, whisk, wheat, wheel

### page 15
write, treasure, bird; light + pie, chair + bear, owl + count

### page 16
a) bridge, b) orange, c) fudge, d) gentle, e) fridge, f) village

### page 18
wren, knot, gnaw; write, knock, gnome, gnarly, wriggle, knife

### page 21
table, towel, comical, loyal, camel, candle, funnel, regal

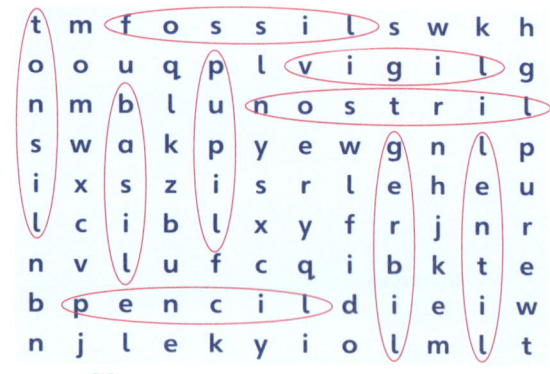

### page 22
[word search with circled words: fossil, vigil, nostril, pencil]

### page 23
glasses, flies, potatoes

### page 24
butterflies, dress, toys, bench, paintbrushes, dominoes, coaches, box, cherry, foxes, bicycles, ostriches, hero, berries

### page 25
worries, tries, cries, fries, dries

### page 26
before th [mother, brother, nothing];
before v [dove, glove, love];
before n [money, honey, monkey]

### page 27
wasp, squash, waffles, wand, watch, squad, squabble, quantity

### page 29
expression, magician

### page 30
danced, dancing; smiled, smiling; cycled, cycling; baked, baking; chased, chasing; taste, tasting
nicer, nicest; larger, largest; wider, widest; cuter, cutest; wiser, wisest; braver, bravest

### page 31
funnier, happiest, prettiest, easier
flying, cried, copying, replied

### page 32
patted, biggest, humming, funny, runner, clapped

### page 33
It's, You're, haven't, We'll
isn't, I'll, she's, doesn't, I'm, we're, they're, can't

### page 34
This is Ada's laptop; This is the cat's bowl; This is my brother's bike
Sam's trophy; the dog's bowl; the girl's sign

### page 35
nonsense words: pration, pluce, shibber, shiggle, tagil, weasure, squim, wamper, pating, radge

### page 36
night, knight; sun, son; here, hear; bee, be; blue, blew; bare, bear; sea, see

### page 37
there, their, They're; two, to, too

### page 39
not left, turn to tighten, rail vehicle, ribbon tie, continue, day and month, tool, rip, gift

### page 42
[word search with circled words: many, told, mind, any, cold, prove, hold, pasta, break, everybody]

### page 44
sore, wrap, can't, children, clues, gnawed; funnier, They're, pretty, people, to, weather

### page 45
There is a gnome in Grandad's garden. It sits on the path beside the grass. It has a blue coat, an orange hat and a little watering can. In winter, Grandad puts a scarf around its neck in case it gets cold. People passing by smile because they think it's funny.

### page 46
antelope, cheetah, crocodile, elephant, giraffe, hippopotamus, lion, monkey, tiger, zebra / apple, banana, carrot, cauliflower, cherries, melon, orange, pepper, potatoes, strawberry

## Punctuation and Grammar

### page 48
Our dog doesn't like getting wet. / It sometimes snows in January. / Giraffes have very long necks. / Kara likes to go ice skating. / The zoo was very busy on Monday. / My cousin plays the guitar really well.
On Saturday we went to visit my grandparents. It was sunny so we ate our lunch in the garden. My little sister Olivia had too much cake and felt ill. We stayed overnight and came back on Sunday. I had fun.

### page 49
Finlay plays football every Saturday. / Aunty Carol bakes the best pies. / London is the capital city of England. / I dropped my icecream on the floor.

### page 51
. / ! / ? / ! / ? / .

### page 52
Is Tokyo the world's largest city?
Are blue whales the largest animals on Earth?

### page 53
Have a glass of water. Go to sleep now.

### page 54
Mum bought apples, oranges, grapes and bananas. / To make the cake you need flour, sugar, chocolate and eggs. / My favourite sports are tennis, cricket and football.
I need to buy new trousers, shoes and socks for school. / The colours of the rainbow are red, orange, yellow, green, blue, indigo and violet. / My school bag is full of notebooks, books, folders and pens.

### page 56
The scared mouse, his hot coffee, her cosy slippers, the friendly old lady, the big purple balloon

### page 58
illness, slowly, spotless, punishment, forgetful; helpful, treatment, darkness, quickly, joyful, careless

### page 59
merriment, lazily, plentiful, penniless, happiness

### page 60
not dressed, not even, not sure; write again, play again, tell again; tie, wrap, wind; unhappy, reread, unsafe, unlock, reuse

### page 61
or, and, so, but, or, and, so, but
I would like to go outside but it's raining.
Lydia was tired so she went to sleep.

### page 62
when, that, when, that / because, if, if, because / Max was allowed to go **when** he had finished his homework. / Grace was cold **so** she put on her coat. / You can buy the jacket **or** you can buy the top. / Ade was hot **because** he had run all the way home.

### page 63
chases, grew, swim, plays, ran, popped

### page 64
brightly, loudly, quickly, softly, sadly, gracefully

### page 65
present, past, present, past / runs → ran / arrives → arrived / collects → collected / play → played / laughs → laughed

### page 66
present progressive, past progressive, past progressive, present progressive
are running → were running / am making → was making / are playing → were playing / is taking → was taking

### page 67

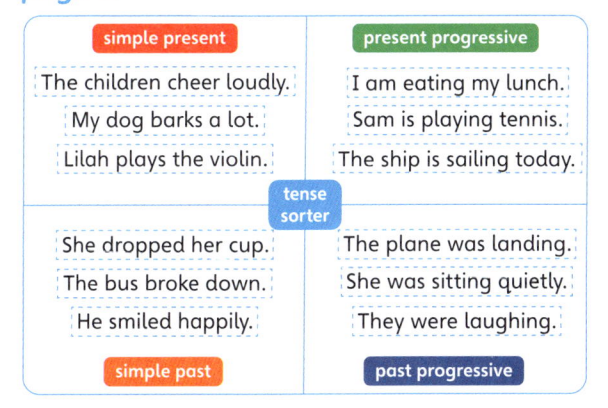

| simple present | present progressive |
|---|---|
| The children cheer loudly. | I am eating my lunch. |
| My dog barks a lot. | Sam is playing tennis. |
| Lilah plays the violin. | The ship is sailing today. |
| **simple past** | **past progressive** |
| She dropped her cup. | The plane was landing. |
| The bus broke down. | She was sitting quietly. |
| He smiled happily. | They were laughing. |

tense sorter

## page 68-70

1) i, saturday, snowy; 2) They built a snowman in the garden. 3) I need a new hat. Find me a new hat. What a nice hat that is! [exclamation] Where can I find a hat? [question]; They had pie, potatoes and peas for dinner. 5) adjective—A word that describes a noun; command—A sentence telling someone to do something; adverb—A word that describes a verb; suffix—A group of letters that can be added to the end of a word; 6) verb, adjective, adverb, noun; 7) big; 8) happy; 9) or, but, because; 10) they're, their, too, to; 11) couldn't, Milo's; 12) played, danced, sparkled

## Reading and Writing

### page 84
persuasive–advert, instructive–recipe, rhyming–poetry, literary–novel

### page 86-87
Ana's sandwich, her dog; to school, excited, pens and pencils [or other sensible answer]; morning/dawn, lake, all day

### page 88-89
Wales, no, no, he is envious; there will be a surprise, excited/joyful, no; miserable/unhappy/sad, she is being bullied/she has no friends at her new school

### page 90-91
at home, to see where Mum is, begged, astronaut, on a space station

### page 92-93
disappointed, they offer to go without a party or cake, Dad acts mysteriously/they hear barking, confused

### page 95-96
grazed—ate grass, peacefully—quietly, stormed away—left angrily, lurking—waiting, scattered—ran off; he pretended there was a wolf, search for the sheep, explained that he felt bored and lonely; liars aren't believed even when they tell the truth

### page 97
no, we can feel it and see it moving the leaves and branches, you and through, I and by

### page 98-99
eight, pink–brink, yellow–mellow, blue–through, green–between; the last line doesn't rhyme so it jolt you/is funny [or other sensible answer]; the wind, colours, both rhyme, they rhyme in different ways/are different lengths/the second poem has a funny ending [or other sensible answer]

### page 100
Ted brushed his teeth, had breakfast with Mum and Dad, they both had coffee, he put his dishes in the dishwasher

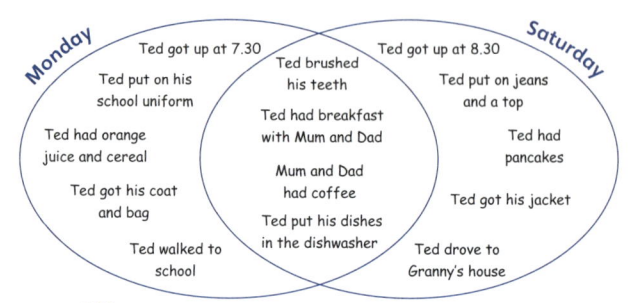

Monday: Ted got up at 7.30, Ted put on his school uniform, Ted had orange juice and cereal, Ted got his coat and bag, Ted walked to school
Both: Ted brushed his teeth, Ted had breakfast with Mum and Dad, Mum and Dad had coffee, Ted put his dishes in the dishwasher
Saturday: Ted got up at 8.30, Ted put on jeans and a top, Ted had pancakes, Ted got his jacket, Ted drove to Granny's house

### page 101
England, his son, Winnie-the-Pooh, the Hundred Acre Woods

### page 103
newspaper article, winds reached 60mph Wiltley recorded 45mm of rain in 24 hours [or other sensible answer], it is factual; the creative writing text, it describes feelings [or other sensible answer], an angry monster; it uses lots of adjectives [or other sensible answer], perfect, brand new, waterproof, strong, sturdy, bright, cheerful, stunning

### page 105
They raised the baby falcons themselves, chick, to tell how a scientist helped birds; 4, 2, 3, 1

### page 107
Northern, Southern, Equator; beach, snow

### page 108

### page 120
[1] Jack and Marcus ... [2] It was a wallet [3] Marcus said, "No!" ... [4] Just then ...

### page 121
Similes–She was as slow as a snail, They fight like cat and dog, I slept like a log; Metaphors–He is my knight in shining armour, My sister is a night owl, Life is a rollercoaster; bat, coal, lion

## page 127

| setting | characters | plot |
|---|---|---|
| a cave in the forest | Mrs Simonds | a book goes missing |
| a sunny beach | Lily and Liam | someone gets a new pet |
| a kitchen | a talking goldfish | someone gets lost |

## page 128
in the woods, Max, Jared and Harris, he has left his jumper behind

# Numbers, Place Value, Addition, Subtraction, Multiplication and Division

## page 136
thirty-nine, twenty-two, ninety-one, seventy-five, sixteen, eighty, forty-eight, fifty-three; 86, 90, 42, 73, 27, 35, 69, 58

## page 137
a) 21, 50, 56, 76, 93; b) 19, 35, 41, 68, 87; c) 16, 28, 30, 52, 77

1. (smiley faces)
2. (base-ten blocks)
3. 4 tens and 3 ones
4. (base-ten blocks)
5. fifty-three
6. (base-ten blocks)
7. 6 tens and 8 ones
8. seventy-seven
9. 86

## page 138
>, <, >, <, >, =, >, <

## page 139
(owl and hedgehog illustrations)

## page 140
| 41 | 22 | 33 | 44 | 49 | 59 | 92 | 25 | 32 | 54 |
| 34 | 17 | 76 | 29 | 62 | 90 | 11 | 74 | 29 | 49 |
| 58 | 72 | 80 | 13 | 14 | 61 | 82 | 16 | 37 | 66 |

1) 92; 2) 19
3) fifty-one, 71, (base-ten blocks)
4) false, true

## page 141
1) 10, 14, 16, 20;
2) 12, 18, 21, 24
4) 25, 30, 35, 45, 50, 60
5) 40, 60, 70, 80, 90

3)
| 0 | 3 | 6 | 9 | 12 | 15 |
| 18 | 21 | 24 | 27 | 30 | 33 |
| 36 | 39 | 42 | 45 | 48 | 51 |

## page 142-143
1) 28, 30, 32, 34; 61, 51, 41, 31; 40, 35, 30, 25; 24, 22, 20, 18; 44, 54, 64, 74;
2) 67, 19, 38, 25; 3) 12, 16; 4) 15, 18; 5) 30, 35; 5) 60

## page 144-145
3, 5, 7, 8, 11, 12, 14, 16, 18
6, 12, 14, 18, 24, 26, 32, 36
6, 15, 21, 30, 36, 41
10, 20, 30, 35, 45, 55, 65, 70, 80, 95

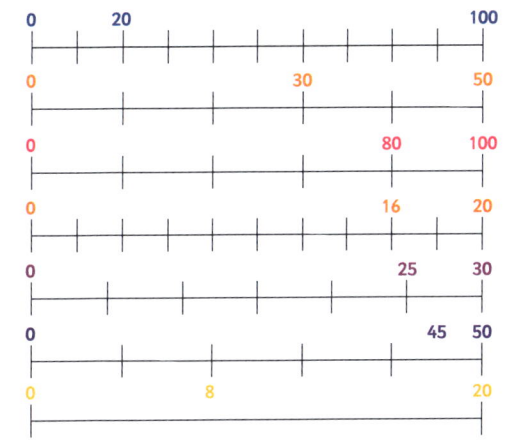

(number lines: 0–20–100; 0–30–50; 0–80–100; 0–16–20; 0–25–30; 0–45–50; 0–8–20)

50, 10

## page 146-7
1) 14, 46, 62, 29
2) (abacus images) 37, 80, 75, 52
3) 65 = 6 tens + 5 ones, 92 = 9 tens + 2 ones, 28 = 2 tens + 8 ones; 3 tens + 3 ones = 33, 7 tens + 0 ones = 70, 8 tens + 6 ones = 86
4) 23, 53, 83, 93; 5) 27, 29, 20, 25; 6) 3 tens + 5 ones = 35; 7) 4 tens + 4 ones = 44

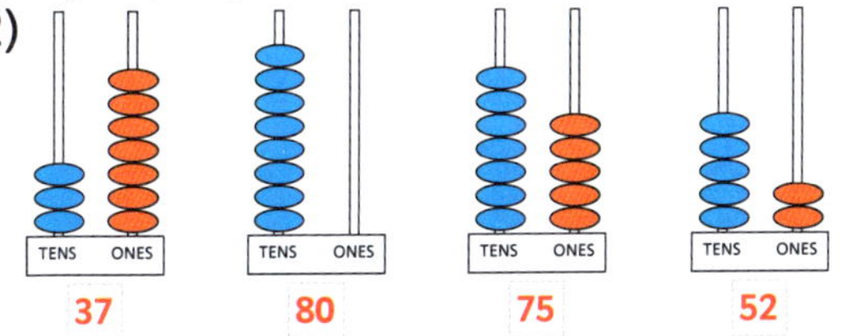

### page 148
1) 25, 20, 52, 50; 2a) 52, b) 20, c) 52, d) 25, e) 50;
3) 30, 36, 60, 63, 4a) 63, b) 30, c) 60, d) 63, e) 60

### page 149

| 25 | 2 tens + 5 ones | 25 = 20 + 5 | |
| 47 | 4 tens + 7 ones | 47 = 40 + 7 | |
| 32 | 3 tens + 2 ones | 32 = 30 + 2 | |
| 58 | 5 tens + 8 ones | 58 = 50 + 8 | |
| 27 | 2 tens + 7 ones | 27 = 20 + 7 | |

23 = 2 tens + 3 ones, 7 tens + 8 ones = 78, 34 = 3 tens + 4 ones, 6 tens + 5 ones = 65, 82 = 8 tens + 2 ones, 4 tens + 9 ones = 49

### page 150
20 + 24 = 44, 10 + 34 = 44, 0 + 44 = 44
40 + 19 = 59, 30 + 29 = 59, 20 + 39 = 59 etc
30 + 32 = 62, 20 + 42 = 62, 10 + 52 = 62 etc
50 + 6 = 30 + 26, 30 + 6 = 10 + 26, 60 + 6 = 50 + 16, 40 + 6 = 20 + 26, 90 + 6 = 60 + 36, 80 + 6 = 40 + 46

### page 152-155
1) Tia, 41; 2) Abdul, 8; 3) Sam – 39 is an odd number; 4) wrong; 5) 30, 40; 6) 91; 7) 40, 8) 27; 9) Tom had 80p, Tilly had 80p, Tania had 95p, Tom spent the most money; 10) 20; 11) 62; 12) 24; 13a) 23, 24, 32, 34, 42, 43; b) various alternatives including 23 < 32, 42 > 24; 14) 6, Smokey

### page 156
(sudoku grids)

### page 158
1) 4, 20; 2) 8, 22; 3) 2, 38; 4) 9, 45; 5) 7, 63

### page 159
6 + 8 = 14, 8 – 6 = 2; 3 + 9 = 12, 9 – 3 = 6;
7 + 7 = 14, 7 – 7 = 0

### page 160-161
a) 14, b) 10, c) 18, d) 7, e) 16, f) 8, g) 19, h) 12, i) 15, j) 8, k) 19, l) 5, m) 16, n) 9, o) 13, p) 2

### page 162
a) 5 + 7 = 12, b) 12 – 7 = 5, c) 7 + 9 = 16, d) 16 – 9 = 7, e) 11, f) 3, g) 16, h) 7, i) 15, j) 8, k) 14, l) 8

### page 163
1) 9 + 5 = 14, 5 + 9 = 14, 14 – 5 = 9, 14 – 9 = 5
2) 10 + 3 = 13, 3 + 10 = 13, 13 – 3 = 10, 13 – 10 = 3
3) 11 + 5 = 16, 5 + 11 = 16, 16 – 5 = 11, 16 – 11 = 5
4) 20 + 15 = 35, 15 + 20 = 35, 35 – 15 = 20, 35 – 20 = 15

### page 164
1) 7 + 6 = 13, 6 + 7 = 13, 13 – 7 = 6, 13 – 6 = 7
2) 10 + 8 = 18, 8 + 10 = 18, 18 – 10 = 8, 18 – 8 = 10
3) 10 – 4 = 2 [8]; 4) 11 + 6 = 16 [5];
5) 7 + 7 = 12 [5]; 6) 11 + 9 = 18 [7]

### page 165
(number matching diagrams and number grid)

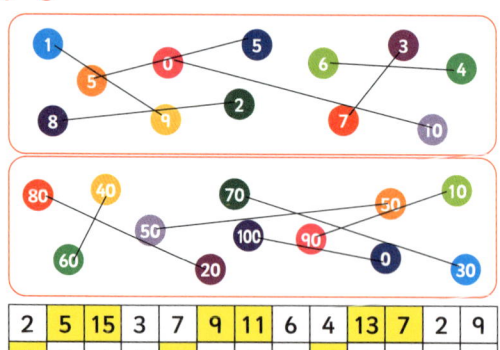

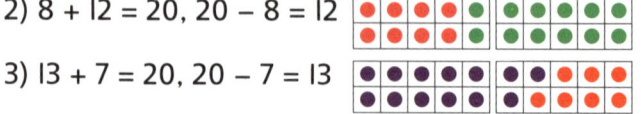

### page 166
1) 11 + 9 = 20, 20 – 9 = 11 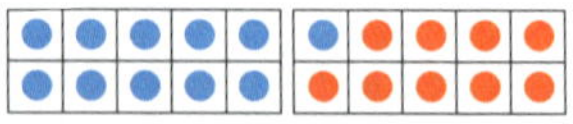
2) 8 + 12 = 20, 20 – 8 = 12
3) 13 + 7 = 20, 20 – 7 = 13
4) 9, 20 – 11 = 9

### page 167
12—22, 53—63, 68—78, 86—96, 75—85;
91—81, 59—49, 47—37, 64—54, 23—13

## page 168
43p, 38p, 79p; 67p, 65p, 37p

## page 169
1) 90ml, 50ml, 80ml; 50ml, 80ml, 20ml;
2) 34, 44, 3) 28, 8

## page 170

## page 171
6 + 3 + 4 = 13, 3 + 6 + 4 = 13, 4 + 3 + 6 = 13 etc
5 + 9 + 2 = 16, 9 + 5 + 2 = 16, 2 + 5 + 9 = 16 etc
8 + 7 + 9 = 24, 7 + 9 + 8 = 24, 9 + 7 + 8 = 24 etc
4 + 0 + 8 = 12, 8 + 0 + 4 = 12, 8 + 4 + 0 = 12 etc

## page 172
10, 19, 12, 15, 9, 17, 18, 13

## page 173
a) true, b) false, c) false, d) true, e) true, f) true

## page 174
Possible answers: 6 + 8 + 7 = 21, 6 + 6 + 9 = 21,
6 + 7 + 9 = 22, 5 + 7 + 9 = 21, 8 + 7 + 9 = 24,
4 + 8 + 9 = 21, 5 + 8 + 9 = 22, 6 + 8 + 9 = 23

Some possible routes:

## page 175
24 + 15 = 39, 57 + 31 = 88, 26 + 33 = 59,
45 + 63 = 108; 13 + 24 = 37, 41 + 17 = 58,
36 + 61 = 97, 25 + 73 = 98

## page 176
Alice–43, Jinny–22, Oliver–55, Jordan–34,
Ren–16, Layla–61; 16 + 22 = 38
Alice and Jordan: 43 + 34 = 77
Oliver and Jinny: 55 + 22 = 77
Ren and Layla: 16 + 61 = 77

## page 177
13 + 21 = 34; 22 + 24 = 46;
12 + 71 = 83; 23 + 46 = 69; 32 + 43 = 75

## page 178
pear and strawberries, mango and banana,
watermelon and orange, grapes and apple
a) true, b) true, c) false, d) false, e) false, f) true; g) 66, h) 68, i) 65, j) 73, k) 69, l) 70

## page 179

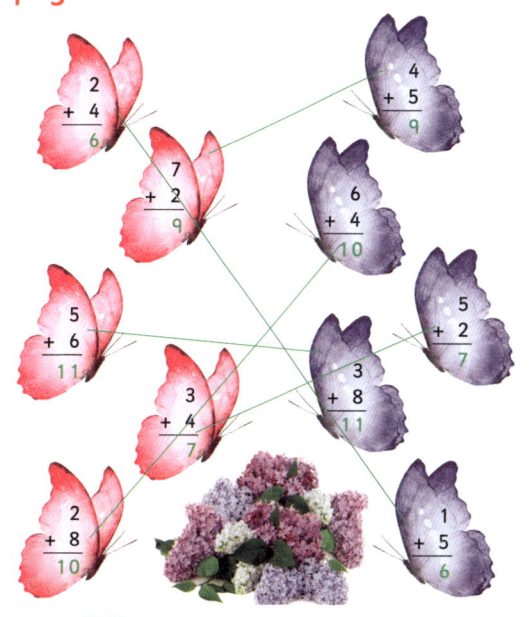

## page 180
a) 69, b) 29, c) 77, d) 67, e) 86, f) 49; g) 86,
h) 95, i) 76, j) 48, k) 98, l) 68

## page 181
a) 15 − 5 = 10, b) 12 − 6 = 6, c) 18 − 7 = 11,
d) 17 − 5 = 12, e) 27 − 6 = 21, f) 39 − 4 = 35;
g) 26 − 4 = 22, h) 69 − 6 = 63, i) 35 − 14 = 21,
j) 68 − 25 = 43

## page 182
16 − 7 = 9; 13 − 5 = 8, 11 − 6 = 5, 14 − 8 = 6,
12 − 3 = 9, 17 − 9 = 8

## page 183
12, 64, 73, 55, 80; 72, 63, 30, 36, 19

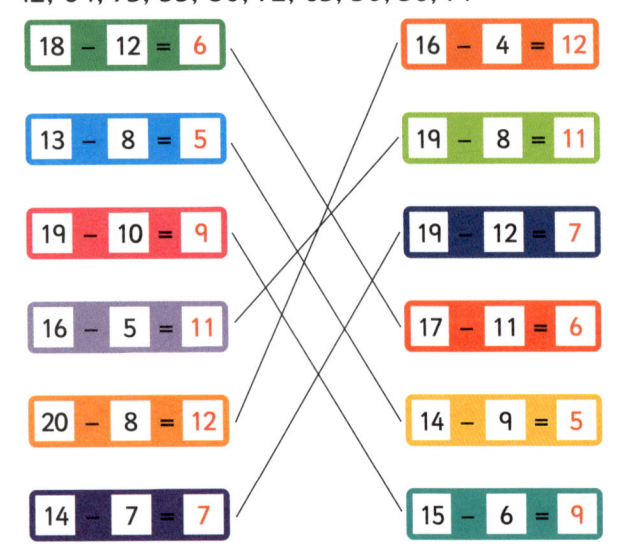

18 − 12 = 6
13 − 8 = 5
19 − 10 = 9
16 − 5 = 11
20 − 8 = 12
14 − 7 = 7
16 − 4 = 12
19 − 8 = 11
19 − 12 = 7
17 − 11 = 6
14 − 9 = 5
15 − 6 = 9

## page 184
15 [A], 9 [B], 4 [C], 12 [D], 17 [E], 5 [H], 8 [I], 13 [O], 10 [R], 16 [S], 1 [T], 14 [U], 18 [W], 7 [Y]
BECAUSE THEY ARE TWO-TIRED

## page 185
14, 44, 13, 13, 43, 66;
45 − 31 = 14; 24 − 12 = 12, 64 − 42 = 22

## page 186
a) 100p − 70p = 30p; b) 100p − 80p = 20p;
c) 100p − 90p = 10p; d) 100p − 20p = 80p;
e) 100p − 40p = 60p; e) 100p − 60p = 40p;
f) yes; g) no

## page 187
a) 16, b) 19, c) 16, d) 18, e) 78, f) 89, g) 79, h) 83, i) 26, j) 49, k) 38

## page 188
a) 72 − 3 = 69, 69 + 3 = 72; b) 94 − 7 = 87, 87 + 7 = 94; c) 86 − 9 = 77, 77 + 9 = 86
d) 88, 78, 68; e) 99, 89, 79; f) 83, 73, 63;
g) 19, 19 + 4 = 23; h) 38, 38 + 3 = 41;
i) 29, 29 + 5 = 34

## page 189
7 − 3 = 4, 9 − 0 = 9, 6 − 6 = 0, 4 − 2 = 2,
5 − 4 = 1, 6 − 2 = 4, 8 − 4 = 4, 9 − 7 = 2,
7 − 5 = 2, 8 − 6 = 2;
8 − 2 = 6, 12 − 4 = 8, 11 − 3 = 8

## page 190
a) 30, 13, 23, 33; b) 100, 20, 30, 40;
c) 80, 18, 28, 38; d) 50, 15, 25, 35;
e) 90, 19, 29, 39; f) 20, 12, 22, 32

## page 191
1) 87, 2) 56, 3) 20g, 4) 23, 5) 12

## page 192-194
1) 16, 2a) −, b) −, c) +, d) +, e) −, f) −, 3) yes, 13p, 4) 19, 5) Tony, 6) 17, 7) 6, 8) 59, 9) 21, 10) £14, 11) 63, 12) 22, 34, 65

## page 196-7
1) 6, 6 x 4 = 24; 2) 7, 7 x 3 = 21; 3) 5, 5 x 5 = 25;
4) 5 equal groups of 10, 50, 50; 5) 3 equal groups of 5, 5 + 5 + 5 = 15, 3 x 5 = 15;
6) 8 equal groups of 3,
3 + 3 + 3 + 3 + 3 + 3 + 3 + 3 = 24, 8 x 3 = 24

## page 198
1) orange squares; 2) toadstools and logs, conkers and scallop shells, acorns and seed pods, pine cones and spiral shells
3)  • • •   • •
4)  • • •   • • •

## page 199
2 x 5 = 10, 5 x 2 = 10; 3 x 5 = 15, 5 x 3 = 15;
4 x 5 = 20, 5 x 4 = 20

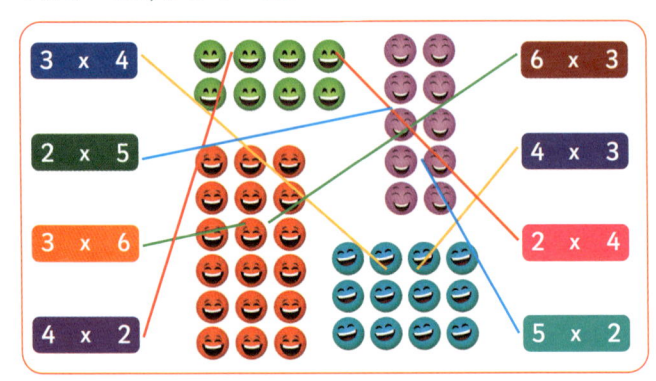

3 x 4, 2 x 5, 3 x 6, 4 x 2, 6 x 3, 4 x 3, 2 x 4, 5 x 2

## page 200
1) 3 sets of 3 biscuits, 3 + 3 + 3 = 9, 3 x 3 = 9;
2) 4 sets of 4 biscuits, 4 + 4 + 4 + 4 = 16, 4 x 4 = 16;
3)

## page 201
2 + 2 + 2 + 2
4 x 2
5 + 5
2 x 5

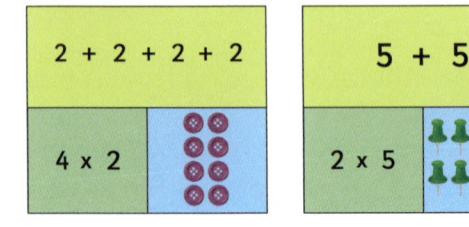

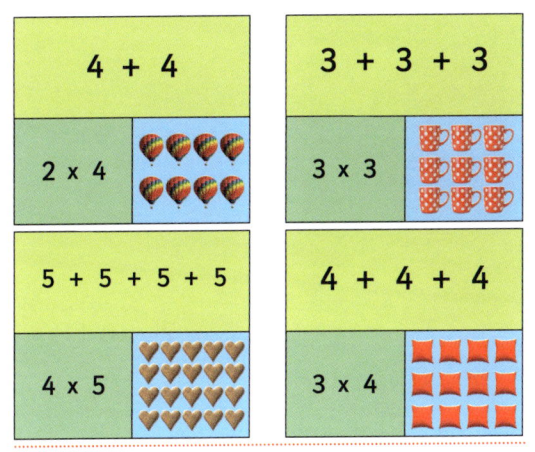

## page 202
a) 4, b) 6, c) 18, d) 14, e) 10, f) 12,
g) 1, h) 11, i) 4, j) 10, k) 12, l) 8

## page 203-5
1a) 2, b) 4, c) 6, d) 8, e) 10, f) 12,
g) 14, h) 16, i) 18, j) 20, k) 22, l) 24

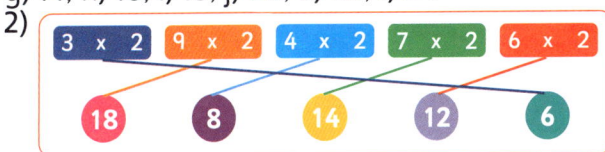

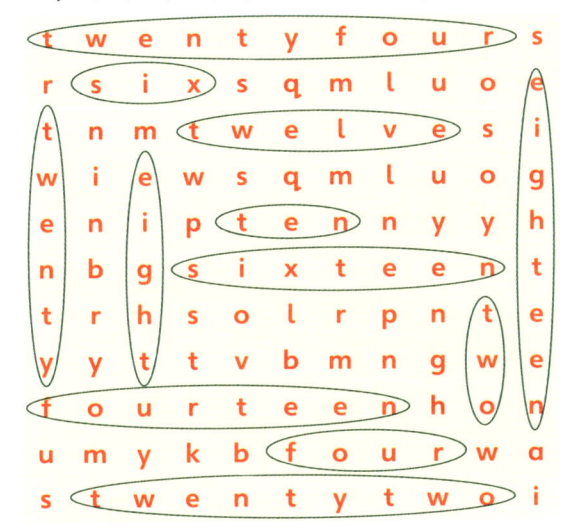

3) 12, 20, 16
4a) 6, 8, 14, 22; b) 2, 12, 4, 16; c) 10, 24, 18, 20

## page 206-8
1a) 5, b) 10, c) 15, d) 20, e) 25, f) 30,
g) 35, h) 40, i) 45, j) 50, k) 55, l) 60
2) 10, 20, 40, 6, 9, 12

4) 25, 35, 15, 55, 40; 5a) 4, b) 35, c) 11, d) 10,
e) 6, f) 15, g) 5, h) 60, i) 9

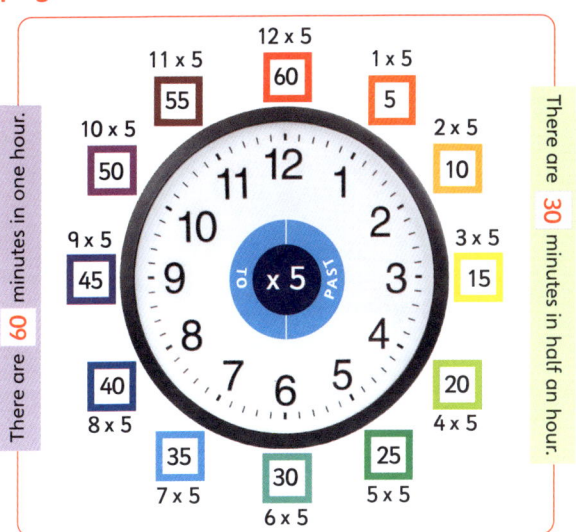

## page 209
10 minutes past 5; 25 minutes to 4

## page 210-212
1a) 10, b) 20, c) 30, d) 40, e) 50, f) 60,
g) 70, h) 80, i) 90, j) 100, k) 110, l) 120
2a) 3, b) 60, c) 10, d) 20, e) 12, f) 80,
g) 7, h) 90, i) 5

4) 50, 90, 100, 2, 6, 3; 5) 60, 80, 30

## page 213
a) 6, 6, 55, 10, 18, 5, 110, 7, 90, 24, 5, 2;
b) 35, 10, 12, 10, 40, 2, 1, 10, 5, 50, 5, 60;
c) 4, 40, 2, 15, 5, 70, 4, 12, 80, 2, 100, 11

## page 214-216
1) 2, 2) 3, 3) 2, 4) 4, 5) 1, 6) 6, 7) 30 ÷ 3 = 10,
8) 20 ÷ 2 = 10, 9) 12 ÷ 4 = 3, 20 ÷ 4 = 5

## page 217
a) 8, b) 12, c) 5, d) 8, e) 4, f) 17, g) 35, h) 14,
i) 10, 10, j) 50, 50, k) 23, 23

## page 218
1a) 7, b) 5, c) 2, d) 4, e) 11, f) 1, g) 5, h) 10,
i) 6, j) 3, k) 8, l) 7; 2) 45 ÷ 9 = 5, 45 ÷ 5 = 9;
3) 60 ÷ 12 = 5, 60 ÷ 5 = 12

## page 219
1a) 4, b) 8, c) 7, d) 10, e) 1, f) 2, g) 3, h) 4,
i) 5, j) 6, k) 7, l) 8; m) 9, n) 10, o) 11, p) 12,
When you divide a number by 10, each digit moves one place to the right to make it 10 times smaller;
2) 90 ÷ 9 = 10, 90 ÷ 10 = 9;
3) 60 ÷ 10 = 6, 60 ÷ 6 = 10

405

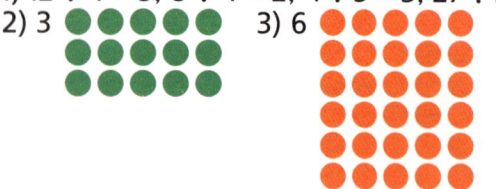

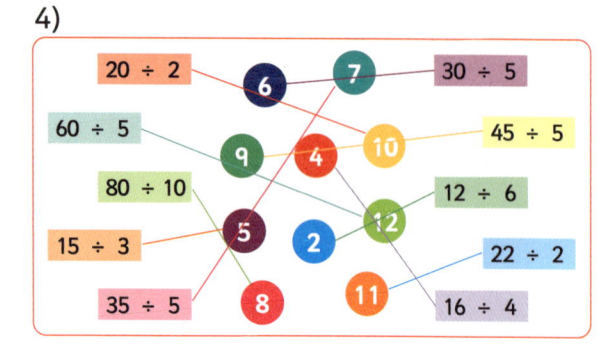

## ANSWERS

### page 220-221
1) 12 ÷ 4 = 3, 8 ÷ 4 = 2, 9 ÷ 3 = 3, 27 ÷ 3 = 9;
2) 3
3) 6

4)
20 ÷ 2 → 10
30 ÷ 5 → 6
60 ÷ 5 → 12
45 ÷ 5 → 9
80 ÷ 10 → 8
12 ÷ 6 → 2
15 ÷ 3 → 5
22 ÷ 2 → 11
35 ÷ 5 → 7
16 ÷ 4 → 4

5) 20 ÷ 5 = 4, 35 ÷ 5 = 7;
6) 10 ÷ 10 = 10 [1], 18 ÷ 2 = 8 [9]

### page 222

### page 223
11, 6, 5, 9, 12, 3, 5, 3, 8, 12, 9, 2, 8, 7, 9, 7, 4, 7, 6, 11, 10, 4

### page 224-226
1) 5; 2) 24, 36; 3) 35 ÷ 7 = 5, 35 ÷ 5 = 7; 4) 12, 30; 5) 20 ÷ 4 = 5; 6) 24; 7) 10 + 5, 5 + 5 + 5 + 5 + 5; 8) 18; 9) FALSE: there are 5 groups of 6 eggs; 10) 40 ÷ 10 = 4, 40 ÷ 4 = 10, 8 x 5 = 40, 5 x 8 = 40, 40 ÷ 8 = 5, 40 ÷ 5 = 8, 10 x 4 = 40, 4 x 10 = 40; 11) 25; 12) 8; 13) 18; 14) 10; 15) 25 minutes past 9; 16) 40

## Fractions, Measurement, Geometry and Statistics

### page 228-229
1) 2, 3, 4; 2a) yes, b) no, c) no, d) no, e) yes, f) yes;
3)
4)
5)
6)

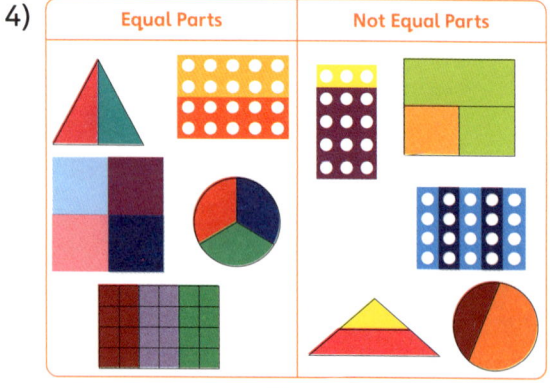

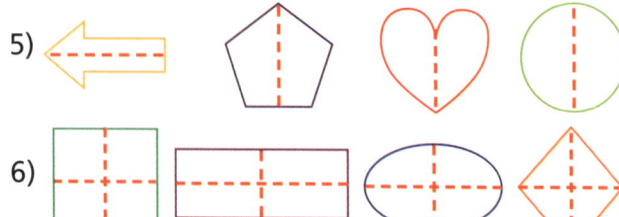

### page 230-231
1) [other alternatives possible]

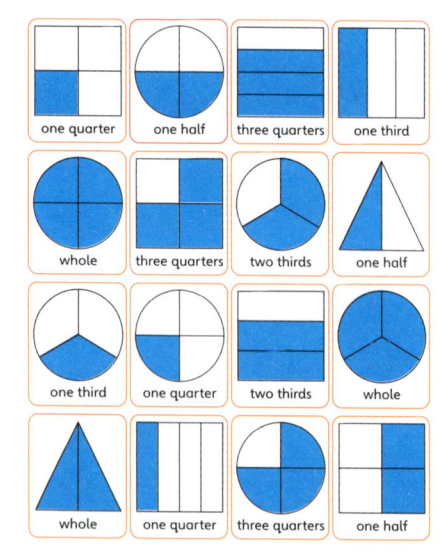

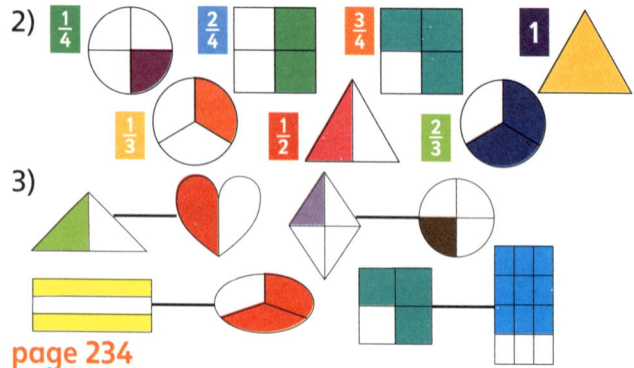

one quarter, one half, three quarters, one third
whole, three quarters, two thirds, one half
one third, one quarter, two thirds, whole
whole, one quarter, three quarters, one half

2) 1/4, 2/4, 3/4, 1
1/3, 1/2, 2/3

3)

### page 234
a) $\frac{1}{4}$ [or $\frac{2}{8}$], b) $\frac{1}{2}$ [or $\frac{3}{6}$], c) $\frac{2}{3}$ [or $\frac{4}{6}$],

# ANSWERS

d) $\frac{1}{4}$ [or $\frac{4}{16}$], e) $\frac{2}{3}$ [or $\frac{6}{8}$], f) $\frac{3}{4}$ [or $\frac{9}{12}$]

### page 235
1) 12, 6; 2) 30, 15; 3) 4; 4) 7; 5) 9

### page 236
1) 16, 4; 2) 20, 5; 3) 3; 4) 6; 5) 12; 6) 25

### page 237
1) 15, 5; 2) 21, 7; 3) 10; 4) 6; 5) 8; 6) 30

### page 238
1) 8, 2; 8, 4; 8, 6; 8, 8; 2) 12, 3; 12, 6; 12, 9; 12, 12
3) 32, 8; 32, 16; 32, 24; 32, 32
4a) 10; b) 14; c) 12; d) 45; e) 20; f) 9;
g) 12; h) 40; i) 40; j) 16; k) 9; l) 22

### page 239
1) low — 5 Emilia, 15 Ade, 20 Tomo, 25 Jamila — high

2a) <; b) =; c) >; d) >; e) =; f) <

### page 240

### page 241-242
1) red, pink, yellow; 2) lime, cucumber;
3) 200g; 4) middle bottle; 5a) 250ml; b) 150ml;
c) 100ml; 6a) 200ml; b) 50ml; f) 100ml

### page 244

| $2\frac{3}{4}$ | 3 | $3\frac{1}{4}$ | $3\frac{2}{4}$ | $3\frac{3}{4}$ | $1\frac{1}{2}$ | 2 | $2\frac{1}{2}$ | 3 | $3\frac{1}{2}$ |
| $5\frac{1}{3}$ | $5\frac{2}{3}$ | 6 | $6\frac{1}{3}$ | $6\frac{2}{3}$ | 9 | $9\frac{1}{4}$ | $9\frac{2}{4}$ | $9\frac{3}{4}$ | 10 |
| 4 | $4\frac{1}{3}$ | $4\frac{2}{3}$ | 5 | $5\frac{1}{3}$ | $7\frac{1}{2}$ | 8 | $8\frac{1}{2}$ | 9 | $9\frac{1}{2}$ |

### page 245-246
1) 15, 30; 2) Molly, £12 + £10 = £22; 3) $\frac{1}{4}$ [or $\frac{3}{12}$];
4) yes, it now weighs 15kg; 5) 1m, 50cm;
6) Charlie, Jamie, Jessica

7) 12, 8

### page 248-251
1) The end of the carrot isn't lined up with the 0; 2) 7, 4; 3) accurately drawn lines; 4) 4.5cm, the white car, the red and yellow cars, the white car; 5) stegosaurus 5cm, tyrannosaurus 7cm, brachiosaurus 10cm; 6) coach, postbox, piano; 7) 2m, 10cm, 20cm; 8) 3m, 30cm

### page 252-253
1a) E–D–A–B–C; b) D; c) >; d) 10m; e) 60m; f) 50m; g) >; 2a) Lottie; b) Alex; c) Sam;
d) Sydney; 3) <, >, <, =, <, >

### page 254-256
1) g, g, kg
2)

| weighs less than 100g | weighs more than 100g |
|---|---|

3) 150g, 300g, 450g, 150g, 600g; 4) 4kg, 2 and a half kg, 1 and a half kg, 2 and a half kg, 4kg; 5a) about 100kg; b) about 120g; c) about 15kg; d) about 7g; e) about 280g; f) about 1g; 6) an orange, because two limes weigh the same as one orange

### page 257-259
1) ml, l, ml; 2) about 2l, about 60l, about 350ml, about 5l, about 1ml; 3) A has less than B, D has more than A, B has more than C, C has more than A, C has less than D, B has less than D; 4) accurately coloured; 5) 75ml, 300ml, 425ml; 6) 3, 10, 2, 20; 7) =, >, <, >, <, <

### page 260
rhino, 410kg, elephant, 500kg, cheetah, cheetah

### page 261-262
1)

2) 20°C, 35°C, 35°C, 85°C, -5°C, 75°C;
3) Moscow, 15°C, 25°C, 21°C, 10°C

## ANSWERS

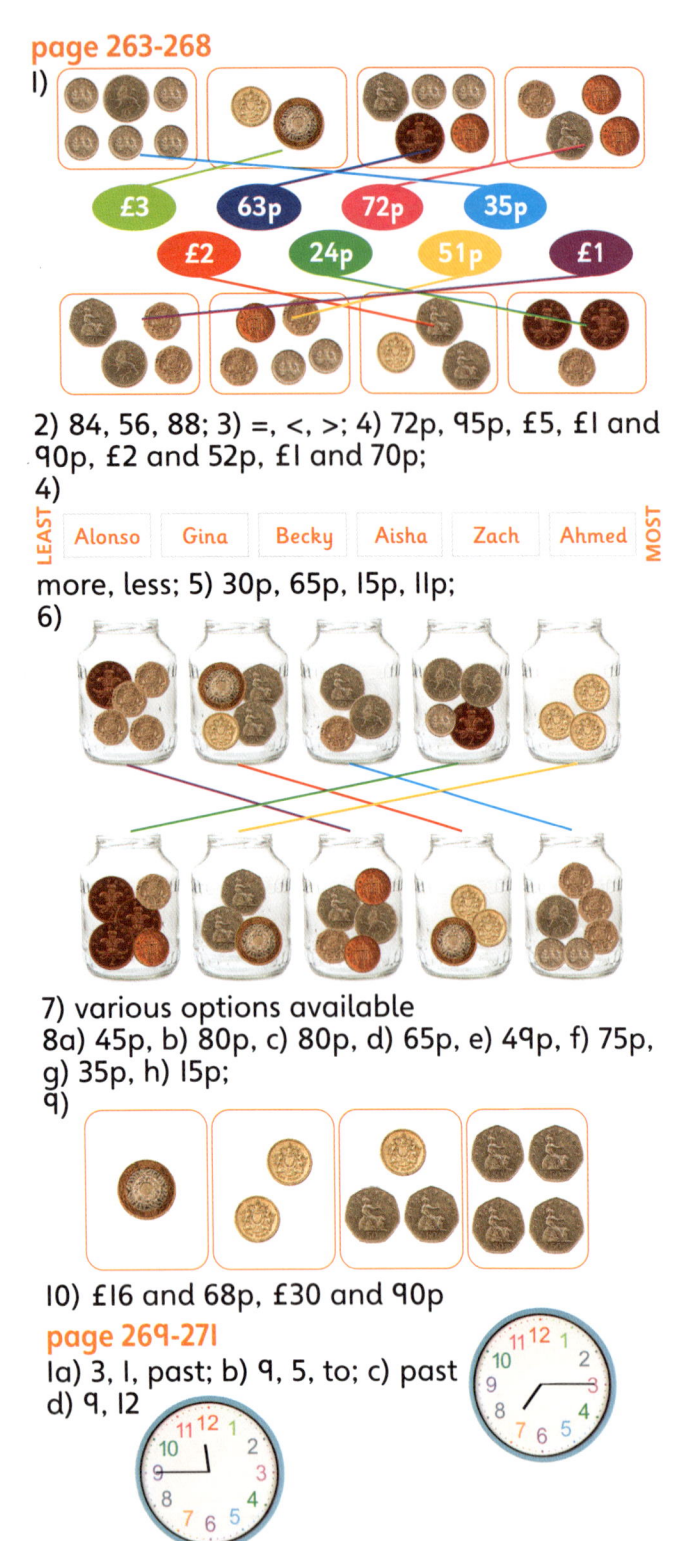

### page 263-268

1) [matching coins to amounts]

2) 84, 56, 88; 3) =, <, >; 4) 72p, 95p, £5, £1 and 90p, £2 and 52p, £1 and 70p;

4) LEAST — Alonso, Gina, Becky, Aisha, Zach, Ahmed — MOST

more, less; 5) 30p, 65p, 15p, 11p;

6) [matching jars]

7) various options available

8a) 45p, b) 80p, c) 80p, d) 65p, e) 49p, f) 75p, g) 35p, h) 15p;

9) [coin images]

10) £16 and 68p, £30 and 90p

### page 269-271

1a) 3, 1, past; b) 9, 5, to; c) past d) 9, 12

2a) quarter past 1; b) quarter to 6; c) quarter past 7; d) quarter to 3; e) quarter past ten; f) quarter to 11;

3) [clocks]

4)
| Minute hand pointing to | 1 | 2 | 3 | 4 | 5 | 6 | 7 | 8 | 9 | 10 | 11 | 12 |
|---|---|---|---|---|---|---|---|---|---|---|---|---|
| Minutes past the hour | 5 | 10 | 15 | 20 | 25 | 30 | 35 | 40 | 45 | 50 | 55 | 60 |

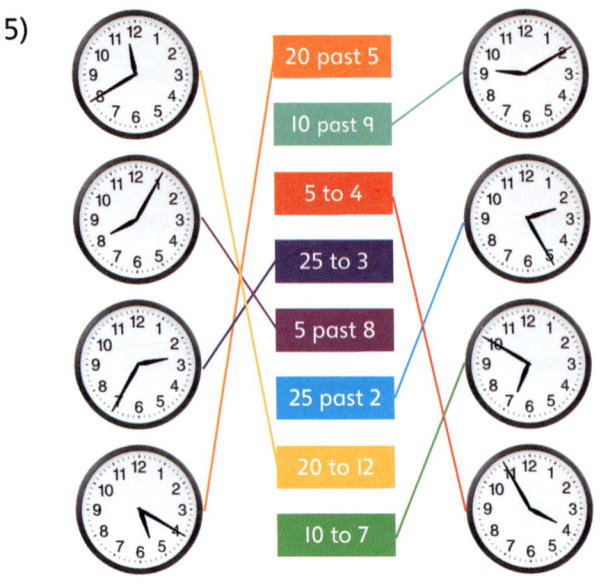

5) [matching clocks to times: 20 past 5, 10 past 9, 5 to 4, 25 to 3, 5 past 8, 25 past 2, 20 to 12, 10 to 7]

### page 272-275

1) washing hands [1], making a bed [2], eating lunch [3], football match [4], day at school [5], family holiday [6]; 2) any suitable answers; 3) 1 hour;

4) [matching: 7 — days in a week; 12 — months in a year; 24 — hours in a day; 60 — minutes in an hour; 60 — seconds in a minute]

5) >, =, >, >, <, >, 6) 31, 30, February;

7) a) 15 minutes b) 10 minutes, c) 25 minutes

8) [clocks]

9a) Pippa; b) Ahmed, 30; c) 35; d) 10; e) Benji; f) [start time and end time clocks]

### page 276-280

1) 16kg; 2) 600ml; 3) 25p, 10p; 4) 54g; 5) 180kg; 6) no, the thermometers have different scales; 7) 10ml; 8) 102kg; 9) 105 minutes; 10) 45ml, 90ml; 11) 350m, 50m; 12) 10, 100ml; 13) Alexi;

408

14)  [clock showing 2:20] 15) 70l, 14; 16) 90g;
17) 75ml; 18) 2kg; 19) £3 and 10p, £1 and 30p;
20) 27

### page 282-285
1a) circle, 1, 0; b) triangle, 3, 3; c) square, 4, 4; d) rectangle, 4, 4; e) pentagon, 5, 5; f) hexagon, 6, 6; g) oval, 1, 0; h) rhombus, 4, 4;
2) square, triangle, rectangle;
3)
4)
5)
6) 3, 4, 1, 2, 5
7) >, >, =, <

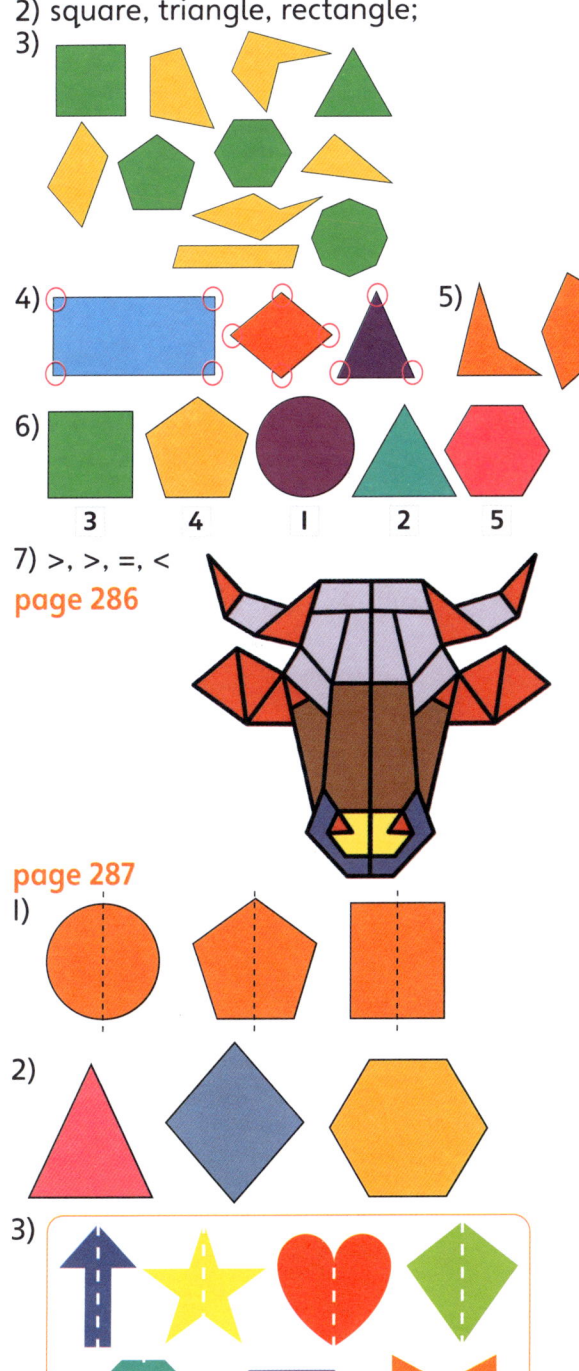

### page 286

### page 287
1)
2)
3)

4) Venn diagram: vertical line of symmetry / 4 sides
5) 
6) 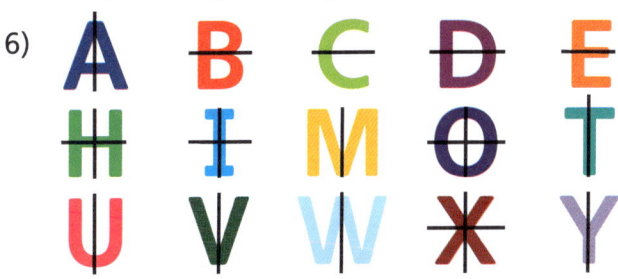 A B C D E H I M O T U V W X Y
7)

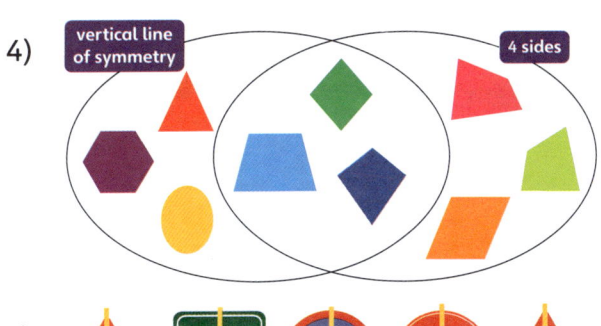

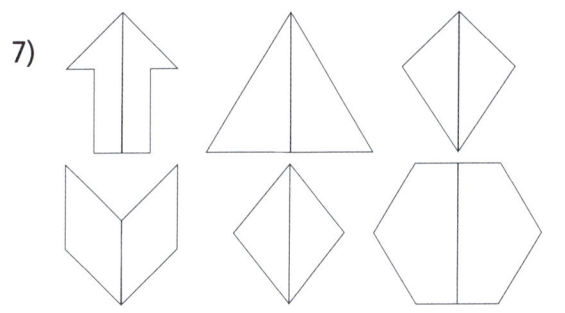

### page 290-295
1) cuboid, 6, 12, 8; cylinder, 3, 2, 0; square based pyramid, 5, 8, 5; cone, 2, 1, 1; cube, 6, 12, 8; sphere, 1, 0, 0; triangular prism, 5, 9, 6;
2) green clue = cube, yellow clue = cuboid, blue clue = cone, red clue = cylinder;
3) square, rectangle, triangle, circle, triangle, square; 4a) cuboid [9], b) triangular prism [2], c) 5, d) 6;
5) Venn diagram: flat surfaces / curved surfaces
6) shapes drawn in correct column;
7) 5, 1, 3, 2, 4

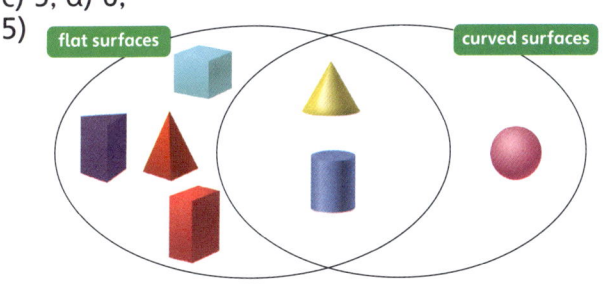

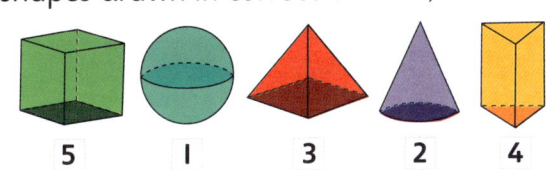

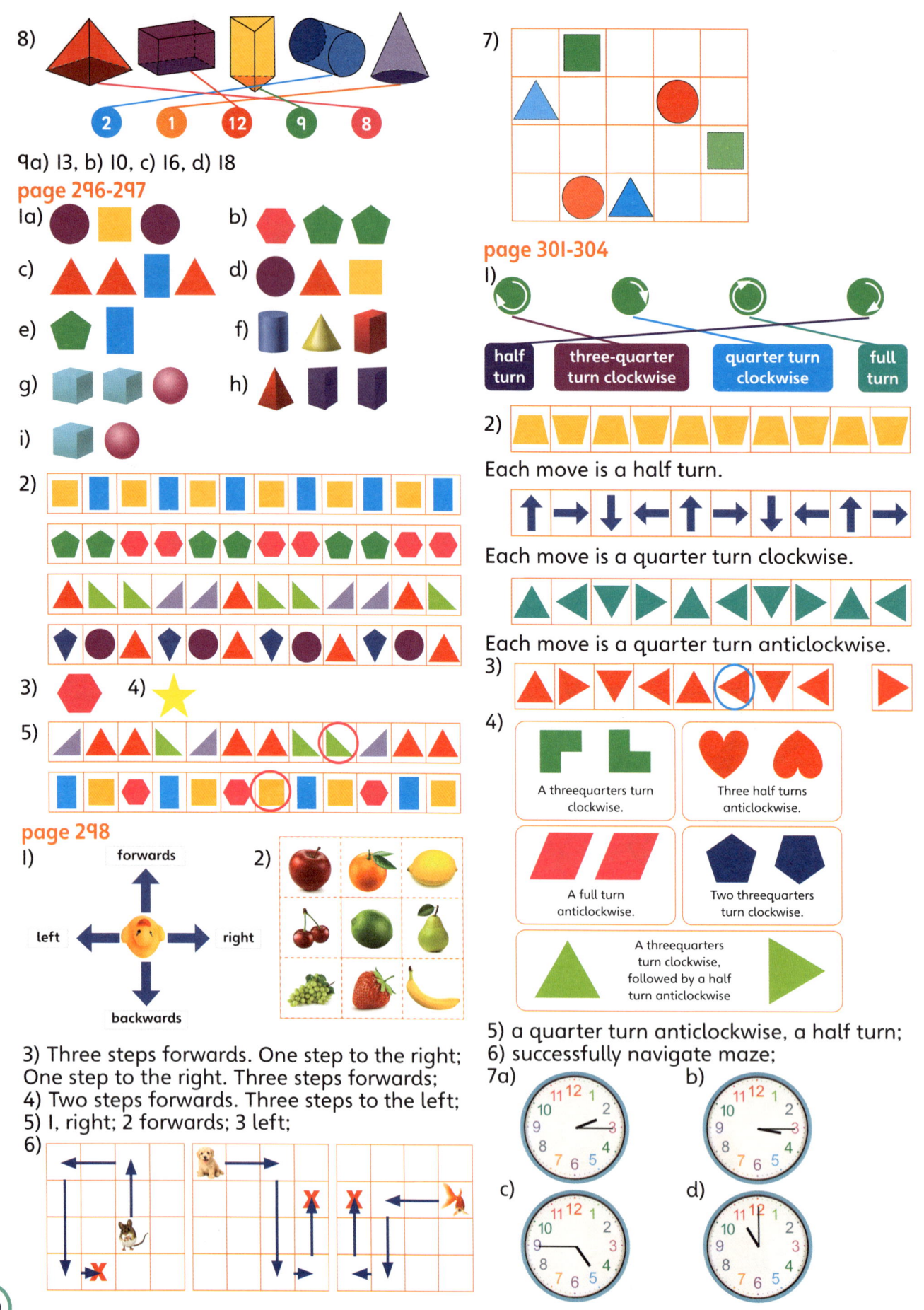

8)

9a) 13, b) 10, c) 16, d) 18

## page 296-297

1a) ... b) ... c) ... d) ... e) ... f) ... g) ... h) ... i) ...

2) ...

3) (red hexagon)   4) (yellow star)

5) ...

## page 298

1) forwards / left / right / backwards

2) (fruit grid)

3) Three steps forwards. One step to the right;
One step to the right. Three steps forwards;
4) Two steps forwards. Three steps to the left;
5) 1, right; 2 forwards; 3 left;
6) (maze diagrams)

7) (grid with shapes)

## page 301-304

1) half turn — quarter turn clockwise; three-quarter turn clockwise — full turn (matching)

2) Each move is a half turn.

Each move is a quarter turn clockwise.

Each move is a quarter turn anticlockwise.

3) (pattern with circled shape)

4) 
- A threequarters turn clockwise.
- Three half turns anticlockwise.
- A full turn anticlockwise.
- Two threequarters turn clockwise.
- A threequarters turn clockwise, followed by a half turn anticlockwise

5) a quarter turn anticlockwise, a half turn;
6) successfully navigate maze;
7a) b) c) d) (clocks)

410

8) East, East

### page 306-309

1)

| Pet | Tally | Total |
|---|---|---|
| Dog | ⦀⦀⦀⦀ ⦀⦀⦀⦀ | 9 |
| Cat | ⦀⦀⦀⦀ ⦀⦀ | 7 |
| Rabbit | ⦀⦀⦀ | 3 |
| Fish | ⦀⦀⦀⦀ | 5 |

pictogram filled out correctly;
2) walking 12, bus 6, car 9, bike 8;
pictogram filled out correctly;
a) 6, b) 3, c) 20, d) 35
3) pink 25, green 10, red 15, blue 30, purple 20;
a) blue, b) green, c) 15, d) 5, e) 20;
4) pictogram completed correctly;
a) birch, b) 30, c) 80, d) 120

### page 310-311

1) puffin 6, emu 1, peacock 3, owl 5, toucan 3, flamingo 2; a) puffin, b) 3, c) 3, d) 3, e) 20;

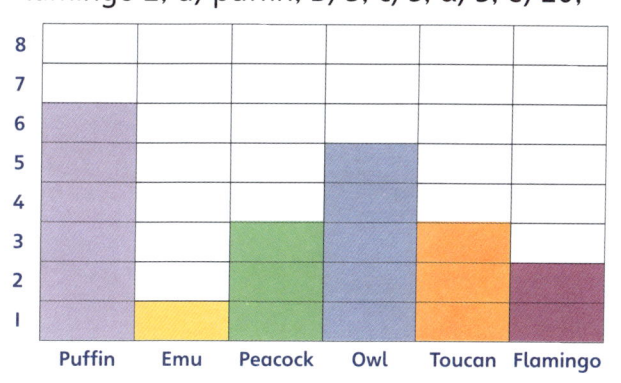

2a) Clara, b) 7, c) Ilana, d) 12

### page 312

a) Emily, b) Tuesday, c) Wednesday, d) 7, e) Jessica, 20

## Science

### page 314

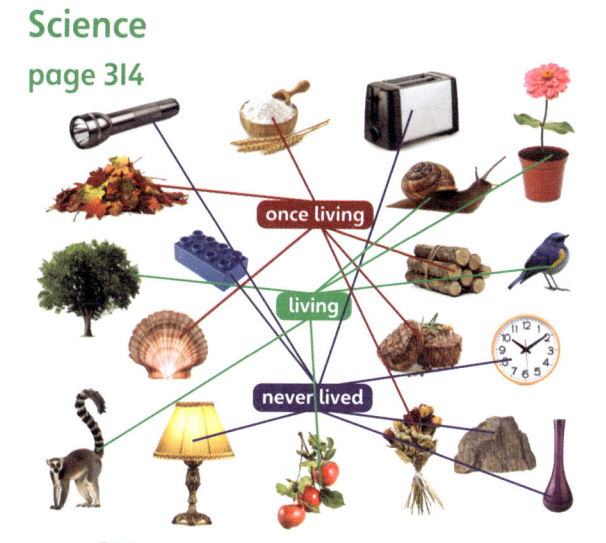

### page 315

a) woodland, deer, moss; b) desert, camel, palm tree; c) ocean, whale, seaweed; d) river, otter, reeds

### page 316

1) (see top of next column)
2)

### page 319

The woodpecker has made a hole in the tree trunk; the termite has built a mound; the prairie dog has dug a burrow

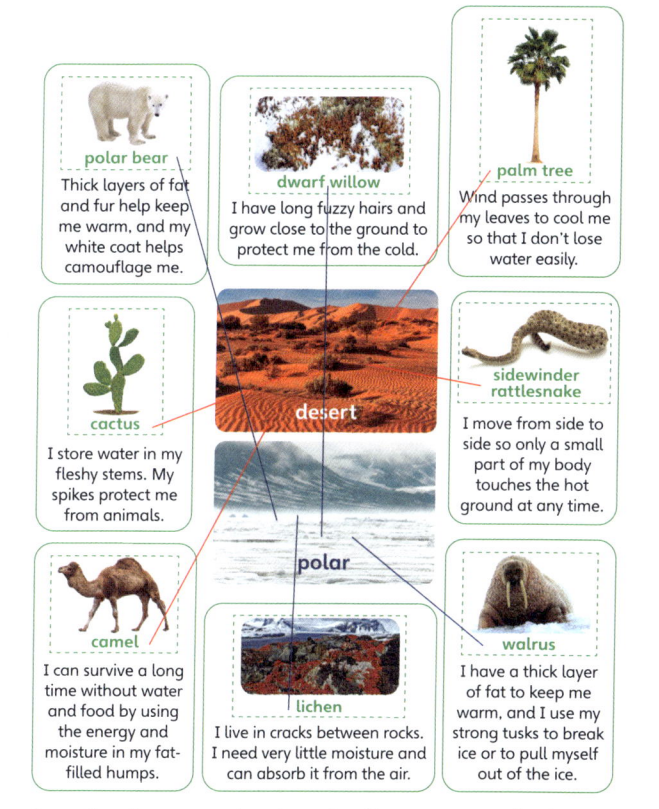

### page 320

a) jaguar, tapir; b) ferns, moss; c) emergent layer; d) canopy layer; e) anaconda or woodpecker

### page 323

nectar, pollen; insets, nests; berries, seeds; shelter, scares

## ANSWERS

### page 324-325
1) [image: matching animals to plants]
2) [image: matching predators to prey]
3) bear—salmon and berries; robin—berries and worm; fox—rabbit and berries; hedgehog—caterpillar and earwig; capuchin monkey—nuts and lizard

### page 326-327
1) sparrowhawk; 2) consumer; 3) kelp;
4a) lettuce [1], slug [2], hedgehog [3], badger [4];
b) grass [1], rabbit [2], fox [3], eagle [4]

### page 328-329
1) [2], [3], [4], [1];
2) [labeled plant diagram: flower, fruit, leaves, stem, roots, seeds]
3) air, water, nutrients, light, warmth; Plants need light and warmth from the sun. Plants need water or they will dry out and die. Many plants get the nutrients they need from soil. Plants need air to breathe and to make food; 4) cactus; 5) water lily;
6) It will become tall and spindly looking for light, and eventually will die.

### page 331
[sequence: 1 seeds, 2 sprouting, 3 seedling, 4 bud, 5 sunflower, 6 withered]

### page 332-333
1) life cycle of a daffodil: dormant → sprouting → roots growing → budding → flowering → withering
2)
- life cycle — the journey of a living thing from beginning to end
- germination — when a seed soaks up water and a new plant begins to grow
- nutrients — a substance that is needed for healthy growth

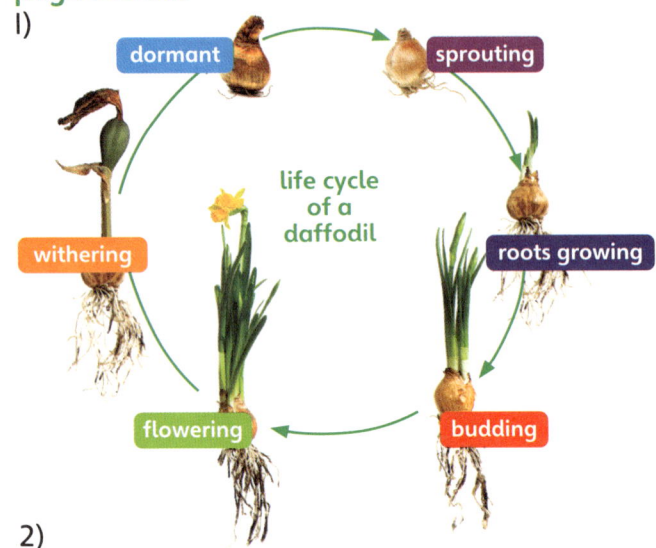

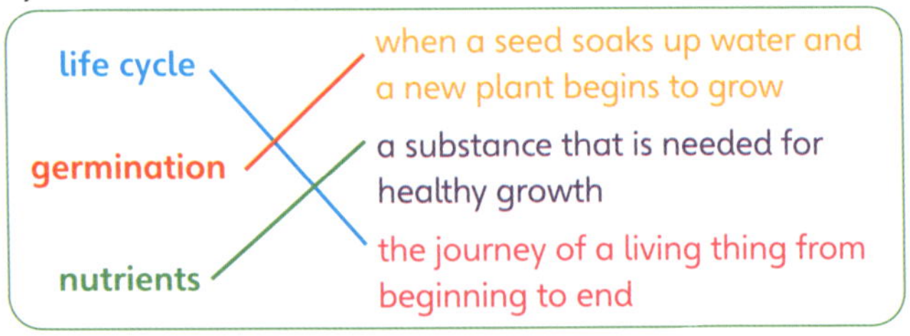

3) water and warmth

### page 334-336
1) [matching adult animals to their young]
2) [matching animals to their eggs/young]

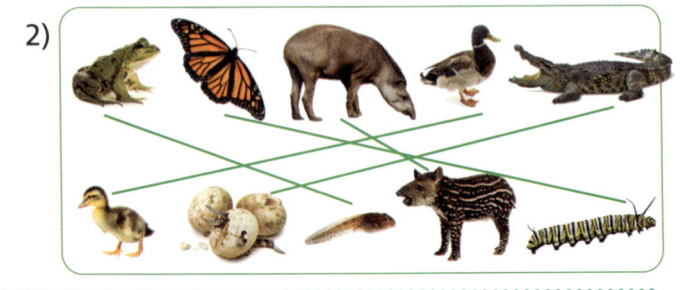

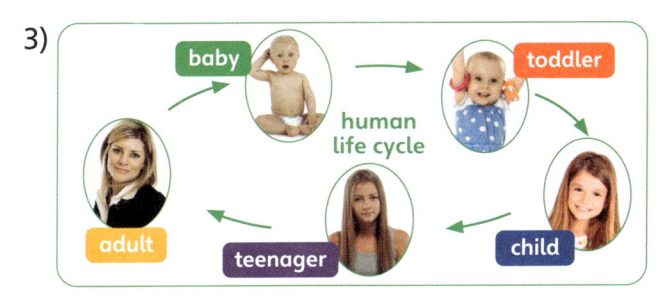

3) baby → toddler → child → teenager → adult (human life cycle)

4) in the sand, 4;

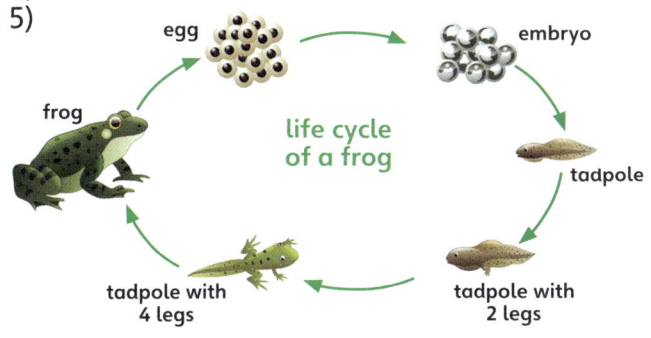

5) life cycle of a frog: egg → embryo → tadpole → tadpole with 2 legs → tadpole with 4 legs → frog

6a) butterfly; b) egg

## page 337-339

1) need—shelter, air (oxygen), water, food; 2) shelter, water, food, air; 3) fish; 4) [matching: dog—bone, spider—fly, bear—fish, bee—clover/flower, cow—grass]

5) beaver—beaver dam, bat—cave, hedgehog—leaves; 6) camel; 7) tiger

## page 340

1) exercise, hygiene, balanced diet; 2) carbohydrates—energy, fruit and veg—sources of fibre, protein—repair, dairy—calcium, fats and sugars—energy; We should eat more of some food groups and less of others; 3) plenty—carrots, grilled chicken, brown rice, salad, broccoli, eggs, fruit, peas

## page 344-346

1) natural—wool, cotton, gold, clay, wood, leather; man-made—plastic, glass, brass, polyester, paper; 2) transparent—opaque, heavy—lightweight, waterproof—absorbent, rigid—flexible; window—transparent, sponge—absorbent, raincoat—waterproof, rope—flexible; 3) t-shirt—fabric, tyre—rubber, mug—clay, wall—brick, water bottle—plastic; 4) Bricks are strong/hard and weatherproof; Plastic is waterproof and lightweight; Rubber is strong/durable and flexible/waterproof; Fabric is lightweight and flexible/soft; Clay is waterproof and rigid/strong. Other answers possible; 5) seat—fabric (soft/flexible), window—glass (transparent), tyre—rubber (durable/waterproof), car body—metal (strong, rigid, durable); 6a) metal, wood, plastic, b) all are waterproof and can be rigid, c) glass might be used for windows, spectacles, cups, containers, vases etc; 7a) it would leak/get wet, b) you wouldn't be able to see through it, c) the water would leak through

## page 347

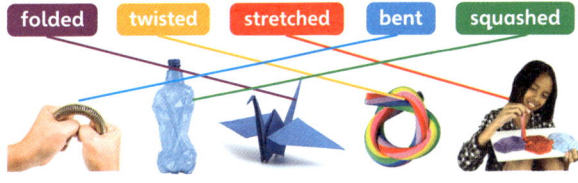

folded — twisted — stretched — bent — squashed

## page 348

waterproof clothing—waterproof and flexible, rubber tyre—flexible and durable, invisible glass—non-reflecting/transparent, rigid, industrial fibres—strong, flexible

# Geography and History

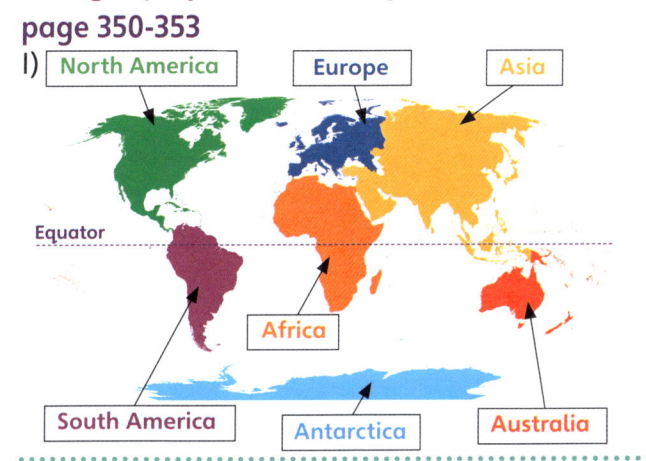

## page 350-353

1) North America, Europe, Asia, Africa, South America, Antarctica, Australia (labelled on world map with Equator)

2a) Atlantic Ocean, b) Indian Ocean, c) Pacific Ocean, d) South America and Australia, e) Antarctica, f) as appropriate; 3) North Pole—coat, scarf, hat, boots, gloves and goggles, Equator—sandals, sunglasses, t-shirt, cap

## page 354-355

1) south, north, west, east, Antarctica, Arctic; 2a) north, south, west, east; b) near to, far from, near to

## page 357

a) in the park; b) the fire station; c) the theatre; d) the park; e) the museum;

# answers

f) Take the first left, and the church is on your left. — **3**
Turn left out of the bus station. — **1**
Turn right at the end of the road. — **2**

## page 359
swimming, petrol station, playground, museum, fast food, telephone, airport, hospital, church, car park (alternatives possible)

## page 360
- industrial park
- main road
- church
- river

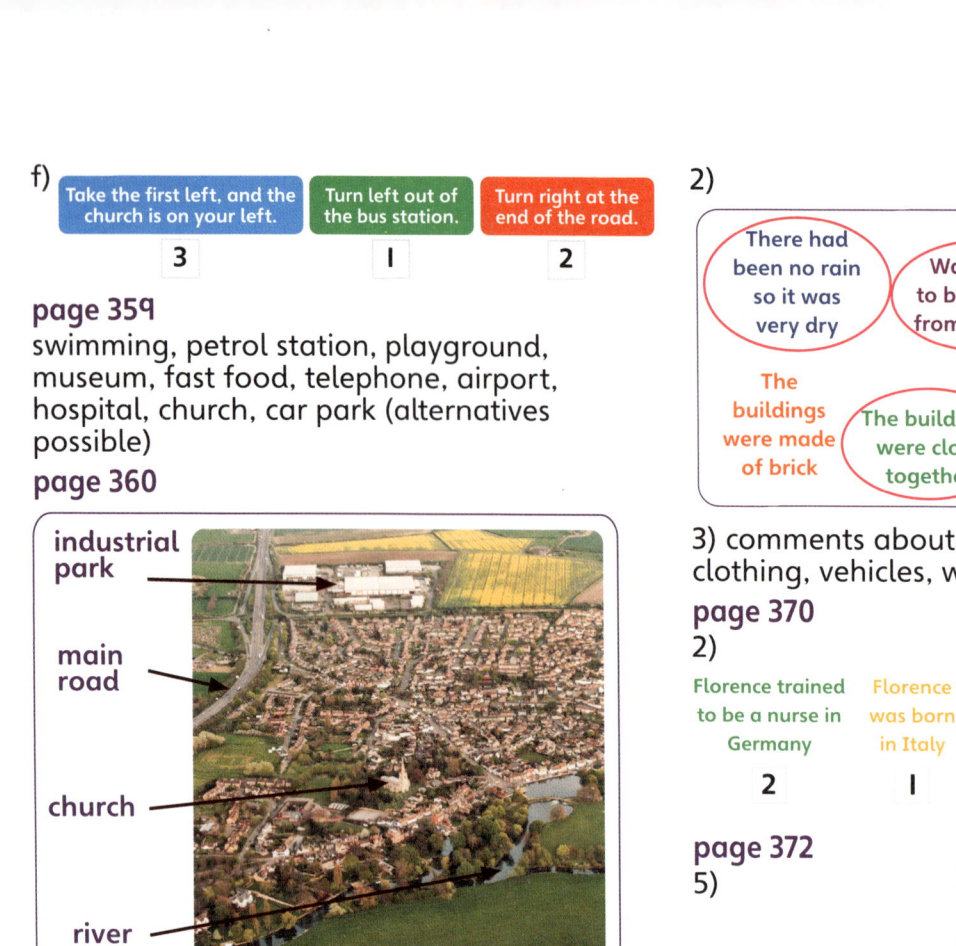

## page 362
1) telephone — *People could talk to others far away.* — **5**
printing press — *Books could be printed quickly and cheaply.* — **2**
cave paintings — *Cave pictures might have been messages.* — **3**
email — *People can access information online.* — **1**
telegraph messages — *People could send messages through wires.* — **4**

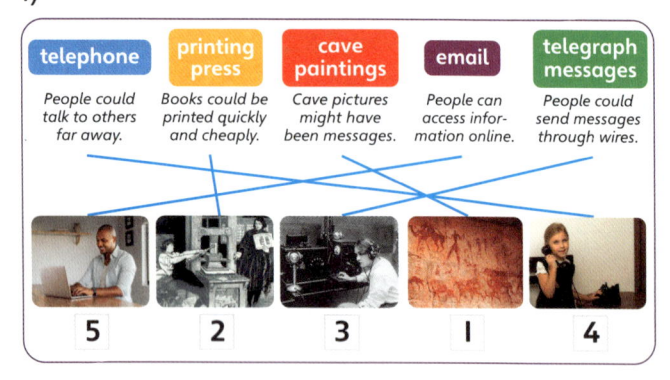

2) print books quickly and cheaply, Morse code; 3) answers could include: phone, email, text messages, letters, video chats etc

## page 364-366
1a) 1666; b) a bakery on Pudding Lane; c) leather buckets, metal hooks and fire squirts; d) four days;

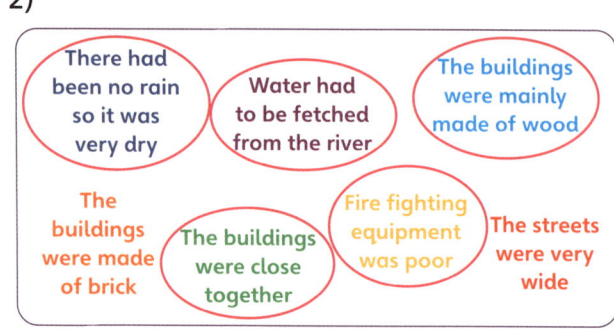

2) Circled (red): There had been no rain so it was very dry; Water had to be fetched from the river; The buildings were mainly made of wood; The buildings were close together; Fire fighting equipment was poor.
Not circled: The buildings were made of brick; The streets were very wide.

3) comments about equipment, protective clothing, vehicles, water access etc

## page 370
2) Florence trained to be a nurse in Germany — **2**
Florence was born in Italy — **1**
Florence set up a nursing school in London — **4**
Florence helped improve the hospital in Scutari — **3**

## page 372
5)
**Florence Nightingale**
- She was known as "the lady with the lamp".
- She trained as a nurse in Germany.
- She saved soldiers during the Crimean War.

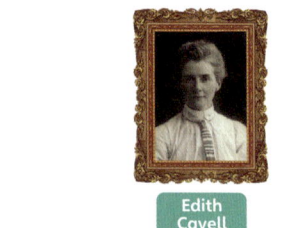

**Edith Cavell**
- She worked in a nursing school in Belgium.
- She saved soldiers during WWI.
- She was arrested and executed for treason.

## Wonders of Learning

# Well done!

You have

# COMPLETED

this

**WORKBOOK**

# CERTIFICATE

Congratulations to:

_____
(name)

for completing this *Wonders of Learning* workbook.

You are a learning star!

What was your favourite part of the book?

What do you want to learn about next?

_____
(parent/helper)

_____
(date)

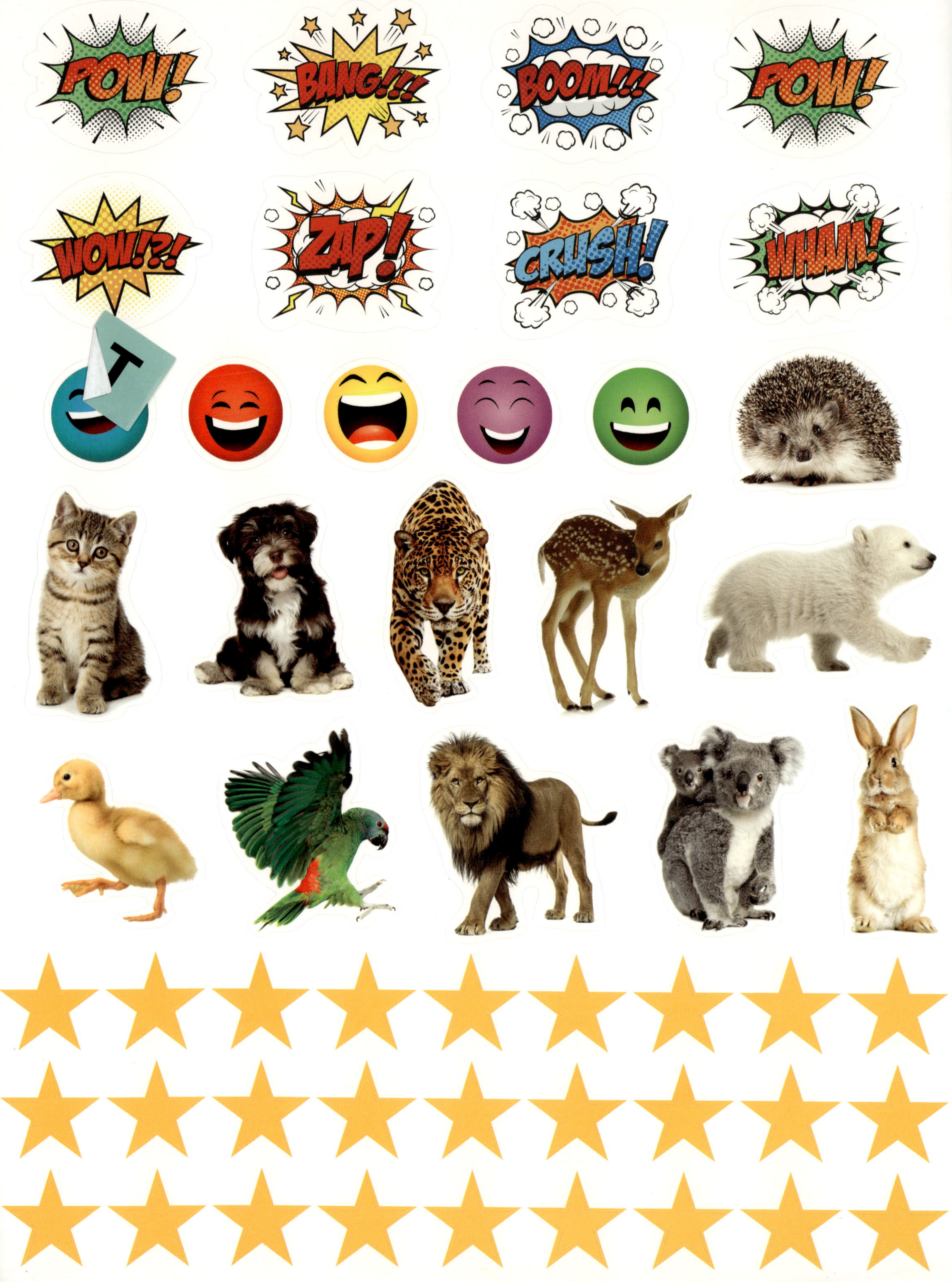
POW!
BANG!!!
BOOM!!!
POW!
WOW!?!
ZAP!
CRUSH!
WHAM!

| A | A | B | B | C | C | D | D | E | E |
| K | K | L | L | M | M | N | N | O | O |
| P | P | Q | Q | R | R | S | S | T | |
| U | U | V | V | W | W | X | X | Y | Y |
| Z | Z | a | a | a | a | b | b | b | c |
| c | c | d | d | d | e | e | e | e | |
| f | f | f | g | g | g | h | h | i | i |
| i | i | j | j | j | k | k | k | l | l |
| l | m | m | m | n | n | n | o | o | o |
| o | p | p | p | q | q | r | r | r | s |
| s | s | t | t | t | u | u | u | v | v |
| w | w | w | x | x | y | y | y | z | z |